THE RISE AND DECLINE OF FUNDAMENTAL RIGHTS IN EU CITIZENSHIP

This book argues that there is an inherent relationship between EU fundamental rights and EU citizenship: they both have the same objective of guaranteeing protection for the individual. This is underpinned by the development of case law in the field by the Court of Justice of the EU (CJEU). Here, however, the author proposes that that relationship has weakened in recent years as the CJEU has entered increasingly sensitive territory in regard to the protection of citizenship rights and fundamental rights.

Writing in the post UK–EU referendum environment, the author argues that this decline is attributable to increasing Euroscepticism, which has worsened since the Eurozone crisis and even more so in light of Brexit, and arguments made that leaving the EU would reduce immigration. This argument is particularly important to note given the rising fears of immigration that underlie much of the dissatisfaction with the EU project: a feeling prevalent not only in the UK. The chapters look at the rights of migrant EU citizens in Member States other than their own, and the guarantees that exist as a matter of protecting their fundamental human rights, which are present alongside rights enjoyed as part of being an EU citizen.

Volume 90 in the Series Modern Studies in European Law

Modern Studies in European Law

Recent titles in this series:

The European Union and Social Security Law
Jaan Paju

The Rule of Law in the European Union: The Internal Dimension
Theodore Konstadinides

The Division of Competences between the EU and the Member States: Reflections on the Past, the Present and the Future
Edited by Sacha Garben and Inge Govaere

Unity in Adversity: EU Citizenship, Social Justice and the Cautionary Tale of the UK
Charlotte O'Brien

The Use of Force and Article 2 of the ECHR in Light of European Conflicts
Hannah Russell

Environmental Crime in Europe
Edited by Andrew Farmer, Michael Faure and Grazia Maria Vagliasindi

Questioning EU Citizenship: Judges and the Limits of Free Movement and Solidarity in the EU
Edited by Daniel Thym

The European Union under Transnational Law: A Pluralist Appraisal
Matej Avbelj

Illegally Staying in the EU: An Analysis of Illegality in EU Migration Law
Benedita Menezes Queiroz

Social Legitimacy in the Internal Market: A Dialogue of Mutual Responsiveness
Jotte Mulder

The EU Better Regulation Agenda: A Critical Assessment
Edited by Sacha Garben and Inge Govaere

Administrative Regulation Beyond the Non-Delegation Doctrine: A Study on EU Agencies
Marta Simoncini

The Interface Between EU and International Law: Contemporary Reflections
Edited by Inge Govaere and Sacha Garben

For the complete list of titles in this series, see 'Modern Studies in European Law' link at www.bloomsburyprofessional.com/uk/series/modern-studies-in-european-law

The Rise and Decline of Fundamental Rights in EU Citizenship

Adrienne Yong

•HART•
OXFORD • LONDON • NEW YORK • NEW DELHI • SYDNEY

HART PUBLISHING

Bloomsbury Publishing Plc

Kemp House, Chawley Park, Cumnor Hill, Oxford, OX2 9PH, UK

HART PUBLISHING, the Hart/Stag logo, BLOOMSBURY and the Diana logo are trademarks of Bloomsbury Publishing Plc

First published in Great Britain 2019

A catalogue record for this book is available from the British Library.

Library of Congress Cataloging-in-Publication data

Names: Yong, Adrienne, author.

Title: The rise and decline of fundamental rights in EU citizenship / Adrienne Yong.

Description: Oxford, UK ; Portland, Oregon : Hart Publishing, 2019. | Series: Modern studies in European law | Based on author's thesis (doctoral - King's College London, 2016) issued under title: The rise and decline of fundamental rights protection in European Union citizenship case law. | Includes bibliographical references and index.

Identifiers: LCCN 2018052062 (print) | LCCN 2018055174 (ebook) | ISBN 9781509917945 (Epub) | ISBN 9781509917938 (hardback)

Subjects: LCSH: Citizenship—European Union countries. | Citizenship—Great Britain.

Classification: LCC KJE5124 (ebook) | LCC KJE5124 .Y66 2019 (print) | DDC 342.2408/5—dc23

LC record available at https://lccn.loc.gov/2018052062

ISBN: HB: 978-1-50991-793-8
ePDF: 978-1-50991-795-2
ePub: 978-1-50991-794-5

Typeset by Compuscript Ltd, Shannon
Printed and bound in Great Britain by TJ International Ltd, Padstow, Cornwall

To find out more about our authors and books visit www.hartpublishing.co.uk. Here you will find extracts, author information, details of forthcoming events and the option to sign up for our newsletters.

FOREWORD

In this work, Adrienne Yong first acknowledges a critical dilemma: how to reconcile the universal objectives of the protection of fundamental rights with the exclusionary nature of the status of citizenship. When this dilemma is translated to the context of the European Union, further complexities inevitably emerge. In particular, questions about the respective competences of the Union and of the Member States, and about the purpose as well as the reach of EU law, have to be confronted.

But Union citizenship rights – consistently characterised in EU law as elements of the 'fundamental status' of nationals of the Member States – and EU fundamental rights share a defining quality too, in the sense that both of these legal frameworks protect substantive rights within the constraints of formal limits and conditions. For Union citizenship, these include the requirements of holding Member State nationality, demonstrating a factor connecting the relevant situation to EU law, and satisfying limits and conditions that the Treaty on the Functioning of the European Union empowers the EU legislature to conceive. For EU fundamental rights, the relevant situation must, again, come within the scope of Union law in the first place, and limits placed on fundamental rights may be justifiable and legitimate where certain conditions are met. The final provisions of the Charter of Fundamental Rights must be recognised in the latter respect; all the more so for present purposes when it is remembered that Article 52(2) requires that rights 'recognised by this Charter for which provision is made in the Treaties' – as Union citizenship rights are – 'shall be exercised under the conditions and within the limits defined by those Treaties'.

This book outlines the respective trajectories of protecting citizenship rights and protecting fundamental rights in EU law; it assesses the extent to which the two have overlapped in reality; and it questions, ultimately, why they have not overlapped more consistently and more deeply. Three important themes can be highlighted from the analysis presented.

First, Union citizenship is characterised and considered as a legal but also social and political concept from the very beginning of and throughout this book. From that perspective, the arguments developed seek to understand the influence of the wider world on the case law of the Court of Justice: aiming to unpick, for example, the implications of the Eurozone crisis on narrowed understandings of collective (financial) solidarity; connections between the rise of Euroscepticism and instances of judicial caution; and the consequences for citizens of the 'age of uncertainty' triggered by the United Kingdom's invocation of the Article 50 TEU process for withdrawal from the European Union. Brexit has necessarily intensified reflections about Union citizenship as a right in and of itself as well as about the rights that Union citizens have or may claim. The interconnectedness of the EU and ECHR legal orders at the domestic level is also shown to be an important issue for affected citizens.

The author poses a question of scalding pertinence when she asks how we might 'convince an entire community who are not united at the outset to believe in a potentially novel conceptual framework'. Legal developments can never, and should not, be artificially insulated from political and social considerations. But neither can they be vulnerably hostage to them. How to find and give effect to the right balance between appropriate responsiveness and misplaced reactiveness is therefore a parallel and perhaps even more critical dilemma pushed to the surface of our thinking by this timely work.

Second, as the discussion across the different chapters of this book consistently reinforces, getting 'in' constitutes the essential threshold that must be crossed in both of the areas of EU law addressed. But what the analysis also confirms is that it is not only the proclaimed limits and conditions that matter, but the judicial interpretation applied to them.

At the present time, the impact of the Charter of Fundamental Rights in horizontal situations is gradually unfolding, further revealing the potential of the Charter as a powerful instrument of rights protection – and more specifically, of rights enforcement. When the Charter is successfully engaged, the implications can be potent. But linking back to the first theme about the impact of the wider world on legal choices, it then becomes clearer why the borders of getting 'in' are protected to different extents at different points in time – under the shadow of different wider world circumstances.

Similarly, in Union citizenship law, a series of recent judgments on extradition shows the considerable added value of belonging to this protected transnational community. The fundamental status of citizenship was also invoked by the Court in support of unilateral revocation of a Member State's intention to withdraw from the European Union.

Where is the line between the prudent containment and calculated suppression of legal power in a polity constructed on the premise of shared competence, on the one hand, but 'for' its citizens, on the other?

Third, the author refers several times to something that she argues can only be restored or strengthened by deeper and more consistent protection of the fundamental rights of Union citizens, by deeper and more consistent overlapping of the narratives that she explores: faith – faith in the concept of Union citizenship itself, and then in the European Union and its legal order more broadly.

In that light, what the book also illustrates is that case law trends rise and fall – and then rise again. In some of the Court of Justice's more recent judgments, there are traces of responsiveness to criticism about the undue detachment of citizenship from the protection of fundamental rights, and from the scope – from the power – of the Charter more specifically: fewer traces yet, perhaps, than the author of the book would wish to see; but traces, nonetheless.

Niamh Nic Shuibhne

ACKNOWLEDGEMENTS[1]

This book is a revised and updated version of my doctoral thesis, which was completed under the supervision of Cian Murphy and Andrea Biondi. Greatest thanks must go to them for their support, encouragement and advice throughout the painful process of the PhD and beyond. I also thank Eleanor Spaventa for setting me down the path of EU citizenship by encouraging me to apply for a PhD and to Niamh Nic Shuibhne and Virginia Mantouvalou for the invaluable comments during my viva which have largely shaped this book. The viva remains to this day the most nerve-wracking experience of my life.

I would like to thank Hart Publishing and all those involved for the opportunity as well as guidance in the process of writing this book. It truly is a dream to become an author and see my thesis become a monograph with such a wonderful and established publisher.

I remain eternally grateful to Hertfordshire Law School for putting their faith in me and giving me my first academic job, and most of all for the friends that I made and people I met there. At the City Law School, I have now grown as a scholar and am grateful for the mentorship in particular from Elaine Fahey, Tawhida Ahmed and Sabrina Germain.

The support and love from my friends were the main things that kept me going. To my Somerset loves, Mathilde Groppo, Emma Perot, Ioanna Hadjiyianni, Justin Koo and Nik Voulgaris, and greatest love especially to Ermioni Xanthopoulou and Laura Lo Coco, my North London neighbours whose homes became my second. I remain ever grateful for the wonderful friendship of Chris Ward, for the sage advice on footnotes from Patrick Murphy,[2] from afar, my Asian superbrain Jen Khoo, and my 90s pop sister Heather Purdie.[3] To the Cambodia girls, Jarrah Hemmant (née Webster) and Lilo Henke, I am grateful that technology will always tell us whether Lilo is still alive. Thanks to every single one of them for enduring the trials, tribulations, anxiety, up and downs, and high and lows that I underwent during the process of writing this book (but mostly when I was not).

To my family, Derryn Yong, Matt Cosad and Tess Cosad. Yosads always, for always having my back.

Finally, the greatest of thanks and love go to my parents. For looking after me no matter how much I wanted to quit, no matter how ridiculous I got, no matter how much grief I gave them, no matter what. Thanks, Mum and Dad.

[1] This would not be a real academic acknowledgement page if it did not have footnotes.
[2] Brexit means Brexit.
[3] 'I have friends, I definitely have friends…'

CONTENTS

ABBREVIATIONS

AG	Advocate General
CJEU	Court of Justice of the European Union
DWA	Draft Withdrawal Agreement
EC	European Community
ECHR	European Convention on Human Rights
ECSC	European Coal and Steel Community
ECtHR	European Court of Human Rights
EU	European Union
TCN	third country national
TEC	Treaty on the European Community
TEU	Treaty on European Union
TFEU	Treaty on the Functioning of the European Union

TABLE OF CASES*

EU

* This book aims to state the law, including cases, as of 1 July 2018.

European Court of Human Rights

UK

1

Examining EU Citizenship and its Relationship with EU Fundamental Rights

I. Introduction

The European Union (EU) introduced the legal, social and political concept of EU citizenship in the Treaty of Maastricht in 1993.[1] Since its inception, a significant number of cases have been heard by the (now) Court of Justice of the European Union (CJEU – hereinafter 'the Court')[2] relating to EU citizenship, and there has been heated discussion and debate in the literature on citizenship. Establishing a European status of citizenship was one of the most prominent non-economic concepts introduced into the EU in the Treaty of Maastricht. This book is a contribution to the expanse of literature on EU citizenship, but is one that adopts a different focus from that currently existing. It is the intention of this study to follow the development of EU citizenship from its origins, prior to its formal introduction in the Treaty of Maastricht, to its current status today, a heated and uncertain time in which the UK seeks to withdraw from the EU entirely and where the interpretation of the enjoyment of citizens' rights is under heavy scrutiny. This analysis will be carried out through an assessment of the Court's case law,[3] with a particular emphasis on the influence of EU fundamental rights throughout. This approach is chosen in order to demonstrate that there has been a rise in the consideration of fundamental rights protection in the Court's case law on citizenship since Maastricht, although now there are signs of a decline in the influence of these fundamental rights. A judicial model for this potential integration will be presented, supported by constitutional developments in fundamental rights protection. However, its limits are also acknowledged, and this is where the political effects are arguably most prominent. It will be argued that the judicial inconsistencies rife in the development of the concept of

[1] Treaty of Maastricht on the European Union [1992] OJ C191/01 (EEC).

[2] Formerly the Court of Justice of the ECSC and then the Court of Justice of the European Communities (CJEC). Under the Lisbon Treaty, it is now the CJEU.

[3] This book considers all case law on EU citizenship up until 1 July 2018.

EU citizenship are linked to the unstable political environment of the EU itself and that this has affected the Court's interpretation of integrating EU fundamental rights into EU citizenship law. This, it will also be argued, will help protect the rights of EU citizens in the UK after its imminent withdrawal from the EU.

The question of an inherent link between EU fundamental rights and EU citizenship law is not a novel one.[4] Because EU citizenship was introduced as a non-economic concept with evident social and political elements, it was compared to other prominent non-economic guarantees in EU law, including the protection of fundamental rights, which is a general principle of EU law.[5] There are inherent similarities between the two concepts. Both are intended to protect interests of the individual, and the effects of the legal principles that guide this also overlap.[6] However, there is a striking difference that is difficult to reconcile. EU fundamental rights derive from a universal foundation of equality,[7] whilst EU citizenship rights are only available upon having exclusive membership to the community.[8] This book will discuss this divergence in the context of the case law in order to examine how the Court managed to interpret this to the benefit of the claimants: citizens of the EU. It will be argued that bringing the scope of EU citizenship law closer to that of EU fundamental rights protection was how this was achieved. However, the law has now more recently retreated to a position more akin to the one that existed at the outset of the introduction of EU citizenship status, somewhat compromising fundamental rights protection in the process. It will be argued that this is normatively and legally inconsistent with the constitutional trajectory that this book will outline. However, it will also be acknowledged that such liberalism as argued for here is hindered by increasingly sensitive politics that influences the legal culture of the Court. This cannot continue, especially in the wake of Brexit, as it risks significantly undermining EU citizenship status, which is supposedly fundamental.[9]

Considerable attention will turn to the political situation facing the EU today – that is, the withdrawal of the UK from the EU. The considerable uncertainty surrounding the effects of Brexit in all areas is particularly damning for citizens' rights, as the UK is also in the midst of its negotiations as to the status of EU citizens within its territory to remain and retain rights after withdrawal.[10]

[4] Siofra O'Leary, 'The Relationship between Community Citizenship and the Protection of Fundamental Rights in Community Law' (1995) 32 *CML Rev* 519.

[5] Judgment of 18 June 1991, *ERT* C-260/89, EU:C:1991:254, para 41.

[6] The principle of non-discrimination in art 18 of the Consolidated Version of the Treaty on the Functioning of the European Union [2008] OJ C115/47 (TFEU) and the principle of proportionality; see Takis Tridimas, *The General Principles of EU Law*, 2nd edn (Oxford University Press, 2006) ch 3.

[7] John Locke, *Two Treatises of Government* (Cambridge University Press, 1963).

[8] Aristotle, *Politics* (Ernest Barker trans, Clarendon Press, 1948).

[9] Judgment of 20 September 2001, *Grzelczyk* C-184/99, EU:C:2001:458, para 31.

[10] Lisa O'Caroll, 'Zero Chance EU Citizens in UK Will Keep Same Rights Post-Brexit, Says Expert' *The Guardian* (13 September 2016), https://www.theguardian.com/politics/2016/sep/13/zero-chance-eu-citizens-keep-same-rights-post-brexit-expert.

The argument to be made here is in favour of protecting and enhancing EU citizenship rights because they are inherently founded upon and linked to fundamental rights protection. This reasoning can be applied to this scenario, and this book intends to provide some clarity to the muddied situation. The argument remains that EU citizenship status is premised upon a wider, more universal level of protection of fundamental rights and that though the UK may be leaving the EU, these safeguards deriving from EU citizenship status are in place to protect the EU citizen. This argument feeds into the current negotiations on the UK joining the single market, and its unwillingness to also commit to the free movement of persons.[11]

EU citizenship, the European construction of a political concept that ordinarily relates to the nation state,[12] was originally found in Article 8 of the Treaty Establishing the European Economic Community (EEC). Citizenship of the EU was established as a status that was granted to: 'Every person holding the nationality of a Member State.'[13] Article 8a EEC then set out the primary substantive rights that citizens would enjoy as part of the privilege of being an EU citizen, including the right to move and reside freely within the EU, amongst other political privileges.[14] It is widely accepted that an EU citizenship status was not a consideration on the minds of the negotiators of the original Treaty of Paris when it was agreed in 1951.[15] It was thus something of a novelty when after over 40 years of focusing on building a common market, a political concept like EU citizenship was introduced into the EU's economic framework.

Whether the introduction of EU citizenship would have the intended effect of uniting the community by providing a status that all individuals in the EU would relate to and understand would inevitably be a struggle at the outset, given the lack of precedent in this regard. The EU was not originally established to fulfil such aims.[16] One of the biggest obstacles still troubling the concept of EU citizenship today derives from the Treaty. The Member States, when drafting the Treaty, made

[11] Simon Nixon, 'Free-Movement Conundrum isn't UK's Only Hurdle to Accessing EU Market' *Wall Street Journal* (21 September 2016), www.wsj.com/articles/free-movement-conundrum-isnt-u-k-s-only-hurdle-to-accessing-eu-market-1474491485.

[12] Derek Heater, *What is Citizenship?* (Polity Press, 1999) 44 describes citizenship as embodying two forms: liberal and civic republican. Liberal citizenship refers to rights; civic republicanism refers to the duties and powers imposed by a government to its citizens. See Engin Isin and Bryan Turner, 'Citizenship Studies: An Introduction' in Engin Isin and Bryan Turner (eds), *Handbook of Citizenship Studies* (SAGE Publications 2002) 1, citizenship comes from the welfare state by default.

[13] Article 8 EEC.

[14] ibid art 8a(1). Article 8b–8e EEC set out political rights, which will not form the subject matter of the discussion in this book.

[15] Treaty of Paris (formerly the Treaty Establishing the European Coal and Steel Community).

[16] See Jürgen Habermas, 'Citizenship and National Identity: Some Reflections on the Future of Europe' (1992) 12 *Praxis International* 255; Hans Ulrich Jessurun d'Oliveira, 'European Citizenship: Its Meaning, its Potential' in Renaud Dehousse (ed), *Europe after Maastricht: An Ever Closer Union?* (Law Books in Europe, 1994).

EU citizenship dependent on first having the nationality of an EU Member State.[17] This meant that EU citizenship was not a free-standing status on its own, which not only had legal implications for the conferral of citizenship rights, but also implications for EU legitimacy and solidarity because it maintained the distinction between Member State nationality and EU citizenship.[18]

On the other hand, the Court introduced EU fundamental rights to the case law as early as 1969.[19] They were originally presented as secondary to the principles governing the internal market. It was not until a year later when the Court declared that fundamental rights were general principles of EU law that they were afforded any formal status in the EU.[20] It made the EU's commitment to non-economic rights official, but did not make fundamental rights as found in the Charter of Fundamental Rights of the EU (hereinafter 'the Charter') fully legally effective.[21] Subsequent case law made clear that the EU was not founded on or solely influenced by human rights considerations,[22] and recent case law has further confirmed that it would be unlikely to ever be exclusively concerned with human rights.[23] This was despite fundamental rights being codified in the Charter and made equal in status to the Treaties themselves.[24] However, it did not diminish the importance or relevance of fundamental rights. The development of fundamental rights case law has steadily widened the scope *ratione materiae* and *ratione personae* since the EU began,[25] and began to overlap with EU citizenship as a result. Given that fundamental rights are inclusive and indiscriminately applicable by their very nature, this was to be expected. For EU citizenship, this expansion was more difficult to acknowledge, despite the concept's scope *ratione materiae* and *ratione personae* also being broadened.[26]

The inherent similarities between EU fundamental rights and EU citizenship rights demand attention. Both share a similar objective – to enhance the

[17] Article 8(1) EEC: 'Every person holding the nationality of a Member State shall be a citizen of the Union.' Article 17 of the Treaty of Amsterdam amending the Treaty on European Union, the Treaties Establishing the European Communities and Related Acts [1997] OJ C340 then added: 'Citizenship of the Union shall complement and not replace national citizenship.' In Art 20 TFEU, this was changed to 'additional to national citizenship'.

[18] Ulrich K Preuss, 'Problems of a Concept of European Citizenship' (1995) 1 *European Law Journal* 267, 275.

[19] Judgment of 12 November 1969, *Stauder v Ulm* C-29/69, EU:C:1969:57.

[20] Judgment of 17 December 1970, *Internationale Handelsgesellschaft* C-11/70, EU:C:1970:114.

[21] Charter of Fundamental Rights of the European Union 83/02 [2010] OJ C83/389.

[22] Judgment of 13 July 1989, *Wachauf* C-5/88, EU:C:1989:321; *ERT* (n 5); Judgment of 26 June 1997, *Familiapress* C-368/95, EU:C:1997:325; Judgment of 11 July 2002, *Carpenter* C-60/00, EU:C:2002:434.

[23] Opinion of 30 September 2010, *Zambrano* C-34/09, EU:C:2011:560, para 155.

[24] See Armin von Bogdandy, 'The European Union as a Human Rights Organization? Human Rights and the Core of the European Union' (2000) 37 *CML Rev* 1307; Piet Eeckhout, 'The EU Charter of Fundamental Rights and the Federal Question' (2002) 39 *CML Rev* 945.

[25] It has been incremental in terms of its enforceability, following a similar development to EU citizenship law.

[26] For a discussion on the changing face of the EU, see Eleanor Spaventa, 'From *Gebhard* to *Carpenter*: Towards a (Non-)Economic European Constitution' (2004) 41 *CML Rev* 743.

protection of an individual's rights as they exist within the context of the EU. However, the nature of citizenship compared to fundamental rights makes this connection contentious. Whilst Heater stated that '[t]he principle of equality cannot, in truth, be discounted in any consideration of the nature of citizenship', it nevertheless 'lies in a tangle of reservations and contradictions'.[27] These contradictions can be traced back to Ancient Greece, where Aristotle's *polis* of citizens was identified as the subject of one of the first concepts of citizenship. He originally reserved all rights and membership of his notion of a *polis* to a specific group of individuals.[28] Though citizenship has now evolved to encompass the community beyond the *polis* into the nation state, this initial emphasis on exclusivity was at odds with fundamental rights. This is because fundamental rights are inherently available to all individuals and are intended to be universal as the EU's manifestation of human rights are today. The question remains as to whether EU citizenship was conceived with this relationship in mind and, if not, why EU citizenship's relationship with human rights in today's EU legal order matters.

II. Linking EU Citizenship and Fundamental Rights

This book will examine the relationship between fundamental rights in the EU and the concept of EU citizenship through an examination of the Court's case law. In order to do so, it will map the development of fundamental rights, codified in the binding Charter, alongside EU citizenship, whose provisions are found in Articles 20–21 of the Treaty on the Functioning of the European Union (TFEU).[29] The similarities between the two concepts of rights – EU fundamental rights and EU citizenship rights – cannot be ignored. Both concepts relate to the protection of the individual and seek to achieve a higher level of protection for them. The promotion of equal treatment of citizens also underpins both concepts. The interaction between the two concepts of rights has seen instances where the Court invoked fundamental rights under the guise of the EU citizenship provisions in order to achieve a coinciding level of protection.[30] The timing of significant developments in both areas also indicated potential for a deeper interaction between the two – in 2009, the Lisbon Treaty made the Charter legally binding in Article 6 of the Treaty on European Union (TEU) and in 2011, the seminal *Zambrano* case made EU citizenship status an independent legal basis for citizenship rights.[31]

[27] Heater (n 12) 82.
[28] 'Polis' meaning city-state from Aristotle (n 8) Book I.
[29] Articles 20–21 TFEU.
[30] See Judgment of 19 October 2004, *Zhu and Chen* C-200/02, EU:C:2004:639; *Carpenter* (n 22); Judgment of 25 July 2008, *Metock and Others* C-127/08, EU:C:2008:449.
[31] Judgment of 8 March 2011, *Zambrano* C-34/09, EU:C:2011:124.

The effect of both developments was to raise the overall status of both non-economic rights against the historically dominant internal market rights. These developments, occurring in succession, represented a shift from an economic to a more political EU, which this book will analyse.

However, the difference between the protection offered by fundamental rights and that of EU citizenship is crucial – fundamental rights have a distinctly wider remit than EU citizenship rights. Citizenship in the EU is only available to individuals who are nationals of the EU Member States, and the case law will show that the Court applied further conditions to the conferral of citizenship rights.[32] Fundamental rights, in contrast, are intended to be universal by their very nature. O'Leary argued that: 'Such a relationship [with fundamental rights] would detract from the orthodox enjoyment of citizenship rights on an exclusionary basis.'[33] She referred to the fact that if exclusive rights for EU citizens became too readily available, this might undermine the entire concept. She thus recognised the potential of their relationship, but seemed uncertain as to how their specific interaction would play out. It is the objective of this book, two decades after O'Leary posed this question, to discuss their interaction. As it stands, the current relationship between fundamental rights and EU citizenship is more asymptotic. This is despite convincing arguments from the literature, Advocates General and even the Court itself that there is a logical, warranted and desirable connection between the two[34] – hence a rise, then a decline. It is the aim of this book to discuss this relationship by looking first at why this divergent relationship has manifested, and why this is unprecedented for the relationship between fundamental rights and EU citizenship. This examination will bring to attention the link between the Court's behaviour and the political atmosphere in the EU, which it will be argued here are connected. However, it does not support this behaviour becoming the norm, especially not in light of the challenges facing the EU as a result of Brexit.

Early on in the judicial development of EU citizenship, the Court issued some striking decisions that spoke to a specific group of individual citizens that had previously been excluded under the internal market.[35] In these cases, the scope *ratione personae* was expanded to include non-economically active citizens, and this also prompted the expansion of the scope *ratione materiae* to include rights more suited to a wider group of individuals who were not economic actors.[36]

[32] This refers in particular to the judicial instruments that the Court used to guide its decision-making process in EU citizenship law; see section IV below.

[33] O'Leary (n 4).

[34] See particularly Opinion of 9 December 1992, *Konstantinidis* C-168/91, EU:C:1992:504; O'Leary (n 4); Percy B Lehning, 'European Citizenship: Towards a European Identity?' (2001) 20 *Law and Philosophy* 239; Eeckhout (n 24); *Zhu and Chen* (n 30).

[35] Judgment of 12 May 1998, *Martinez Sala* C-85/96, EU:C:1998:217; *Grzelczyk* (n 9); Judgment of 17 September 2002, *Baumbast* C-413/99, EU:C:2002:493.

[36] This included the right to equal treatment for all citizens irrespective of economic activity; as seen in *Sala*, this included equal treatment to social welfare, residency rights and family rights which also fell under the protection of fundamental rights.

Naturally, it led to more social factors being considered by the Court in citizenship law, with fundamental rights being the most relevant example. As the judicial interaction between fundamental rights and EU citizenship law in the Court became more pronounced,[37] fundamental rights were expected to naturally fall into the category of considerations for the Court. Given that all Member State nationals are EU citizens and all EU citizens enjoy fundamental rights, this seemed a reasonable assumption. Furthermore, during this time, fundamental rights themselves as a separate discourse were also becoming constitutionalised, therefore also supporting a hypothesis that this book will make that the Court's behaviour is linked to its political environment, which influences the way it decided cases.[38]

It was a slow process of constitutional acceptance for the fundamental rights *acquis*, whose development progressed because of the Court's case law.[39] In 2000, the discourse had developed enough to justify codification in a Charter of Fundamental Rights. However, until 2009, this Charter was not yet legally binding.[40] The EU evidently struggled to redefine itself as a political and social entity with broader, non-economic, functional objectives, and the slow development of fundamental rights protection is evidence of this struggle. However, though a strong constitutional relationship between fundamental rights and EU citizenship was foreseeable, the problem that underlies this book is that of the tension between the two concepts. This existed despite the concepts sharing the common goal of bettering protection for all individuals in the EU. The differences between two such interrelated concepts is down to the core of the rights themselves – the universal nature of fundamental rights contradicts the idea of the political 'right to have rights' in a polity like a community of citizens.[41] The natural theory of rights, which form the basis of human rights,[42] is inconsistent with the idea of political membership being a prerequisite of rights conferral.[43] This is what EU citizenship is based on. Because fundamental rights and citizenship both have the same objective of guaranteeing the legal protection of their subjects, they are inherently linked. The struggles behind both concepts actually derive from the boundaries erected by the EU's constitutional framework in being restricted to applying only when the case falls within its ascribed territory. The difference is

[37] See *Carpenter* (n 22); *Zhu and Chen* (n 30); Judgment of 9 January 2007, *Jia* C-1/05, EU:C:2007:1.

[38] See section III below on legal culture.

[39] See *Internationale Handelsgesellschaft* (n 20); *Wachauf* (n 22); *ERT* (n 5); *Familiapress* (n 22).

[40] Article 6(1) TEU.

[41] The 'right to have rights' comes from Hannah Arendt, *Totalitarianism: Part Three of the Origins of Totalitarianism* (Harcourt Brace Jovanovich, 1968). See Samantha Besson, 'The Right to Have Rights: From Human Rights to Citizens' Rights and Back' in Marco Goldoni and Christopher McCorkindale (eds), *Hannah Arendt and the Law* (Hart Publishing, 2012); and Alison Kesby, *The Right to Have Rights: Citizenship, Humanity, and International Law* (Oxford University Press, 2012) for analysis.

[42] Locke (n 7). It is beyond the scope of this book to debate natural law theories; therefore, this is the position assumed.

[43] This is the civic republican model of citizenship, supported by Aristotle.

that the ideal scope of protection that a concept of fundamental rights embodies is broader and more inclusive as compared to citizenship, whilst EU citizenship has been restricted to benefiting only the EU citizens themselves.[44]

Inherent disparities in the relationship between fundamental rights and EU citizenship emerged as obstacles to the relationship's further development because both concepts had to remain within the strict boundaries of EU law. The scope *ratione personae* of EU citizenship was limited from the outset, with EU citizenship rights only being available to nationals of EU Member States. With the advent of the Lisbon Treaty, binding fundamental rights in the Charter would be able to form the legal basis for further expansion of the scope *ratione materiae* of EU citizenship. However, this too faced difficulties. Though universal in principle, EU fundamental rights are nonetheless also restricted to operating strictly within the scope of EU law, in accordance with Articles 51–54 of the Charter. Therefore, though the Court sought to broaden the remit of EU citizenship law by linking it with fundamental rights, it still could not escape the restrictions erected by the EU's constitutional structure, a struggle that was also present in the judicial discourse of the citizenship concept. The difficulty is that, normatively, rights should transcend territorial boundaries, but both EU fundamental rights and EU citizenship are unable to do so.

A. Understanding EU Fundamental Rights

This section will begin by consolidating the rise of fundamental rights in the EU. By tracing its history, the analysis will uncover the fact that fundamental rights struggled initially to find relevance in the economic EU. However, unlike for citizenship, the Court has more successfully overcome the obstacles it faced initially in the context of fundamental rights protection, culminating in the Charter of Fundamental Rights becoming legally binding in the Lisbon Treaty. The Charter provides a foundation for the claims made in this book regarding a deeper relationship between itself and EU citizenship. It is argued that the potential constitutional effects of making the Charter binding will encourage greater affiliation with EU citizenship status, because rights protection is more effective if the EU governing framework is perceived to be legitimate.[45] The book will discuss the relationship between the two concepts and their stark differences as interpreted by the Court in order to explain the divergence when interpreting both concepts.

[44] This is the reason that the judicial instruments of the genuine link test and purely internal situations rule emerged (see section IV below).

[45] See Marcus Horeth, 'No Way Out for the Beast? The Unsolved Legitimacy Problem of European Governance' (1999) 6 *Journal of European Public Policy* 249, 259; Erik Oddvar Eriksen and John Erik Fossum, 'Europe in Search of Legitimacy: Strategies of Legitimation Assessed' (2004) 25 *International Political Science Review* 435, 437; Andrew Moravcsik, 'Reassessing Legitimacy in the European Union' (2002) 40 *Journal of Common Market Studies* 603, 616.

In the context of this book, fundamental rights do not refer to the broad political concept of human rights; rather, they are defined as the human rights that the EU has accepted as part of its legal framework. For this reason, they primarily derive from the Charter of Fundamental Rights, which has drawn heavily on the European Convention on Human Rights (ECHR).[46] Human rights and fundamental rights are distinguished because they differ in terms of their scope. Both rights are universal, but fundamental rights are unique to the EU and applicable only when within the remit of EU law.[47] Controversially, EU fundamental rights are not always wholly 'human' in nature. What is typically considered a human right, typified by the rights enshrined in the ECHR, are not the only rights protected in the Charter.[48] The Charter also protects rights such as workers' rights, property rights and business rights, and this broad range is subject to criticism.[49] However, the justification remains that the EU is not a nation state and its commitments have not always been orthodox human rights guarantees. The EU has other priorities that are duly reflected in the Charter, though it should be noted this has not meant ignoring the most basic of human rights and liberties.[50]

In the early years of the Treaty of Paris, there was no thought given to rights that were not economic in nature. Fundamental rights in the EU were mainly interpreted as those that protected commercial and financial interests.[51] There is a distinction to be made between the Charter's binding nature and the legal enforceability of EU fundamental rights more generally. EU Treaty drafters decided to make fundamental rights in the Charter binding, and this was limited not only in terms of substance, but also in terms of scope. However, before this, the Charter existed as soft law, and fundamental rights were enforceable through the Court's interpretation of how they are to apply as a general principle of EU law. It would appear that there was a desire to maintain the established financial integrity and solidarity of the original Treaty, thereby prompting restrictions on such novel non-economic rights.[52] However, despite these modest beginnings, the Charter

[46] Convention for the Protection of Human Rights and Fundamental Freedoms (European Convention on Human Rights, as amended).

[47] Articles 51–54 of the Charter.

[48] For example, arts 15, 16 and 17 of the Charter primarily refer to employment rights, the right to conduct a business and the right to property. The ECHR presents human rights, whilst the Charter presents EU fundamental rights; therefore, the difference between the two is their specificity and target audience, as well as their substance.

[49] Gráinne de Búrca, 'The Drafting of the EU Charter of Fundamental Rights' (2001) 26 *European Law Review* 126, 134; David Anderson and Cian C Murphy, 'The Charter of Fundamental Rights' in Andrea Biondi, Piet Eeckhout and Stefanie Ripley (eds), *EU Law after Lisbon* (Oxford University Press, 2012).

[50] The Charter of Fundamental Rights directly transposes all of the ECHR's rights and then adds other rights; see 'EU Charter of Fundamental Rights', http://ec.europa.eu/justice/fundamental-rights/charter/index_en.htm.

[51] Articles 16 and 17 of the Charter.

[52] ibid arts 51–54.

has now gained legally binding status, providing the Court with a stronger legal foundation from which EU fundamental rights protection can derive. This chapter will demonstrate why this should have inspired a stronger constitutionalisation of fundamental rights in EU citizenship law.

Tridimas argued that the human rights rhetoric did not exist as part of a commitment to social standards, but rather to expand the scope of the Treaty and improve legitimacy.[53] One of the first cases on fundamental rights in 1969 was *Stauder v Ulm*, which concerned a challenge to a Commission decision that allowed butter to be sold at a reduced price under a social welfare scheme. The Court found that the Commission decision did not infringe fundamental rights, marking the first time that it recognised that Member States' constitutional principles and EU fundamental rights both existed and were related, but remained distinct.[54] Consistent with Tridimas' statement, *Stauder* was the first case to establish that fundamental rights could, and would, broaden the remit of the Treaty. Tridimas also suggested that the conferral of greater rights, particularly fundamental rights, would improve the EU's perceived legitimacy. The EU was inspired by national constitutional principles, and later international treaties,[55] but EU fundamental rights remained their own separate concept at the outset. This book adopts Tridimas' argument regarding legitimacy, which was one of the reasons for committing to the fundamental rights and EU citizenship relationship in the first place.

The connection made by Tridimas between a broader scope of fundamental rights and improved perception of EU legitimacy is supported primarily because it is consistent with the nature of fundamental rights themselves. Use of the term 'fundamental' is indicative of its significance. The philosophy behind rights in general will not be discussed in this book,[56] but rather the focus will be on their legal effects in the EU. The broader the scope of fundamental rights protection offered, the greater its potential effect on a citizen's life in the EU. This protection stems from the EU institutions. EU citizenship's role in this is to strengthen ties between the individual and the EU community through the conferral of a common EU citizenship status. If the protection of fundamental rights can encourage a stronger perception of EU legitimacy amongst its citizens, then the EU citizenship status becomes the identifiable connection between the EU and its individual citizens, and in this manner becomes of relevance.[57]

The Court has played a crucial role in broadening the scope of fundamental rights over the years. Various cases in the development of EU fundamental rights can help assess what the Court's intentions appeared to be in relation to

[53] Tridimas (n 6) 298.
[54] *Stauder v Ulm* (n 19) para 7.
[55] Judgment of 14 May 1974, *Nold* C-4/73, EU:C:1974:51.
[56] See Peter Jones, *Rights* (Macmillan, 1994) for discussion on rights in political theory.
[57] See Gráinne de Búrca, 'The Quest for Legitimacy in the European Union' (1996) 59 *MLR* 349, 356.

fundamental rights protection, and how effective it was in legitimising the EU as an institution when broadening the scope of fundamental rights. As mentioned above, one of the first cases on fundamental rights in the EU, *Stauder v Ulm*, highlighted that the Court has had the capacity to legally acknowledge fundamental rights at the outset, despite the economic nature of the EU. The judgment itself was only eight paragraphs long, with fundamental rights asserted at the end. However, as a statement from the Court in 1969, it demonstrated a willingness to accept that non-economic rights existed within the EU. Yet, what the expectation would be going forward was not clear.

Internationale Handelsgesellschaft followed from this to confirm a year later that fundamental rights were guaranteed as general principles of EU law and had to be adhered to throughout the EU.[58] The case concerned a system of financial deposits established by the EU, which the German court believed to be in contravention of its own national law. The Court noted that for the sake of uniformity, it could not allow national law to override EU law; however, this did not mean that it should not thoroughly consider whether there was an 'analogous guarantee inherent in Community law … [that had] been disregarded' and confirmed that fundamental rights could be inspired by national law.[59] EU fundamental rights then developed as the EU grew and its objectives changed to become more political in nature in the early 1990s.

In *Wachauf*, 20 years after *Stauder*, the Court clarified that national laws implementing EU laws 'are not absolute … but must be considered in relation to their social function'.[60] *Wachauf* concerned a milk farmer who sought compensation under German law for having to discontinue his milk production when his farm's tenancy ended. Compensation was denied because the original landlord had withdrawn consent for it. The Court noted that it would be an infringement of fundamental rights not to allow the farmer, a lessee of the land, to be rewarded for 'the fruits of his labour'.[61] This was especially as he did not have the option to extend the lease. Requiring there to be 'a sufficiently wide margin of appreciation to apply those rules in a manner consistent with the requirements of the protection of fundamental rights',[62] the case was further acknowledgement by the Court of fundamental rights and their legal effects. However, acknowledging their existence still did not guarantee their legal effectiveness. The Court simply confirmed the existence of fundamental rights as general principles of EU law.[63]

[58] *Internationale Handelsgesellschaft* (n 20) para 4.

[59] ibid.

[60] *Wachauf* (n 22) para 18.

[61] ibid para 19.

[62] ibid para 22.

[63] Gráinne de Búrca, 'Fundamental Human Rights and the Reach of EC Law' [1993] *OJLS* 283, 298. For further discussion, see Frank I Michelman, 'Human Rights and the Limits of Constitutional Theory' (2000) 13 *Ratio Juris* 63.

This adds to the claim that the rights discourse still seemed to remain buried underneath more pressing internal market matters.[64]

ERT is frequently cited as the first case that accepted and established a standard for fundamental rights, with the Court stating that 'fundamental rights form an integral part of the general principles of law' and that the EU itself 'cannot accept measures which are incompatible with observance of the human rights thus recognized and guaranteed'.[65] This case, which was decided in 1991, specifically referred to Article 10 ECHR on the freedom of expression, as it concerned the legality of a Greek monopoly on television services. However, the Court in *ERT* also addressed the application of EU fundamental rights in general. This statement by the Court is evidence of its commitment to fundamental rights, emphasising that there was an obligation to consider these rights as part of the EU's guarantees.[66] It raised the profile of fundamental rights in the EU, but was still not a formal legal guarantee, and the Court in *ERT* did not specify which fundamental rights fell within the remit of the Treaty.

By 1991 and the *ERT* case, it was clearer what message the Court intended to convey in comparison to when it first passed judgment on fundamental rights in 1969. It had been 22 years since *Stauder v Ulm* was decided, and initially there had been a sense of uncertainty as to whether the EU would truly embrace this rights-based discourse and whether it had the legal tools to do so, exacerbated by a lack of any constitutional guarantees in the Treaty on binding fundamental rights.[67] This uncertainty may have contributed to the slow progress towards integrating the notion of fundamental rights protection into the Court's decision-making process. However, in the same year that the European Council drafted the Maastricht Treaty, a more convincing statement in *ERT* was finally presented. From its actions, it was possible to infer that the Court was aware of the discussions and political and social elements to be introduced in Maastricht. The Court in *ERT* built on its judgment in *Wachauf* to confirm the growing non-economic influences of the political atmosphere on its decision-making.[68] This resulted in a clarified statement of commitment to fundamental rights, until the Lisbon Treaty made the Charter binding in 2009.

These cases are evidence of a slow but gradual development of the fundamental rights language in the Court's judgments. Changes were seen in the Court when interpreting fundamental rights consistent with the constitutional developments

[64] See Stephen Weatherill, 'After *Keck*: Some Thoughts on How to Clarify the Clarification' (1996) 33 *CML Rev* 887 for the debate dominating the early 1990s in the internal market and the free movement of goods.

[65] *ERT* (n 5) para 41.

[66] Jason Coppel and Aidan O'Neill, 'The European Court of Justice: Taking Rights Seriously?' (1992) 12 *Legal Studies* 227, 234.

[67] See de Búrca (n 63) for a particularly Irish perspective in relation to ECHR rights; Philip Alston and Joseph Weiler, 'An "Ever Closer Union" in Need of a Human Rights Policy: The European Union and Human Rights' in Philip Alston (ed), *The EU and Human Rights* (Oxford Univeristy Press, 1999).

[68] *ERT* (n 5) para 41.

of the EU itself, for only when the EU Treaty drafters were ready to embrace a greater political dialogue with fundamental rights did these rights become judicially substantiated.[69] Although it is recognised that the Court was not as effective in terms of fundamental rights conferral compared to, perhaps, the potential of the binding Charter of Fundamental Rights, what it did do in *ERT* in terms of fundamental rights protection should certainly not be discounted. The enthusiasm of the Court in constitutionally recognising fundamental rights and then confirming this by balancing these interests against the fundamental freedoms demonstrated that its promises in this regard were not empty. This is in direct contrast to the less warmly received EU citizenship provisions. Whilst fundamental rights did not change the face of the EU immediately, their impact on EU law was undeniable.[70]

The principles of conferral, subsidiarity and proportionality as found in Article 5 TEU are the principles that set the boundaries for the operation and application of EU law,[71] underpinning the protection of fundamental rights and also EU citizenship. It is well known that EU citizenship status is limited, restricted from the outset only to nationals of the EU Member States. The Court applied further restrictions as to the scope *ratione personae* and *ratione materiae* on the rights conferred under citizenship status in its case law.[72] Fundamental rights, however, presented a more complicated paradox. As the human rights of the EU, they were perceived to be normatively universal in nature.[73] Yet, the reality is that because the EU itself is defined by its borders and territory, the concept of fundamental rights was limited to protecting situations that have a link with EU law. Though the rights themselves are guaranteed, they cannot be relied upon unless the situation brings them under the scope of EU law. When fundamental rights were made binding in the Charter, expectations for a relationship with EU citizenship were raised even further. However, instead of being integrated, the Court found a way to legally sidestep having to address fundamental rights in the context of citizenship.[74] This did not help the EU's legitimacy and solidarity objectives, or its goals of integration and becoming closer to its citizens.

[69] As proven by the cases discussed previously in this section spanning 1969 to 1992.

[70] Especially considering their influence in the internal market, see Judgment of 12 June 2003, *Schmidberger* C-112/00, EU:C:2003:333; Judgment of 14 Oct 2004, *Omega* C-36/02, EU:C:2004:614. *cf* Judgment of 11 December 2007, *Viking* C-438/05, EU:C:2007:772; Judgment of 18 December 2007, *Laval* C-341/05, EU:C:2007:809.

[71] Article 5 TEU.

[72] Proportionality assessments would also have the effect of limiting the scope of EU citizenship; see *Baumbast* (n 35); Judgment of 18 July 2006, *De Cuyper* C-406/04, EU:C:2006:491.

[73] See James Griffin, 'First Steps in an Account of Human Rights' (2001) 9 *European Journal of Philosophy* 306.

[74] See criticism of *Zambrano* in Niamh Nic Shuibhne, 'Seven Questions for Seven Paragraphs' (2011) 36 *European Law Review* 161; Loïc Azoulai, '"Euro-Bonds": The *Ruiz Zambrano* Judgment or the Real Invention of EU Citizenship' [2011] *Perspectives on Federalism* 31; Roderic O'Gorman, '*Ruiz-Zambrano, McCarthy* and the Purely Internal Rule' [2011] *Irish Jurist* 221; Hanneke van Eijken and Sybe de Vries, 'A New Route into the Promised Land? Being a European Citizen after *Ruiz Zambrano*'

B. Legitimacy and Solidarity in the EU

Integration is the crux of the development of the EU and, as such, permeates all areas. In EU citizenship law, specific objectives have been identified under the umbrella of integration as those necessary to achieve successful EU integration. They are legitimacy of the EU generally and solidarity between EU citizens. It has been challenging for the EU to foster solidarity within its community of citizens when this community is made up of individuals from 28 different Member States. Civic nationalists attribute legitimacy of a nation state to a longer and richer cultural history.[75] This places the EU at a disadvantage, for its history as a supranational entity pales in comparison. Ensuring that the policies and legislation under the Treaties also respect national autonomy has long been a concern of the EU, so much so that it has been codified into the citizenship provisions themselves – EU citizenship 'shall complement' nationality,[76] now 'additional to' it in Lisbon.[77] Maintaining this stark distinction between nationality and EU citizenship status has emphasised the individual's national identity to the potential detriment of the creation of a common European identity.[78]

EU solidarity has also been inhibited because of the relationship that citizens have with their own nation state, and the national solidarity created therein. The struggle that EU citizenship faces is that it is 'growing in the shadow of nationalism'.[79] This relates back to the idea that making EU citizenship dependent on nationality was an obstacle to the concept's development. Solidarity underpins the democratic and political choices of any governing authority, though it may not be widely cited as part of the nation state's reasoning.[80] The actions of the nation state in protecting its own citizens and building its own communities to achieve national solidarity long precedes the advent and goals of European citizenship. The citizen's feeling of solidarity being attributed to the nation state is inherent in national Member States, yet has to be painstakingly fostered in the EU. Exacerbated by European citizenship's dependence on nationality, this has made it somewhat secondary to the national status.

Whilst Member States agreed to limit their sovereignty when joining the European Coal and Steel Community (ECSC) because they would significantly benefit

(2011) 36 *European Law Review* 704; Anja Wiesbrock, 'Disentangling the "Union Citizenship Puzzle"? The *McCarthy* Case' (2011) 36 *European Law Review* 861.

[75] See David Miller, *Citizenship and National Identity* (Polity Press, 2000); and David Miller, *On Nationality* (Clarendon Press, 1995) for more on civic nationalism.

[76] Article 8a EEC.

[77] Article 20(1) TFEU.

[78] Furthermore, nationality is an exclusive national competence; see Judgment of 7 July 1992, *Micheletti* C-369/90, EU:C:1992:295.

[79] Jürgen Habermas, 'Citizenship and National Identity' in Bart van Steenbergen (ed), *The Condition of Citizenship* (SAGE Publications, 1994) 257.

[80] Alexander Somek, 'Solidarity Decomposed: Being and Time in European Citizenship' (2007) 32 *European Law Review* 787, 788.

from it,[81] the introduction of EU citizenship did not include this same reciprocity outright, especially in terms of financial gain. This is perhaps another reason why there has been little EU solidarity generated from the concept, despite the development and changes. In many states, the nation state is the entity with which citizens have a principal affiliation.[82] The EU's goals for solidarity amongst its citizens are unlikely to be realised in the same way as those of a Member State precisely because it is not a nation state. For this reason, there is value in trying to establish a different basis upon which to foster solidarity of the EU.

Differences in the EU are particularly prevalent not only between the 28 Member States that (currently) make up the EU, but also in differences between each individual citizen. This book will not discuss the psychology of the identities of individual citizens. Instead, it notes that Member State autonomy must be respected in relation to their prerogatives concerning their own unique nationality and separate national identity. In contrast, the objective for EU citizenship when it was first negotiated by the EU institutions was to create a platform from which to generate solidarity within the community. This by its nature opposed Member States' interests in guarding their very different national identities. Identity and solidarity are both strengthened when individuals are able to share common values and beliefs. For this reason, EU citizenship had to aim to foster a common EU identity amongst its citizens to break the bounds of nationalism.[83] It is this dependence on nationality that has proven to be an obstacle in the development of EU citizenship's relationship with fundamental rights, which will be considered below.

A political EU would need to give citizens a voice in certain EU affairs.[84] Sacerdoti believed that 'a Europe based on solidarity and democracy where the citizens are the key actors'[85] would be able to truly depart from the internal market focus. A European citizenship would have been suitable for this as 'the content of citizenship is something of a black box which is constrained only by the limits of administrative imagination'.[86] Its flexibility allowed it to be moulded to suit the

[81] See Robert Dahl, *Democracy and its Critics* (Yale University Press, 1989) and his definition of democracy as a reciprocal relationship. Amy Gutmann and Dennis Thompson, 'Why Deliberative Democracy is Different' (2000) 17 *Social Philosophy and Policy* 161 believe that there is room to debate the parameters of this relationship.

[82] See Isin and Turner (n 12) 2 and n 75 above for theories on this.

[83] D'Oliveira (n 16) 139 discusses this in terms of voting; David Held, *Democracy and the Global Order: From the Modern State to Cosmopolitan Governance* (Stanford University Press, 1995) 58 discusses it in terms of national identity existing to bind people together and enhance state power.

[84] Jo Shaw, *The Transformation of Citizenship in the European Union: Electoral Rights and the Restructuring of Political Space* (Cambridge University Press, 2007) particularly believed in voting and representation for this.

[85] Giorgio Sacerdoti, 'The European Charter of Fundamental Rights: From a Nation-State Europe to a Citizen's Europe' (2002) 8 *Columbia Journal of European Law* 37, 52.

[86] Elspeth Guild, 'Does European Citizenship Blur the Borders of Solidarity?' in Elspeth Guild, Cristina Gortázar and Dora Kostakopoulou (eds), *The Reconceptualization of European Union Citizenship* (Martinus Nijhoff, 2014) 190.

EU's objectives. However, if it simply extended workers' rights like the Court had been seen to do in the context of the fundamental freedoms,[87] it would be underwhelming and would contradict what would appear to be the intention that the Treaty negotiators had for an EU manifestation of a political citizenship concept – namely, legitimacy and solidarity within the EU.

It is clear that 'the outer limits of EU free movement law are inherently fragile',[88] given the number of developments that have tested these boundaries and led to a broadening of the scope of the Treaty.[89] Therefore, for the sake of legitimacy, it would be wise for the Court not to push these boundaries too much and risk permanent upset to the balance between the EU and its Member States. This is what it struggled with throughout its development. As Tridimas argues, without legitimacy and solidarity between citizens, establishing democracy becomes a more difficult task.[90] What this book purports to argue in the realm of citizenship, legitimacy and solidarity is that the benefits of citizenship status would be enhanced through the application of fundamental rights, now with a firm legal basis in the Charter. The scope of fundamental rights is the best example of boundaries between national territories being transcended, and acknowledging that national authorities are more willing to compromise for protection of such rights is more reason for this book to support it in the quest for EU legitimacy and EU solidarity.[91]

However, the reality is not so simple or straightforward. The political atmosphere surrounding the Court's decision making has proven to be an obstacle in current interpretations of citizenship law. This will be explained by the discourse in this book on the development of fundamental rights in EU citizenship law. There is a distinct difference between human rights and EU fundamental rights, the main issue being their scope *ratione personae*. EU fundamental rights cannot be universal in scope like human rights for the reasons established earlier. Similarly, EU citizenship rights are not as broad as EU fundamental rights. Though their convergence would broaden the potential for the scope of EU citizenship to expand, this book will demonstrate that there has been a divergence in the interaction between the two concepts of rights due to the increasing unstable political situation in the EU. For a time, convergence appeared likely through activist

[87] See Judgment of 7 July 1992, *Singh* C-370/90, EU:C:1992:296 and the discussion of it in ch 2.

[88] Daniel Thym, 'The Elusive Limits of Solidarity: Residence Rights of and Social Benefits for Economically Inactive Union Citizens' (2015) 52 *CML Rev* 17, 39.

[89] This is true for all four fundamental freedoms of movement: in goods – see Judgment of 24 November 1993, *Keck and Mithouard* C-267/91, EU:C:1993:905; Judgment of 10 February 2009, *Commission v Italy (Trailers)* C-110/05, EU:C:2009:66; in services – see Judgment of 23 November 1995, *Alpine Investments* C-394/93, EU:C:1995:400; in persons – see Judgment of 6 June 2000, *Angonese* C-281/98, EU:C:2000:296; Judgment of 15 December 1995, *Bosman* C-415/93, EU:C:1995:463; and in capital – see arts 63–64 TFEU.

[90] Tridimas (n 6) 298.

[91] Karen J Alter, *Establishing the Supremacy of European Law: The Making of an International Rule of Law in Europe* (Oxford University Press, 2001) 61.

Court interpretations;[92] however, recent cases indicate that this is no longer the case.[93] The Court's decision-making process has been central to the developments in both fundamental rights and EU citizenship, and its case law is the focus of this book.

C. The Role of the Court

This book argues that the Court created expectations early on in the development of both fundamental rights and EU citizenship, separately as well as when both concepts were invoked together. Interpretations came not only from analysing the case law, but also from considering Opinions by Advocates General and aligning the objectives of the concepts with the changing face of the economic EU. There were also legitimacy and solidarity concerns that both fundamental rights and EU citizenship would have the potential to contribute to as part of developing a more political EU.[94] The aims underlying this progress were arguably those of fostering solidarity within the identified EU community and improving the legitimacy of the provisions to which they were subject.

The turning point for recent landmark cases in EU citizenship and fundamental rights is the Lisbon Treaty. This is where this book identifies that the relationship comes closest to a potential convergence. Amongst these cases are also three Opinions that have been instrumental in developing the relationship between fundamental rights and EU citizenship by suggesting and advocating directions that the Court could adopt. Arguments presented particularly in the early Opinions support this book's line of reasoning for a stronger relationship between fundamental rights and EU citizenship. Advocate General (AG) Jacobs in *Konstantinidis* supported their relationship as a way to enhance the legitimacy of both concepts.[95] This set a precedent for EU citizenship before it was formalised in the Treaty, and linked it early on to fundamental rights.

Though *Konstantinidis* was a case on the free movement of services, AG Jacobs nonetheless makes reference to non-economic rights enjoyed inherently as part of

[92] The most indicative case for this was Judgment of 2 March 2010, *Rottmann* C-135/08, EU:C:2010:104; however, see also *Carpenter* (n 22); Judgment of 2 October 2003, *Garcia Avello* C-148/02, EU:C:2003:539; and *Zhu and Chen* (n 30).

[93] Judgment of 5 May 2011, *McCarthy* C-434/09, EU:C:2011:277; Judgment of 15 November 2011, *Dereci* C-256/11, EU:C:2011:734; Judgment of 8 November 2012, *Iida* C-40/11, EU:C:2012:691; Judgment of 10 October 2003, *Alokpa* C-86/12, EU:C:2013:645; Judgment of 6 December 2012, *O, S and L* C-356/11 and C-357/11, EU:C:2012:776.

[94] See Lehning (n 34); Armin von Bogdandy et al, 'Reverse Solange: Protecting the Essence of Fundamental Rights against EU Member States' (2012) 49 *CML Rev* 489; Moravcsik (n 45); Joze Strus and Nina Persak, 'The Charter of Fundamental Rights and EU Citizenship: The Link with EU Law Re-examined' in Elspeth Guild, Cristina Gortázar and Dora Kostakopoulou (eds), *The Reconceptualization of European Union Citizenship* (Martinus Nijhoff, 2014).

[95] *Konstantinidis* (n 34).

being an individual in the EU. He states that declaring 'civis europeus sum' ('I am a European citizen') is entitlement enough to the guarantees under fundamental rights protection.[96] Decided a little under a year before the Maastricht Treaty came into effect, the Opinion is a precursor to the introduction of citizenship status and its relationship with fundamental rights. The significance of the *Konstantinidis* Opinion is that it brings the question of fundamental rights to the fore after – and indeed during – a time of dominance of the internal market. It is the first clear expression of an intention to foster a closer relationship between fundamental rights and the citizen being protected as a citizen. At this point, there was little enforceable protection for non-economic actors.[97]

It took the Court nearly six years after *Konstantinidis* to expand the scope *ratione personae* of EU citizenship to include non-economically active citizens and then for it to expand the scope *ratione materiae* to follow suit.[98] After this, many cases were referred asking for clarification on the rights of non-economically active citizens. This lasted until the mid-2000s. In 2007, following this boom of cases,[99] AG Colomer delivered his Opinion on the developing relationship between fundamental rights and EU citizenship in *Petersen*.[100] After much deliberation, he noted that the Court had been successful in its attempts to make citizenship status relevant against the backdrop of the more prominent EU internal market. Instead of relying on the fundamental freedoms, AG Colomer argued that it was entirely possible to envisage that individuals were protected irrespective of their economic activity because of the way in which EU citizenship had been interpreted, raising not only its own status, but also that of fundamental rights. This Opinion demonstrates that to interpret case law as indicating what AG Colomer calls 'homo civitatis' as opposed to 'homo economicus' was supported.[101]

The notions of *homo civitatis* and *homo economicus* come from analysing the state of the citizenship case law at the time of the Opinion in 2007 and comparing it to the early 1990s, when AG Jacobs' Opinion in *Konstantinidis* was delivered. This book will make clear that prior to the introduction of political elements to the EU, the Court primarily considered citizens *homo economicus* – in their economically active capacity. This excluded many citizens such as those who were not non-economically active by choice, like children, or disabled individuals.

[96] ibid para 46.

[97] Unless they were family members of workers; see Regulation (EEC) No 1612/68 of the Council of 15 October 1968 on freedom of movement for workers within the Community [1968] OJ L257/2.

[98] See *Sala* (n 35) and the introduction of equal treatment for social welfare for non-economically active migrant citizens.

[99] Between 1998 and 2007, the judicial instruments governing EU citizenship law emerged in *Sala* (n 39); *Grzelczyk* (n 9) (on non-discrimination); Judgment of 15 March 2005, *Bidar* C-209/03, EU:C:2005:169; *Baumbast* (n 35); Judgment of 7 September 2004, *Trojani* C-456/02, EU:C:2004:488 (on proportionality and the genuine link test); *Carpenter* (n 22); *Garcia Avello* (n 92) (on purely internal situations); *Zhu and Chen* (n 30) (on fundamental rights). These will be discussed more fully in section IV below.

[100] Opinion of 11 September 2008, *Petersen* C-228/07, EU:C:2008:281.

[101] Judgment 11 September 2008, *Petersen* C-228/07, EU:C:2008:494, para 15.

With the impetus of EU citizenship status, the Court has been able to bring these citizens, and more, within the scope of the Treaty's protection. As AG Colomer argued, 'the Court has transformed the paradigm of *homo economicus* into that of *homo civitatis*'.[102] *Homo civitatis* thus put no emphasis on economic activity, so all subjects were recognised simply as EU citizens rather than as workers in the EU. This was acknowledged to be a broader perspective, and included those who would not necessarily have benefited originally.[103] It will also be argued in this book that the reason for this was the growing relevance of fundamental rights, initially through the principle of non-discrimination and then more widely.[104]

Following on from this explicit statement of approval of the Court's more liberal direction from AG Colomer, in 2010, AG Sharpston issued her Opinion in the seminal *Zambrano* case, which has become as significant as the case itself.[105] This Opinion, alongside the preceding cases and literature, has cemented the position taken in this book of promoting an expansive scope *ratione personae* and *ratione materiae* of EU citizenship because of the way in which its relationship with fundamental rights had been developing. It is acknowledged that the case law did not always portray such a relationship operating so coherently and, indeed, did not demonstrate what AG Colomer considers as supporting a *homo civitatis* approach, or what AG Jacobs meant by declaring *civis europeus sum*. For this reason, this book will begin by assessing the original position adopted by the Court not only before Lisbon but also before the Maastricht Treaty in order to draw out the stark differences and to identify from where this book's line of reasoning derives.

The EU's early history was dominated by a focus on establishment of the internal market. Though this was an approach that was suitable at the time to the original objectives and goals of the European Economic Community (EEC), as it broadened to encompass other competences, it became clear this this was not always appropriate. In particular, when political and social elements were introduced to the economic EU, the dichotomy between old approaches to the new subject matter became evident. This can be seen in the citizenship case law when comparing the Court's methodology pre- and post-1998,[106] with *Sala* in 1998 being used as the point of reference.[107] The Lisbon Treaty is the next indicator of change in the EU citizenship development, thereby demarcating three 'ages' of citizenship.[108]

[102] ibid.

[103] ibid.

[104] After non-discrimination, legal residency rights became more prominent and after this, the rights of family members of EU citizens, particularly if they were not EU nationals.

[105] *Zambrano*, Opinion of AG Sharpston (n 23).

[106] It was only in 1998 with the *Sala* case that citizenship status was considered to have been substantiated, despite it being established in 1993.

[107] *Sala* (n 35).

[108] Niamh Nic Shuibhne, 'The Third Age of EU Citizenship' in Phil Syrpis (ed), *The Judiciary, the Legislature and the EU Internal Market* (Cambridge University Press, 2012).

III. The Legal Culture of the Court

It is clear from the discussion thus far that it is the Court that determines the relationship between fundamental rights and EU citizenship. It is through the case law that both concepts have developed, and rights under the Treaty have been substantiated. Examining the Court's behaviour in many similar yet different cases provides an insight into its legal culture, and it is this legal culture that explains and justifies many of the claims made in this book. This refers not only to the relationship between fundamental rights and EU citizenship, but also to the decisions made in each separate concept that directed their development, informed by the EU's ever-changing constitutional landscape. It is important to consider how the Court came to adopt such a culture and why this has added to the expectations for EU citizenship and fundamental rights.

To understand the EU's legal culture, we must understand legal culture itself. This is a notably difficult task.[109] Friedman describes legal culture as 'ideas, values, expectations and attitudes towards law and legal institutions, which some public or some part of the public holds'.[110] It is also understood that legal culture 'can serve to capture an essential intervening variable in influencing the type of legal changes which follow on large social transformations'.[111] Acknowledging both the Court's legal culture and the factors that influence this culture helps to explain its behaviour, especially in EU citizenship law. It should be noted that the Court reacts to the political atmosphere in which it operates in order to ensure respect for Member States' autonomy, which has led to apparent shifts throughout the developments in terms of how the Court undertakes its decision making depending on the subject matter of the cases on which it issues judgment. This perpetuates inconsistency, but has become a recognised characteristic of the Court.

The role of the Court as a check on the EU institutions was identified as early as when the EU was the ECSC, and since then this role has grown.[112] Alter argues that, unsurprisingly, when the Court first emerged as a supranational player in the EU's constitutional legal order, national courts were extremely wary of its judicial powers and influence over their own governance. If the CJEU was perceived to be infringing national prerogatives, this would be an affront to national sovereignty.[113] The Court would react to this negative reception by somewhat

[109] Roger Cotterrell, 'The Concept of Legal Culture' in David Nelken (ed), *Comparing Legal Cultures* (Dartmouth Publishing, 1997).
[110] Lawrence M Friedman, 'The Concept of Legal Culture: A Reply' in David Nelken (ed), *Comparing Legal Cultures* (Dartmouth Publishing, 1997) 34.
[111] David Nelken, 'Using the Concept of Legal Culture' (2004) 29 *Australian Journal of Legal Philosophy* 1.
[112] Alter (n 91) 6.
[113] ibid 54.

judicially retreating.[114] For this reason, in early citizenship case law, the Court applied the legal reasoning of cases in the internal market, appearing to anticipate negative reaction from Member States for attempting anything different. At the time of the introduction of EU citizenship, the EU internal market was also being established,[115] and demanded more attention. For the Court, it was the more familiar option, and choosing to defer to it was a symptom of its legal culture. However, this eventually changed, hence it being perceived as inconsistent in its decision-making process.

Though informed early on by the economics of the then ECSC, the Court did seek to achieve one everlasting common objective: 'deeper integration through law'.[116] EU law is shaped by hard law,[117] a number of soft instruments[118] and the Court's interpretations. It is a unique mélange of the common and civil law.[119] For this reason, the Court could not avoid being influenced by external politics, especially from its 28 Member States.[120] It had to remain an institution sensitive to its subjects for ultimately it aimed to achieve an integrated EU. Precedent does not bind the Court;[121] rather, it is defined by its unpredictability. However, Schmidt argues the opposite, in that 'its overarching interest in the consistency of case law, often backed by litigants' support for the existing path, imply that the [CJEU] generally follows precedent'.[122] This is a further symptom of the Court's legal culture. Legal certainty is the ideal, but it is notably more difficult to achieve in the EU because of political factors that influence judicial decisions, hence the disparities and differing opinions.

The CJEU's legal culture is thus defined as follows. It is the culture of the Court to be cautious when dealing with certain sensitive subject matters, such as those which did not form the basis of the original ECSC. This effectively covers all non-economic issues, from the political to the social. However, it is also in its nature to be judicially activist when the political atmosphere suits it, such as around

[114] This is evident in the inconsistencies of the Court throughout citizenship, for example, in the area of student maintenance after *Bidar*; see Judgment of 18 Nov 2008, *Förster* C-158/07, EU:C:2008:630.

[115] Article 3 EEC.

[116] Andreas Grimmel, '"This is Not Life as it is Lived Here": The European Court of Justice and the Myth of Judicial Activism in the Foundational Period of Integration through Law' [2014] *European Journal of Legal Studies* 62, 63.

[117] Article 288 TFEU.

[118] See Linda Senden, *Soft Law in European Community Law* (Hart Publishing, 2004).

[119] See William Tetley, 'Mixed Jurisdictions: Common Law v Civil Law (Codified and Uncodified)' (1999) 60 *Louisiana Law Review* 677.

[120] A particularly good example is the Judgment of 11 November 2014, *Dano* C-333/13, EU:C:2014:2358 case on the free movement of non-economically active citizens in today's Eurosceptic environment. See ch 5 for more details.

[121] See Clifford J Carrubba, Matthew Gabel and Charles Hankla, 'Judicial Behavior under Political Constraints: Evidence from the European Court of Justice' (2008) 102 *American Political Science Review* 435.

[122] Susanne K Schmidt, 'Who Cares about Nationality? The Path-Dependent Case Law of the ECJ from Goods to Citizens' (2012) 19 *Journal of European Public Policy* 8, 9.

when the Maastricht Treaty came into force, when non-economic elements were first officially introduced to the EU. This prompted inconsistency in the judicial reasoning of the Court as it struggled to balance its original objectives with its new ones, inciting criticism given the challenges of balancing two starkly opposed objectives. For this reason, in several areas – EU citizenship most pertinently – the Court has not followed a clear trajectory in its case law. Therefore, despite choosing to depart from adopting a rights-based *acquis* in recent cases, there was still a possibility that this could change, especially because the Lisbon Treaty had now made the Charter binding.[123]

A stronger fundamental rights discourse as it applies to EU citizenship is a desirable outcome of the Court's case law. A rights-based *acquis* speaks more directly to protection of the individual. It is consistent with the goals of greater EU integration and is argued to possibly even be an expected outcome in the political context of a rights-based EU. The fundamental rights discourse and its normative foundations should have influenced the Court's legal culture more, given indications from its previous case law that this was a possibility.[124] However, it appears that other political factors have now altered the constitutional context of the Court, explaining why it has not met expectations.[125] Furthermore, these recent political factors have had the effect of deferring more to Member States' interests than those of the EU. Nelken is thus correct in stating that legal culture identifies the variable that is the determinant for legal change.[126] This book argues that in the citizenship and fundamental rights relationship, there are three variables. The first is the Maastricht Treaty and the introduction of political and social policies where the Court became more accepting of the protection of non-economic values, and the second is the eurozone crisis which instigated the rise of Euroscepticism and the Court's more cautious tone.[127] A possible third can also be argued to be developing at present: the recent advent of the British vote to leave the EU has prompted a possible Brexit variable, which will also be discussed.

It has long been recognised that if anything could quell the criticism surrounding a judicially activist Court, it would be the implementation of fundamental rights. It is an area where national courts are more willing to compromise.[128] Though it would seem that the Court is activist in order to achieve the objectives related to integration, it does not pursue these goals at the expense of ignoring the interests of national courts. As Grimmel puts it, 'it is about understanding the rules of the game, not just the motives of the players, or the way the game shapes their

[123] Article 6 TEU.

[124] See *Garcia Avello* (n 92); *Zhu and Chen* (n 30); *Carpenter* (n 22).

[125] This book hypothesises that it is the eurozone crisis that has incited these sentiments, which will be discussed in ch 5.

[126] Nelken (n 111) 8.

[127] See the discussion in ch 5.

[128] Alter (n 91) 61.

thoughts and actions'.[129] The rules of the Court's game, namely its legal instruments and wider objectives, are flexible. Though a commitment to integration is ever-present, there are no hard rules or strict direction. This has its benefits but also disadvantages. It supports a relationship between EU citizenship and fundamental rights, but also highlights disparities in the case law and perpetuates legal uncertainty. However, as this book will outline, fundamental rights have not been integrated into EU citizenship law as expected.

Alter argues that 'if Member States ultimately accepted this transfer [of competences], it must be because at some level they desired it'.[130] This can be said to be true of fundamental rights in particular. This seemed to be the case in EU citizenship, especially after the Court overcame obstacles in the first age to produce the vast amount of case law in the second. EU citizens accumulated a great number of rights and, importantly, access to these rights was made less cumbersome as the process became less concerned with economic activity. What instead emerged were legal instruments that were applied to shift the focus of the law to other emerging general principles of EU law, and the Court's role was to create legal rules in the case law that would help determine whether the facts warranted protection under such principles guaranteed by citizenship law. As such, under citizenship, a set of rights, rules, principles and tests have emerged, and these have shaped the legal order in the EU under EU citizenship. Their development underlies the analysis in this book.

IV. Judicial Instruments in EU Citizenship Law

As the arbiter of EU law, the Court is tasked with applying legal principles and establishing legal rules in order to best guarantee the protection and rights enshrined in the Treaty. There is relative flexibility in terms of how this should be done, given the lack of an EU constitution as well as the EU not following civil or common law,[131] which evidently has its strengths and weaknesses. One of the main strengths is that if the principles, rules or tests applied at the outset are then considered unsuitable for the broader objective of the provisions, the Court can bring about a normative shift to change the constitutional landscape to work better in its favour. It is arguable that this is what happened in EU citizenship. However, it is less desirable for overall legal certainty, and has been problematic in relation to citizenship for being unpredictable and disadvantageous to citizens who sought such rights. This book labels the principles, rules and tests applied by the Court

[129] Grimmel (n 116) 63.
[130] Alter (n 91) 182.
[131] Subject of course to the general principles of EU law, most notably, conferral, subsidiarity and proportionality in art 5 TEU.

under the notion of legal or judicial instruments, and identifies five used throughout the course of citizenship's development: the principles of non-discrimination, proportionality, the genuine link test, the purely internal situations rule and the deprivation of genuine enjoyment test.

In order to clarify the nomenclature used to describe the principles, rules and tests employed by the Court in its decision-making process, it is important to distinguish legal principles from rules, and rules from tests. Tridimas notes that '[p]rinciples provide justification for concrete rules' whilst a 'rule answers the question "what" whereas a principle answers the question "why"'.[132] Under citizenship law, there are several rules for the different notions of why the Court should endeavour to grant protection to its subjects, the EU citizens, particularly if they were non-economically active. There are also many legal principles in citizenship that have Court-generated rules and tests to determine whether the factual scenario falls under its remit so as to guarantee protection of the relevant legal principle. The term 'judicial instruments' is therefore used as a catch-all for the various methods the Court applies in its reasoning EU citizenship case law. It is due to the subtle but present differences in terms of the application of these identified instruments that they are considered as 'instruments'. The first and most prominent legal principle in the operation of EU citizenship law concerns non-economically active citizens and whether they deserve rights under citizenship by virtue of the legal principle of non-discrimination.

A. The Principle of Non-discrimination (Article 18 TFEU)

The principle of non-discrimination is a constitutional principle in EU law. It is also a right enshrined in Article 18 TFEU, which states that 'any discrimination on grounds of nationality shall be prohibited'.[133] This reference to nationality is indicative of the integrationist agenda of the EU, for above all else, equality is sacrosanct in an entity that aims to unite 28 different Member States under one supranational umbrella of governance. Given the importance of this constitutional legal principle, it was foreseeable that the Court would eventually apply this principle to empower the citizen. This was especially after it became clear that the provisions were limited in scope to the economically active. It is this legal principle that has shaped a large part of EU citizenship case law. Reading this principle with the status of EU citizenship was a significant judicial achievement because it was used to legally recognise that economic actors were not the only subjects of EU law, thereby expanding the scope *ratione personae* of citizenship.

[132] Tridimas (n 6) 2.
[133] Article 18 TFEU.

The principle of non-discrimination dominated the case law for most of the history of EU citizenship, which is a testament to its judicial weight. The principle itself protected the wider community of citizens and was clearly the cornerstone of the citizenship development, as well as in the EU generally. Because of its respected and accepted status in the EU, it was easy for the Court to apply such rules to enhance the status of citizenship and for this legal reasoning to quickly become the norm throughout. It is argued that the growth of this principle also indicated an underlying intention to engage more fully with fundamental rights, and is thus a prelude to its later rise throughout citizenship. However, it should be noted that this principle has faded into the background of judicial decisions of late because of recent developments like the *Zambrano* case,[134] which saw a shift in norms directed away from non-discrimination and economic activity, and towards an independent legal basis of EU citizenship.

B. The Principle of Proportionality

The second most common legal principle in EU citizenship case law is the principle of proportionality, another general EU constitutional principle. The formula to determine if actions taken by the EU institutions would be proportionate is whether the provision has a legitimate aim and if the provision is necessary, suitable and the least intrusive means to achieving the identified aim.[135] In EU citizenship, this principle has proven itself to be a strong ally in balancing the interests of the Member States against the liberal integrationist nature of EU citizenship. By framing it under such a flexible principle, it can be interpreted to the benefit of either the Member States (protecting their resources) or the citizens (protecting their individual rights). This book will show that this principle has been interpreted to the benefit of both parties[136] and became especially relevant after non-discrimination was introduced as a legal principle.

The Court's decision to read non-discrimination and the status of being a EU citizen together to empower the non-economically active citizen has been broadly well received, but at the time of its introduction, there were concerns that this risked going beyond the norms established prior to this – namely, judicial norms that shaped the fundamental freedoms.[137] The introduction of the principle of proportionality helped mitigate these fears. This was through adding flexibility to the judicial process, as the proportionality assessment applied by the Court often saw economic interests balanced against non-economic interest (primarily social or political rights). Though also employed widely in the internal market,

[134] *Zambrano* (n 23) para 42.
[135] Tridimas (n 6) 139.
[136] See the discussion in *Trojani* (n 99) and *De Cuyper* (n 72). *cf Bidar* (n 99); and *Förster* (n 114).
[137] See the discussion after *Keck* in Weatherill (n 64).

AG Jacobs notes that in relation to proportionality, 'there are few areas of Community law, if any at all, where that is not relevant'.[138] Like non-discrimination, it was also foreseeable that it would be applied to EU citizenship law, and has also become a widely relied upon source of justice for the Member State and citizens alike. The Court's approach to proportionality in EU citizenship was markedly favourable to the citizen at first,[139] and this contributed significantly to expanding the scope of the citizenship provisions, making room for fundamental rights considerations. More recently, however, the Court has been more cautious about exhibiting such liberalism, arguably reacting to the EU's state of crisis.[140]

C. Protecting National Welfare Systems and the 'Genuine Link' Test

As the Court alluded to in its application of the principles of non-discrimination and proportionality, there was a strong need for the EU institutions to guarantee respect for national interests and national autonomy. This was a feature of the legal culture of the Court, encouraged by provisions in the Treaty.[141] When the Court began to interpret EU citizenship law and upset this long-held legal tradition, there had to be safeguards in place. This worked both ways, for the EU also sought to employ safeguards for the larger numbers of free-moving citizens seeking welfare after *Sala*. Given the Court's inclination to protect its market over its citizens, this would also benefit them in appearing to strike a balance between broadening the scope of the Treaty for non-economically active citizens, but also avoiding situations where moving for the sole reason of benefits was the intention.[142] This situation would be akin to capitalising on the EU's commitments to its citizens, and would simply become unfeasible without restrictions, given a Member State's finite resources.

Therefore, in order to protect Member States' national welfare systems, the Court introduced the 'genuine link' test and the 'unreasonable burden' criteria. It was in *Baumbast* that the Court first introduced the terminology of being an unreasonable burden. It stated that in order to be able to qualify for rights under the Treaty in relation to citizenship, claimants had to prove that they were not

[138] Opinion of 6 April 1995, *Commission v Greece* C-120/94, EU:C:1995:109, para 70.

[139] Eleanor Spaventa, 'Earned Citizenship: Understanding Union Citizenship through its Scope' in Dimitry Kochenov (ed), *EU Citizenship and Federalism: The Role of Rights* (Cambridge University Press, 2017).

[140] Mark Dawson and Floris de Witte, 'Constitutional Balance in the EU after the Euro-Crisis' (2013) 76 *MLR* 817, 821. On the crisis more generally, see Alicia Hinarejos, 'Fiscal Federalism in the European Union: Evolution and Future Choices for EMU' (2013) 50 *CML Rev* 1621.

[141] Article 4(2) TEU.

[142] The Court has recently upheld this notion in *Dano* (n 120), which has generated a significant amount of media attention given the current Eurosceptic political atmosphere.

being unduly burdensome on the host state's finances.[143] It was effectively a manifestation of the strict economic criteria for claiming citizenship rights that existed at the outset.[144] This would be assessed after the citizen proved that they had a genuine link with the host society, and was a test that national courts had the freedom to determine the limits of. The genuine link test was often a residency requirement, which in itself raised several different legal questions under non-discrimination and proportionality.[145]

The genuine link test and the unreasonable burden criteria both stem from balancing interests under proportionality, and are the representative protective measures for the conservative view of EU citizenship law. It is also a way for the Court to consider not only EU interests, but also those of the Member States, as well as the political implications of such decisions. This was not only as they pertained to the EU, but also as they extended into national legal autonomy. However, it has served as a useful legal instrument to establish what the boundaries of the scope of EU citizenship are more clearly, although it is evident from the case law that the Court's interpretations have not always been consistent. Like the other instruments identified above, the genuine link test lends itself to this kind of flexible interpretation. Fundamental rights occasionally found protection through the medium of the genuine link test. Recently, though, the test has been more narrowly interpreted, with the Court emphasising being an unreasonable burden more than proving a genuine link.[146]

D. The 'Purely Internal Situations' Rule

Related to the genuine link test is the 'purely internal situations' rule. One of the strict guarantees under EU law is that it will not engage or interfere with anything that falls outside its scope, and there are different rules depending on the provision to determine whether a case falls within its scope or not.[147] In the context of EU citizenship, the test that determines if there is a purely internal situation derives directly from the rules governing the fundamental freedoms – the cross-border test. If the claimant had not moved from one Member State to another, they would not trigger the Treaty or rights under Article 21 TFEU. Their claim

[143] *Baumbast* (n 35) para 90.

[144] In the three 1990 Residency Directives, Council Directive (EEC) 90/364 of 28 June 1990 on the right of residence [1990] OJ L180/26; Council Directive (EEC) 90/365 of 28 June 1990 on the right of residence for employees and self-employed persons who have ceased their occupational activity [1990] OJ L180/28; Council Directive (EEC) 93/96 of 29 October 1993 on the right of residence for students [1990] OJ L180/59, claimants were required to demonstrate sufficient resources and comprehensive health insurance.

[145] See the debate in *Bidar* (n 99) and Judgment of 11 July 2002, *D'hoop* C-224/98, EU:C:2002:432, discussed in ch 2.

[146] Judgment of 21 December 2011, *Ziolkowski* C-424/10, EU:C:2011:866; Judgment of 19 September 2013, *Brey* C-140/12, EU:C:2013:565; *Dano* (n 120).

[147] Articles 4 and 5 TEU.

would remain the sole authority of the home Member States' national courts, hence a 'purely internal' situation. Because the EU cannot act where it has not been conferred any competence to act,[148] this test did not seem to raise any issues, especially when employed in the internal market.[149] However, it had several purported effects for citizenship in particular.

The first effect was that employing this principle was an opportunity to add legal certainty to an increasingly convoluted area of case law. Like the genuine link test, it also provided a clearer demarcation for where the boundaries of the scope for EU citizenship lay. This was welcomed. Second, instead of grappling with difficult situations and sensitive issues like fundamental rights, the purely internal situations rule allowed the Court to declare that the matter was wholly outside the scope of its competences. This would ensure respect for the outer limits of EU law, which was especially timely given the concerns that, after *Sala*, these boundaries were being tested.[150] However, the problems that this raised in the citizenship context was whether it was a suitable test to apply to a non-economic concept aiming to protect non-economic legal rights.[151]

The effect of the purely internal situations rule and the genuine link test in strengthening the positions of citizens who satisfied their respective standards for falling under the Treaty further corroborated the Court's support for EU citizenship status carrying rights for a greater scope of individuals within the EU. Given that both principles were flexible and balanced in a normative sense, it was up to the Court to clarify what its intentions would be going forward. As ever, this was both positive and negative. This book will analyse what the trend of the Court was in this regard, as well as its legal ramifications and what this change means for the future of citizenship, considering particularly its relationship with fundamental rights. The purely internal situations rule has been especially criticised because it is inconsistent with the guarantees under the principle of non-discrimination. Whether this test should remain in EU citizenship law will also be discussed in this book.

E. The 'Deprivation of Genuine Enjoyment' Test

The deprivation of genuine enjoyment test is the most recent and least developed of the five judicial instruments applied by the Court in EU citizenship law. It emerged from the decision in *Zambrano* and represented a significant change in direction for the constitutional development of EU citizenship. Non-discrimination

[148] ibid art 5.

[149] The wording of art 34 TFEU dictates that a cross-border element is necessary.

[150] See Michael Dougan, 'Expanding the Frontiers of European Union Citizenship by Dismantling the Territorial Boundaries of the National Welfare States?' in Catherine Barnard and Okeoghene Odudu (eds), *The Outer Limits of European Union Law* (Hart Publishing, 2008).

[151] This will be discussed in ch 2. The problem being referred to is the issue of reverse discrimination.

had dominated judicial developments for the majority of citizenship history, but as the principle itself increasingly became the legal norm in citizenship cases, it began to lose its significance as a specific judicial instrument driving the development of EU citizenship. Furthermore, the widespread, almost tacit, acceptance of non-discrimination of EU citizens had begun to suggest that there was a possibility that EU citizenship need not rely upon free movement and the cross-border test before actually seeking to rely on its provisions – it was becoming its own independent legal basis for the application and enjoyment of EU citizenship rights.

The Court in *Zambrano* explicitly confirmed that EU citizenship status under Article 20 TFEU had become an independent legal basis for rights under Article 21 TFEU.[152] Many commentators hailed this introduction, as EU citizenship was finally liberated from the internal market and principles like those governing the existence of the cross-border test.[153] This had been hinted at in many Court cases prior to this, though not explicitly.[154] In order to rely upon EU citizenship provisions after *Zambrano*, the Court declared that if a citizen had been deprived of the genuine enjoyment of their rights under EU citizenship, then they would be able to exercise their rights as an EU citizen and claim protection from this deprivation. What it meant in principle was that there was no longer a need to consider a breach of non-discrimination to trigger the Treaty.

However, what was missing then was a thorough classification of what it meant to be deprived of the genuine enjoyment of one's rights. The Court in *Zambrano* left this open. Given the liberalism exhibited by the Court that led to it declaring EU citizenship status an independent legal basis for rights, there was an expectation that interpretations of the deprivation of genuine enjoyment test would adopt a similar style of reasoning. This book argues that fundamental rights in the Charter should be a factor in the assessment of whether a citizen has been deprived of the genuine enjoyment of their rights or not, especially given the Charter's now binding status in the Lisbon Treaty. However, in the cases after *Zambrano*, the trajectory of the Court no longer points towards integration of fundamental rights into EU citizenship law. This book will thus analyse the application of this test by the Court as it pertains to its decision to reject a fundamental rights *acquis*, and what this says about the current legal culture of the Court.

[152] *Zambrano* (n 23) para 42.

[153] Schmidt (n 122); Peter van Elsuwege, 'Shifting the Boundaries? European Union Citizenship and the Scope of Application of EU Law – Case No. C-34/09, *Gerardo Ruiz Zambrano v Office national de l'emploi*' (2011) 38 *Legal Issues of Economic Integration* 263; Robin Morris, 'Case C-34/09 *Gerardo Ruiz Zambrano v Office National de l'Emploi* (ONEm), Judgment of the Court (Grand Chamber) of 8 March 2011, Not Yet Reported' (2011) 18 *Maastricht Journal of European and Comparative Law* 179; van Eijken and de Vries (n 74).

[154] See *Garcia Avello* (n 92); *Zhu and Chen* (n 30); *Carpenter* (n 22); *Rottmann* (n 92).

V. The Three Ages of EU Citizenship

Nic Shuibhne coined the notion of 'ages' of citizenship. She separated the case law of citizenship into three distinct time periods by identifying when the Court adopted distinctly different judicial reasoning in its decisions. She also identified two events in citizenship's historical timeline that were the clear driving forces behind the shifts in normative judicial thinking. The first is the *Sala* case, a widely accepted landmark of EU citizenship law, which demarcated when the first age of *homo economicus* reasoning ended and when the second age of *homo civitatis* reasoning instead began. The second is the introduction of the only other formally codified legal instrument specific to EU citizenship, the Citizenship Directive 2004.[155] Nic Shuibhne argued that the specificity of the provisions and codification of principles in the Directive led the Court down a different judicial route, and this now drives the Court's decision-making process. Whilst this book adopts the notion of distinct periods of normative reasoning exemplified by the Court to demarcate 'ages' of citizenship, it will not use the same indicators to separate the ages. Instead, it argues that the Lisbon Treaty and the binding status of the Charter have changed the Court's judicial direction. Therefore, in reference to the three 'ages' of citizenship, this book identifies the first age to be case law before *Sala* in 1998, the second age to be the decade of citizenship case law after 1998 leading up to 2009, and the third age to capture the case law after the Lisbon Treaty entered into force.

At this juncture, it may be worth noting that this book has been written in a very interesting political timeframe for the EU itself as well as for various Member States. It marks the first time that a Member State has chosen to trigger the withdrawal provision, Article 50 TEU, and begin the process of withdrawing as a Member State of the EU.[156] In this regard, it seems relevant to also add a 'fourth' age: the Brexit age. The UK's EU referendum vote's outcome in mid-2016 has led to a flurry of activity within the EU and the UK as they negotiate the very complicated and unprecedented process of withdrawal. There have been a great number of serious effects on many different areas. One of the most controversial has been the area of citizens' rights in the context of fundamental rights protection. This has gone hand in hand with the discussion applicable human rights protection post-Brexit, and also forms a large part of this book's analysis.

However, returning to the earlier history of citizenship, what can be said to be a dominant feature of the cases in the first age of citizenship is that they can also be situated within the scope of the internal market. However, this character

[155] Council Directive 2004/38/EC of 29 April 2004 on the right of citizens of the Union and their family members to move and reside freely within the territory of the Member States amending Regulation (EEC) 1612/68 and repealing Directives 64/221/EEC, 68/360/EEC, 72/194/EEC, 73/148/EEC, 75/34/EEC, 75/35/EEC, 90/364/EEC, 90/365/EEC 93/96/EEC [2004] OJ L158/77.

[156] Letter from Theresa May to Donald Tusk (29 March 2017).

is criticised because the Court used approaches already employed under the fundamental freedoms to advance EU citizenship. The Court was seen to apply internal market principles to situations that would otherwise have fallen under citizenship case law by extending the scope of workers' rights.[157] It continued with this even after citizenship was introduced,[158] giving rise to concerns that the status was nothing more than an empty political statement.[159] The protection of fundamental rights had been a general principle of EU law for many years, and only later did the Court decide that these rights should be protected where relevant.[160] Cases on fundamental rights did not distinguish between the economically active and inactive. However, the Court in pre-1998 EU citizenship case law seemed to favour those who had contributed economically.[161] It will be argued that the reason for this is part of the legal culture of the Court, which is defined by the influence the political situation has on its decision making.[162]

The doubts surrounding EU citizenship before 1998 primarily derive from comparing the provisions' scope *ratione personae* and *ratione materiae* to the scope of the fundamental freedoms in the internal market. Because the Court simply extended workers' rights in scenarios concerning citizenship for a time after EU citizenship status was established, it appeared to replicate what was already in existence. This neither differentiated nor legitimised EU citizenship status. The legitimisation of the status was all the more crucial, especially given the novelty of a political EU. By failing to substantiate EU citizenship as its own concept and constantly requiring it to be linked with internal market values, the original objective of an indiscriminate and uniting status within the exclusive EU community was lost. Furthermore, because the scope of fundamental rights was significantly broader in terms of also protecting the economically inactive, it seemed incongruous that the scope of EU citizenship was more limited if the two concepts were to interact coherently.

The second age of EU citizenship for this book starts in 1998 and ends in 2009. Citizenship's restrictive scope *ratione personae* and *ratione materiae* were gradually broadened in these 11 years. It did not happen immediately; the gradual disintegration of strict ties to the fundamental freedoms seemed difficult at the beginning. However, after *Sala* and *Grzelczyk* were decided, and the Court in

157 *Singh* (n 87).

158 Much had to do with the existence of the criteria in the Residency Directives which pre-dated EU citizenship status; see (n 144).

159 See d'Oliveira (n 16); O'Leary (n 4); Ulrich K Preuss, 'Two Challenges to European Citizenship' (1996) 44 *Political Studies* 534; Carole Lyons, 'A Voyage around Article 8: An Historical Evaluation on the Fate of European Union Citizenship' (1997) 17 *Yearbook of European Law* 135.

160 See *Internationale Handelsgesellschaft* (n 39); *ERT* (n 39).

161 See *Singh* (n 87).

162 This was discussed in section III above.

Grzelczyk declared that 'Union citizenship is destined to be the fundamental status of nationals of the Member States',[163] a new direction for citizenship became clear. This was applied most effectively in cases in the early to late 2000s and culminated in the codification of the Citizenship Directive 2004/38. After many years of steady case development for EU citizenship law, the Court also began to introduce the idea of fundamental rights to its decisions,[164] which strengthened the position of both concepts and the future constitutionalisation in the Lisbon Treaty of fundamental rights.

When the Lisbon Treaty came into force in 2009, fundamental rights permeated a vast number of areas of the EU, which included cases where fundamental rights would not previously have featured.[165] When the Charter was raised in equal status to the Treaties, the Court could legally raise concerns of fundamental rights and require that the rights be adhered to. EU citizenship complemented fundamental rights, more so after cases like *Chen*, which applied fundamental rights reasoning to citizenship rights.[166] The *Zambrano* case, which was about third-country national (TCN) family members and derived rights to residency, was one of the first opportunities to link fundamental rights in the binding Charter and EU citizenship provisions. The claimants in *Zambrano* believed that their situation was comparable to that of the claimants in *Chen*. By invoking their claim not only to EU citizenship rights to residency but also to the fundamental right to private and family life,[167] the claimants in *Zambrano* were in a good position for a favourable decision. However, whilst the Zambrano family were successful on this occasion, the outcomes of cases following this have restricted *Zambrano* to its facts. This prompted speculation in the literature as to why this was the case, given how fundamental rights and EU citizenship had developed up to this point.[168]

Fundamental rights in EU citizenship featured heavily in AG Sharpston's Opinion on *Zambrano*, adding to the criticism that followed from the case itself when the Court did not engage with the question of clarifying the relationship between fundamental rights and EU citizenship.[169] It was especially anticipated

[163] *Grzelczyk* (n 9) para 31.

[164] This was also complemented by the codification of fundamental rights in 2000 in the Charter of Fundamental Rights, which were indicative of a progressive step for the constitutionalisation of fundamental rights in the EU.

[165] See, for example, Judgment of 19 January 2010, *Kücükdeveci* C-555/07, EU:C:2010:21 in relation to age discrimination; Judgment of 6 September 2012, *Deutsches Weintor* C-544/10, EU:C:2012:526 in relation to in business and marketing.

[166] *Zhu and Chen* (n 30).

[167] Article 7 of the Charter.

[168] Wiesbrock (n 74) 872; Niamh Nic Shuibhne, '(Some of) the Kids are All Right' (2012) 49 *CML Rev* 349, 363; Stanislas Adam and Peter van Elsuwege, 'Citizenship Rights and the Federal Balance between the European Union and its Member States: Comment on *Dereci*' (2012) 37 *European Law Review* 176, 189.

[169] See Adam and van Elsuwege (n 168); von Bogdandy et al (n 94); Wiesbrock (n 74).

after the Lisbon Treaty equated the status of the Charter to its own Treaties. Van Eijken and de Vries even argued that 'rather than extending the scope of application of fundamental rights, *Ruiz Zambrano* may just as well entail a "levelling down" of fundamental rights protection in the Member States'[170] because of the questions raised by the judgment. This was particularly difficult to reconcile when considering other areas of the EU where there was a proliferation of fundamental rights and expansion of the EU's scope of competence, which demonstrated the impact that the Lisbon Treaty's new provisions had on the EU's legal order.[171] In EU citizenship, case law subsequent to *Zambrano* was not as accommodating to fundamental rights or to clarifying the new independent legal status as established by the Court in *Zambrano*.[172]

Fundamental rights, especially for citizenship cases, were a way in which the Court further legitimised the status of EU citizenship. In common scenarios where claimants were TCN family members of EU citizens and did not have rights under EU law, fundamental rights and newly liberalised EU citizenship status had the potential and capacity to bring these TCNs within the scope of the Treaty. Having allowed this in cases in the past, it did not continue to do so in the third age.[173] It is argued that the reason for such hesitance recently is because the Court has been unable to find a concrete solution to the tensions finally being recognised because of the new constitutional nature of both concepts – the universality of fundamental rights against the exclusive nature of citizenship. The expansion of the scope *ratione personae* and *ratione materiae* of citizenship in line with fundamental rights protection has been halted. This book argues that it presents a regression of sorts.

It is thus the main objective of this book to look at the developments in a relationship between fundamental rights in the EU and the concept of EU citizenship through the Court's case law. The discussion will first follow the development of EU citizenship from its beginnings, where initially the Court mostly interpreted citizenship rights as an extension of economic rights. It will argue that despite these economic beginnings, there was an underlying fundamental rights discourse that drove the development. It will then follow the case law to demonstrate that gradually, the scope *ratione materiae* and *ratione personae* of EU citizenship was expanding and fundamental rights were becoming more explicit in the Court. This is argued to be directly related to the constitutionalisation of fundamental rights as a concept on its own, which this book will also discuss in relation to its impact on EU citizenship. This generated legitimate anticipation for a more

[170] Van Eijken and de Vries (n 74) 718.

[171] See *Kücükdeveci* (n 165); *Deutsches Weintor* (n 165); Judgment of 26 February 2013, *Melloni* C-399/11, EU:C:2013:107; Judgment of 26 February 2013, *Fransson* C-617/10, EU:C:2013:105; Judgment of 18 July 2013, *Kadi II* C-584/10, EU:C:2013:518.

[172] See n 93 above.

[173] See *Zhu and Chen* (n 30). *cf Zambrano* (n 23).

integrated relationship between the two concepts of rights and is designated as the rise of fundamental rights in EU citizenship. Recently, however, the development has taken a different turn. This book will ultimately argue that there is a possible correlation between the Court's behaviour and the EU's political situation due to the eurozone crisis, which is the hypothesised reason for a decline in fundamental rights protection in EU citizenship. It will also argue that this cannot continue in the discussion on EU citizens' rights in the UK after withdrawal. An integrated fundamental rights and EU citizenship relationship has disappointingly not materialised, and at the heart of these contentions is the Court's legal culture.

A. The Age of Uncertainty: The UK's Withdrawal from the EU

As mentioned above, it is important to highlight that there is a potential 'fourth' age of citizenship that has been brought about by the unprecedented decision of the UK to withdraw as a Member State of the EU, having officially triggered Article 50 TEU on 29 March 2017. This has started the countdown of a two-year negotiation period, which as it stands at the time of writing is currently under way between EU and UK representatives. It is not the aim of this book to retrospectively analyse reasons for the EU referendum result. It will instead situate the question of how to negotiate and govern a fair and just Brexit for EU citizens in the context of their citizenship rights and their deserved protection of human rights after the UK is no longer bound by EU law. Whilst a fairly crucial question, this has thus far proven to be a controversial topic because of the sheer difficulty in coming to a middle ground between what the EU and the UK seem to normatively agree is a good compromise for EU citizens' rights.

What has been a particularly difficult part of the process of withdrawal so far is that everything related to Brexit is dominated by uncertainty. It is apt to consider this 'fourth' age as the age of uncertainty, since even the discussion to follow this book will be somewhat tentative. The entire process so far has been subject to considerable change and debate in a very short space of time. Whilst this is the nature of law in any case, it has been more pronounced during the Brexit negotiations and is worth highlighting here as a result. However, there are some things which are less uncertain in the UK's withdrawal from the EU. These are its external obligations – particularly to human rights protection – which are unaffected by the UK's withdrawal. In the human rights context, this is a reference to the ECHR, which will play a stronger role once the EU's framework no longer applies.[174]

[174] See ch 6.

VI. Methodology and Outline of the Analysis

This book takes an approach that has been described as a 'history of the present'.[175] It does not purport to simply describe past and present, but rather to contextualise the current situation in its past to help explain why certain phenomena have occurred today. For this reason, the book's ultimate conclusion addresses why fundamental rights, though now deriving from an explicit and legally enforceable foundation in the Charter, have not been able to legitimise and substantiate the now-independent EU citizenship status. The answer can be found by looking at the five guiding legal instruments of EU citizenship – the principle of non-discrimination, the principle of proportionality, the genuine link test, the purely internal situations rule and the deprivation of genuine enjoyment test – and other general principles that shaped EU citizenship, fundamental rights and their founding entity, the EU. When speculation surrounding the meaning of EU citizenship status occurred in 1998, it was said that 'putting historical contexts of experience, expectation and practice into perspective contributes to understand the contextualised meaning of citizenship of the Union'.[176] This is the approach that will be taken in this book.

By looking at the history of citizenship case law in the EU, the Court can be seen to have reshaped several general principles and judicial instruments in EU law, putting their orthodox interpretations under stress. Though this unorthodox approach was met with some hostility at the outset, this eventually became the accepted approach adopted by the Court. Normative shifts in the mindsets of the EU institutions had to occur in order for this to happen. It was a slow process because the designers of the EU had originally set out an economic, not political, direction for the EU. Furthermore, the Court had to respect the specific boundaries laid down by the Treaties to protect national Member States' authorities. The Court succeeded in reshaping the scope of some of the judicial instruments through its interpretation of provisions in EU citizenship case law. However, more recently, the trend has indicated that there are questions surrounding these interpretations, particularly of principles and rules related to EU fundamental rights. If this is to continue, then serious questions need to be addressed in relation to the status of EU citizens in the UK after it exits the EU. The argument is that there is a resistance to a shift away from integrating fundamental rights and EU citizenship.

This book is also written in the age of Brexit, and therefore the notion of a 'history of the present' is still relevant as it carries out this analysis. Another objective of this book is therefore to situate the analysis on the relationship between fundamental rights in the EU and EU citizenship status in the context of the UK's

[175] David Garland, *The Culture of Control: Crime and Social Order in Contemporary Society* (University of Chicago Press, 2012) 2.

[176] Antje Wiener, *'European' Citizenship Practice* (Westview Press, 1998) 12.

withdrawal from the EU. This involves looking at the plans for treatment of EU citizens in the UK (and, more tangentially, British citizens in the EU) post-Brexit and analysing whether these are consistent with human rights protection that will still exist after withdrawal. This is rather than lamenting the loss of the EU framework of rights, as this book does not intend to look backwards at the political events that have led to the Brexit vote or attempt to rationalise them. Instead, as a dynamic process subject to change, this book is a fluid analysis of an ever-changing process looking at the static rights and obligations that will exist post-Brexit to account for the dynamisms of the withdrawal process. It is therefore more forward-looking, at least in the context of Brexit.

However, the earlier parts of the book, particularly Chapter 2, will explain the early interaction of the Court with the rights under EU citizenship. Prior to EU citizenship developing its own judicial instruments, the Court relied heavily on the internal market values of fundamental freedoms to determine how EU citizens would enjoy EU citizenship rights under Article 21 TFEU. This approach was found to be unsuitable to the aims behind a political concept like EU citizenship.[177] By considering whether there was an obstacle to free movement to determine whether EU citizenship rights were triggered, it seemed that the Court did not distinguish between protection offered by the fundamental freedoms and protection under citizenship status. It was unable to move away from this market-based reasoning until 1998. The legal principle of non-discrimination in Article 18 TFEU was introduced in *Sala* to replace the obstacle to free movement.[178] Instead of being economically active, the citizen needed only to be legally resident. The Court found a successful balance in emphasising legal residency and non-discrimination, recognising that limiting citizenship provisions to an elite group of individuals would be against a citizenship status aimed at uniting its community. This idea is supported by the increasing number of direct references to fundamental rights by the Court, particularly under Article 8 ECHR, which entails rights to respect for family life and rights to one's identity.

Chapter 3 moves on to focus on fundamental rights pre-Lisbon and its rise in the case law of EU citizenship. It emerged after the Court had established non-discrimination for social welfare and residency as part of the scope *ratione materiae* of EU citizenship, and when the scope *ratione personae* had been extended to citizens who were legal residents in Member States other than their home states. This chapter will analyse the three AG Opinions identified earlier as being the first indicators of a potential relationship between fundamental rights and EU citizenship. There is a noticeable rise in the fundamental rights questions, especially on TCN family members and the right to family life, from Article 8 ECHR and its

[177] See Christian Tomuschat, 'Case C-85/96, *María Martinez Sala v Freistaat Bayern*, Judgment of 12 May 1998, Full Court [1998] ECR I-2691' (2000) 37 *CML Rev* 449.

[178] Citizenship rights also extended to include social welfare benefits for ex-workers who were legally resident in the host Member State as part of the principle of non-discrimination.

equivalent in Article 7 of the Charter of Fundamental Rights. It is argued that there is a correlation between the rise of fundamental rights in the EU generally and its influence in the Court in cases on citizenship.

Chapter 4 presents the first signs of the decline of fundamental rights in EU citizenship law after its notable rise. The focus here will be on this phenomenon of regression after progressing towards integrating fundamental rights protection into EU citizenship status. Anticipation was built initially in the *Rottmann* case, which led to AG Sharpston's Opinion in *Zambrano*, and then the highly anticipated *Zambrano* judgment itself. This chapter will analyse these developments individually to emphasise how indicative they were to the original hypothesis of an integrated rights discourse in citizenship jurisprudence. These cases are the culmination of the fundamental rights and EU citizenship relationship. Attention will then turn to the cases of *McCarthy* and *Dereci* that immediately followed *Zambrano*. Looking closely at these cases will highlight the slow but gradual disconnect between fundamental rights in EU citizenship despite the apparent indications from the anticipation surrounding *Zambrano*. There is also a contemporary contextualisation of the discussion thus far with a focus particularly on the current case law. From this, it becomes especially clear that what the Court decided to implement in the jurisprudence of *McCarthy* and *Dereci* was not an exceptional line of reasoning. Most recurrently in the context of conferring welfare benefits to non-economically active individuals, this chapter will demonstrate that the Court is departing from favouring an empowerment of the individual through protection of fundamental rights to now deferring more to Member States' own national interests.

Chapter 5 will offer a potential explanation for this in the context of the increasing Euroscepticism amongst Member States and the political crises this has instigated. Because its legal culture is known to be influenced by the political atmosphere in which it operates, this book argues that there is a strong correlation between the eurozone crisis, rising nationalism and increasing Euroscepticism, and the decline of fundamental rights in EU citizenship. It seeks to analyse the history of the present set out in the previous chapters and to address the question posed at the outset – why, despite becoming binding and constitutionalised in the Lisbon Treaty, has the Charter failed to have the intended impact on EU citizenship case law in the Court? It will suggest a solution and note its limits. It argues that the reason why the relationship between fundamental rights and EU citizenship has not met expectations is that despite both fundamental rights and EU citizenship becoming noticeably more constitutional, the Court is unlikely to fully integrate the two sets of rights because this would expand the scope of the Treaty too much. Although there were legitimate expectations set by the Court in case law leading to this hypothesis,[179] another unforeseen factor has changed the direction for

[179] Particularly strong examples include *Zhu and Chen* (n 30); *Garcia Avello* (n 92); *Carpenter* (n 22); Judgment of 4 June 2009, *Vatsouras* C-22/08, EU:C:2009:344.

the Court. This has led to the most surprising of the developments – the UK's vote to leave the EU. This chapter will provide clarity to a confusing situation to argue that EU citizens' rights should be preserved in a defensible manner, even to the exiting UK authorities. The idea is entirely premised on the protection of EU fundamental rights, which has fallen by the wayside in more areas than just citizenship.

Chapter 6 is the Brexit chapter, which will continue in the vein of being a 'history of the present', with a heavier focus on the present. However, because of the book's political context, this chapter will be more forward-looking than the others. The analysis of the EU citizenship and fundamental rights case law as a rise and decline is pertinent for this discussion because of the patterns that can be identified between the two distinct legal authorities – the UK and the EU. In particular, the decline in the fundamental rights discourse is argued to have done no favours for the UK's perception of the value of EU citizenship status and its rights. As such, whilst there can be no proven correlation between the vote in favour of exiting the EU from the British electorate and the CJEU's declining interest in engaging with fundamental rights protection, the argument is that it suggests an overall undermining of human rights in general. The chapter will also consider the justice of Brexit for EU citizens, as their rights are at stake and there are a number of human rights mechanisms that should be of relevance. In particular, this needs to be made more clear to the negotiators, otherwise there could be grave consequences. However, the overall underlying argument that this chapter is intended to further support is that of this book.

There is tension between fundamental rights being universal in nature and EU citizenship rights promoting EU exclusivity. This much is clear. The situation is made even more complicated having to respect boundaries established by the EU. Fundamental rights are universal; however, they must still remain within the boundaries of EU law.[180] In EU citizenship case law, the Court has not confirmed that fundamental rights are freestanding rights in and of themselves.[181] Instead, it opted to adhere strictly to the boundaries set out in the Charter, as well as to adopt a narrow interpretation of what an independent legal basis of rights for EU citizenship means after *Zambrano*. This book will explain that there is underlying irreconcilable tension for reasons uncovered by the historical account of the development of both concepts, by assessing their political objectives and by explaining their situation with the unique supranational entity that is the EU. This will uncover that the rise and decline of fundamental rights is potentially linked to the EU's own constitutional developments; the rise occurred during a more

[180] There are limitations on fundamental rights in the EU in terms of the scope of their application, especially in arts 51–53 of the Charter.

[181] In fact, in Opinion of 12 December 2013, *O and B; S and G* C-456/12 and C-457/12, EU:C:2013:842, it is confirmed that they are not.

positive time where fundamental rights were becoming more constitutional and the scope of citizenship was expanding, whilst the decline presented itself when the EU began to face greater economic troubles and, later, political ones as well. This is an unacceptable change of position, and attention must return to the protection of fundamental rights in the light of Brexit if the EU intends at all to argue a defensible position to protect its citizens in the territory of the UK.

2

The Progressive Empowerment of EU Citizens through Judicial Instruments and Fundamental Rights

I. Introduction

The EU did not, at first, involve a transnational citizenship status. The original six Member States sought primarily to build greater economic ties between themselves. For a time, they considered little else. It was only after the ECSC became the EEC that the institutions began to address the political and social gaps that had been created by their narrow focus on the market. Amongst the various non-economic measures introduced[1] was the establishment of European citizenship.[2] Though a seemingly bold political statement, its effect was minimal at first. The concept received mixed reviews from the commentary as to whether it was simply a 'cosmetic exercise'[3] or whether it would truly represent the politicisation of the EU.[4] Long preceding the introduction of citizenship was also the gradual emergence of fundamental rights considerations in economic areas,[5] which prompted significant discussion as to a more non-economic constitutional framework for the EU. This is argued to be the driving force behind creating a European status of citizenship.[6]

[1] Of most relevance would be social policy in arts 5–6 EEC and the various Protocols on Social Policy.

[2] Article 8a EEC.

[3] Siofra O'Leary, 'The Relationship between Community Citizenship and the Protection of Fundamental Rights in Community Law' (1995) 32 *CML Rev* 519, 537. See also Michael Dougan, 'The Constitutional Dimension to the Case Law on Union Citizenship' (2006) 5 *Inter Alia* 77, 78.

[4] See Carole Lyons, 'A Voyage around Article 8: An Historical Evaluation on the Fate of European Union Citizenship' (1997) 17 *Yearbook of European Law* 135; Sybilla Fries and Jo Shaw, 'Citizenship of the Union: First Steps in the European Court of Justice' (1998) 4 *European Public Law* 533; Jo Shaw, 'The Interpretation of European Union Citizenship' (1998) 61 *MLR* 293.

[5] Beginning with the Judgment of 17 December 1970, *Internationale Handelsgesellschaft* C-11/70, EU:C:1970:114, then Judgment of 12 November 1969, *Stauder v Ulm* C-29/69, EU:C:1969:57, then Judgment of 13 July 1989, *Wachauf* C-5/88, EU:C:1989:321, then Judgment of 18 June 1991, *ERT* C-260/89, EU:C:1991:254.

[6] There was an Inter-governmental Conference on a political union held as part of the Maastricht negotiations which promoted greater European integration. See 'Treaty of Maastricht on European Union', http://europa.eu/legislation_summaries/institutional_affairs/treaties/treaties_maastricht_en.htm.

EU citizenship has had both positive and negative legal and political effects since its inception. However, its successes have not been the main focus of contemporary debates. The reason for this lies in EU citizenship's history and its many changes over the years. Provisions protecting free-moving workers in the EU under its internal market rules preceded EU citizenship law.[7] These provisions have been influential to the development of the EU law generally, and citizenship law in particular has taken inspiration from the application of these rights in its own discourse. Though this economic element of citizenship law is less prominent today, its roots remain in the internal market. It is in part due to EU citizenship status that citizens are no longer perceived solely as workers.[8] However, this did not detract from the fact that the CJEU struggled to politicise the EU from the outset, and arguably still faces some of the same issues today. Institutional loyalty to original EU internal market values has prevented the Court from rejecting this approach completely.[9] Where the Court has struggled to balance economic priorities of the EU against the individual rights of the EU citizen, it has led to some legal uncertainty. This chapter will examine these difficulties in light of the objectives of a citizenship of the EU, but also in relation to its relationship with fundamental rights.

This book argues that a relationship between EU citizenship and fundamental rights was an expectation raised by the Court in its case law, especially when they featured both citizenship rights and fundamental rights. When introducing this argument, a brief background of citizenship will be discussed, for early on in the citizenship literature and case law, there has been very little explicit indication of interaction with fundamental rights. However, what can be shown instead is an innate willingness to expand beyond the market and into acknowledging the influence of other non-economic values like fundamental rights. This is argued to underlie the subtle but evident steps made by the Court to depart from utilising internal market reasoning in cases on EU citizenship, since fundamental rights and citizenship share several common objectives.

Since the Schuman Declaration,[10] one of the EU's primary objectives has been to generate solidarity within the community of united EU Member States and their citizens. It is argued that all EU provisions – including both fundamental rights and citizenship – are created with this objective in mind as the EU aims to bring together its diverse community of individuals.[11] However, solidarity between

[7] Article 45 TFEU and Regulation (EEC) No 1612/68 of the Council of 15 October 1968 on freedom of movement for workers within the Community [1968] OJ L257/2.

[8] It is argued that the fundamental rights influence from the early 1970s was also a factor underlying this decision.

[9] See, most recently, Judgment of 11 November 2014, *Dano* C-333/13, EU:C:2014:2358; Judgment of 15 September 2015, *Alimanovic* C-67/14, EU:C:2015:597; *Garcia-Nieto* C-299/14 (ECJ, 25 February 2016) demonstrating the political pressure the Court faced in ch 4.

[10] Robert Schuman, *Schuman Declaration* (9 May 1950).

[11] The Preamble to the TFEU states not only the intention of an 'ever closer Union', but also 'intending to confirm the solidarity which binds Europe'.

citizens of the EU remains elusive to this day.[12] On the one hand, financial solidarity was established as a clear objective to all parties at the outset. The Treaty of Paris mandated economic cooperation between the Member States.[13] This prominent economic element has been developing since the EU began.[14] On the other hand, efforts to generate political and social solidarity have been more recent, minimal and less successful. When political and social EU concepts were introduced, many were functional solutions to resolve issues that were not considerations for Member States originally.[15]

For this reason, when provisions that lacked economic elements were introduced – such as the EU's political citizenship status – they appeared underdeveloped and normatively weaker in the EU's constitutional framework.[16] A citizenship status shared by all EU Member State nationals might have encouraged solidarity. However, this encouragement has not been the solution to the EU's greater democratic problems.[17] If EU citizenship status is considered to bring about greater EU democracy, then it is argued that the EU is still struggling, given the criticism of citizenship and its superficial changes.[18] These have weakened the overall legitimacy of the EU's institutional power in social and political areas like citizenship.[19] In the same vein, the enforcement of rights has also been undermined, as these rights were not given the necessary attention as compared to rights that were reserved for the economically active. EU citizenship status thus struggled to find its place in a very crowded internal market.

When citizenship was introduced by the Maastricht Treaty in 1993, the EU institutions had been facing problems of a democratic deficit attributable to the EU's newly politicised nature.[20] In many ways, the Treaty was representative of

[12] This book defines solidarity as encompassing two facets: the financial, and the social and political.

[13] Treaty of Paris (formerly the Treaty establishing the European Coal and Steel Community).

[14] The Treaty of the European Economic Community (EEC Treaty) is the best indicator of this, with the EC (at the time) dedicating a whole Treaty to furthering these goals.

[15] See Preamble of the Treaty of Paris; and *Schuman Declaration* (n 10) for the original goals and intentions for the ECSC.

[16] This is particularly evident in the slow drawn-out process of the constitutionalisation of fundamental rights.

[17] This primarily refers to the democratic deficit. The Lisbon Treaty has taken some measures to try and address this problem, for example, the increased involvement of national parliaments, known as the yellow/orange card subsidiarity warning mechanism and the gradual increased role of the European Parliament. This is evident in the ordinary legislative procedure in art 294 TFEU and the judicial review system in art 263 TFEU. However, these mostly attend to the EU's democratic deficit rather than being legal resolutions to the legitimacy problems.

[18] Jürgen Habermas, 'Citizenship and National Identity: Some Reflections on the Future of Europe' (1992) 12 *Praxis International* 255, 264ff; Ulrich K Preuss, 'Two Challenges to European Citizenship' (1996) 44 *Political Studies* 534.

[19] On the democratic deficit, see Marcus Horeth, 'No Way out for the Beast? The Unsolved Legitimacy Problem of European Governance' (1999) 6 *Journal of European Public Policy* 249; and Andrew Moravcsik, 'Reassessing Legitimacy in the European Union' (2002) 40 *Journal of Common Market Studies* 603 for an initial indication of these issues.

[20] See Brigitte Boyce, 'The Democratic Deficit of the European Community' (1993) 46 *Parliamentary Affairs* 458; John D Occhipinti, 'Whither the Withering Democratic Deficit? The Impact of the

measures taken to address this lack of democracy,[21] with EU citizenship being one example of a concept with the potential to address democratic imbalances brought about by the relationship that the EU had with its Member States.[22] The intention was that EU citizenship should have been a status that empowered the citizen to feel more like they were involved with the EU, as it granted rights not only to residency and free movement but also to representative democracy.[23] However, the EU is not a purely international organisation or a federal governing body – it is a supranational entity. This is one reason for the strained relations between itself and its constituent Member States. This chapter will introduce citizenship cases that focused on the market to explain the difficulties of the Court in departing from its market-centric approach initially. Then, it will turn to the key citizenship decisions, with a particular emphasis on their fundamental rights aspects through the lenses of the judicial instruments. It will discuss the principles of non-discrimination, proportionality, the genuine link test and the purely internal situations rule as they relate to the subject matter of cases in the first age and early in the second age. In this manner, it will become clear that underlying the citizenship development is an inherent consideration for the protection of fundamental rights.

The legal principle of non-discrimination is the foundation for EU citizenship status becoming an independent legal basis for rights today.[24] It was the principle applied by the Court in the *Sala* case that brought non-economically active citizens and rights to equal treatment for social welfare benefits within the scope of the Treaty. The principle of proportionality and the genuine link test are considered as checks on the application of the principle of non-discrimination, for non-discrimination has been applied by the Court and has frequently favoured the citizen in lieu of protecting the EU's economic objectives.[25] It will be argued that the way in which the Court interprets these instruments raised expectations that the future interpretation of these judicial instruments should allow individuals to enjoy certain rights, especially because they are EU citizens by

Lisbon Treaty on the Area of Freedom, Security and Justice' [2013] *Cambridge Review of International Affairs* 1; Robert E Goodin, 'Enfranchising All Affected Interests, and its Alternatives' (2007) 35 *Philosophy and Public Affairs* 40; Teija Tiilikainen, 'The Problem of Democracy in the European Union' in Esko Antola and Allan Rosas (eds), *A Citizen's Europe: In Search of a New Order* (SAGE Publications, 1995).

[21] The official EU website (http://europa.eu/eu-law/decision-making/treaties/index_en.htm) states that its purpose was to 'introduce elements of a political union (citizenship, common foreign and internal affairs policy)'.

[22] Richard Bellamy and Alex Warleigh, *Citizenship and Governance in the European Union* (Bloomsbury, 2005) 3.

[23] Articles 22ff TFEU.

[24] Judgment of 8 March 2011, *Zambrano* C-34/09, EU:C:2011:124.

[25] The first example of this is Judgment of 12 May 1998, *Martinez Sala* C-85/96, EU:C:1998:217, but other examples include Judgment of 7 September 2004, *Trojani* C-456/02, EU:C:2004:488; Judgment of 23 March 2004 *Collins* C-138/02, EU:C:2004:172; and Judgment of 19 October 2004, *Zhu and Chen* C-200/02, EU:C:2004:639.

virtue of Article 20 TFEU.[26] Residency is also introduced as a factor determining whether rights should be conferred upon EU citizens who have moved, and with it the purely internal situations rule. This rule, it will be shown, somewhat limits the scope of the Treaty, but is flawed, and it will be argued that its application by the Court has not demonstrated enough consideration to fundamental rights protection.

The chapter is structured as follows. Section II follows the empowerment of citizens' rights as seen through the lenses of three judicial instruments – the principles of non-discrimination, proportionality and the genuine link test. Through non-discrimination initially, slowly but surely, the Court began to protect a broader category of citizens because of EU citizenship status under Article 20 TFEU, but also because of underlying fundamental right objectives which this discussion will draw out. Then, through proportionality assessments and the genuine link test, the growing fundamental rights *acquis* will be highlighted in relation to non-discrimination in order to demonstrate how this has further empowered the EU citizen. Then, the discussion will turn to the purely internal situations rule, which, in contrast to the other three judicial instruments, the Court has used as a tool to limit the scope of EU citizenship. The rule emerged out of the Court's consideration of legal residency as a factor determining the conferral of citizenship rights. However, this analysis will also highlight why the interpretation of the rule itself and its application do not support enhanced fundamental rights protection.

II. Empowering the EU Citizen

One set of rights identified as having shaped the material scope of EU citizenship is the conferral of social welfare benefits to free-moving citizens. The first notable free-moving citizen in the EU that existed prior to the existence of EU citizenship status was the free-moving worker, under the free movement of labour – Article 45 TFEU – in the internal market. With this provision and other instruments already in existence to govern the rights of this particular group of individuals in the EU,[27] it was expected that a political and social concept like citizenship would have a different scope of protection.[28] It purported to be wider in scope as a status

[26] See case law on students, including Judgment of 20 May 2010, *Zanotti* C-56/09, EU:C:2010:288; Judgment of 4 October 2012, *Commission v Austria* C-75/11, EU:C:2012:605; Judgment of 25 October 2012, *Prete* C-367/11, EU:C:2012:668; Judgment of 18 July 2013, *Prinz and Seeberger* C-523/11, EU:C:2013:524; Judgment of 24 October 2013, *Thiele Meneses* C-220/12, EU:C:2013:683; Judgment of 24 October 2013, *Elrick* C-275/12, EU:C:2013:684.

[27] Article 45 TFEU and Regulation 1612/68.

[28] Peo Hansen and Sandy Brian Hager, *The Politics of European Citizenship: Deepening Contradictions in Social Rights and Migration Policy* (Berghahn Books, 2013) 205.

available to all nationals of all EU Member States. The Court, however, began by interpreting the personal scope of citizenship as only extending to those who were economically active. This greatly resembled, if not wholly transposed, the legal effect of the free movement of persons under the internal market.

It will be argued that this approach, deriving from the treatment of the internal market's fundamental freedoms and transposed onto EU citizenship law, is unsuitable. This is mainly due to differences in scope between the two concepts. The scope of the fundamental freedoms is restricted to applying only to economic actors, protecting rights guaranteed by the internal market. Conversely, EU citizenship status as it applies to all nationals of all EU Member States would not logically purport to exclude individuals purely on the basis of their economic activity. In this manner, citizenship draws closer similarities with the scope of fundamental rights protection. In the broader understanding of a political concept like this, it would be a more acceptable supposition.[29] EU citizenship can be distinguished by its direct links with fundamental rights protection, which the development of EU citizenship over time will show can stand up against the longer-standing economic influences, which derive from the original aims of the Treaty of Paris.

The approach taken by the Court in the early 1990s can be explained by looking to the legal culture of the Court before and after EU citizenship status was introduced. The Court's decision making appears to be influenced by external politics, which could explain its conservative behaviour when initially interpreting the political concept of EU citizenship. Though it was capable of implementing a normative shift towards protection of rights like citizenship and fundamental rights, the Court was also cautious about it.[30] Initially, there were some signs of engaging with fundamental rights, which supports the argument that although fundamental rights were not the Court's primary consideration, they did play a role. This established foundations for more explicit interactions between this set of rights and EU citizenship in later case law.

A. Workers and Family Life

The case of *Singh* is often discussed in citizenship literature despite it pre-dating the introduction of the status in the EU by three years.[31] It is included in this

[29] Recall the Aristotelian definition of citizenship in Aristotle, *Politics* (Ernest Barker trans, Clarendon Press, 1948) Book I, which is premised on exclusivity of membership to the defined *polis*.

[30] There were only four cases on citizenship between 1993 and 1998: Judgment of 7 July 1992, *Singh* C-370/90, EU:C:1992:296; Judgment of 7 July 1992, *Micheletti* C-369/90, EU:C:1992:295; Judgment of 5 June 1997, *Uecker and Jacquet* C-64/96 and C-65/96, EU:C:1997:285; and Judgment of 24 November 1998, *Bickel and Franz* C-274/96, EU:C:1998:563.

[31] *Singh* (n 30). See, amongst others, Dimitry Kochenov and Richard Plender, 'EU Citizenship: From an Incipient Form to an Incipient Substance? The Discovery of the Treaty Text' (2012) 37 *European Law Review* 369; Henri de Waele, 'EU Citizenship: Revisiting its Meaning, Place and Potential' (2010)

analysis as a comparator for pre- and post-Maastricht behaviour in the Court regarding non-economic rights and statuses, but, more importantly, to bring to attention the early influence of fundamental rights protection. The right to private and family life features in this case, deriving from Article 8 ECHR.[32] This element was noted by the Court and became a factor in their final decision, although the legal basis cited was the rights of free-moving workers under Regulation 1612/68.[33] The decision in *Singh* thus highlights not only that the Court is willing to engage with elements of fundamental rights, but also brings to light the pre-existence of relevant provisions that already encompassed elements of fundamental rights protection.

The claimant, Mr Singh, was a third country national (TCN) married to a British citizen. After working in Germany for two years, the couple returned to the UK to open a business together. Mr Singh was granted leave to remain as a spouse of a British national. Several years later, a deportation order was issued against the claimant, prompted by his wife initiating divorce proceedings, leading to an initial *decree nisi* of divorce against him. The question referred asked whether the claimant had derived rights to remain with his wife, an employed EU citizen, prior to their divorce being finalised. She had exercised her right to free movement and worked in another Member State, thus triggering Treaty protection. The Court decided that irrespective of Mr Singh's non-EU nationality, the rights of his wife as a worker returning to her home state were such that he could derive a right to residency.

In this decision, the Court placed a lot of weight upon economic activity. The effect would be to allow economically active EU citizens to accrue a wide array of benefits and not only for themselves. This would appear to establish a hierarchy of individuals whom the Court considered to be able to benefit from the Treaty's protection, which was unsurprising given the EU's historical foundations. However, under Regulation 1612/68, these 'benefits' already included workers' family rights. Raising the question of a social element of family life before EU citizenship status existed foreshadowed that the future discussion of citizenship rights might further involve these considerations. The fact that the Regulation already protected this fundamental right proved that it was not a novel suggestion. However, it was the way in which the Court engaged with the provision solely in the context of workers' rights that indicated greater potential still for fundamental rights protection to be influential in other situations.

For this reason, the *Singh* case serves to demonstrate that even as early as pre-Maastricht, considerations such as family life fell within the scope of the

12 *European Journal of Migration and Law* 319; Niamh Nic Shuibhne, 'The Resilience of EU Market Citizenship' (2010) 47 *CML Rev* 1597.

[32] Convention for the Protection of Human Rights and Fundamental Freedoms (European Convention on Human Rights, as amended), art 8.

[33] Regulation (EEC) No 1612/68 of the Council of 15 October 1968 on freedom of movement for workers within the Community [1968] OJ L257/2.

provisions on the free movement of workers. It is argued that given the existence of an EU citizenship status and guarantees of protection under fundamental rights, the Court should extend this protection to all citizens. However, this form of 'market citizenship' exhibited by the Court in *Singh* was most consistent with an approach deriving from the internal market and workers' rights.[34] In the case itself, the Court did not explicitly cite rights to family life as the legal basis for its decision. Importantly, however, the acknowledgement of citizens being more than just workers and engaging with the right to private and family life supports the discussion going forward as to an underlying fundamental rights thread.[35]

It later became clear that promoting and valuing economic activity was inconsistent with the principle of equality promoted by citizenship status. The focus on the economically active was narrow, and evidently excluded many non-economically active individuals.[36] This further substantiated the criticism that EU citizenship status was merely cosmetic because it did not add to the rights already available to citizens.[37] The Court's justification for extending workers' rights became less acceptable as the EU became less economic and more political. In order to convince the Court to consider provisions that promoted political and social rights more, there had to be a push from the judiciary, especially because these rights had already been constitutionalised.[38] This argument was substantiated by subtle references to fundamental rights, whose protection also formed part of the political and social policies that had emerged out of Maastricht.[39]

The objective of introducing an EU citizenship status should have been to extend the scope of protection of EU law to individuals who were not already protected by the fundamental freedoms in the internal market. It is argued that EU citizenship status could be differentiated from the values and rights under the internal market if the Court placed greater emphasis on fundamental rights hinted at initially in *Singh*, but not executed. It had to avoid comparing the economic

[34] Michelle Everson, 'The Legacy of the Market Citizen' in Jo Shaw and Gillian More (eds), *New Legal Dynamics of the European Union* (Oxford University Press, 1995). Interestingly, Nic Shuibhne (n 31) still believes the label should be applied today.

[35] *Singh* (n 30) para 20.

[36] This included disabled individuals and children most obviously. However, this also disproportionately excluded carers of children who did not otherwise have full-time employment and who were often women.

[37] Annette Schrauwen, 'European Union Citizenship in the Treaty of Lisbon: Any Change at All' (2008) 15 *Maastricht Journal of European and Comparative Law* 55.

[38] Alec Stone Sweet, 'The European Court of Justice and the Judicialization of EU Governance' (2010) 5 *Living Reviews in EU Governance* 5, 17.

[39] In the late 1990s and early 2000s, the *ERT* (n 5) case had been decided. This case was the closest the EU had at the time to a firm commitment to fundamental rights until the introduction of the original Charter of Fundamental Rights of the European Union 83/02 [2000] OJ C364/01. There were also social and employment policies introduced into Maastricht, such as the Justice and Home Affairs (JHA) pillar, the Protocol on Social Policy, and the Protocol on Economic and Social Cohesion.

activity to economic inactivity of its citizens. It appeared for some time that the Court was unable to adjust to this fundamental rights *acquis* because it had become its culture to defer somewhat to Member States' autonomy. This was supplemented by the fact that the political atmosphere right after Maastricht did not allow for this in the wake of the developments in establishing an economic and monetary union and the internal market.[40]

It is for this reason that this book does not support the market citizenship model as a normative framework for the development of citizenship law. The model operates on the assumption of complete harmonisation; moreover, it asks for claimants to demonstrate financial solidarity and limits rights on this basis. The book does not reject the notion that EU citizenship began as a market-based form of citizenship, but agrees that a 'thesis of market citizenship does not mean that we should stop striving for the evolution or even transformation of EU citizenship'.[41] Preuss describes the Court's extension of workers' rights in citizenship as a functional choice.[42] For this reason, many parties still relied upon the fundamental freedoms before considering whether citizenship can provide a solution. Functional as it may have become, it was in *Martinez Sala* in 1998 that the Court granted rights to a non-economically active citizen, raising more elements of fundamental rights.[43]

B. Non-discrimination as a Fundamental Right

In *Martinez Sala*, a Spanish citizen living in Germany wanted to claim child benefits in her host state after being economically inactive for some years. She was precluded from doing so by national law, which required the claimant to 'have German nationality, a residence entitlement or a residence permit'.[44] After determining that Mrs Sala was indeed non-economically active, the Court decided that EU law – and, more specifically, EU citizenship – precluded Member States from disallowing social welfare benefits purely on the basis that the claimant was not a national. *Sala* was the first instance where the Court drew upon the legal principle of non-discrimination on the grounds of nationality[45] as part of 'the limitations and conditions laid down in this Treaty and by the measures adopted to give it effect'.[46] By reading this general principle of EU law with the rights conferred as a citizen of the EU, Mrs Sala could rightfully enjoy equal treatment for social welfare

[40] This refers mostly to the process of setting up the common euro currency and European Central Bank between 1995 and 1998.
[41] Nic Shuibhne (n 31) 1628.
[42] Preuss (n 18).
[43] *Sala* (n 25).
[44] ibid para 16.
[45] Article 18 TFEU.
[46] Originally in art 8a EC and carried into the revised editions of the Treaties up to Lisbon.

because she was legally resident. Denying her this would be a direct contravention of non-discrimination, irrespective of her economically inactive status, and would also be disproportionate.

It is widely recognised that the Court's decision to empower the non-economically active legally resident citizen, particularly through employing the principle of non-discrimination, put 'flesh on the bones of European Union citizenship'.[47] This interpretation is especially supportive of the argument that fundamental rights protection had enjoyed a greater role in the Court's judicial reasoning, which was notable for occurring in the case that set the judicial and constitutional tone for citizenship going forward. Mrs Sala was granted these rights because of her status as an EU citizen from Article 20 TFEU and legal residency from Article 21 TFEU, the denial of which would have been disproportionate, considering the objective of 'desiring to deepen the solidarity between their peoples'.[48] In effect, the Court's judicial reasoning was sound as to the invocation of strong legal principles that justified the more prominent role fundamental rights played, manifesting through the general principle of non-discrimination and proportionality.

Henceforth, non-discrimination became the principle for all EU citizens to rely upon in order to be conferred rights under the Treaty if they could prove they were legally resident. It was the tool the Court needed in order to legitimately enhance the status of EU citizenship without interfering excessively with unspoken precedent, which was more akin to protection of the economic fundamental freedoms. It helped to shift norms ingrained in the Court's legal culture that did not support the EU's political development. Establishing that citizens could claim rights in this way also began to diminish the importance of conditions under the Residency Directives, a positive step towards equalising the status of all citizens in the EU. This set the groundwork for later more explicit involvement with fundamental rights because at the time, as a general principle of EU law, the principle of non-discrimination had to be respected.[49] This was also the case for fundamental rights and it is argued that this connection proved to be an effective way to promote such non-economic rights.

The *Sala* case was the first occasion where the concept of EU citizenship was interpreted by the Court as being able to stand on its own. By departing from strict market values, rights deriving from EU citizenship status under Article 20 TFEU were given another legal basis under Article 18 TFEU, the principle of non-discrimination, which expanded both the scope *ratione materiae* and *ratione personae* of the status.[50] However, the Court in *Sala* was not considered radical,

[47] A phrase borrowed from Siofra O'Leary, 'Putting Flesh on the Bones of European Union Citizenship' (1999) 24 *European Law Review* 68.

[48] Preamble, Treaty of Maastricht.

[49] *Internationale Handelsgesellschaft* (n 5).

[50] Albeit always dependent on nationality, as art 20 TFEU requires.

did not create any new rights[51] and seemed keen to avoid any backlash that its non-market-based reasoning might incite. Its reasoning was clearly grounded in legal principles that were suited to furthering social and political solidarity, and shifted the focus of the Court to protection under fundamental rights. Because it broadened the scope *ratione materiae* and *ratione personae* of the provisions under EU citizenship, the focus was more on the citizen than on the worker. Unlike in *Singh*, where the family life element was more directly related to fundamental rights, here the Court suggested less focus on the market and more on non-economic factors such as rights to non-discrimination. In holistic assessments employing this principle, it is argued that room was thus created which allowed for the accommodation of fundamental rights.

Interestingly, despite the judgment in *Sala*, some cases after it were decided in part, if not entirely, on the basis of the applicant being economically active.[52] However, cases that are of more interest are those that rejected extending workers' rights in favour of empowering the citizen using Article 20 TFEU and Article 18 TFEU instead. The Court in *Sala* emphasised that the right to non-discrimination had to be prioritised in its assessment of its conferral of citizenship rights, especially for non-economically active individuals. The Court could then consider other factors and give effect to fundamental rights considerations. It was later in *Grzelczyk* that the Court consolidated this approach, declaring that:

> Union citizenship is destined to be the *fundamental status* of nationals of the Member States, enabling those who find themselves in the same situation to enjoy the same treatment in law irrespective of their nationality, subject to such exceptions as are expressly provided for. (Emphasis added)[53]

By building on the principle in *Sala*, the Court developed a more coherent and separate line of reasoning that was more suited to the developing status of EU citizenship, away from the internal market and more towards fundamental rights.

The *Grzelczyk* case quickly became one of the most well-known cases in EU citizenship because of its application of legal principles first introduced in *Sala*, as well as for the statement above on the fundamental status of EU citizenship. *Grzelcyzk* was a case concerning a French student in Belgium. The claimant

[51] A Castro d'Oliveira, 'Workers and Other Persons: Step-by-Step from Movement to Citizenship – Case Law 1995–2001' (2002) 39 *CML Rev* 77.

[52] See Judgment of 23 November 2000, *Elsen* C-135/99, EU:C:2000:647; Judgment of 8 July 2004, *Gaumain-Cerri and Barth* C-502/01 and C-31/02, EU:C:2004:413; Judgment of 16 December 2004, *MY v ONP* C-293/03, EU:C:2004:821; Judgment of 21 February 2006, *Hosse* C-286/03, EU:C:2006:125; Judgment of 11 January 2007, *ITC* C-208/05, EU:C:2007:16; Judgment of 11 September 2007, *Hendrix* C-287/05, EU:C:2007:494; Judgment of 4 December 2008, *Zablocka-Weyhermuller* C-221/07, EU:C:2008:681; Judgment of 16 July 2009, *Von Chamier-Glisczinski* C-208/07, EU:C:2009:455; Judgment of 23 February 2010, *Ibrahim* C-310/08, EU:C:2010:80; Judgment of 23 February 2010, *Teixeira* C-480/08, ECLI:EU:C:2010:83; Judgment of 5 May 2011, *Bartlett* C-537/09, EU:C:2011:278; Judgment of 19 July 2012, *Reichel-Albert* C-522/10, EU:C:2012:475; *Prete* (n 26).

[53] Judgment of 20 September 2001, *Grzelczyk* C-184/99, EU:C:2001:458, para 20.

worked part-time during his studies, but ceased working in his final year and instead claimed benefits to support himself. The question referred asked whether under Regulation 1612/68, Mr Grzelczyk could be considered a worker and, if not, how he could legally claim the social welfare normally reserved for workers. The Court found first that Mr Grzelczyk was not a worker at the time of claiming the benefit. However, the conditions attached to the grant were directly discriminatory on the grounds of nationality because they were reserved for Belgian nationals only.

Given that Mr Grzelczyk had been declared a non-worker at the time of claiming the benefit, it would appear that this was the perfect opportunity to apply *Sala*'s judicial reasoning as an EU citizen under Article 20 TFEU, who moved and resided in another Member State under Article 21 TFEU, and whose fundamental rights under the principle of non-discrimination and Article 18 TFEU would be protected. The judgment clarified that although Mr Grzelczyk did not have worker status, this should not preclude him from relying on EU citizenship and fundamental rights, as he was a legal resident in the host Member State. The *Grzelczyk* judgment then set out the mantra that would be repeated in the subsequent years in citizenship case law that 'Union citizenship is destined to be the fundamental status of nationals of the Member States',[54] whilst also confirming that exercising free movement as a student does not warrant a loss of citizenship rights.[55] This represented a further expansion of both the scope *ratione personae* and *ratione materiae* of EU citizenship.

However, the Court was careful to set limits on this expansion. It emphasised that declaring EU citizenship a fundamental status did not translate into an unrestricted right to cross-border social welfare benefits, applying the limitation set out by *Sala* that the claimant had to have moved and been legally resident in the Member State in question in order to be eligible for equal treatment in social welfare. Mr Grzelczyk satisfied the criteria set by the host Member State, apart from being a national. The legal residency criteria are thus described as a compromise in relation to both parties, because they benefited the claimant and protected the Member State.[56] In other words, Article 18 TFEU read with Article 20 TFEU prevailed to confer rights on Mr Grzelczyk, but was still subject to valid restrictions under proportionality for one's legal residency status deriving from Article 21 TFEU. This appeared to be a satisfactory balance, respecting the principle of non-discrimination and considerations of fundamental rights, but also the limits and conditions placed on adopting this approach as set out in the citizenship provisions themselves.[57]

[54] ibid para 31.

[55] ibid para 36.

[56] Michael Dougan and Eleanor Spaventa, 'Educating Rudy and the (Non-)English Patient: A Double-Bill on Residency Rights under Article 18 EC' (2003) 28 *European Law Review* 699, 703.

[57] Anne Pieter van der Mei, 'Freedom of Movement and Financial Aid for Students: Some Reflections on *Grzelczyk* and *Fahmi and Esmoris-Cerdeiro Pinedo Amoris*' (2001) 3 *European Journal of Social Security* 181, 190.

To further corroborate the conviction of the *Grzelczyk* case and fundamental status of EU citizenship, the Court repeated its statement in many subsequent judgments.[58] The legal effect of the fundamental status translated into citizens enjoying many substantive benefits and tangible rights over time, mostly those that emphasised that they were to be considered as citizens rather than just workers. Declaring that EU citizenship status under Article 20 TFEU was the fundamental status of all citizens and accepting the principle of non-discrimination gave the Court the opportunity to involve fundamental rights considerations through this now well-established and accepted legal basis. By emphasising the fundamentality of citizenship to all EU citizens irrespective of economic activity or nationality, a relationship between fundamental rights and EU citizenship, as is the proposed hypothesis for this book, became a more foreseeable reality.

It was by declaring EU citizenship status under Article 20 TFEU to be the fundamental status of all Member State nationals in *Grzelczyk* that it can be argued here that the Court appears to suggest that there could be greater emphasis on EU citizenship as an independent legal status in itself. At this point, there were safeguards and conditions imposed by Member States before the rights under Article 21 TFEU were conferred, thereby necessitating references to the EU citizen's legal residency. However, this declaration was a clearer indication of the Court's view of the importance of the status of EU citizenship, particularly separate from other statuses as recognised by the EU institutions. Substantiating the concept of one's citizenship in the EU rather than focusing on how best to achieve pragmatism and functionality for rights conferral emphasised the empowerment of the EU citizen, thereby allowing greater room for protection under the guise of fundamental rights. In this way, the EU citizen could potentially be empowered not by their movement, residency or worker status, but rather because they were simply an EU citizen.

However, what the meaning of holding such a fundamental status was had to be clarified before its citizens could appreciate its benefits and rights. After *Grzelczyk*, there were many preliminary rulings on various different situations of non-economically active citizens.[59] Conditions that were being challenged were

[58] See Judgment of 11 July 2002, *D'hoop* C-224/98, EU:C:2002:432; Judgment of 17 September 2002, *Baumbast* C-413/99, EU:C:2002:493; Judgment of 2 October 2003, *Garcia Avello* C-148/02, EU:C:2003:539; *Collins* (n 25); Judgment of 29 April 2004, *Orfanopoulos and Oliveri* C-482/01 and C-493/01, EU:C:2004:262; C-224/02 *Pusa* [2004] ECR I-5763; *Chen* (n 25); Judgment of 15 March 2005, *Bidar* C-209/03, EU:C:2005:169; Judgment of 7 July 2005, *Commission v Austria* C-147/03, EU:C:2005:427; Judgment of 12 July 2005, *Schempp* C-403/03, EU:C:2005:446; Judgment of 12 September 2006, *Spain v UK* C-145/04, EU:C:2006:543; Judgment of 9 November 2006, *Turpeinen* C-520/04, EU:C:2006:703; Judgment of 7 June 2007, *Commission v The Netherlands* C-50/06, EU:C:2007:325; Judgment of 11 September 2007, *Schwarz* C-76/05, EU:C:2007:492; Judgment of 11 September 2007, *Commission v Germany* C-318/05, EU:C:2007:495; Judgment of 16 December 2008, *Huber* C-524/06, EU:C:2008:724; Judgment of 23 April 2009, *Ruffler* C-544/07, EU:C:2009:258; Judgment of 1 October 2009, *Gottwald* C-103/08, EU:C:2009:597; *Zanotti* (n 26); Judgment of 21 July 2011, *Stewart* C-503/09, EU:C:2011:500; *Commission v Austria* (n 26).

[59] See alongside the cases discussed in this chapter: Judgment of 15 September 2005, *Ioannidis* C-258/04, EU:C:2005:559; Judgment of 23 October 2007, *Morgan and Bucher* C-11/06 and C-12/06,

not always directly discriminatory. The Court began to more consistently adapt the principles of proportionality and non-discrimination to different situations to be as broad as possible, which had the perceived effect of paving the way for a more explicit fundamental rights discourse to emerge. However, fundamental rights were still subsumed under the principle of non-discrimination, with the principle used as a tool to indicate that the thread existed, but not independently. The Court was willing to introduce different elements to its case law, and fundamental rights seemed the logical justificatory approach for promoting non-economic values.

There were many opportunities for the Court to capitalise on the declaration of a fundamental status of EU citizenship, including clarifying who could rely on the status to determine whether this would be an expansion of the scope *ratione personae* of EU citizenship, and implicitly also of its scope *ratione materiae* and fundamental rights.[60] In other judicial systems such as England and Wales, a court being faced with similar factual situations would be prompted to apply precedent and decide the matter consistently.[61] However, with no practice of such precedent in the EU, the Court can more easily distinguish one case from the next to develop the law. This approach has diminished legal certainty, despite making progress in expanding the scope of EU citizenship. Looking specifically at applications of the principles of proportionality and genuine link test further substantiates the argument that the fundamental status of EU citizenship intended to encompass more protection of an EU citizen's fundamental rights.

C. Fundamental Rights Protection through Proportionality

After *Sala* and *Grzelczyk*, the principle of non-discrimination became accepted as an inherent part of the Court's decision making in citizenship cases. It was by virtue of these judicial instruments that the Court could declare that EU citizenship was destined to be the fundamental status of all citizens of the EU, as well as introducing a fundamental rights discourse early on. The cases that came after the fundamental status declaration in *Grzelczyk* were all directed at clarifying and understanding the novelty of a political and social conception of EU citizenship.

EU:C:2007:626; Judgment of 22 May 2008, *Nerkowska* C-499/06, EU:C:2008:300; *Commission v Austria* (n 58); Judgment of 13 April 2010, *Bressol* C-73/08, EU:C:2010:181; Judgment of 14 June 2012, *Commission v The Netherlands* C-542/09, EU:C:2012:346; *Commission v Austria* (n 26); Judgment of 21 February 2013, *LN* C-46/12, EU:C:2013:97.

[60] A logical expansion of the scope *ratione materiae* is thought to occur with any expansion of the scope *ratione personae* because with a broader group of citizens falling under the Treaty, a broader range of rights more suited to their needs would also need to be protected, subject to restrictions, as set out in the Treaty provision itself. However, any deeper integration would require more cooperation from the Member States as to the extent of EU citizenship's scope *ratione materiae*.

[61] Rupert Cross and JW Harris, *Precedent in English Law* (Clarendon Law Series 1991); Neil Duxbury, *The Nature and Authority of Precedent* (Cambridge University Press, 2008).

To do this, the Court employed two particular judicial instruments – the focus on proportionality and to a lesser extent the genuine link test. Fundamental rights protection can be seen to emerge from the way in which the Court undertook and still undertakes proportionality assessments. Under the guise of these assessments, it was able to justify factoring such fundamental rights into account. The flexibility of proportionality in practice has painted a picture of the jumbled EU citizenship development as it entered the core of the second age of EU citizenship. However, it still had the effect of expanding the scope *ratione personae* of Article 21 TFEU, and its casuistic assessments of individual situations have impacted many citizens who would have previously been denied rights.[62] The argument is that underlying all of these judicial interpretations is the growing potential of fundamental rights considerations.

The *Baumbast* case was one of the first examples of the Court applying proportionality to the interpretation of the specific economic criteria under EU citizenship for residency. Hailbronner argued that 'Union citizenship and the principle of proportionality are used to rewrite the rules laid down in secondary Community law'.[63] In *Baumbast*, legal residency and its principles were at the centre of consideration by the Court.[64] Mr Baumbast, who lived and worked in the UK, had sufficient resources and comprehensive health insurance for himself and his family, but the insurance was from Germany. When applying to renew their UK residency permits, the family were rejected because the authorities considered the German health insurance to be insufficient under the EU's residency criteria for not being 'comprehensive' enough; it did not cover emergencies. Decided soon after *Sala* and *Grzelczyk*, there was still a need to clarify the exact parameters of the scope of EU citizenship, particularly under Article 21 TFEU, both *ratione materiae* and *ratione personae*.[65] The question posed by the national court essentially sought to confirm whether denial of legal residency on the basis of this minor detail was acceptable under an assessment of proportionality.

There are several important factors in the *Baumbast* case. First, the entire Baumbast family were involved, suggesting the potential relevance of the right to private and family life. Second, non-discrimination, proportionality and the genuine link test determined the final outcome, and these three judicial instruments can be said to raise fundamental rights arguments. Finally, EU citizenship had

[62] *D'hoop* (n 58); *Baumbast* (n 58); *Orfanopoulos and Oliveri* (n 58); *Collins* (n 25); *Garcia Avello* (n 58); *Commission v Austria* (n 58); *Chen* (n 25); *Trojani* (n 25); *Bidar* (n 58); *Ioannidis* (n 59); Judgment of 26 October 2006, *Tas Hagen and Tas* C-192/05, EU:C:2006:676; *Morgan and Bucher* (n 59); *Nerkowska* (n 59); *Huber* (n 58); Judgment of 18 November 2008, *Förster* C-158/07, EU:C:2008:630; Judgment of 25 July 2008, *Metock and Others* C-127/08, EU:C:2008:449 all occurred in the first and second ages of EU citizenship and underwent proportionality assessments.

[63] Kay Hailbronner, 'Union Citizenship and Access to Social Benefits' (2005) 42 *CML Rev* 1245, 1251.

[64] *Baumbast* is a joint decision with the case of *R*, the facts of which will not be considered here.

[65] See Christian Tomuschat, 'Case C-85/96, *María Martinez Sala v Freistaat Bayern*, Judgment of 12 May 1998, Full Court [1998] ECR I-2691' (2000) 37 *CML Rev* 449; O'Leary (n 47).

now introduced a right of free movement and residency to all individuals within the EU, irrespective of their economic activity.[66] This was supported by the fundamental status of EU citizenship. The Court stated that there was no longer a need to be pursuing an economic activity in order to fall within the scope of the Treaty. However, if the claimants had been economically active and their economic activity ceased, this did not mean that they also ceased to have rights.[67] This extended the scope *ratione materiae* of rights under Article 21 TFEU read with Article 18 TFEU.

Proportionality was the cornerstone of the *Baumbast* decision. By considering necessity, suitability and the least restrictive alternatives for the family's situation,[68] the Court decided that simply lacking emergency health insurance was a disproportionate reason to deny them their rights to residency. The Court also required the claimants instead to prove they were not an 'unreasonable burden on the public finances of the host Member State',[69] a condition under the genuine link test. The unreasonable burden criteria received some negative reception when it was first introduced because it seemed to create obstacles for EU citizens when claiming EU citizenship rights.[70] It was because Mr Baumbast could satisfy the financial criteria of having sufficient resources and had been a worker for some time that the Court considered him and his family not to be unreasonable burdens.[71]

O'Gorman argues that this approach of applying the genuine link test and unreasonable burden criteria stems from the concept of financial solidarity.[72] The proportionality assessment allowed the Court to apply economic criteria and balance the Member States' interests against the Baumbast family's interests.[73] O'Brien further argues that the genuine link test 'implies the retention of national privilege',[74] with the burden being on the claimant to prove that they were integrated into the host society, rather than the national Member State having to guarantee non-discrimination of all migrating EU citizens. It seemed that avoiding creating unreasonable burdens on public finances was the compromise struck

[66] *Baumbast* (n 58) para 81.

[67] ibid para 83.

[68] See Takis Tridimas, *The General Principles of EU Law*, 2nd edn (Oxford University Press, 2006) 136.

[69] *Baumbast* (n 58) para 90.

[70] See Charlotte O'Brien, 'Real Links, Abstract Rights and False Alarms: The Relationship between the ECJ's "Real Link" Case Law and National Solidarity' (2008) 33 *European Law Review* 643; Alexander Somek, 'Solidarity Decomposed: Being and Time in European Citizenship' (2007) 32 *European Law Review* 787.

[71] *Baumbast* (n 58) para 93.

[72] Roderic O'Gorman, 'The Proportionality Principle and Union Citizenship' [2009] *Mitchell Working Papers 1/2009*, 4.

[73] There is a possibility that the CJEU simply wants to consider all options potentially available; however, it directly mentioned these aspects in *Baumbast* and it is clear that they played a significant role in the decision.

[74] O'Brien (n 70) 654.

for Member States that were concerned with the expansionist agenda of the EU for citizenship.[75] However, it is argued here that though Mr Baumbast's status as an EU citizen seemed secondary to his primary status as a worker with sufficient resources,[76] it is what the Court does not say that is important here.

The Court in *Baumbast* emphasised restrictions for invoking one's status as an EU citizen through the application of judicial instruments aimed at protecting national welfare systems. It established rules for the operation of the EU citizenship status, confirming that they did not intend to allow unrestricted access to citizenship rights by declaring it a fundamental status. The Court appeared unable to decouple itself from the original economic freedoms and interests therein.[77] It is argued that the reason that the unreasonable burden criteria seems protectionist in nature is that it is a symptom of the Court's legal culture. It is acknowledged that it seemed flawed for the Court to apply legal instruments that restricted the application of citizenship provisions appearing to favour the state over the individual. However, using proportionality, the genuine link test could be interpreted as flexible for either party. In the case itself, much like in *Singh*, the judgment would determine residency for the ex-worker EU citizen's family members. Ultimately, the Court accepted that Mr Baumbast being an ex-worker was enough to bring his rights to family life to the fore. This is interestingly despite O'Brien's more negative outlook on the situation itself.[78]

There is no explicit reference to family life in this case, but the outcome would have undoubtedly affected this. Therefore, by virtue of a proportionality assessment and satisfying the genuine link test, the Court decided in favour of the claimant for this. In line with its politicised nature, its interpretations of the judicial instruments had to strike a balance and appease both parties. However, it is argued that the way in which this has been approached is nonetheless supportive of fundamental rights. Because the family rights of workers and ex-workers were long accepted under Regulation 1612/68 and in the previous Residency Directive 90/364,[79] the claimants' rights under Article 18 TFEU extended to the Baumbast family as well. The genuine link test simply substantiated the legitimacy of Mr Baumbast's claim. It was applied in several later cases on citizenship,[80] which will see its interpretation evolving as a tool not to deter citizens from enjoying rights, but rather to justify greater consideration given to fundamental rights.

[75] *Baumbast* (n 58) para 90.

[76] See Castro d'Oliveira (n 51).

[77] Nic Shuibhne (n 31) 1598.

[78] O'Brien (n 74).

[79] As cited by the Court in *Baumbast* (n 58) para 92.

[80] See *Chen* (n 25); *Trojani* (n 25); Judgment of 10 July 2008, *Jipa* C-33/07, EU:C:2008:396; Judgment of 2 March 2010, *Rottmann* C-135/08, EU:C:2010:104; Judgment of 8 December 2011, *Ziebell* C-371/08, EU:C:2011:809; Judgment of 4 October 2012, *Byankov* C-249/11, EU:C:2012:608; Judgment of 19 September 2013, *Brey* C-140/12, EU:C:2013:565.

D. Proving a Genuine Link

The subject matter of cases where the Court applied the genuine link test primarily concerns two types of individuals: those seeking work and students. In some cases, students would have completed their studies and then would have sought work.[81] In the cases that explicitly mentioned a genuine or real link, the Court ruled in favour of the claimant, requiring national courts to reassess criteria for claiming such welfare in order for them to also adhere to the genuine link principle in light of the fundamental status of EU citizenship and, incidentally, also fundamental rights.[82] Having to prove a genuine link with the host society, which is flexible in principle, has thus proven more effective than not for protection of the individual citizen. The breadth of factors that this genuine link assessment can bring under the Court's remit is especially progressive for fundamental rights, particularly when bolstered by non-discrimination and proportionality.

This positive interpretation of the genuine link test allows an interesting comparison to be made with some more critical appraisals of it, which are perceived to be too deferential to Member States' interests.[83] Looking to its actual interpretation in the case law, the legal reality reveals a different picture. Though the principle was an obstacle to claiming rights on the face of it, the opposite effect has been seen in the Court, with claimants who could prove a genuine link actually able to make a better claim to be conferred rights under the Treaty. With the overall objective of the EU to achieve deeper integration, the Court's interpretation can be justified. Incidentally, this has brought to light the fact that because citizens are not to be treated simply as workers, their fundamental rights must be protected as well as a matter of adherence to the general principles of EU law.

Emphasis in these cases will be to demonstrate that individuals should not be recognised only as workers, but also as citizens with rights – both citizenship and fundamental rights. The Court has invoked the judicial instruments as legal bases for its actions when interpreting the effect of fundamental rights through citizenship. The genuine link test has also been used this way, first introduced in *D'hoop*.[84] In *D'hoop*, the claimant had left her home state of Belgium for secondary education in France, and then returned to attend university in Belgium. After finishing her studies, she sought a Belgian tide-over allowance for those looking for work (the 'minimex'). The Belgian authorities argued that because she had completed her secondary education overseas, she was ineligible for the grant. This was despite her Belgian nationality and obvious legal residency as a national of the Member State in question.

[81] *D'hoop* (n 58); *Ioannidis* (n 58); *Prete* (n 26).

[82] *Commission v Austria* (n 58); Judgment of 4 June 2009, *Vatsouras* C-22/08, EU:C:2009:344; *Stewart* (n 58); *Commission v The Netherlands* (n 59); *Thiele Meneses* (n 26).

[83] See O'Brien (n 70).

[84] *D'hoop* (n 58).

The decision of the Court in *D'hoop* is straightforward. The claimant was easily able to prove a genuine link with the host society, given that she was a national. However, the Belgian rules for the minimex were inherently easier for nationals to satisfy, thus amounting to indirect discrimination under Article 18 TFEU, which was protected by reference to Article 20 TFEU, as in *Sala* and *Grzelczyk*. Indirect discrimination, a common internal market principle,[85] is the term used for situations where the discrimination is not so explicit as to refer specifically to the exclusion of individuals based on their nationality, but has the same kind of effect. In this case, requiring that the minimex would only be available to those who had completed secondary school in Belgium indirectly favoured Belgians. Though it did not specific exclude non-nationals, it was still discriminatory. At this point, the discrimination would also raise fundamental rights considerations. Ms D'hoop's situation is unique as most cases under citizenship have concerned the migrant non-national EU citizen, and was thus more straightforward to judge because she was a national. It was also important to acknowledge that the genuine link test and the principle of proportionality were related and informed one another's assessments.[86] The Court's approach in *D'hoop* supported a more liberal citizenship status, influenced by fundamental rights under the principle of non-discrimination, and was therefore not radically different than the same considerations in prior cases.

The *Trojani* case was more difficult in that the claimant was not a worker in the conventional sense of the term and this initially prevented his claim to the same minimex grant succeeding before the national court.[87] The claimant, a French national, was residing in a Salvation Army hostel in Belgium as part of a socio-occupational reintegration programme and was doing odd jobs in exchange for lodging and a nominal amount of money. The conditions for worker status in the EU required the work to be genuine and real if done for payment.[88] After *Grzelczyk*, it was held that Mr Trojani would likely fall under the Treaty irrespective of his worker status as a legally resident EU citizen. The Court required an assessment of conditions for legal residency in accordance with the principle of proportionality as it did in *D'hoop*, but ultimately decided in the claimant's favour.[89] The effect of *Trojani* was to expand the scope *ratione personae* and *ratione materiae* of EU citizenship after the *D'hoop* case, demonstrating that the Court's justification therein should be applied to non-nationals as well. It re-emphasised the importance of legal residency as a precondition for citizenship rights under Article 21 TFEU, concurrently reinforcing the notion that being a citizen of the EU under Article 20 TFEU also inherently required fundamental rights to be protected through non-discrimination and proportionality.

[85] See Tridimas (n 68) 69 for a definition in the context of equality and race discrimination.

[86] Dora Kostakopoulou, 'European Union Citizenship: Writing the Future' (2007) 13 *European Law Journal* 623, 637.

[87] *Trojani* (n 25).

[88] ibid para 18.

[89] ibid para 46.

A similar situation concerning the worker status of a non-economically active claimant was seen in *Collins*. An Irish citizen sought jobseeker's allowance after moving to the UK to find work.[90] His situation was different from Mr Trojani's as he clearly did not qualify as a worker and was also only temporarily legally resident. Though not a worker, the Court decided that his status as a (temporary) legal resident would nonetheless mean that consideration should be given to his rights as an EU citizen. This meant applying the genuine link test to determine if as a work-seeker, he had enough of a connection with the host society to justify a conferral of equal treatment to social welfare.[91] The decision ultimately granted the claimant his rights and had the intended effect of emphasising that by virtue of Article 20 TFEU, rights were available under Article 21 TFEU. However, these rights also derived from other legal foundations, such as fundamental rights. Protection of fundamental rights through the principle of non-discrimination is triggered because of EU citizenship status under Article 20 TFEU. Moreover, demonstrating that rights have been exercised under Article 21 TFEU justifies bringing the EU concept of fundamental rights within the scope of the EU citizenship. The more the Court allowed non-economically active individuals to fall within the scope *ratione personae* of EU citizenship, the stronger the connection made to protection of fundamental rights.

D'hoop, *Trojani* and *Collins* thus served the aggregated purpose of demonstrating in particular that there was an implicit connection being fostered between EU citizenship and fundamental rights because of the number of non-economic values increasingly being acknowledged by the Court. Though none of the cases mentioned it, looking at the development retrospectively, the gradual shift from market values to social policy indicates that this was the *acquis* underlying the decisions. It is arguably a subtle connection, in that by no longer only concerning itself with workers' rights, the Court was able to focus on the citizen and their rights to non-discrimination and proportionality, which were linked to whether they were truly connected to the Member State they were claiming protection from. At the centre are fundamental rights, because it is these rights which are the most important, particularly when economic activity is removed as the development's primary consideration.

It is here where an observation can be made as to the influence of fundamental rights seen thus far. There is a growing link between the fundamental status of citizenship and fundamental rights because of the recognition and guaranteed protection afforded to non-economically active citizens in the Court. Though the genuine link test seems to emphasise that it is Article 21 TFEU that determines whether Article 18 TFEU and other rights are conferred, the decisions actually reflect the fact that Article 20 TFEU is the justification for why

[90] *Collins* (n 25).
[91] ibid para 70.

these non-economically active citizens were nonetheless protected for non-discrimination, proportionality and for recognising citizens' fundamental rights. Noting this, one particularly relevant category of non-economically active citizens was students, which the *Bidar* case established the rules for in terms of claiming cross-border student maintenance. It is an especially important decision in the context of students, for students make up a large proportion of individuals within the EU with a great propensity to move, but are less likely to have been or become economically active and fall under the definition of a worker. They would therefore be most likely to be the types of claimants who would benefit from being guaranteed general protection under fundamental rights, general principles of EU law and EU citizenship rights to residence and movement. It was a good opportunity for the Court to demonstrate further commitment to fundamental rights through citizenship.

Dany Bidar was a French student who, after living and completing secondary education in the UK, sought a loan for higher education there. The questions referred concerned whether, first, his student loan fell under the Treaty as part of Article 18 TFEU rights to equal treatment and, second, whether he himself fell under the Treaty as a non-economically active citizen. The question of whether the student loan fell under the Treaty was confirmed by the Court.[92] Regarding the scope *ratione personae* of EU citizenship and Mr Bidar himself, the Court stated that although the Member States are required to guarantee equal treatment under Article 18 TFEU to legal residents as per *Sala*, they could attach conditions to confirm that the claimant himself had a 'genuine link with the society of that State' before conferring the benefit on him.[93] They maintained their disapproval of discriminatory criteria for benefits, but confirmed that conditions requiring a genuine link to society were valid to protect the financial integrity of a Member State's welfare system, as long as they were proportionate.[94]

The effects of *Bidar* are threefold. First, equal treatment for student maintenance and other forms of student finance were included under the scope *ratione materiae* of EU citizenship, and free-moving economically inactive migrants who were moving to other Member States were included under the scope *ratione personae*.[95] Second, having to grant equal treatment for such categories of social welfare meant that it was acceptable for the Member State to implement a test based on proving a genuine link with the host society before claiming such rights.[96] Third, the conditions the Member States put on claiming rights as guaranteed by Article 18 and 21 TFEU had to be proportionate to the objectives sought. This effectively excluded conditions that were indirectly discriminatory.[97]

[92] *Bidar* (n 58) para 31.
[93] ibid para 55.
[94] ibid para 57.
[95] ibid para 31.
[96] ibid para 57.
[97] ibid para 61.

The principles of non-discrimination, proportionality and the genuine link test are employed in this case to demonstrate the true effectiveness of the Court in substantiating and legitimising the status of EU citizenship, but also for bringing to light, again, that simply being an EU citizen under Article 20 TFEU raises fundamental rights considerations. This is determinative in the case law.

The genuine link test is the main preoccupation in *Bidar*. However, it is the way in which the genuine link test is employed that sets the tone for fundamental rights protection within citizenship law. Though Article 21 TFEU forms the basis of this test, the Court in *Bidar* recognised that it was not as simple as proving legal residency, hence requiring a proportionality assessment for the relevant 'genuine link' conditions. This suggests that Article 20 TFEU and fundamental rights have played a more substantial role, as had been suggested throughout when previously considering *D'hoop*, *Trojani* and *Collins*. The Court is able to justify departing from the strictness of the genuine link test by employing a broad proportionality assessment, which emphasises equal treatment. However, the emphasis on equal treatment under Article 18 TFEU is supported by the need to protect one's fundamental rights, rights that citizens enjoy by virtue of Article 20 TFEU. For this reason, fundamental rights protection is argued to underlie the true meaning of Article 20 TFEU and the fundamental status of being an EU citizen.

The normative shift as it stood from the Court in *Sala* was that legal residency should confer rights to non-discrimination in the territories of host Member States. Legal residency was a right granted by virtue of EU citizenship status under Article 21 TFEU and existed hand in hand with the rights to free movement. It became a condition for claiming further rights under citizenship, as well as a replacement for the strict economic criteria of sufficient resources and comprehensive health insurance.[98] On its own, the idea of being able to attain legal residency in another EU Member State simply because of Article 20 TFEU encouraged greater cross-border movement. It was a gateway to many rights other than social welfare. EU citizenship status under Article 20 TFEU and legal residency from Article 21 TFEU read together with the principle of equal treatment and non-discrimination under Article 18 TFEU was an important influential factor in proportionality assessments. This helped to substantiate the status of being an EU citizen, moving towards a broader acceptance of the individual as a citizen with fundamental rights.

The idea of residency gained traction in EU citizenship because it did not prioritise territorial borders or financial integrity of the individual Member States over the social and political solidarity that EU citizenship fosters. Rather, it provided a common basis from which to cultivate a common European identity based upon fundamental rights, initially manifesting in the form of the principle of non-discrimination. The principle of proportionality is respected through this

[98] *Sala* (n 25) para 60.

approach, as it involves a balancing act intended to provide a fair outcome. The non-discrimination principle was also stretched beyond the realm of social welfare rights and it is argued that this was a result of a greater willingness to engage with fundamental rights. By considering that legal residency under Article 21 TFEU was a reason to confer citizenship rights, a shift towards more explicit rights-based reasoning adopted by the Court emerged. It is through this justified and considered approach that fundamental rights protection will be argued to have become a valid and important consideration for the Court in EU citizenship law. In this manner, fundamental rights protection did not appear to be an overtly radical solution.

EU citizenship status facilitates movement across borders and residence in other Member States under Article 21 TFEU; therefore, using legal residency to determine whether individuals can enjoy the benefits of EU citizenship is appropriate.[99] Considering residency rather than the economic activity of citizens particularly expanded the scope *ratione personae* of EU citizenship. As the Court noted in *Grzelczyk*, EU citizenship was the fundamental status of *all* EU citizens, not simply economically active individuals. A requirement of legal residency was thus a legitimate and broader condition for conferral of rights under the Treaty. By expanding the scope *ratione personae* of EU citizenship, the scope *ratione materiae* would also have to expand to be consistent with the growing number of individuals within the remit of EU law. This would encourage a move towards more explicit consideration of fundamental rights because the Court would have to apply rights such as equal treatment to a wider range of individuals in more varied situations. However, it should be noted that this expansion of EU citizenship law did begin to test the boundaries of the EU framework, hence the establishment of the purely internal situations rule.

III. Cross-border Residency

Residency is a malleable concept in EU citizenship law. Because it is a right as well as a condition for the conferral of other rights, it has proved to be a powerful legal tool. It fell squarely within the scope of EU citizenship law and was applied to further the development of EU citizenship itself. The Court was more inclined early on to grant rights of residency to those who had worked, which was to be expected, considering there was more established financial solidarity between the EU and its Member States than political solidarity.[100] As seen earlier,

[99] See Tomas Hammar, *International Migration, Citizenship and Democracy* (Gower, 1990); William Rogers Brubaker, 'Membership without Citizenship: The Economic and Social Rights of Noncitizens' in William Rogers Brubaker (ed), *Immigration and the Politics of Citizenship in Europe and North America* (Rowman & Littlefield, 1989).

[100] See *Singh* (n 30) and *Grzelczyk* (n 53), where the Court preferred worker provisions over the citizenship rights.

after its decision in *Sala*, the Court's stance noticeably loosened. It began to consider not only the ordinary EU citizen's rights to residency, but their family's rights as well. This was a notable expansion as it demonstrated a willingness to acknowledge individuals beyond their economic activities, and tested the limits of the EU's territorial jurisdiction by occasionally allowing non-EU nationals to fall within its scope. This was a result of protection guaranteed under the fundamental right to private and family life.[101]

The CJEU drew inspiration from the rights under Regulation 1612/68, the primary difference being that EU citizenship law had to engage with the rights of family members both from inside the EU as well as later and more controversially those from outside. The question then became whether the scope *ratione materiae* would be interpreted as extending residency to non-EU citizens' family members, a question of fundamental rights. It was also concerned with whether under scope *ratione personae*, the EU could truly justify bringing non-EU nationals within its scope, even though this respected the fundamental right to family life. The role that politics plays in the Court's decision making for EU citizenship will become more evident in this discussion. The concept of EU citizenship had already struggled to find its place in the crowded legal order of the EU without having to consider non-EU citizens' rights.[102] For reasons of respecting competing national and supranational interests, the Court had to apply a judicial instrument that was balanced and flexible in relation to both parties.

Residency used to be based upon satisfying economic criteria under three Residency Directives in 1990.[103] These Directives stipulated that in order to be considered a legal resident, the claimant had to prove they had sufficient (financial) resources and comprehensive health insurance. They would then be able to claim residence and employment rights, which were also offered to their families as long as the family also had sufficient resources and comprehensive health insurance.[104] This was notably less generous than workers' family rights in Regulation 1612/68. The Citizenship Directive 2004/38 then came into force in 2006, repealing all three former Residency Directives and streamlining the application of the three separate legal instruments with the objective of improving the overall application of EU citizenship.[105] As the final Commission Report

[101] Protected by art 8 ECHR, but later also included in the Charter of Fundamental Rights in art 7.

[102] See discussions on the future of EU citizenship in Jo Shaw, 'The Many Pasts and Futures of Citizenship in the European Union' (1997) 22 *European Law Review* 554; Samantha Besson and André Utzinger, 'Introduction: Future Challenges of European Citizenship: Facing a Wide-Open Pandora's Box' (2007) 13 *European Law Journal* 573.

[103] Council Directive (EEC) 90/364 of 28 June 1990 on the right of residence [1990] OJ L180/26; Council Directive (EEC) 90/365 of 28 June 1990 on the right of residence for employees and self-employed persons who have ceased their occupational activity [1990] OJ L180/28; Council Directive (EEC) 93/96 of 29 October 1993 on the right of residence for students [1990] OJ L180/59.

[104] Articles 1(1) and 2(2) of Directive 90/364, Directive 90/365 and Directive 93/96.

[105] *Third report from the Commission to the Council and the European Parliament on the application of Directives 93/96, 90/364, 90/365 on the right of residence for students, economically inactive and retired Union citizens* (COM (2006) 0156 final, European Commission).

on the Directives noted, Directive 2004/38 'marks a major step forward in the evolution of the right of free movement from simple economic right to the concrete expression of a real Union citizenship'.[106] Slowly, it also became less relevant to establish legal residency as a condition for these rights. This foreshadowed the later liberation and independence of the EU citizenship status, also driven by the need to promote fundamental rights.[107]

When considering EU citizenship case law and the rights derived therein before the Directive supposedly codified these decisions, it would appear that non-economically active citizens would have a greater chance of claiming rights by going directly to the Treaty rather than the Directive. The burden of demonstrating sufficient resources and comprehensive health insurance had already proven to be a significant barrier for many a non-economically active claimant. By retaining this in the Directive, it seemed to restrict itself from being relied upon by the broader scope of citizens who had been brought under the Treaty by Article 20 TFEU and fundamental rights. It was also difficult to reconcile treating citizens as simply citizens, as EU citizenship status intended (rather than as workers), and that the Court was legitimising this by granting greater deference to EU fundamental rights. Hailbronner described the situation as a 'diverse picture' because 'the basic distinction between economically and non-economically active citizens has not been given up'.[108] During the second age of citizenship, clarification on this was much sought-after.

A. The Purely Internal Situations Rule

The saga begins with *Uecker and Jacquet*,[109] a case on the exercise of free movement. The Court asked whether exercising free movement determined whether rights were within the scope *ratione materiae* of EU citizenship and whether an individual fell within the scope *ratione personae*, rather than simply by virtue of their EU citizenship under Article 20 TFEU. *Uecker and Jacquet* concerned two TCN claimants who were living in Germany, married to German nationals and working. The duration of their employment contracts was limited, which they contested under Article 11 of Regulation 1612/68 protecting spouses of EU citizens' rights to work. The question was thus whether they fell under the scope of the Regulation, which would have afforded them protection as family of

[106] ibid 8.

[107] See Editorial, 'Two-Speed European Citizenship? Can the Lisbon Treaty Help Close the Gap?' (2008) 45 *CML Rev* 1; Loïc Azoulai, '"Euro-Bonds" The *Ruiz Zambrano* Judgment or the Real Invention of EU Citizenship' [2011] *Perspectives on Federalism* 31; Roderic O'Gorman, '*Ruiz-Zambrano*, *McCarthy* and the Purely Internal Rule' [2011] *Irish Jurist* 221.

[108] Hailbronner (n 63) 1258.

[109] *Uecker and Jacquet* (n 30).

the migrant EU citizen workers.[110] Therefore, the claimants' biggest obstacle was triggering rights under the Treaty. Though the rights clearly existed, Ms Uecker and Ms Jacquet had both not moved.[111]

It was here where the notion of a 'purely internal situation' first emerged and, with it, the corresponding cross-border test. The purely internal situations rule allowed the Court to determine where the boundaries of its competences lay and what the scope of the Treaty's legal effects was by looking at whether there had been a border crossed between Member States. The Court utilised this instrument in citizenship case law and as a result of its widespread use, the test became the norm applied throughout the main part of citizenship's development.[112] Considering the purely internal situations rule will further corroborate the notion that politics was rife in the case law of the Court. Legal culture in the Court had not yet been redefined as completely separate from the internal market.[113] The Court did not appear ready to spring what would be perceived to be a judicially activist ruling upon Member States. This was unsurprising when considering that the development was still only in its second age and was beginning to gain attention amongst the more demanding questions surrounding the interpretation of the four fundamental freedoms.[114] However, this did not mean that fundamental rights were to be forgotten.

Uecker and Jacquet, which was decided the year before the *Sala* case, is indicative of the Court's initial concerns surrounding boundaries and limitations to triggering rights under the Treaty. It is argued that limits on the scope *ratione personae* and *ratione materiae* of EU citizenship was a preoccupation of the Court after the *Baumbast* case not only confirmed the effect of *Sala* and *Grzelczyk* on future citizenship cases for non-economically active citizens, but also after it applied the proportionality principle to questions on granting rights to non-discrimination and to substantiate the fundamental status of EU citizenship and better protect fundamental rights. The Court found itself under pressure from rules governing the internal market to restrict the application of such provisions to situations that would merit conferral of rights under Articles 18 and 21 TFEU, particularly when citizenship was still developing.[115] Employing a rule originally applied in the

[110] Interestingly, the claimants did not refer to their spouses' EU citizenship status, though it was mentioned by the Court in the operative part of the judgment itself. It should be noted that they mentioned it to set aside its application, given that the case itself did not trigger any Treaty rights because there had been no cross-border movement by the spouses or the claimants; ibid para 23.

[111] ibid para 18.

[112] *Garcia Avello* (n 58); Judgment of 11 July 2002, *Carpenter* C-60/00, EU:C:2002:434; *cf Rottmann* (n 80).

[113] See Nic Shuibhne (n 31) and her views on whether EU citizenship has ever departed from market citizenship.

[114] The overlap that *Collins* and *Trojani* presented for workers and citizenship rights indicates the beginning of this.

[115] See Dougan (n 3) 78, who describes the proportionality test as 'context-sensitive', with the Court often employing a 'familiar "light touch"'.

internal market,[116] the purely internal situations rule and cross-border test were applied in citizenship law to exclude cases that did not have a link with EU law from falling under the scope of the Treaty. Much like the intended effects of the genuine link test, the purely internal situations rule and cross-border test provided a way for Member States to avoid engaging with the protection of citizenship rights by arguing that the situation fell outside the scope of the Treaty's jurisdiction.

Though the Court in *Grzelczyk* and *Sala* set the foundations for the further expansion of the scope of EU citizenship, the EU institutions, and particularly the Court, still had to protect the integrity of Member State welfare systems. EU citizenship as an independent status may have been considered too federal,[117] prompting questions of competences and hierarchies of status. The Treaty itself ensured that EU citizenship was always dependent on Member State nationality.[118] The Court also confirmed that nationality would always be an exclusive Member State competence.[119] This helped to preserve the exclusivity of the status of EU citizenship.[120] Without the prerequisite of having nationality of one or more of the 28 EU Member States, the EU citizenship status itself risked becoming diluted and over-inclusive.[121] By being dependent on nationality, EU citizenship cleaved to Westphalian territorial boundaries of the nation state.[122] It is this reasoning that underpins the purely internal situations rule.

Nowadays, an argument has been put forward that the growth of globalisation and multiculturalism has rendered the Westphalian framework less appropriate.[123] The emphasis in the EU's legal order on transcending territorial boundaries supports this in principle. The emphasis on borders is contrary to the integration goals of both the market and citizenship, especially when the Court was so insistent on eliminating barriers to free movement within the EU under the four fundamental freedoms. These particular drawbacks of the purely internal

[116] From the wording in art 34 TFEU 'between Member States'.

[117] Christoph Schönberger, 'European Citizenship as Federal Citizenship: Some Citizenship Lessons of Comparative Federalism' (2007) 1 *European Review of Public Law* 19, 67 notes that though early considerations of EU citizenship hinted that it was federal, this has never been carried forward. Early federalism did not look kindly upon economically inactive citizens.

[118] Article 20 TFEU.

[119] On this, see *Micheletti* (n 30) and Judgment of 20 February 2001, *Kaur* C-192/99, EU:C:2001:106 cf. *Rottmann* (n 80).

[120] Norbert Reich, 'Union Citizenship: Metaphor or Source of Rights?' (2001) 7 *European Law Journal* 4.

[121] Dora Kostakopoulou, *The Future Governance of Citizenship* (Cambridge University Press, 2008) 127.

[122] The Peace of Westphalia was a treaty that formed the foundation of the state system in Europe. See Andreas Osiander, 'Sovereignty, International Relations, and the Westphalian Myth' (2001) 55 *International Organization* 251.

[123] On this, see Will Kymlicka, *Multicultural Citizenship: A Liberal Theory of Minority Rights* (Clarendon Press, 1995); Rainer Bauböck, 'Global Justice, Freedom of Movement and Democratic Citizenship' (2009) 50 *European Journal of Sociology* 1; Janna Thompson, 'Community Identity and World Citizenship' in Daniele Archibugi, David Held and Martin Köhler (eds), *Re-imagining Political Community: Studies in Cosmopolitan Democracy* (Stanford University Press, 1998).

situations rule are what truly allowed fundamental rights to grow, for the constitutional gaps created by the inconsistencies in the rule's application are where the Court was able to fit in fundamental rights protection, and this has proven especially effective.

EU fundamental rights in citizenship have manifested primarily under the right to private and family life in Article 8 ECHR, later consolidated in the EU's Charter of Fundamental Rights in Article 7,[124] and at the margins of the considerations of respect for the principles of non-discrimination, proportionality and interpretations of the genuine link test. Arguably, the principle of non-discrimination itself is also a manifestation of EU fundamental rights protection.[125] The intention here is to demonstrate greater emphasis of the Court's respect for family life as it considers residency rights. However, the analysis will also highlight increasing references to citizens' identities. This element of the fundamental right to private and family life became prevalent in the second age after the scope *ratione materiae* of rights under Article 21 TFEU was expanded by the Court. It represents the Court's increasingly flexibility in its understanding of this right, consistent with the nature of fundamental rights and the fundamental status of EU citizenship generally. Rather than simply being isolated examples of marginal fundamental rights considerations, the cases towards the end of the second age began to resemble more of a trend.

B. Respect for Family Life and Identity

Purely internal situations are governed by the cross-border test in the same way that the genuine link test is determined by the unreasonable burden criteria. In order to bring a citizenship case within the scope of the Treaty to allow claimants to exercise their citizenship rights, the claimant had to prove that they had moved across EU territorial borders, subsequently triggering the Treaty. Without this, the case would be under the sole jurisdiction of the national Member State. Given that non-negotiable territorial borders and the jurisdiction of the EU is an important principle to adhere to in the legal order of the Court, this restriction is justified.[126] However, this section will examine the extent to which this test has been undermined and has lost its relevance and conviction in the Court's legal culture, especially as fundamental rights – particularly the respect for family life and identity – has become a valid consideration in EU citizenship case law.

One case that encompassed a clear fundamental rights element early on is the case of *Garcia Avello*.[127] This is also a case where the Court is seen to create a

[124] Charter of Fundamental Rights of the European Union 83/02 [2010] OJ C-83/389, art 7.

[125] Not only was this enshrined in art 18 TFEU, but EU fundamental rights were protected in *Stauder v Ulm* and later *ERT* as general principles of EU law.

[126] Article 5 TEU.

[127] *Garcia Avello* (n 58).

cross-border element in order to allow its specific factual situation to fall under the Treaty's scope *ratione personae* and *ratione materiae*. The outcome was deferential to fundamental rights, but it is argued here that this was a conscious choice made by the Court, demonstrating its belief in the influence of these rights. A Belgian father, Spanish mother and their children, who had dual nationality, lived in Belgium. They applied to the Belgian authorities to register the children with the surname consisting of both the mother and father's surnames, as was traditional in Spain. This was refused, as Belgians adopted paternal surnames only. There were several issues at hand, first relating to whether this amounted to discriminatory treatment as protected by Article 18 TFEU and, if it did, how it would come within the scope of EU law. The children claiming rights in Belgium had been born there and had not yet exercised their free movement rights – there was no cross-border element and was therefore an exclusively national question.

The judgment does not struggle with questions surrounding the legal residency of the claimants, as their residency statuses were confirmed and granted by virtue of their rights under Articles 20 and 21 TFEU. Rather, it was a question of free movement and the exercise of this right to trigger further rights under the Treaty that arose because the claimants were EU citizens, namely Article 18 TFEU. Respecting several fundamental principles of dual nationality,[128] the expectation would be such that the EU did not have jurisdiction to allow the children their rights under citizenship to equal treatment because the Treaty had supposedly not been triggered by their lack of movement. However, the Court held that the situation was within the scope of EU law because it would be an impediment to the children's future movement and exercise of fundamental freedoms if the Belgian authorities denied them registration of their surnames.[129] Their identities could be compromised if not. Therefore, a potential cross-border element was established to allow the case to fall within the scope of Article 21 TFEU.

It was important for the Court to reiterate the principle established in *Uecker and Jacquet*, that: 'Citizenship of the Union … is not … intended to extend the scope *ratione materiae* of the Treaty also to internal situations which have no link with Community law.'[130] However, it then argued that the fact that the children were nationals of a Member State, yet resident in another, did provide a valid link with the Treaty. This preceded later discussion of the citizens' rights to Article 18 TFEU, in which AG Jacobs' Opinion was raised in relation to identity rights under the right to private (and family) life.[131] Accounting for 'the scale of migration within the Union',[132] it was extremely likely that these EU citizens would

[128] *Micheletti* (n 30) para 10.
[129] *Garcia Avello* (n 58) para 42.
[130] ibid para 26.
[131] Opinion of 22 May 2003, *Garcia Avello* C-148/02, EU:C:2003:311, quoted in the judgment in para 36.
[132] *Garcia Avello* (n 58) para 42.

want to move eventually, and this could not be ignored. It was this argument that convinced the Court to declare that in order to protect the citizens' potential rights to move in the future, their identities and therefore surnames had to be consistent, thereby affording them rights to non-discrimination as to the Belgian rules on surnames.

It is argued that though there was an emphasis on free movement rights and not punishing individuals in the EU for exercising their rights to free movement as guaranteed by the Court earlier in *Grzelczyk*, the true intention was that of protecting the claimant's identity rights. The decision was a novel one, as the scenario would otherwise have been considered a purely internal situation – a Belgian law challenged by its own (non-moving) nationals. However, the claimants had very firmly established their claim to EU citizenship status by also arguing that the Court should take consideration of the fact that the children were dual EU nationals, strengthening the argument that they would be likely to move in the future.[133] It was this element of identity that the Court interpreted as allowing them to enjoy a very broad range of rights even without exercising free movement. However, framing the decision under Articles 18 and 21 TFEU did not distract from the true intention of the judgment – that of protecting the fundamental right to private life.

Three observations can be made from this case. First, *Garcia Avello* contradicts the Court's decision in *Uecker and Jacquet*, which had been clear about purely internal situations and crossing borders in order to trigger the Treaty.[134] The difference is that the Court in *Garcia Avello* cited AG Jacobs' argument regarding identity rights, and the case facts almost exclusively concern EU citizenship and fundamental rights. The Court referred very little to economic rights. Therefore, and second, it brought social rights under the scope of protection under the Treaty, as well as extending EU citizenship's scope *ratione personae* to non-moving legal residents. Because protection under EU citizenship was 'ascertained by identifying *who* are seen as members and on *what* basis they are included',[135] *Garcia Avello* appeared to be a significant development. Finally, confusion over one's identity that would hinder a potential move overseas to exercise fundamental freedoms, further strengthened by the fact that the children were dual nationals, was the first instance where the Court considered identity as a fundamental right to be protected under the Treaty.[136]

[133] ibid para 43.

[134] However, some limits do apply. See Judgment of 21 September 1999, *Wijsenbeek* C-378/97, EU:C:1999:439 on showing passports not being an obstacle and *Jipa* (n 80) on public policy and security invocation for justifications.

[135] Espen Olsen, 'Work, Production, Free Movement and Then What?' *EUI Working Papers 2006/08*, 3.

[136] The first time that the fundamental right to identity was noted in the Court was by AG Jacobs in Opinion of 9 December 1992, *Konstantinidis* C-168/91, EU:C:1992:504, paras 31ff, but the Court's ultimate decision did not employ this particular reasoning.

An alternative view of *Garcia Avello* could argue that it was not that the Court ignored the purely internal situations rule, but rather that it (like most other cases in EU citizenship) expanded the scope of citizenship to include situations where the crossing of borders had not yet occurred. Therefore, it was a clarification on the limits of the cross-border test, which contributed to a different interpretation of the rule.[137] This different perspective, like in situations involving the genuine link test, favoured the fundamental and citizenship rights of individual citizens. The Court adopted a liberal interpretation that widened the scope *ratione personae* of citizens who fell under the Treaty's protection, thus highlighting the importance of the protection of fundamental rights, yet still empowering the citizen as a 'moving' citizen. This was despite the physical 'movement' across borders itself being pre-empted by the Court in lieu of accepting that fundamental rights were the underlying reason for the ultimate decision.

Therefore, though the purely internal situations rule had the potential to become a strict rule in practice, the Court was willing instead to transcend this boundary and broaden the remit of what it meant to be within or outside the scope of a purely internal situation. This was to the benefit of the citizens claiming rights, broadening the scope *ratione materiae* of Article 20 TFEU. The justification for this was the right to private and family life. It also seemed futile to attempt to uphold the cross-border test, in particular to govern purely internal situations, as it diminished the value of equal treatment,[138] but also did not give way to fundamental rights protection. It could also be argued that because the purely internal situations rule derived out of the jurisprudence on the fundamental freedoms, it was unable to capture the intricacies that involving citizens inherently introduced.[139]

Garcia Avello may have been considered an anomaly in terms of protecting the fundamental right to private life through identity until the decision in *Grunkin and Paul.*[140] *Grunkin and Paul* concerned the double-barrelled surname of a German national. The surname was registered in Denmark where the claimant was born, but subsequently was not recognised under German law. The claim surrounded rights to non-discrimination concerning this refusal. In relation to the purely internal situations rule, the Court applied its reasoning from *Garcia Avello* in that the Treaty was triggered because the claimant, a German national, was living in Denmark and therefore was no longer in a 'purely internal' situation.[141]

[137] This was later confirmed by *Carpenter* (n 112). See Peter Oliver and Wulf-Henning Roth, 'The Internal Market and the Four Freedoms' (2004) 41 *CML Rev* 407, 418.

[138] Siofra O'Leary, 'The Past, Present and Future of the Purely Internal Rule in EU Law' [2010] *Irish Jurist* 13, 16.

[139] See *Rottmann* (n 80); Peter Van Elsuwege, 'Court of Justice of the European Union European Union Citizenship and the Purely Internal Rule Revisited Decision of 5 May 2011, Case C-434/09 *Shirley McCarthy v Secretary of State for the Home Department*' (2011) 7 *European Constitutional Law Review* 308, 317.

[140] Judgment of 14 October 2008, *Grunkin and Paul* C-353/06, EU:C:2008:559.

[141] ibid para 17.

However, unlike in *Garcia Avello*, the claimant was not being discriminated by the German authorities on the grounds of nationality as he was himself German, but rather it was the 'serious inconvenience' to the claimant that would be central to the reasoning and most indicative of deference to a fundamental rights discourse in EU citizenship.[142] This notion of a 'serious inconvenience' is central and becomes an important point later on. In *Grunkin and Paul*, if the claimant's surname as registered in Denmark was not recognised by the German authorities, it would leave him liable to confusion surrounding his identity and thus amount to an obstacle in his private life. This was the same situation in *Garcia Avello* for the two children with double-barrelled surnames in Spain, but not in Belgium where they were currently residing.

The Court dedicated most of its judgment in *Grunkin and Paul* to clarifying its arguments surrounding this point of an interference to private and family life manifested by identity,[143] with the effect of demonstrating that the right to private life under identity was clearly the focal point of its decision-making process, without ever stating this explicitly. Importantly, the purely internal situations rule clearly did not pose an obstacle in this case. The Court was able to enhance fundamental rights considerations through a loose interpretation of the purely internal situations rule in principle, and it is this which supports the argument here that it is the drawbacks of the rule itself that has truly empowered the fundamental rights of EU citizens. From this, an argument began to emerge that the purely internal situations rule was losing relevance in EU citizenship development in order to make way for EU fundamental rights[144] and was increasingly criticised for appearing to have 'lost the plot, allowing, in an arbitrary manner, ever more remote or tenuous links to trigger the application of EU law'.[145]

C. An Increasingly Tenuous Cross-border Link

The purely internal situations rule was established in order to curtail the excessive expansion of the scope of EU citizenship after *Sala* and *Grzelczyk*. However, as noted above, in the face of EU fundamental rights, the rule began to play a notably diminished role in the Court's eyes. The trend was turning against emphasising the limits erected by the judicial instruments employed in the first age and early in the second age, and more towards fundamental rights. There was especially little resistance as regards the purely internal situations rule and the cross-border element in particular. The *Garcia Avello* case was preceded by *Carpenter* and

[142] ibid para 29.

[143] ibid paras 23ff.

[144] This element of identity rights as an EU fundamental right was later reiterated by the Court in Judgment of 22 December 2010, *Sayn-Wittgenstein* C-208/09, EU:C:2010:806; and Judgment of 12 May 2011, *Runevič-Vardyn and Wardyn* C-391/09, EU:C:2011:291.

[145] O'Leary (n 138) 29.

MRAX,[146] neither of which was centrally concerned with EU citizenship status, but rather more with the right to private and family life under Article 8 ECHR. The discussion of these two cases will bring to light the flaws of the cross-border test in view of the importance afforded to this fundamental right in the EU.

The key example that demonstrated how tenuous a cross-border link can be in reality is the *Carpenter* case, which was framed in the context of the free movement of services.[147] The scope of EU citizenship had changed from being based on rights under the internal market to being based on its own rights to EU citizenship.[148] However, it did not do so without being scrutinised for the way in which it brought these claimants under the scope of the Treaty, namely through tenuous 'cross-border' links. In the *Carpenter* case, an economically active British citizen married a TCN after she had overstayed her permitted entry to the UK. Upon threat of deportation, Mrs Carpenter argued that if she left, it would affect her husband's family life and his ability to provide services overseas. He would have to move to live with her or, if not, be separated from his family. If he were to go to live with them, it would be somewhere outside the EU. This would mean that his work in the EU in which he was currently engaged would no longer be available to him. The Court found that there was a breach of his rights because breaking up his family would deter him from moving to provide services. Interestingly, the Court in *Carpenter* does not mention the fundamental status of EU citizenship. However, if the claim was framed as seeking to achieve internal market integration, it would seem peculiar.[149] Therefore, in order to protect Mr Carpenter and protect his family, the Court had to invoke fundamental rights read with the free movement of services and apply arguably activist judicial reasoning to bring his claim within the scope of the Treaty.

In *Carpenter*, the right to family life as protected by Article 8 ECHR was a consideration, but not the main reason for the conferral of rights. It was difficult to frame *Carpenter* under the fundamental freedoms, though the Court seemed to suggest that this was the case.[150] Whilst there was a fundamental freedom to be exercised and the right to family life was protected under the ECHR, there was no link between the two concepts. Spaventa suggested that the Court might have used the fundamental status of being an EU citizen to bridge this normative gap.[151] It would also mean that it was no longer a purely internal situation.

[146] C-459/99 *MRAX* [2002] ECR I-6591.

[147] *Carpenter* (n 112).

[148] See Opinion of 11 September 2008, *Petersen* C-228/07, EU:C:2008:281.

[149] Oliver and Roth (n 137) 419; Dora Kostakopoulou, 'Ideas, Norms and European Citizenship: Explaining Institutional Change' (2005) 68 *MLR* 233, 254.

[150] Niamh Nic Shuibhne, 'EU Citizenship after Lisbon' in Diamond Ashiagbor, Nicola Countouris and Ioannis Lianos (eds), *The European Union after the Treaty of Lisbon* (Cambridge University Press, 2012) 149.

[151] Eleanor Spaventa, 'From *Gebhard* to *Carpenter*: Towards a (Non-)Economic European Constitution' (2004) 41 *CML Rev* 743, 767.

Though this could explain the thinking behind its decision, it was nonetheless difficult to reconcile the emphasis on Mr Carpenter's future cross-border movement. It detracted significantly from the value of the test as a way to demarcate the competences of the Court. However, what this did do was to highlight the inconsistency of trying to justify the case under the internal market, and that the core of the decision was actually protection of fundamental rights, which was brought to light by the fact that Mr Carpenter was an EU citizen.

Soon after the *Carpenter* case was decided, the Court was faced with the *MRAX* case, in which several issues surrounding the right to family life, particularly of TCNs, were at hand. This was a case entirely concerned with rights to family life and was therefore a pertinent example in the context of empowering EU fundamental rights through EU citizenship status after the *Carpenter* decision. Indeed, the Court was clear in reiterating that the law under the internal market's fundamental freedoms 'is not applicable to situations not presenting any link to any of the situations envisaged by Community law',[152] thereby ensuring that again, the purely internal situations rule was upheld. In this case, the MRAX organisation challenged Belgian laws published in a circular of August 1997. The questions asked to do with fundamental rights violations were raised because of the rules laid out in the circular, rather than being preoccupied with the specifics of proving a cross-border element should the scenarios raised occur in reality.

There were two main problems noted by MRAX. First, Belgium claimed to be able to turn away TCN spouses of EU citizens at their border if they could not prove they had the requisite documentation – namely, a valid visa. The Court was adamant in this case as to emphasising rights as to family life. It cited *Carpenter*, as well as Regulation 1612/68, the rights to a worker's family in order to justify its decision.[153] This would confirm the prior assessments of cases as to the influence of this provision in encouraging the proliferation of the fundamental rights *acquis*. Importantly, the Court held that Belgium had the right to ask for documentation of the relevant TCN family members entering to join their families and, if this was not supplied, to send them away. However, it remained the case that if the TCN family member did provide the required proof of family ties and identity, but not a visa, they could not automatically be sent away at the border. The reason for this, amongst others, was to protect Article 8 ECHR rights to family reunification.

The second problem concerned situations where TCNs failed to comply with the legal formalities of residency in Belgium prior to becoming spouses of EU citizens, and thereafter sought rights based upon their new spousal status. Though proportionate penalties were accepted for failure to comply with Belgian

[152] Judgment of 25 July 2002, *MRAX* C-459/99, EU:C:2002:461.
[153] ibid para 53.

laws as to legal residency, it was held that it was disproportionate to deny rights to residency if this is regarded as the only reason.[154] Therefore, if the TCN spouse was able to prove identity and familial ties, this was reason enough to afford flexibility in the rules surrounding the conferral of legal residency and its formalities. The *MRAX* case scenarios discussed were purely hypothetical; however, it was clear from the reasoning employed that the fundamental right to family life – and, in particular, family reunification – had assumed such significance that it justified greater weight being afforded to these elements when assessing proportionately if it was acceptable to confer or deny rights to enter, remain and reside.

The important point to note about both *Garcia Avello* and *Carpenter* is that static citizens could now rely on the citizenship provisions. The *MRAX* case, on the other hand, was the legal foundation needed to justify the Court further capitalising upon fundamental rights irrespective of a cross-border element. Read cumulatively, this would appear to suggest that fundamental rights could be read independently of movement and instead by virtue of EU citizenship status. It is clear that these cases casted especial doubt over the relevance of the cross-border test and highlighted the arbitrary nature of the crossing of borders to trigger such fundamental protection.[155] It was not only the free-moving citizen who required and deserved protection under EU citizenship. If EU citizenship was truly the fundamental status of all nationals of the EU Member States that it purported to be, it would not exclude citizens who did not exercise free movement.[156] By its very nature, this necessitated a thorough consideration for fundamental rights reflected by the Court's decision making.

The arguments raised by the Court in *Carpenter* then carried through to *MRAX* both drew upon the longer-established Article 8 ECHR, the right to private and family life, and, to a lesser extent, the Charter of Fundamental Rights and its equivalent Article 7.[157] What is relevant for the discussion in the context of the CJEU case law is the longer history of the protection of this right in the European Court of Human Rights (ECtHR), particularly as to family reunification, which was decided earlier than the establishment of EU citizenship status.[158] In *Matthews v UK*,[159] the ECtHR held that Member States were liable for breaches of fundamental rights in the context of EU law, even though the EU was not a contracting party. This made it clear that though the EU had not acceded to the

[154] ibid para 78.

[155] Eleanor Spaventa, 'Family Rights for Circular Migrants and Frontier Workers: *O and B, and S and G*' (2015) 52 *CML Rev* 753, 754; O'Brien (n 70) 661; Catherine Jacqueson, 'Union Citizenship and the Court of Justice: Something New under the Sun? Towards Social Citizenship' (2002) 27 *European Law Review* 260, 281.

[156] Leonard FM Besselink, 'Dynamics of European and National Citizenship: Inclusive or Exclusive?' (2007) 3 *European Constitutional Law Review* 1, 2.

[157] Because around the time of *Carpenter* and *MRAX* the Charter had only been in existence for a few years, it is argued that the true influence remained primarily with the ECHR at this point.

[158] *X and Y v UK* [1977] ECHR 3; *Abdulaziz* (1985) 7 EHRR 471.

[159] *Matthews v UK* [1999] ECHR 12

Convention, this did not allow it to escape liability for breaches of human rights. It thereby justified bringing fundamental rights protection as the Court did in the cases just discussed to the forefront of its decision making. Nowadays, there are several case law developments on this matter of accession since the EU called for it in the Lisbon Treaty;[160] however, the core of the argument remains that leading up the early 1990s, the right to private and family life under Article 8 ECHR embodied a strong persuasive element of family reunification and it is this approach that is most suitable for the foundations of the argument here.

The definition of 'family life' as interpreted by the ECtHR had been accepted as notably broad.[161] The standard in the ECtHR was therefore of preventing 'arbitrary interference' to family life, a deliberately wide notion.[162] As Connelly notes: 'This approach to the interpretation of Article 8 reflects a liberal view of rights.'[163] The Court seems to have drawn upon this and aligned itself with the ECtHR's approach, as evidenced by cases at the end of the second age. The status of the Charter was such that it was legally non-binding and had yet to make a significant impact. It was in this way that EU fundamental rights began to grow in constitutional significance in scenarios concerning EU citizenship status, where the Court was presented with relevant opportunities to capitalise upon such rights because of the EU citizens involved, and their rights. This is arguably the legal foundation behind the decisions in *Carpenter* and *MRAX* initially, and the later more explicit reference to Article 8 ECHR in the *Chen* case confirms this.

In 1982, the Court first mentioned family members and their rights to residency under the Treaty.[164] This would seem to be consistent with many of the cases on family life before the ECtHR as well, thus also confirming that the CJEU may have been more influenced than it appeared where elements of fundamental rights were present. The Court stated that the Treaty provisions 'cannot be applied to cases which have no factor linking them with any of the situations governed by Community law … Such is undoubtedly the case with workers who have never exercised the right to freedom of movement within the Community'.[165] It confirmed that the boundaries established to protect the integrity of the EU's jurisdiction were firm, and this set an expectation that it would be difficult for such a disconnected and non-EU notion as TCNs to be brought within the scope of the Treaty. However, what the Court in *Chen* did instead was notable in terms of connecting EU fundamental rights, particularly of respect for family life,[166] to

[160] See *Bosphorus Airways v Ireland* (2006) 23 EHRR 1.

[161] Hugo Storey, 'The Right to Family Life and Immigration Case Law at Strasbourg' (1990) 39 *ICLQ* 328, 334.

[162] AM Connelly, 'Problems of Interpretation of Article 8 of the European Convention on Human Rights' (1986) 35 *ICLQ* 567, 570.

[163] ibid 571.

[164] Judgment of 4 November 1997, *Morson and Jhanjan* C-35/82 and C-36/82, EU:C:1997:517.

[165] ibid paras 16 and 17.

[166] *Chen* (n 25).

EU citizenship status under Article 20 TFEU. It built upon the cases discussed earlier and adds to the argument that the purely internal situations rule had become too restrictive to accommodate the growing constitutional influence of EU fundamental rights.

Mrs Chen, a Chinese national married to another Chinese national who frequently travelled to the UK for work, was due to give birth. She travelled to Northern Ireland, where she knew that her baby would gain Irish nationality. After the baby was born, mother and daughter then returned to Wales, where the British authorities subsequently denied Mrs Chen a residency permit because her daughter, an EU citizen by virtue of the Republic of Ireland's *jus soli* rules, was not exercising any rights under the Treaty and could thus not rely on them to allow her mother to derive residency as a dependent family member.[167] The facts of the case emphasised the extent of newborn baby Chen's reliance on her mother to demonstrate how imperative it was that her mother remained to care for her. The national court also put forward the question of whether it would have to consider rights under the ECHR regarding private and family life, and non-discrimination.[168]

Several questions were posed aside from the primary one regarding the scope of EU citizenship – those of purely internal situations, exploiting the Irish citizenship rules to attain nationality and hence EU citizenship, and the minimum age for exercising Treaty rights. The purely internal situations rule was sidestepped by citing the reasoning adopted in *Garcia Avello* and *Grunkin and Paul*, in that simply by reason of being born in the Member State in question and having not exercised free movement yet was not persuasive in denying rights as an EU citizen, but more importantly, to fundamental rights. The Court then considered if the fundamental status of EU citizenship and fundamental rights would be sufficient to grant the TCN mother a derived right of residency.[169] The Court noted that baby Chen was not a financial burden because her parents had sufficient resources and comprehensive health insurance for her.[170] Then, through an assessment of proportionality, Mrs Chen was ultimately accepted as the primary carer of a very dependent EU citizen and was thus allowed to derive a right to indefinite residence to remain and care for her young daughter, who could certainly claim her rights under citizenship irrespective of her age.[171]

The breadth of the decision in the *Chen* case had both positive and negative effects. The Court accepted that without her mother looking after her, baby Chen

[167] See Dimitry Kochenov and Justin Lindeboom, 'Breaking Chinese Law – Making European One: The Story of *Chen*, Or: Two Winners, Two Losers, Two Truths' in B Davies and F Nicola (eds), *EU Law Stories* (Cambridge University Press, 2017) for a rather more dramatic exposé of the *Chen* case.

[168] *Chen* (n 25) para 22.

[169] The *jus soli* argument was rebutted by maintaining the exclusivity of nationality as a competence of Member States, and the notion of minimum age was set aside for lacking any legal basis.

[170] *Chen* (n 25) para 28.

[171] ibid para 20.

would be hindered from exercising her right to freely move and reside in the EU. However, protecting baby Chen's free movement rights were not the claimant's primary intention; rather, the case appeared to be about allowing Mrs Chen's right of residency in the UK with her daughter, given the personal implications of separating a family.[172] The situation is made more complicated because her mother was a TCN. It is here where fundamental rights become a valid argument for granting citizenship rights. There was otherwise no connection with economic rights or activity. In order to achieve the desired outcome for the claimant, the Court would have to adopt a starkly different mindset than it had done prior to this based on the approach under the fundamental freedoms. It was the opportunity for the Court to demonstrate its ability to depart from internal market reasoning and towards adopting a more fundamental rights-based *acquis*, as had been seen in *Garcia Avello*, *MRAX* and *Carpenter*, particularly in the context of family life.

The *Chen* decision had several important effects. First, it suggested that solidarity was established between the EU and its citizens because access was granted to fundamental rights through the status of EU citizenship under Article 20 TFEU.[173] This supported a more independent legal basis for EU citizenship rights.[174] However, and second, it brought TCNs within the scope of Article 21 TFEU, which could have been perceived to undermine the legitimacy of EU citizenship status as it would dilute its exclusive nature. Nonetheless, it is argued that the CJEU appears to have drawn from the approach adopted by the ECtHR as regards the right to private and family life, which is confirmed by the cases discussed earlier as to this developing rights *acquis*.[175] Finally, the approach taken by the CJEU in *Chen* represented the first instance of it embracing a distinctly different approach. Given the conviction of fundamental rights and the fundamental status of EU citizenship, there was potential for this line of legal reasoning and culture to continue in the future development of EU citizenship law.

The Court refrained from mentioning fundamental rights in its judgment, though they seemed instrumental to the outcome. This was unsurprising as it had yet to do so in citizenship cases, but was a missed opportunity for the EU citizenship and fundamental rights relationship to become more explicit. Nonetheless, this case linked Article 20 TFEU, the status of EU citizenship, and EU fundamental rights, particularly under Article 8 ECHR, in the most unequivocal way

[172] Jean-Yves Carlier, 'Case C-200/02, *Kunqian Catherine Zhu, Man Lavette Chen v Secretary of State for the Home Department*' (2005) 42 *CML Rev* 1121, 1125.

[173] See Michael Dougan and Eleanor Spaventa, '"Wish You Weren't Here …" New Models of Social Solidarity in the European Union' in Michael Dougan and Eleanor Spaventa (eds), *Social Welfare and EU Law* (Bloomsbury, 2005).

[174] See Francis G Jacobs, 'Citizenship of the European Union: A Legal Analysis' (2007) 13 *European Law Journal* 591, 595.

[175] Considering *Uecker and Jacquet* (n 30) and *Morson and Jhanjan* (n 164), this would not have been an expected outcome.

seen thus far. However, in terms of the rights to residency, *Chen* expanded the scope *ratione materiae* and *ratione personae* for dependent TCN family members of EU citizens allowing derived rights of residency as a result of proven dependency to protect free movement rights. The Court justified its decision by stating that 'provisions laying down a fundamental principle such as that of the free movement of persons must be interpreted broadly'.[176] Though this is not the expression of intent for fundamental rights that was predicted initially,[177] the Court hinted that it would soon become a more regular and influential feature.[178]

Commentators began to identify the potential for some substantial normative changes in the Court's legal culture applied to citizenship case law, which would take EU citizenship very far from where it began.[179] Slowly but surely, the case law exhibited changes in the legal culture of the Court when interpreting the rights under EU citizenship. Many judgments indicated a growing relationship with fundamental rights because of the expanding scope of EU citizenship and broad interpretations of the effects and rights under Article 20 TFEU.[180] These were embraced positively by the commentary and were taken as a sign of a more liberalised political EU.[181] Starting from only the economically active to the economically inactive, scope *ratione personae* of Article 21 TFEU now extended to non-EU citizens. Furthermore, the non-EU citizen appears to have a potentially justifiable legal basis for enjoyment of rights from *Chen*, deriving from increasingly constitutionalised fundamental rights protection.

It is clear at this point as well that economic activity as part of the Court's justification for conferral of rights under Article 21 TFEU no longer held as much significance as had previously been the case. The reasons for the demise of economic activity as a condition to claiming EU citizenship rights are the same ones that can be applied to discount the cross-border test. The test unjustifiably excluded a number of citizens who could not cross borders, for whatever reason. Again, this became too restrictive and discriminatory because the notion of movement across borders was notably arbitrary.[182] The status of EU citizenship would not be able to live up to its expectations of being a fundamental status if the test continued to be

[176] *Chen* (n 25) para 31.

[177] See the criticism by Bernard Hofstotter, 'A Cascade of Rights, or Who Shall Care for Little Catherine? Some Reflections on the *Chen* Case' [2005] *European Law Review* 548, 571 that *Chen* was 'dogmatically unsatisfactory and merely instrumental to the result pursued'.

[178] *Metock and Others* (n 62) and Judgment of 5 September 2012, *Rahman* C-83/11, EU:C:2012:519 also held family to be of importance to enjoying citizenship rights, though they were both decided upon the protection of this right specifically.

[179] See Spaventa (n 151); Eleanor Spaventa, 'Seeing the Wood Despite the Trees? On the Scope of Union Citizenship and its Constitutional Effects' (2008) 45 *CML Rev* 13; Dougan (n 3).

[180] See the cases discussed above, as well as *Baumbast* (n 58); *Metock and Others* (n 62); Judgment of 9 January 2007, *Jia* C-1/05, EU:C:2007:1; *Carpenter* (n 112); and *Chen* (n 25).

[181] See Editorial (n 107).

[182] See Alina Tryfonidou, 'In Search of the Aim of the EC Free Movement of Persons Provisions: Has the Court of Justice Missed the Point?' (2009) 46 *CML Rev* 1591 for criticism as it pertains to reverse discrimination.

interpreted this way. It was a period of confusion during the mid-2000s midway through the second age of EU citizenship that Dougan and Spaventa describe as 'veritable kaleidoscope of welfare rights and principles'.[183] This was exacerbated by the problem of reverse discrimination, which arose as a consequence of the application of the purely internal rule and the cross-border test.

D. The Problem of Reverse Discrimination

There is an inherent downside of the purely internal situations rule and the cross-border test apart from their inability to truly account for EU fundamental rights considerations. Requiring claimants to prove they had moved across borders to claim rights under EU law raised the problem of reverse discrimination. Reverse discrimination occurs in respect of the disadvantageous position into which a host state's own nationals are placed as compared to non-nationals, the moving EU citizens. Because individuals are required to prove a cross-border element to claim rights under EU law, any national who has not moved would not be able to claim this protection, which by its very nature acts as an additional layer of protection for individuals. Therefore, being excluded under the scope *ratione personae* of Article 21 TFEU for simply failing to move across borders established a hierarchy where it appeared more beneficial to be a moving EU citizen because of the greater number of rights available to these individuals.

The problem of reverse discrimination adds to arguments for abolishing the cross-border test as a way to determine the boundaries of the scope *ratione personae* of EU citizenship. It is clear that it was an unsuitable test, given that it came from the internal market originally, where, for example, alternative tools existed to resolve reverse discrimination effects on the consumption of foreign goods over national goods.[184] However, in the context of human lives – especially those that the EU are committed to protecting by virtue of the fundamental status of EU citizenship and EU fundamental rights – this problem was highly unsatisfactory. At the time of *Garcia Avello* and *Carpenter*, there was no obvious solution, though the AGs had raised the issue in their Opinions.[185]

In case law, the Court often left the question of reverse discrimination to the national courts, which then had to assess rights of their nationals under the ECHR to resolve the issue.[186] With the EU in the process of accession to the ECHR and the Treaty encompassing a new fundamental rights dimension,[187] the dynamic of

[183] Dougan and Spaventa (n 173) 182.

[184] In terms of the free movement of goods, alternative marketing and advertising methods exist nationally to counteract the effects of reverse discrimination on national goods.

[185] See Opinion of 20 February 2002, *D'hoop* C-224/98, EU:C:2002:103; and Opinion of 13 September 2001, *Carpenter* C-60/00, EU:C:2001:447.

[186] O'Leary (n 138) 14.

[187] Article 6(2) TEU.

this solution could have changed significantly. The discussion will evolve in light of the constitutionalisation of fundamental rights in the Charter in the Lisbon Treaty. What this analysis aimed to uncover was that during this second age of citizenship, though *Grzelczyk* had indicated what the direction for citizenship was to be in its declaration of the fundamental status, the Court had yet to develop a consistent discourse even when using residency as the legal basis for the conferral of rights. As a result, the case law that emerged from the first half of the second age was a disorderly mix of judicial reasoning that drew from the internal market, as well as incomplete pictures of what the Court perceived the new discourse on the fundamental status of EU citizenship should be. This uncertainty was then codified into Directive 2004/38 and is the reason for the lack of confidence shown in this chapter in relation to its ability to support greater fundamental rights protection. However, recognising the shortcomings of the purely internal situations rule serves to highlight that fundamental rights protection had been considered of such importance that even the Court in its application of the judicial instrument could not fully appreciate the potential of these rights.

IV. Conclusion

Thym accurately summarised the state of the law today, 26 years after the introduction of EU citizenship status. He recognised that 'Union citizenship may have created an overarching status, but it did not reverse the idiosyncrasies of the different layers of free movement law, which have been historically accumulated in a process of stratification'.[188] Recognising this, it was now clear that the internal market had been left behind in favour of non-economic foundations under the Treaty provisions for citizenship. This chapter has discussed that both prior to the status of EU citizenship being established as well as afterwards, a fundamental rights discourse has been present in and influential on the citizenship discussion. By means of the judicial instruments of non-discrimination, proportionality, the genuine link test and even the purely internal situations rule, the Court's case law interpretations have moved the development away from its roots in the internal market. It has grown into what is seen now as a widespread proliferation of the effects of the status of EU citizenship under Article 20 TFEU and implicitly, as a result, fundamental rights protection.

The *Sala* case was identified as the turning point for EU citizenship because the Court was able to adopt a different legal basis for the conferral of rights to citizens outside of those who were actors in the internal market. This was carried through to the *Grzelczyk* case, where it was held that EU citizenship was destined to be

[188] Daniel Thym, 'The Elusive Limits of Solidarity: Residence Rights of and Social Benefits for Economically Inactive Union Citizens' (2015) 52 *CML Rev* 17, 43.

the fundamental status of all nationals of EU Member States. Most pertinently, this appeared to be true for the non-economically active citizen and marked a departure from the judicial approaches under the four fundamental freedoms. Individuals without worker status (such as students) were frequently the claimants, and these cases contributed to determining what it really meant to have the 'fundamental' status of EU citizenship – effectively, not only of rights under Article 21 TFEU read with Article 18 TFEU, but also of fundamental rights more broadly (though perhaps less explicitly).

This chapter has also discussed the development of discourse surrounding the legal residency of EU citizens under Article 21 TFEU, the demise of the purely internal situations rule. This has contributed to the slow rise of EU fundamental rights in citizenship case law. It has been argued that this derived from cases on identity rights as well as respect for family life under Article 8 ECHR, the right to private and family life. This longer established right before the ECtHR has also been noted as a potential foundation for the Court's later decisions and approach adopted, particularly towards the end of the second age. The next chapter will draw upon fundamental rights in particular to examine the constitutionalisation of fundamental rights as a discourse on its own and within the growing EU citizenship development, to argue that the increasing number of references to fundamental rights in citizenship law correlates to the increasing dominance of fundamental rights in the EU's constitutional framework.

3

The Growing Potential of EU Citizenship's Relationship with Fundamental Rights

I. Introduction

It has been established by prior analysis that having legal residency should grant rights to social welfare and equal treatment through the principles of non-discrimination and proportionality. This also included applying rules on purely internal situations and establishing a genuine link with the host state. Later, this expanded and Article 20 TFEU started to be used as the legal basis for conferring citizenship and fundamental rights as well. Fundamental rights implications were increasingly referred to by the Court in tandem with citizenship rights. This had become especially evident through the Court's consideration of identity rights and respect for family life, but also the ECHR case law on family life under Article 8 ECHR. The protection of fundamental rights has been underlying much of the progress mentioned made to date.

Two Advocate General (AG) Opinions discussed fundamental rights early on in citizenship which this chapter will draw attention to – AG Jacobs in *Konstantinidis* in 1992[1] and AG Colomer in *Petersen* in 2008.[2] As the scope of EU citizenship law widened to include more types of citizens and a broader set of rights, the Court has implicitly suggested that there may be a possibility of EU citizenship status becoming an independent legal basis for claiming such rights.[3] It will be argued that this is in part due to the rise of fundamental rights. Then, AG Sharpston's Opinion in *Zambrano* in 2010 will be used to examine the later development of EU citizenship and fundamental rights, and to show how perspectives on citizenship have changed over time according to the Advocates General.[4] AG Sharpston's Opinion is particularly critical of the Court avoiding answering questions on fundamental rights. She proposes a solution that this book supports of an independent legal

[1] Opinion of 9 December 1992, *Konstantinidis* C-168/91, EU:C:1992:504.

[2] Opinion of 11 September 2008, *Petersen* C-228/07, EU:C:2008:281.

[3] See Eleanor Spaventa, 'Seeing the Wood Despite the Trees? On the Scope of Union Citizenship and its Constitutional Effects' (2008) 45 *CML Rev* 13.

[4] Opinion of 30 September 2010, *Zambrano* C-34/09, EU:C:2011:560.

status for citizenship. She also asks the Court to clarify the relationship between fundamental rights and citizenship.

The questions raised by AG Sharpston in her Opinion are pertinent to clarify the situation in the context of what has been evident in the citizenship case law concerning the rise of fundamental rights protection. Therefore, there was great anticipation surrounding the eventual *Zambrano* judgment, which was somewhat satisfied when the Court finally confirmed that EU citizenship status was an independent legal basis for the conferral of citizenship rights. The fifth judicial instrument governing citizenship was also established in this case, so Articles 20–21 TFEU were now subject to proving that a citizen had been deprived of the genuine enjoyment of their rights. It will be argued that all this has been to the credit of the development in the Court, which has slowly but surely raised the status of fundamental rights protection in cases of citizenship rights.

The chapter is structured around the three identified AG Opinions used as case studies to examine the gradual development of fundamental rights and EU citizenship. Spanning from 1992 to 2010, each represents a different time period for the EU citizenship jurisprudence. For this reason, it is pertinent to look closely at how attitudes in the Court have shifted over time. In this manner, the fundamental rights thread comes to the fore. The main cases that have paved the way towards fundamental rights protection in EU citizenship case law will be reviewed in light of the AG Opinions and the underlying rhetoric of fundamental rights they allude to in the context of pre- and post-Lisbon developments. Finally, the *Zambrano* case itself will be examined, though notably in a cautious light.

II. Fundamental Rights in EU Citizenship Pre-Lisbon

The previous chapter demonstrated that fundamental rights protection has been present in the case law of the Court for some time. This is by virtue of the application of the principle of non-discrimination, the principle of proportionality, the genuine link test and, to an extent, interpretations of the purely internal situations rule. All of these developments pre-dated the Lisbon Treaty, the benchmark identified earlier in this book as one of the key turning points for constitutional fundamental rights. This is because the Charter of Fundamental Rights did not become binding until the Lisbon Treaty, despite having existed for nine years beforehand. However, as the cases in the previous chapter showed, this did not mean that there were no indications that a fundamental rights discourse did not exist or that there was no appetite for one in the Court's deliberations.

This aim of this section is to trace the history of discussion in the Court surrounding the relationship between fundamental rights and EU citizenship, building upon Chapter 2's initial prelude to these rights in the context of EU citizenship. First, it will present AG Jacobs' Opinion in *Konstantinidis*, which occurred prior to the formal establishment of citizenship. AG Jacobs is the first to link fundamental rights and citizenship status, representing the initial rise of fundamental rights in citizenship. Then, it will clarify how the general discourse in the previous section led to the Court's consideration of family life and identity as it pertains to citizenship status under Article 20 TFEU. AG Colomer's Opinion in *Petersen* will be considered after this to present a more optimistic view of the further potential of fundamental rights, focusing on what the Court had achieved since the status was first introduced and how this relates to the general EU fundamental rights development as well.

A. AG Jacobs' Opinion in *Konstantinidis* (1992)

The AG Opinion in *Konstantinidis* is chosen as a case study because it is the most explicit indication of the potential that fundamental rights was perceived to have in light of the protection guaranteed by a non-economic EU. The Advocate General already brought the two concepts together before citizenship status existed, confirming their inherent relationship and emphasising their significance early on. The general EU fundamental rights development is argued to have had a hand in AG Jacobs' Opinion, given the recognisable consideration the Court had attributed to these rights leading up to Maastricht. Citing *ERT* as his authority,[5] AG Jacobs laid out a clear formula for the application of fundamental rights before they were legally binding in the Charter and raised the status of fundamental rights applied to EU citizenship for the first time.

The *Konstantinidis* case concerned a question on the free movement of services. Mr Konstantinidis was a Greek national working in Germany who argued that the incorrect transliteration of his name from its original in Greek was affecting his identity and ability to provide services, given that he was a self-employed masseur.[6] AG Jacobs separated the question into three issues: first, whether there was discrimination and if this was acceptable; second, whether the question on compromising identity fell within the scope of EU law to trigger fundamental rights protection; and, third, whether there was a breach of the identified fundamental right. A classic 'Community' approach was offered, first considering whether there was a breach of the fundamental freedoms of movement (based upon discrimination), which would then allow for fundamental rights considerations through the approach of the Court in *ERT*, and then how it could be shown that the claiment's fundamental rights had been breached. Bringing fundamental rights under the remit of the Treaty through the internal market would have been the most common approach in the past. However, AG Jacobs still argued that there was a justified reason to link fundamental rights with citizenship in the case.

[5] *Konstantinidis* (n 1) para 42.
[6] ibid.

AG Jacobs noted that the claimant 'is entitled to say "*civis europeus sum*" and by being a European citizen, this should allow the claimant to oppose violations of his fundamental rights'.[7] Though he initially applied rules under the free movement of services, he approved the application of fundamental rights as well, arguing that they could and should be invoked irrespective of the claimant's exercise of the fundamental freedoms.[8] To further substantiate his point, he broadened the interpretation of certain existing fundamental rights to include protection of one's name and identity,[9] and convincingly rebutted three potential arguments against allowing such fundamental rights to prevail, despite previously stating that fundamental rights were not the central issue in the case.[10] Safjan described the Opinion as a 'forecast' for citizenship status triggering protection of fundamental rights in future.[11]

AG Jacobs' recognition of the problems surrounding his declaration of *civis europeus sum* and his consideration of solutions is most commendable. The main issue of reverse discrimination is still controversially a concern today.[12] Fundamental rights guarantees exacerbated the problem of reverse discrimination against static citizens because of their non-discriminate nature. They must not be limited to the strict confines of the specific EU Member States, must not depend on borders being crossed by individuals and do not derive from economic provisions that limit their scope. Fundamental rights are available to all EU citizens, irrespective of their worker status, financial means or nationalities.[13] However, because they do not distinguish between nationals and migrant EU citizens, it was entirely possible that this would amount to more benefits for EU citizens as compared to national citizens of a host Member State. This occurred when it was the EU citizen rather than the national citizen who triggered a situation where EU law applied. This frequently occurred in EU citizenship law, where EU citizens who moved fell under the Treaty and could claim EU citizenship rights, yet static national citizens lost out in comparison.[14]

[7] ibid para 46. 'Civis europeus sum' means 'I am a European citizen'.

[8] ibid para 42.

[9] ibid para 41.

[10] The three arguments are: first, that non-discriminatory measures (including fundamental rights) being a breach of the Treaty would be inconsistent with the Court's current case law; second, that there is a risk of reverse discrimination; and, third, that there would be too much overlap between the Court's case law and the ECHR case law.

[11] Marek Safjan, 'Areas of Application of the Charter of Fundamental Rights of the European Union: Fields of Conflict?' [2012] *EUI Working Paper 2012/22*, 2.

[12] Even whether it is relevant today remains unsettled.

[13] Of course, this is strictly within the EU context. As fundamental rights are a branch of human rights, it would seem that they should be universally applicable where territory is no boundary. However, as this book is limited to the EU, thus necessitating limiting fundamental rights to being applicable in the EU within the boundaries of EU law, this is the main limitation placed on fundamental rights. These territorial boundaries have to be taken for granted.

[14] In EU citizenship law, this is a direct result of the emphasis placed on the cross-border test, so any EU citizens who have moved and thus become eligible to claim EU citizenship rights are automatically placed in a better position compared to those who have never moved.

AG Jacobs made some pertinent points in his Opinion regarding reverse discrimination in the context of the free movement of goods, which could have been applied to the concerns in EU citizenship and fundamental rights law. The seminal case of *Cassis de Dijon* in goods saw the Court accepting that non-discriminatory measures also breached the Treaty.[15] Accepting this would also mean accepting any and all consequences of broadening the scope of the Treaty, such as problems like reverse discrimination. AG Jacobs stated this matter-of-factly as an expected and non-negotiable consequence. Applying this reasoning to EU citizenship law, it was also possible that the status enhanced by fundamental rights protection could justify setting aside the reverse discrimination conundrum in favour of promoting the relationship between EU citizenship and fundamental rights. To do so would truly demonstrate a commitment to adopting a more rights-based *acquis* across the EU, but especially in the context of political and social concepts like citizenship.

Others believed that the elimination of the cross-border test would have resolved the problems of reverse discrimination entirely,[16] for it is the requirement of movement that brought about this problem to begin with. In the Opinion itself, AG Jacobs noted that:

> Once it is accepted that the Treaty requires more than the abolition of discrimination, it follows *ex hypothesi* that a Member State may in certain circumstances be obliged to treat producers or workers from other Member States more favourably than it treats its own producers and workers.[17]

This statement asserted the potential irrelevance of the cross-border test and the purely internal situations rule in light of accepting greater fundamental rights protection even before the Court applied these instruments in cases after *Konstantinidis*. Equal treatment, which governed the above statement, was already protected as a fundamental right and as a general principle of the EU. Therefore, the above statement could be interpreted today as prophesising that if the general fundamental rights discourse grew in the context of citizenship, the cross-border test may slowly be overshadowed by the guarantees of protection of rights. The EU fundamental rights discourse had grown, already somewhat validating AG Jacobs' hypothesis.

What AG Jacobs appeared to argue in 1992 is that citizens as citizens should eventually be able to claim rights protection without looking to rely upon rights in the internal market or any other similar economic prerequisites. In 2007, he

[15] Judgment of 20 February 1979, *Cassis de Dijon* C-120/78, EU:C:1979:42.

[16] Camille Dautricourt and Sebastien Thomas, 'Reverse Discrimination and Free Movement of Persons under Community Law: All for Ulysses, Nothing for Penelope?' (2009) 34 *European Law Review* 433; see also Dominik Hanf, 'Reverse Discrimination in EU Law: Constitutional Aberration, Constitutional Necessity, or Judicial Choice' (2011) 18 *Maastricht Journal of European and Comparative Law* 29 for other solutions, such as looking to national law.

[17] *Konstantinidis* (n 1) para 49.

himself argued that the *Konstantinidis* case appeared to broaden the scope of EU citizenship, despite it not being a citizenship case.[18] Legal bases in the Treaties and the constitutionalised EU fundamental rights discourse support the predictions of 1992 today, and for this reason, Lawson rightly cautions that AG Jacobs' Opinion, 'revolutionary as its implications may be, does not come out of the blue'.[19] It is supported by the discussion on the constitutional development of fundamental rights in other areas of the EU, which prompted a slow but eventual judicial recognition of these rights in EU citizenship cases. AG Jacobs' contribution served more as the first time that the idea was formally presented amongst the predominantly economic atmosphere of the EU at the time, and is significant retrospectively as coming close to predicting how the EU would eventually play out politically in regards to fundamental rights.

The Opinion has been chosen to highlight that even before the EU had guaranteed any political rights or established EU citizenship, the direction that the EU was heading towards encompassed fundamental rights considerations. It foreshadowed the potential of fundamental rights in the EU, which would logically be strengthened by a formal EU citizenship status, and moreover by a binding Charter. This section will now assess the Court and the rise of fundamental rights considerations, proven through its own decision to integrate them into citizenship. There was anticipation surrounding this relationship because of how fundamental rights had developed in the EU generally. These cases will show that the Court appears wary of excessive further expansion of the scope of EU citizenship rights, but does eventually recognise that it could not ignore fundamental rights entirely. It began to exhibit more signs of accepting greater fundamental rights protection towards the end of the second age.

B. The Rise of Fundamental Rights Protection in EU Citizenship

With the case of *ERT* decided in 1991 and the Maastricht Treaty establishing EU citizenship status only two years later, it is argued that EU citizenship has long had a solid foundation upon which to develop its citizen-centric reasoning based on fundamental rights protection. As mentioned previously, the ideal situation would be that EU citizens could claim fundamental rights purely by virtue of being EU citizens, for this is most consistent with the general nature of human rights from which the concept derives. How this ideal sits in the context of the judicial instruments will be considered here, as will whether it can be realised in the current

[18] Francis G Jacobs, 'Citizenship of the European Union: A Legal Analysis' (2007) 13 *European Law Journal* 591, 604.

[19] Rick Lawson, 'Case C-168/91, *Christos Konstantinidis v Stadt Altensteig-Standesamt*, Judgment of 30 March 1993 [1993] 3 CMLR 401, not yet reported in ECR' (1994) 31 *CMLR* 395, 405.

EU framework and against the more restrictive values these instruments seek to uphold. A relationship between fundamental rights and EU citizenship became more foreseeable as both discourses grew more prominent. However, this did not occur immediately.

It was some time before the Court adopted a regular and obvious fundamental rights discourse in citizenship case law, despite AG Jacobs' Opinion in 1992. As the previous chapters have discussed, there was a thread underlying many cases, but none so explicit until later. The first case under EU citizenship that mentioned fundamental rights was *Kaur* in 2001.[20] The *Kaur* case was a question on the fundamental right for national citizens to be allowed to re-enter their home Member State. The case was ultimately not decided upon this right, but rather on whether the claimant was actually a national of the Member State in question. Nationality law was an exclusive competence of the Member States, so did not trigger the Treaty.[21] Furthermore, the case was decided wholly under the free movement of workers. This approach resembled that adopted by the Court early on when it attempted to balance fundamental rights against the internal market,[22] demonstrating slow progress for the fundamental rights discourse even in citizenship. For this reason, it is argued that the influence of fundamental rights was almost negligible in the early 2000s after they first emerged in the Charter, which was evident by the sparse number of cases as well as the lack of analysis of this element in operative parts of the judgments themselves.[23]

However, it is argued that although the Court did not outwardly defer to fundamental rights in their judgments early on, the consideration was still present nonetheless. For this reason, *Garcia Avello* and *Chen* stand out in the context of respect for family life, and regarding identity, *Garcia Avello* stands out again, this time with *Grunkin and Paul*. These cases were the first substantial indicators of a growing fundamental rights discourse because they were the first instances where the fundamental right to private and family life could be specifically pinpointed and identified in EU citizenship law.[24] Furthermore, it was by virtue of their status as EU citizens that they enjoyed rights, rather than free-moving individuals, whether workers or not. Especially in comparison to the cases preceding them,

[20] Judgment of 20 February 2001, *Kaur* C-192/99, EU:C:2001:106.

[21] Judgment of 7 July 1992, *Micheletti* C-369/90, EU:C:1992:295.

[22] On this, see John Morijn, 'Balancing Fundamental Rights and Common Market Freedoms in Union Law: *Schmidberger and Omega* in the Light of the European Constitution' (2006) 12 *European Law Journal* 15.

[23] Even prior to this, references to the Charter were not especially abundant, though they were not non-existent. The other notable cases are *Kaur* (n 20); Judgment of 29 April 2004, *Orfanopoulos and Oliveri* C-482/01 and C-493/01, EU:C:2004:262; Judgment of 11 July 2002, *Carpenter* C-60/00, EU:C:2002:434; Judgment of 23 September 2003, *Akrich* C-109/01, EU:C:2003:491. *Baumbast* mentioned fundamental rights once, but did not consider this extensively. Judgment of 12 September 2006, *Spain v UK* C-145/04, EU:C:2006:543 considered the fundamental right to vote.

[24] James D Mather, 'The Court of Justice and the Union Citizen' (2005) 11 *European Law Journal* 722, 740.

these were more promising towards establishing a stronger bond between the EU institutions and their citizens, creating greater solidarity through the guarantees of fundamental rights.[25] It particularly helped to substantiate the status of EU citizenship under Article 20 TFEU, for legal residency had been underlying the EU citizenship jurisprudence up to this point. Whilst this was acceptable in principle regarding proportionality and the genuine link test, what the fundamental rights discourse rather emphasised was that Article 20 TFEU provided a sufficient link with the Treaty to allow for the protection of fundamental rights.

The *Garcia Avello* case, decided a year before *Chen*, was a unique set of facts which ultimately led to the conferral of equal treatment rights to have a joint patronymic and matronymic surname for two EU citizens in Belgium who had not yet crossed borders. Most notable about this case was that it was decided upon the potential hindrance to exercising free movement in future if, for example, their names were not recognised in another Member State. The other influential factor was protection of the right to private and family life under Article 8 ECHR, or Article 7 of the Charter, in terms of needing to respect rights to one's identity. By allowing potential movement to suffice to trigger the Treaty, it appeared to broadly construe requirements under the cross-border test, making it seem almost inconsequential. It was clear that fundamental rights were not outside the remit of consideration for the Court in *Garcia Avello*, but that it was still cautious about expressing this in terms that would not be fully appreciated by its wider judicial audience in other Member States.

The role of the cross-border test and purely internal situations rule was significantly diminished in *Garcia Avello*. This has been discussed in the previous chapter. It is argued that the treatment of these judicial instruments by the Court in this way was to achieve a particular outcome related to fundamental rights. The Court sought to grant non-discrimination rights to the claimants who were EU citizens, but yet to exercise their rights to free movement as children. The question on accepting the right to a name can be linked to the *Konstantinidis* Opinion, where AG Jacobs argued that the very matter fell under the protection of the ECHR regarding respect for one's identity.[26] It seems that this was considered here. As noted previously, the Court's interpretation of the purely internal situations rule was to set boundaries for individuals who did not trigger the Treaty by means of movement. This avoided excessive intrusion into national Member State authority.[27] However, such a broad construction of the rule in this case appears to undermine its original intention, thereby bringing into question whether this judicial instrument retained relevance in the face of a growing fundamental

[25] Alina Tryfonidou, 'Family Reunification Rights of (Migrant) Union Citizens: Towards a More Liberal Approach' (2009) 15 *European Law Journal* 634, 649.

[26] *Konstantinidis* (n 1) paras 31–44.

[27] On this broadly, see Niamh Nic Shuibhne, 'Free Movement of Persons and the Wholly Internal Rule: Time to Move On?' (2002) 39 *CML Rev* 731.

rights discourse.[28] With the ideal being that an EU citizen should enjoy fundamental rights protection for simply being an EU citizen, the purely internal situations rule appears to be an obstacle.

Though the Court in *Garcia Avello* avoided confronting fundamental rights directly, the *Chen* case presented a situation where it was forced to do so, an early example of a liberal interpretation of EU citizenship rights.[29] The Court in this situation went against orthodox understandings of EU law to allow the claimant mother, a TCN, the right to reside in order to remain to care for her infant daughter, an EU citizen. The questions referred by the national court in *Chen* mentioned fundamental rights, thereby demonstrating the slow but steady development towards this eventual recognition as part of one's status as an EU citizen under Article 20 TFEU. However, it should be noted that ultimately, the CJEU did not expressly engage with the respect for family life under Article 8 ECHR. The outcome appeared to reflect some consideration of fundamental rights, but formally this was not the legal basis used. The reason for this is likely to be attributed to the TCN family element and the Court's adherence to the principle of conferral.[30] A proportionality assessment based upon the child's – an EU citizen's – rights was undertaken instead.

In *Chen*, the requirements of the genuine link test seemed to have also been relaxed in order to accommodate the rights to family life of the infant claimant to have her TCN mother reside in the EU to care for her. It had the effect of ensuring that the Court remained within the scope of the Treaty. It was more evident in *Chen* than in *Garcia Avello* that fundamental rights were influential to the Court's ultimate decision because of the factual situation itself, and actually being a matter of keeping a family together. Originally, the genuine link test and the unreasonable burden criteria were applied to set boundaries on citizenship rights. In *Chen*, the unreasonable burden criterion was satisfied because the family were workers and could prove they had plentiful resources to remain in the country. Therefore, although a fundamental rights element is evident, satisfying the unreasonable burden criteria may have been more convincing to the Court.[31]

[28] See Peter Van Elsuwege, 'Court of Justice of the European Union European Union Citizenship and the Purely Internal Rule Revisited Decision of 5 May 2011, Case C-434/09 *Shirley McCarthy v Secretary of State for the Home Department*' (2011) 7 *European Constitutional Law Review* 308; Peter van Elsuwege, 'Shifting the Boundaries? European Union Citizenship and the Scope of Application of EU Law: Case No. C-34/09, *Gerardo Ruiz Zambrano v Office national de l'emploi*' (2011) 38 *Legal Issues of Economic Integration* 263 for comments on this in cases in the third age, where this idea became more definitive.

[29] Bernard Hofstotter, 'A Cascade of Rights, or Who Shall Care for Little Catherine? Some Reflections on the *Chen* Case' (2005) 30 *European Law Review* 548; Jean-Yves Carlier, 'Case C-200/02, *Kunqian Catherine Zhu, Man Lavette Chen v Secretary of State for the Home Department*' (2005) 42 *CML Rev* 1121.

[30] Article 5(1) TEU.

[31] Dimitry Kochenov and Justin Lindeboom, 'Breaking Chinese Law – Making European One: The Story of *Chen*, or: Two Winners, Two Losers, Two Truths' in B Davies and F Nicola (eds), *EU Law*

There was no explicit mention of fundamental rights; however, Carlier has noted that the stringent application of rules on nationality and residency requirements could lead to a contravention of rights under the ECHR for TCNs.[32] There were arguments that pointed towards the overall consideration for the Court being of family life, supported by the growing fundamental rights discourse in the EU.

In 2008, a situation on rights to family life and residency finally arose for the Court to confront in *Metock*, in which the application of Directive 2004/38 was of central consideration.[33] The claimants were four TCNs seeking residency who were married to EU citizens residing in Ireland. They were denied residency for not satisfying a prior residency requirement. The CJEU in *Metock* confirmed that 'the Community legislature recognised the importance of ensuring the protection of the family life of nationals of the Member States'.[34] For this reason, the Directive precluded Irish legislation from requiring prior lawful residence before conferring such spousal residency rights. The provision itself seemed consistent with the genuine link test at the outset, and the Court had upheld similar requirements previously.[35] However, it noted that this had to 'be reconsidered', for now it was important to protect fundamental rights.[36]

It is important to analyse the effects of the *Metock* case. This case is an example of the consolidated support for fundamental rights being integrated into EU citizenship law just before Lisbon came into force, with the Court's reasoning in it described as 'an important tool in cases where the Member States seek to use the Directive in novel restrictive ways'.[37] Indeed, as the Directive had already been previously discounted as a reliable indication of the direction for the future of EU citizenship law, the judgment in *Metock* would further demonstrate the impetus towards fundamental rights integration with EU citizenship status. The Court refers directly to case law that respected rights to family life previously,[38] thereby confirming the argument here that these cases were indicative of a fundamental rights trajectory in citizenship. More importantly, it also builds upon the clarification of standards as to family rights protection set by the *MRAX* case six years earlier, before the Directive had come into being.

The Court addressed the defence raised by the Member State authorities in *Metock* of controls on immigration from TCNs.[39] It discussed the exact wording of the Directive's provisions on this matter, but also emphasised the assessment

Stories (Cambridge University Press, 2017). The authors undertake an extensive story-like assessment of the facts of the case in this article and to what extent this affected the outcome.

[32] Carlier (n 29) 1130.

[33] Judgment of 25 July 2008, *Metock and Others* C-127/08, EU:C:2008:449.

[34] ibid para 56.

[35] ibid para 58 mentions the case of *Akrich* (n 23).

[36] *Metock and Others* (n 33) para 58.

[37] Cathryn Costello, '*Metock*: Free Movement and "Normal Family Life" in the Union' (2009) 46 *CML Rev* 587, 602.

[38] *Metock and Others* (n 33) para 56.

[39] ibid para 70.

of proportionality in accepting such arguments in regards to the purely internal situations rule and confirming that matters without a link to EU are not within the scope of the Treaty,[40] as well as the respect it must afford to Article 8 ECHR.[41] The Court's assessment of the entire situation had the ultimate effect of demonstrating that the arguments presented by Ireland were obstacles to the claimant's rights to family life. Through a closer analysis of the Directive's wording as well as a convincing assessment of the protection of the fundamental right to private and family life, it was possible to interpret the provisions flexibly and allow rights under the Directive not to be an obstacle to claims made in the case as to rights for the TCN family members to enter and reside in the EU.

The *Metock* case became a stronger, clearer indication of the influence of fundamental rights protection under Article 8 ECHR, especially after the decisions in *Garcia Avello* and *Chen*. It provided a valid legal foundation from which future cases in the area could also draw upon, much like the influence the ECtHR cases had for the CJEU. Respect for family life was not the only fundamental right recognised by the Court, and later in 2008 the case of *Grunkin and Paul* was decided, almost factually identical to *Garcia Avello* in terms of it being a question on the recognition of a surname registered in another Member State. The Court cited the same provisions of free movement to guarantee protection under Articles 21 and 18 TFEU rather than fundamental rights. However, the element of identity rights was noted as an important factor in the development of EU citizenship, particularly because of how the case was ultimately decided. Read cumulatively with *Carpenter* and *MRAX*, but most importantly with *Garcia Avello* and *Metock*, the decision in this case several years later demonstrates that the Court was not prepared to ignore EU fundamental rights completely because of EU citizenship status. In *Grunkin and Paul*, more emphasis was placed on the identity element of the case than in *Garcia Avello* and it is argued that this is an incremental result of the cases which have been instrumental in developing the fundamental rights *acquis* in EU citizenship.

Grunkin and Paul deserves especial mention in this chapter also in regards to links drawn with identity and the *Konstantinidis* Opinion, as well as *Garcia Avello* and after *Metock* in the context of the rise of fundamental rights in citizenship. AG Jacobs had alluded to the right to respect for one's identity as a subset of the right to respect for private and family life in 1992. These rights become relevant now, interpreted in the same way by the Court in *Garcia Avello* and *Grunkin and Paul*. These cases corroborate AG Jacobs' original interpretation of the fundamental right. In general, cases on the right to respect for family life rather than cases on the right to respect for private life come before the Court.[42] This is possibly because

[40] ibid para 77.

[41] ibid paras 79; 89.

[42] Judgment of 19 October 2004, *Zhu and Chen* C-200/02, EU:C:2004:639; *Carpenter* (n 23); *Metock and Others* (n 33).

family life often involves the expansion of the scope *ratione personae* of the EU citizenship provisions. This is more controversial as a concept as compared to identity rights because of the involvement of TCNs. Certainly, the effects of accepting that rights of TCNs may be covered under the scope *ratione materiae* of EU citizenship have greater consequences overall for EU legitimacy and solidarity. However, the recognition of identity rights adds to the discussion here in terms of mapping the rise of fundamental rights in EU citizenship case law. Noting that *Metock* was decided only three months earlier, the extensive analysis of the obstacles to the claimant's identity clearly demonstrates an intention to allow fundamental rights to be influential to the final decision, as necessitated by Article 20 TFEU.

It is evident now that the fundamental rights influence in citizenship case law was starting to become more prominent, especially given specific facts that demanded attention for family life and identity rights. From this, the analysis will now examine AG Colomer's Opinion in *Petersen*, for instead of focusing on fundamental rights, he focused on the citizenship development more generally to note that 'the free movement of persons [has become] the movement of free citizens'.[43] Because he looked at the development of citizenship as a whole, the Advocate General noted a favourable development towards embracing fundamental rights. His Opinion follows logically from this analysis, but is also a precursor to the discussion on post-Lisbon fundamental rights as well.

C. AG Colomer's Opinion in *Petersen* (2008)

Although the fundamental rights and EU citizenship development has been slow, the citizenship development itself has nonetheless made significant gains since AG Jacobs' Opinion in 1992 until 2008, when AG Colomer issued his Opinion in *Petersen*. This period saw the Court's decisions in *Sala*, in *Grzelczyk*, in *Baumbast* and in *Garcia Avello*, *Chen*, *Carpenter* and *MRAX*, which meant that the legal principles of non-discrimination, proportionality, the genuine link test and the purely internal situations rule had been established. The Opinion in *Petersen* noted that since *Sala*, citizenship 'has gathered unprecedented momentum' by extending its protection to those who were not necessarily the original benefactors under the Treaty.[44] It is this which suggests that some progress was being made towards substantiating EU citizenship status as having its own individual value and set of rights. This section will consider AG Colomer's optimism about the normative changes and how this led into the third age of citizenship.

An extensive discussion of the *Petersen* Opinion has not been common in EU citizenship literature because the judgment is decided entirely upon the provisions

[43] *Petersen* (n 2) para 28.
[44] Judgment of 11 September 2008, *Petersen* C-228/07, EU:C:2008:494, para 15.

of the free movement of workers.[45] However, AG Colomer undertook an extensive review of the citizenship case law in his Opinion, which supports the hypothesis of this book. The Advocate General argued that because there had been so many developments in terms of how citizens understood citizenship through the Court's judgments, it indicated that the Court had shifted its legal culture more towards accepting social and political normative judicial reasoning. The justification for this was to improve the individual's personal situation in the EU.[46] Citing several cases that validated AG Jacobs' *civis europeus sum* declaration,[47] he argued that the combined effect of this was to clarify that the concept of free movement of persons was its own legal construct, whereas before it was attached to the internal market. AG Colomer's observation is that there was less reliance on the fundamental freedoms and more on the EU citizenship provisions, thus prompting the Court to consider adopting this approach in the *Petersen* case.

AG Colomer advanced a different approach to AG Jacobs in his Opinion, focusing not on the economic value of the citizens in question, but simply their rights as legally relevant individuals in the EU. Because of this, he argued that decisions should be based more on individual situations, bringing into consideration fundamental rights as well and noting that 'the Court has transformed the paradigm of *homo economicus* into that of *homo civitatis*',[48] meaning that economic activity was no longer the deciding factor in rights conferral. This was consistent with the idea that there was no need to be so reliant upon the free movement of workers to protect oneself under the Treaties. Therefore, where there were elements concerning fundamental rights, or 'democratic factors of belonging to a political community',[49] AG Colomer argued that this should be used to determine when citizenship provisions applied rather than the fundamental freedoms. It is noted that '[l]egal scholarship undoubtedly served as an inspiration for his opinion' as well,[50] further substantiating that he was not the only one arguing for a stronger fundamental rights influence in the citizenship discourse.[51]

The underlying message of AG Colomer's Opinion is an answer to why individuals in the EU have been afforded greater protection under the umbrella of

[45] See Koen Lenaerts, 'European Union Citizenship, National Welfare Systems and Social Solidarity' (2011) 2 *Jurisprudencija* 397 for a workers-based assessment.

[46] *Petersen* (n 2) para 16.

[47] Judgment of 17 September 2002, *Baumbast* C-413/99, EU:C:2002:493; *Carpenter* (n 23); Judgment of 15 March 2005, *Bidar* C-209/03, EU:C:2005:169; Judgment of 26 October 2006, *Tas Hagen and Tas* C-192/05, EU:C:2006:676; Judgment of 23 October 2007, *Morgan and Bucher* C-11/06 and C-12/06, EU:C:2007:626.

[48] *Petersen* (n 2) para 15.

[49] ibid para 36.

[50] Anja Wiesbrock, 'The Self-Perpetuation of EU Constitutionalism in the Area of Free Movement of Persons: Virtuous or Vicious Cycle?' (2013) 2 *Global Constitutionalism* 125, 138.

[51] For other examples that also argued for a stronger fundamental right discourse in EU citizenship case law, see Jacobs (n 18); Sara Iglesias Sánchez, 'Fundamental Rights and Citizenship of the Union at a Crossroads: A Promising Alliance or a Dangerous Liaison?' (2014) 20 *European Law Journal* 464.

a previously exclusively economic EU. He called it 'European belonging',[52] the element of 'belonging' expressed materially for being part of the EU community.[53] This would directly involve citizens in the EU's political community. The establishment of EU citizenship status was the catalyst for this change,[54] inspiring a new direction for the EU and introducing political objectives that AG Colomer argued were able to co-exist with the original economic objectives. Because the focus shifted from economic rights to individual rights, greater attention had to be devoted to protecting fundamental rights as well. It would be the role of the Court to confirm whether this was feasible, which would involve an unequivocal acceptance of the political nature of citizenship and its rights, the development of which is wholly unaffected by the economic fundamental freedoms and their prior influences on citizenship. The constitutionalisation of the protection of fundamental rights supported the claim that this could have occurred.

AG Colomer considered the value of fundamental rights and the fact that AG Jacobs recognised the value of fundamental rights for the Court's decision-making process. He noted that this had been adopted in the subsequent case law.[55] Despite the legal principle of non-discrimination governing both workers' and citizens' rights, the scope of citizenship status is inherently intended to be broader because the principle applies to all EU citizens. This reasoning was consistent with that of fundamental rights and justified what AG Colomer did in his Opinion by connecting the two and declaring that 'the focus of attention has shifted to the individual'.[56] He also argued that in determining a question under the fundamental freedoms, 'maximum protection' should be afforded through the fundamental citizenship status.[57] This confirmed that there was a need for a distinction between the approach under the fundamental freedoms and that of citizenship, and therefore also greater room for fundamental rights considerations.

Though AG Colomer presented an 'erudite opinion' on the citizenship approach for the *Petersen* case, '[t]he Court's failure to respond to the Advocate General's interesting arguments concerning the relationship between Article [45 TFEU] and the Citizenship provisions leaves open this issue for further case law'.[58] Therefore, although it was demonstrative of a shift in the legal culture towards non-economic rights, it did not represent a complete departure. Unlike AG Jacobs, AG Colomer in *Petersen* did not propose any radical changes to the current face of the EU; rather, he outlined his interpretation of the current state of the law in regards to

[52] *Petersen* (n 2) para 31.
[53] This default position is established by EU citizenship status (art 20 TFEU).
[54] ibid arts 22ff.
[55] *Petersen* (n 2) para 17.
[56] ibid para 28.
[57] ibid para 36.
[58] Mel Cousins, 'Overview of Recent Cases before the European Court of Human Rights and the European Court of Justice (May–September 2008)' (2008) 10 *European Journal of Social Security* 295, 299 and 300.

the relationship between the internal market and EU citizenship, with the addition of fundamental rights. AG Colomer's position as compared to AG Jacobs indicated that the perceived value of fundamental rights as applied under EU citizenship provisions had changed since 1992 and that there was certainly room for further developments, especially in regards to a fundamental rights and EU citizenship relationship.

III. Fundamental Rights in EU Citizenship Post-Lisbon

The gradual development of both EU citizenship law and fundamental rights was indicative of a constitutionalisation of individual rights protection in the EU. The development of EU fundamental rights reached its peak when it was codified in the Lisbon Treaty, which affirmed that it was not only the EU institutions themselves that approved of the new fundamental rights discourse, but also the Member States when they were able to agree on the final draft of the Treaties.[59] In EU citizenship law, the development peaked when the status became an independent legal basis for the conferral of rights without crossing borders in the seminal case of *Ruiz Zambrano*. After this, a trend emerged where cases on fundamental rights in EU citizenship mostly concerned rights to family life.[60] National courts required further clarification on how to interpret the new judicial instrument introduced in *Zambrano* of the deprivation of genuine enjoyment test in these situations.

The Court had hinted at an independent EU citizenship status most prominently in the *Rottmann* case after Jacobs predicted this outcome four years earlier.[61] They seized the opportunity in *Zambrano* to make this a reality. It is thought that this

[59] See the failed Treaty Establishing a Constitution for Europe [2004] OJ C310.

[60] The other cases post-Lisbon have been on student maintenance – see Judgment of 20 May 2010, *Zanotti* C-56/09, EU:C:2010:288; Judgment of 4 October 2012, *Commission v Austria* C-75/11, EU:C:2012:605; Judgment of 25 October 2012, *Prete* C-367/11, EU:C:2012:668; Judgment of 18 July 2013, *Prinz and Seeberger* C-523/11, EU:C:2013:524; Judgment of 24 October 2013, *Thiele Meneses* C-220/12, EU:C:2013:683; Judgment of 24 October 2013, *Elrick* C-275/12, EU:C:2013:684; Judgment of 26 February 2015, *Martens* C-359/13, EU:C:2015:118 – and Directive 2004/38 where there has been a cross-border element present: see Judgment of 23 November 2010, *Tsakouridis* C-145/09, EU:C:2010:708; Judgment of 6 September 2012, *Czop and Punakova* C-147/11, EU:C:2012:538; Judgment of 4 October 2012, *Byankov* C-249/11, EU:C:2012:608; Judgment of 16 October 2012, *Hungary v Slovak Republic* C-364/10, EU:C:2012:630; Judgment of 8 November 2012, *Iida* C-40/11, EU:C:2012:691; Judgment of 19 September 2013, *Brey* C-140/12, EU:C:2013:565; Judgment of 16 January 2014, *Onuekwere* C-378/12, EU:C:2014:13; Judgment of 16 January 2014, *MG* C-400/12, EU:C:2014:9; Judgment of 16 January 2014, *Reyes* C-423/12, EU:C:2014:16; Judgment of 10 July 2014, *Ogieriakhi* C-244/13, EU:C:2014:2068; Judgment of 18 December 2014, *McCarthy and Others* C-202/13, EU:C:2014:2450; Judgment of 12 March 2014, *O and B; S and G* C-456/12 and C-457/12, EU:C:2014:135.

[61] Jacobs (n 18) 595.

was also an opportunity to put fundamental rights in the spotlight. *Rottmann* did not consider this element. The Opinion of AG Sharpston in *Zambrano* asked the Court to address these unanswered questions. Her Opinion is a more recent one that supports an enhanced fundamental rights and EU citizenship relationship. The Opinion provided a thorough overview of the state of EU citizenship, whilst also highlighting the constitutional gaps that the Court still needed to resolve.

A. Post-Lisbon, but Pre-*Zambrano*

The Lisbon Treaty came into force at the end of 2009, but the *Zambrano* judgment was decided in March 2011, just over a year later. In between this time, there were some important cases that warrant attention because of their references to fundamental rights protection. It is these cases, in particular the *Rottmann* case, which built greater anticipation that there was to be a judgment from the Court which finally brought together fundamental rights protection and EU citizenship rights. Identity rights in particular were a common theme in these pre-Lisbon, pre-*Zambrano* cases. From these cases, it was understood that the manifestation of the right to private and family life was a right well accepted by the Court in cases concerning the rights of EU citizens. This was yet more evidence of the upwards trajectory of the fundamental rights and EU citizenship relationship.

Identity rights, as initially established by *Garcia Avello* and *Grunkin and Paul*, were discussed in two cases decided within six months of each other after the Lisbon Treaty came into force. It is argued that the fact that they occurred after the Lisbon Treaty consolidates the arguments presented in the previous chapter as to the developing fundamental rights *acquis*, specifically here in the context of identity rights. In both cases, like in the previous scenarios, the focus is on the recognition of surnames and the discrepancies in different Member States. In *Sayn-Wittgenstein*,[62] the claimant referred explicitly to rights under Article 8 ECHR and in *Runevič-Vardyn*, the claim was premised upon equal treatment.[63]

Sayn-Wittgenstein, decided in December 2010, was a case concerning an Austrian national residing and working in Germany, whose surname – Fürstin von Sayn-Wittgenstein – was registered in Austria and subsequently used in Germany after her adoption. Austrian law then abolished titles of nobility added to surnames – in this case, 'Fürstin von' – and required the claimant to correct her registered surname to Sayn-Wittgenstein. The claimant argued this was an interference of the enjoyment of rights under Article 8 ECHR, which was justified by Austria in light of *Grunkin and Paul*. It was held that it did not amount to a serious inconvenience, given that removing 'Fürstin von' would not make the

[62] Judgment of 22 December 2010, *Sayn-Wittgenstein* C-208/09, EU:C:2010:806.
[63] Judgment of 12 May 2011, *Runevič-Vardyn and Wardyn* C-391/09, EU:C:2011:291.

name materially different. The question was whether rights under citizenship were violated because of the Austrian laws on non-noble titles in surnames, which was accepted in Germany after her adoption, but nonetheless went against the constitutional law of her home Member State, Austria.

There are two important features of the *Sayn-Wittgenstein* case. First, the Court noted that 'the referring court does not consider it necessary to state in what capacity the applicant in the main proceedings resides in Germany'.[64] Therefore, it was purely by reason of her status as an EU citizen under Article 20 TFEU that this seems to have triggered the referral by the national courts to bring EU citizenship closer to its liberated independent status. Second, in the judgment, the Court referred to Article 7 of the Charter, now binding in Lisbon, alongside Article 8 ECHR[65] to argue that 'confusion and inconvenience are liable to arise'[66] if the claimant was required to change her surname. Therefore, the Austrian law represented an obstacle to Article 21 TFEU (free movement) and Article 18 TFEU (equal treatment), the latter of which is notably also a right in the Charter.[67] The fundamental rights element was clearly a factor, with the Court empowered by the Lisbon Treaty and previous threads of rights enjoyment in the second age of citizenship especially.

This case then set an example for the *Runevič-Vardyn* case decided in May 2011. A Lithuanian national with the surname Runevič (on her birth certificate) married a Polish national with the surname Wardyn in Lithuania. On the marriage certificate, she was registered as Runevič-Vardyn because the Lithuanian alphabet did not recognise the letter W. Living in Belgium, she then applied to change her name on her birth certificate to Runiewicz and both her and her husband's names on the marriage certificate, hers to Runiewicz-Wardyn and his to include the Polish diacritical marks,[68] which was denied. Citing the fundamental status of citizenship[69] and noting the claimants' rights under Articles 21 and 18 TFEU and rights to private and family life under Article 7 of the Charter and Article 8 ECHR from *Sayn-Wittgenstein* especially, the 'serious inconvenience' as to identity had to be determined in order to amount to a breach under Article 21 TFEU.[70] Of the three questions referred as to the name on her birth certificate, on her marriage certificate and her husband's diacritical marks, the Court denied the first and last changes, but allowed the national court to decide how best to address the claim to a change of the claimant's married name under proportionality.[71]

[64] *Sayn-Wittgenstein* (n 62) para 41.
[65] ibid para 52.
[66] ibid para 66.
[67] ibid para 89. Equal treatment is upheld in art 20 of the Charter.
[68] 'Lukasz Pawel' to 'Łukasz Paweł'.
[69] *Runevič-Vardyn and Wardyn* (n 63) para 60.
[70] ibid para 75.
[71] ibid para 94.

This concept of a 'serious inconvenience' has been mentioned in other CJEU cases, particularly when interpreting the right to private and family life.[72] This has been mostly when it is not the traditional manifestation of family life, as seen for example in *Chen*, *Metock* and *Carpenter* in terms of families being separated and seeking reunification.[73] This reference to serious inconveniences increasingly appears to be a consistent approach applied by the Court, in that it has become a criterion for analysis of whether there has been a breach of the right to private and family life in the context of identity. The way in which it has been interpreted thus far has also afforded great flexibility to the national legal authorities. As van Eijken notes, 'this "hands-off approach" is quite remarkable'.[74] The Court leaves the ultimate decision up to the national courts to determine if a serious inconvenience has arisen. However, here it is the recognition of the identity rights, and references to Article 7 of the Charter is what is significant about this case, particularly after the build-up to it in *Garcia Avello*, *Grunkin and Paul* and *Sayn-Wittgenstein*.

Another way in which this idea of a serious inconvenience can be interpreted is that given that there is a slight shift in approach as to embracing the fundamental rights discourse in the third age, applying such a deferential concept is also recognised as a potential prelude to the later decline of fundamental rights protection as exhibited after *Zambrano*. This approach has allowed national legal authorities a significant amount of breadth to determine what they consider to be a breach of the right to private and family life, and more ease in which to potentially disregard fundamental rights claims. Nonetheless, because the rights under the Charter and the ECHR were now included in the operative parts of judgments in EU citizenship case law, it demonstrated that there had been a constitutional shift towards fundamental rights rather than the Court being solely preoccupied with the rights under Article 21 TFEU. It is this which makes way for an independent legal basis of rights under Article 20 TFEU, which *Rottmann* most obviously first suggested could be acceptable.

Rottmann as a case on its facts alone is an anomaly. It was not closely connected to the fundamental freedoms or with EU citizenship status. Dr Rottmann, originally an Austrian national, sought naturalisation in Germany. Austria did not allow dual citizenship, so he had to surrender his Austrian nationality when he began the process of German naturalisation. However, Germany discovered that Dr Rottmann had an undisclosed criminal record and suspended his naturalisation. This would have left him stateless if it was carried through. Dr Rottmann

[72] Judgment of 2 October 2003, *Garcia Avello* C-148/02, EU:C:2003:539; Judgment of 14 October 2008, *Grunkin and Paul* C-353/06, EU:C:2008:559.

[73] *Chen* (n 42); *Metock and Others* (n 33); *Carpenter* (n 23).

[74] Hanneke van Eijken, 'Case C-391/09, *Malgožata Runevič-Vardyn and Lukasz Pawel Wardyn v Vilniaus miesto savivaldybes administracija and Others*, Judgment of the Court (Second Chamber) of 12 May 2011' (2012) 49 *CML Rev* 809, 819.

brought proceedings against Germany, arguing that EU law should protect him from losing EU citizenship status, which would mean intervening in the process of a Member State's determination of the EU citizens' own nationality. In a bold judgment, the CJEU required the national court to carry out a proportionality assessment on the effect of withdrawing naturalisation on EU citizenship status in light of the deception exhibited by Dr Rottmann, despite questions on nationality being an exclusive national competence.

Controversy surrounded the *Rottmann* ruling because at first glance, it seemed to contradict the rulings in *Micheletti*[75] and *Kaur*,[76] where nationality was strictly upheld to be a matter for the Member States only. It appeared to be an unfair balance in the division of competences established by the EU when Article 20 TFEU was drafted.[77] By requiring that decisions on naturalisation should consider their impact on EU law, a Member State's exclusive competence to decide matters relating to nationality would be brought under the remit of EU law. The Court attempted to avoid potential conflict by stating that the effect of withdrawing the claimant's naturalisation would independently affect his rights under EU law, thereby requiring national courts to consider whether it would be proportionate to withdraw his naturalisation in regards to EU citizenship. AG Poiares Maduro made a strong argument in his Opinion on *Rottmann* for the fact that nationality itself was outside the Treaty's scope, but conditions for nationality affecting EU citizenship should fall within.[78]

The principle of proportionality was the cornerstone of this ruling, for without an assessment of both parties' interests and consideration of the consequences of such a decision for both, the Court could lose its legitimacy. It was prudent to avoid this if possible, given the issues surrounding the EU's constitutional 'competence creep', especially here where it directly impinged on nationality laws.[79] In this scenario, proportionality favoured the status of EU citizenship and it being the fundamental status of EU citizens. However, in *Rottmann*, it went one step further, appearing to prioritise, above all, this fundamental status and to require that the Member State undertake a proportionality assessment to determine if denying the claimant German naturalisation in his situation would be disproportionate to the outcome of him losing EU citizenship status. This decision understandably attracted a lot of negative attention because of what it purported to require Member States to do in light of their own laws on nationality.

[75] *Micheletti* (n 21).

[76] *Kaur* (n 20).

[77] Dimitry Kochenov, 'Two Sovereign States vs a Human Being: CJEU as a Guardian of Arbitrariness in Citizenship Matters' [2011] *EUI Working Paper* RSCAS 2011/62.

[78] Gerard-René de Groot and Ngo Chun Luk, 'Special Issue EU Citizenship: Twenty Years on. Twenty Years of CJEU Jurisprudence on Citizenship' (2014) 15 *German Law Journal* 821, 828.

[79] Stephen Weatherill, 'Competence Creep and Competence Control' (2004) 23 *Yearbook of European Law* 1.

Savino is one such critic, arguing that: 'The Court of Justice cannot depart from the letter of the Treaty in order to satisfy post-national anxieties.'[80] AG Poiares Maduro had noted this same concern in his Opinion,[81] where EU citizenship's dependency on nationality in the Treaty seemed to him to be crucial, although he offered an alternative solution that the Court adopted in its judgment. The effect of this ruling would be to suggest for the first time that EU citizenship status could be an independent legal basis for claiming rights. However, it had yet to truly revolutionise citizenship by officially emancipating it from the cross-border test. The Court's proportionality assessment was difficult to reconcile with previous approaches it had adopted simply because it alluded to a new way of triggering the Treaty provisions on citizenship that did not involve crossing borders.[82] The situation was exacerbated because it dealt with an exclusive Member State competence.

Golynker also commented on the broad-brush approach of the Court that allowed Dr Rottmann rights under citizenship. She noted that the Court also took into account the future potential effect of him losing both Member States' nationalities, but that it would be consistent with empowering the fundamental status of EU citizenship as the Court had declared in *Grzelczyk*.[83] There was no mention of the Treaty being triggered by having crossed borders to be in Germany from Austria, and the Court also drew independently upon the EU citizenship status and being potentially unable to exercise citizenship rights without first having Member State nationality. It considered EU citizenship status fundamental enough to be an independent legal basis for claiming rights and brought an excluded area within the Treaty's scope. However, there was no mention of fundamental rights or the cross-border test, thereby confirming little in regards to the judicial approach going forward.

Dougan notes in the context of *Rottmann* that: '[a]gainst the Member State, the Court's chief weapon is the proportionality test.'[84] The proportionality principle has been used throughout the history of citizenship cases before the Court to allow a number of different values to influence the decision-making process, one of the most prominent being fundamental rights considerations. By utilising this principle, the Court could also bring fundamental rights considerations into citizenship law legitimately without the cross-border test as an obstacle. The justification

[80] Mario Savino, 'EU Citizenship: Post-national or Post-nationalist? Revisiting the *Rottmann* Case through Administrative Lenses' (2011) 23 *European Review of Public Law* 39, 44.

[81] Opinion of 30 September 2009, *Rottmann* C-135/08, EU:C:2009:588, para 15.

[82] See contributions by Jo Shaw et al, 'Has the European Court of Justice Challenged Member State Sovereignty in Nationality Law?' [2011] *EUI Working Paper* RSCAS 2011/62.

[83] Oxana Golynker, 'The Correlation between the Status of Union Citizenship, the Rights Attached to it and Nationality in *Rottmann*' [2011] *EUI Working Paper* RSCAS 2011/62, 19.

[84] Michael Dougan, 'The Bubble that Burst: Exploring the Legitimacy of the Case Law on the Free Movement of Union Citizens' in Maurice Adams et al (eds), *Judging Europe's Judges* (Hart Publishing, 2013) 135.

would be the fundamentality of both the status of EU citizenship and fundamental rights themselves. Although the Court did not engage with such an assessment in the judgment, if citizenship status became an independent legal basis for rights, the implications for these rights is argued to be that constitutional fundamental rights in Article 6 TEU could be integrated into the Court's assessment of rights under EU citizenship status. However, because there was no mention of this, speculation increased as to the effects of this new provision three months after it came into force.[85]

The *Rottmann* case epitomises the pinnacle of the expansion of the scope *ratione materiae* and *ratione personae* of EU citizenship since *Sala* first intimated that it was non-discrimination that should govern EU citizenship rights, not economic activity. However, one question still remained: is it 'now misleading to describe Union citizenship as secondary, or dependent'?[86] The CJEU maximised the protection afforded to its citizens by virtue of Article 20 TFEU and appeared to allow EU citizenship status to be an independent legal basis for claiming rights. By doing so, it substantiated and legitimised the provisions under Articles 20–21 TFEU and came closer to fostering true European solidarity. However, it is crucial that the judgment's criticism is also acknowledged because it ran the risk of having the opposite effect on solidarity and legitimacy in the EU because of the activism it seemed to encourage.[87] This would challenge the aims and fundamental nature of EU citizenship.[88] It was particularly an issue of reverse discrimination, because it could 'undermine the equality of rights within the national bond between Member States and their nationals'.[89] Without knowing what the CJEU's exact intention for the *Rottmann* ruling was, it was unclear whether it was more positive than negative. Greater clarification was sought, especially in terms of the relationship of EU citizenship with fundamental rights, given the Court's silence on this matter here.

B. AG Sharpston's Opinion in *Zambrano* (2010)

Zambrano is a case that dealt directly with TCN family members and the rights to residency of these individuals as they pertained to protecting the right to private and family life of EU citizens. It also raised the question of non-moving citizens and their rights under the Treaty without crossing borders. The judgment also

[85] See Juliane Kokott and Christoph Sobotta, 'The Charter of Fundamental Rights of the European Union after Lisbon' [2010] *EUI Working Papers, Academy of European Law 2010/6*.

[86] Gareth Davies, 'The Entirely Conventional Supremacy of Union Citizenship and Rights' [2011] *EUI Working Paper* RSCAS 2011/62, 9.

[87] For a discussion of judicial activism, see Dougan (n 84).

[88] Gerard-René de Groot and Anja Seling, 'The Consequences of the *Rottmann* Judgment on Member State Autonomy: The European Court of Justice's Avant-Gardism in Nationality Matters' [2011] *European Constitutional Law Review* 138, 145.

[89] Golynker (n 83).

settled the question of when the Directive or the Treaty provisions applied, though notably this was not the concern of AG Sharpston in her Opinion. From the outset, AG Sharpston emphasised her intention to discuss the broader questions posed by *Zambrano*, for she acknowledged it as the golden opportunity for the EU citizenship concept to clarify its relationship with fundamental rights.

The claimants in *Zambrano* were a Colombian couple who lived in Belgium after seeking asylum there. The couple had three children, two of whom were born in Belgium and by *jus soli* rules attained Belgian nationality and therefore EU citizenship status. Mr Zambrano sought a residency permit but was rejected, yet could not leave Belgium because of a *non-refoulement* clause preventing Belgium from forcing his return to Colombia during a period of civil unrest. He found work for a time, but after losing his job sought unemployment benefits, which were denied because he was not a legal resident. He thus claimed he had derived rights to residency as in *Chen* and *Garcia Avello*, because of his two EU citizen children, who like the children in *Garcia Avello* had not yet exercised their rights to free movement, but like baby Chen were dependent on their TCN parents.

AG Sharpston raised a number of questions that all concerned the bigger picture for EU citizenship in her Opinion in *Zambrano*. First, she asked broadly what the concept of an EU citizenship should entail. Second, a question concerning the independent legal status of citizenship and operation of purely internal situations was posed. Third, the notion of a breach of fundamental rights, and whether TCN family members were excluded from benefiting from the rights specifically under the right to private and family life, was considered.[90] The issues are especially pertinent post-Lisbon and after the claim that the EU now recognises the free movement of citizens rather than the free movement of consumers.[91] This analysis will focus on these questions and if there is now 'true citizenship, carrying with it a uniform set of rights and obligations, in a Union under the rule of law … [where] respect for fundamental rights must necessarily play an integral part'.[92]

AG Sharpston described fundamental rights as a 'leitmotif running through all three questions'.[93] What would be considered under the scope *ratione materiae* of the fundamental right to family life is relatively clear – these were mostly citizenship rights, such as residency and non-discrimination.[94] The scope *ratione personae* was different. AG Sharpston argued that the scope *ratione personae* has not only protected the EU citizen themselves, but has been extended to indirectly cover TCN family members – this was the case in *Carpenter* under the free

[90] *Zambrano* (n 4) para 2.

[91] As *Petersen* (n 2) established earlier.

[92] *Zambrano* (n 4) para 3.

[93] ibid para 53.

[94] When the law on fundamental rights was still in its early stages, in *Konstantinidis* (n 1), AG Jacobs took pains to meticulously analyse whether identity constituted an interference with the right to private and family life, and eventually deciding that it did indeed fall under its remit; see paras 31ff.

movement of services and then in *Chen* under EU citizenship.[95] Whether fundamental rights protection meant that TCN family members could be included within the scope *ratione personae* of citizenship remained to be uncovered. The rights of TCN family members, mostly to residency, became the central question of the third age.

i. Residency Rights and Third Country Nationals

Residency rights of TCNs is a controversial topic by its nature because TCNs are outside the scope *ratione personae* of citizenship prima facie. However, there were situations in which this principle could be circumvented. In the Opinion on the *Panayotova* case on the rights of TCNs connected to the EU, AG Poiares Maduro made the claim that:

> Aliens, by the very nature of a political community, cannot benefit from all the rights granted to the citizens of that political community, but it is precisely for the same reason that they deserve added judicial protection where rights granted to them are affected by decisions of the same political community.[96]

This statement appeared to be a justification for affording rights to TCNs. It was especially relevant considering the EU's solidarity objectives for the established community of EU citizens, whose rights to private and family life were to be protected under the binding Charter. Rights to residency for TCNs were realised in the *Chen* case and later in *Metock*.[97] The *Zambrano* case was decided at an opportune moment because it presented a chance to settle the speculation surrounding EU citizenship law and fundamental rights, and also demonstrated how the application of the Court's judicial instruments in citizenship would change with the integration of these rights.

Zambrano was timely because 'the Court had already largely done away with the requirement to demonstrate a clearly identifiable, physical, cross-border movement in order to rely on the rights derived from Union citizenship' in cases before this such as *Carpenter*, *Chen* and *Rottmann*.[98] Therefore, AG Sharpston asked whether citizenship rights should now entail a combined right to residence (movement and residence together), a sequential right to residence (movement *then* residence) or an independent right to residence (movement and residence separately).[99] It would be redundant for both the free movement of persons under the internal market and citizenship in the EU to operate as concurrent concepts if they were identical in terms of scope and effect. Therefore, the combined right to residence,

[95] *Zambrano* (n 4) para 57.
[96] Opinion of 19 February 2004, *Panayotova* C-327/02, EU:C:2004:110, para 47.
[97] *Metock and Others* (n 33).
[98] Anja Wiesbrock, 'Union Citizenship and the Redefinition of the "Internal Situations" Rule: The Implications of Zambrano' (2011) 12 *German Law Journal* 2077, 2084.
[99] *Zambrano* (n 4) para 80.

which in effect was the same as those conferred under Regulation 1612/68, was not the answer for citizenship.

Similarly, the sequential right to residence seemed to be what resulted from applying the cross-border test. It was clear that AG Sharpston did not believe that the cross-border test should be the basis upon which EU citizenship rights applied. When movement is chosen as the trigger for EU citizenship rights: '[l]ottery rather than logic would seem to be governing the exercise of EU citizenship rights.'[100] Crossing borders in order to trigger the Treaty encouraged too arbitrary a conferral of rights. Criticism on previous case law such as *Carpenter* and *Garcia Avello* supported this,[101] and was AG Sharpston's reason for rejecting the sequential right to residence as well. By focusing more on the protection of fundamental rights, it justified supporting her final option, an independent right to residence. Therefore, in support of the independent legal basis of EU citizenship rights, the independent right to residence is most desirable.[102]

In previous cases where circumvention of the cross-border element proved convincing, EU citizenship status and the fundamental nature of it proved to be determinant for whether the claimant was able to frame their case under EU law or not.[103] By framing the question in terms of protection of fundamental rights rather than movement as required by the cross-border test, the status not only becomes independent but also more consistent with a rights-based *acquis*. It is this again which AG Sharpston found convincing for the Zambrano family, leading her to boldly recommend that 'the Court now recognise[s] the existence of that free-standing right of residence'.[104] The potential effect that a free-standing right of residence could have on fundamental rights would be significant because legal residence was a broader basis upon which to confer rights, especially as compared to movement across borders.

ii. Fundamental Rights

If a free-standing right of residence emerged from the Court in the *Zambrano* case, it would mean that claimants could be better protected because of their claim to fundamental rights. It was now less cumbersome to trigger the Treaty for this.

[100] ibid para 88.

[101] See Dautricourt and Thomas (n 16); Charlotte O'Brien, 'Real Links, Abstract Rights and False Alarms: The Relationship between the ECJ's "Real Link" Case Law and National Solidarity' (2008) 33 *European Law Review* 643.

[102] This would be akin to denizenship, most famously championed by Tomas Hammar, 'Denizen and Denizenship' [2003] *New Concepts of Citizenship* 93; and William Rogers Brubaker, 'Membership without Citizenship: The Economic and Social Rights of Noncitizens' in William Rogers Brubaker (ed), *Immigration and the Politics of Citizenship in Europe and North America* (Rowman & Littlefield, 1989).

[103] Judgment of 24 November 1998, *Bickel and Franz* C-274/96, EU:C:1998:563; Judgment of 12 July 2005, *Schempp* C-403/03, EU:C:2005:446; *Garcia Avello* (n 72), which are interestingly all citizenship cases.

[104] *Zambrano* (n 4) para 101.

However, it was not the same as fundamental rights being free-standing rights on their own. AG Sharpston noted that its application is constrained by the principle of conferral,[105] and the concept of fundamental rights is an EU concept whose protection overlaps at both the national and European levels. However, importantly, this did not mean that fundamental rights were not available for claimants who had not exercised their rights under the Treaty, such as if they were too young to move and reside freely in the EU under Article 21 TFEU.[106] To deny this would contradict the very core of fundamental rights, especially given the EU's commitment to these individual rights and liberties in the Preamble, as well as Article 2 TEU: 'Such contingent protection of rights is the antithesis of the way in which contemporary democracies legitimise the authority of the State.'[107] Therefore, not only would it be hypocritical in regards to fundamental rights, but it could also negatively affect EU legitimacy.

The idea of linking fundamental rights and EU citizenship within the legitimate legal framework of the EU is as follows. Because fundamental rights have to adhere to the principle of conferral and remain within the boundaries erected by the Charter,[108] there had to be a valid legal basis for invoking these rights. Making EU citizenship an independent legal basis for rights thus made it a valid legal foundation upon which fundamental rights protection could derive. The fact that the Charter was now binding made this link an even stronger one. It was consistent with the idea of the 'right to have rights'.[109] If the Court could bring the individual under the scope of the Treaty, and more specifically under EU citizenship provisions, then the citizen should be able to rely upon their Charter rights. Because this had already been seen in *Carpenter* and *Chen*, there was a legitimate expectation going forward that this would become the norm. AG Sharpston asked the Court to clarify the parameters of this expectation in her Opinion.

AG Sharpston advanced the argument that 'EU fundamental rights should protect the citizen of the EU *even if such competence has not yet been exercised*'.[110] She proposed three advantages of doing so. First, it would do away with the cross-border test, whilst also ensuring that the EU remained within its competences.[111] Second, it would also encourage greater consistency in the EU-wide application of fundamental rights.[112] Finally, it would enhance the fundamental status of EU citizenship because 'only seamless protection of fundamental rights under EU law in all areas of exclusive or shared EU competence matches the concept

[105] ibid para 162.
[106] ibid para 163. This is a direct reference to the *Chen* case and the Zambrano children's situation.
[107] ibid para 165.
[108] Charter of Fundamental Rights of the European Union 83/02 [2010] OJ C-83/389, arts 51ff.
[109] Hannah Arendt, *Imperialism: Part Two of the Origins of Totalitarianism* (Harcourt Brace Jovanovich, 1968) 171.
[110] *Zambrano* (n 4) para 163.
[111] ibid paras 167–68.
[112] ibid para 169.

of EU citizenship'.[113] Interestingly, the Opinion ended on a more cautious note, as AG Sharpston predicted that the CJEU would postpone answering many of the questions posed in her Opinion because of their sensitive nature, nonetheless warning of the inevitability of having to respond to them at some point.[114] Her prediction proved true, though it did not serve to mitigate the criticism surrounding the actual *Zambrano* judgment when it emerged later in 2011.

C. An Independent Legal Basis for Citizenship Rights

Compared to the lengthy Opinion from AG Sharpston, the *Zambrano* judgment itself is a short, unenthusiastic discussion criticised as 'just seven slender paragraphs of "reasoning"'.[115] In these seven paragraphs, the Court signified important constitutional changes for citizenship, especially regarding judicial instruments. It confirmed that EU citizenship status was now an independent legal basis for claiming rights under Article 21 TFEU. It also confirmed that if there happened to be a cross-border element, both Directive 2004/38 and Articles 20–21 TFEU would be able to govern the situation. If there was no cross-border element, it no longer excluded the situation from the Treaty at the outset; instead, rights came from Article 21 TFEU only. This resolved the question of the application of Directive 2004/38. The Court in *Zambrano* then introduced a new judicial instrument to determine when EU citizenship rights were applicable – the deprivation of genuine enjoyment test. This test was the judicial instrument that defined most of the cases in the third age. However, for the fundamental rights relationship, it was less progressive, for the Court chose not to clarify the test's relationship with the protection of fundamental rights, despite an extensive discussion in the Opinion as well as in the literature and history preceding this case.

In the first paragraph of the *Zambrano* judgment, the Court interpreted the provisions under Directive 2004/38 very literally to find that only crossing borders would trigger its provisions. There was no cross-border element in *Zambrano*, so Directive 2004/38 did not apply. The second paragraph confirmed that although they did not fall under the Directive's application, both children of the Zambrano family born in Belgium still enjoyed EU citizenship status.[116] In the third paragraph, the CJEU reiterated the fundamental status of EU citizenship from *Grzelczyk*, which it argued justified bringing the Zambrano children within the remit of the Treaty, despite lacking a cross-border element. In the

[113] ibid para 170.

[114] This is raised again in her more recent Opinion; see Opinion of 12 December 2013, *O and B; S and G* C-456/12 and C-457/12, EU:C:2013:842.

[115] Niamh Nic Shuibhne, 'Seven Questions for Seven Paragraphs' (2011) 36 *European Law Review* 161.

[116] The family had a third child who was a Colombian national and was not a claimant in the case.

fourth paragraph, it interpreted what the fundamental status protected, stating that national provisions should not deprive EU citizens of the genuine enjoyment of their citizenship rights found in Article 21 TFEU. This was followed by an agreement that the *Zambrano* situation contravened Article 21 TFEU as interpreted under the deprivation of genuine enjoyment test, because the children would be unable to stay in Belgium without their parents, which was reminiscent of the situation in *Chen*. Having to leave the EU amounted to being 'unable to exercise the substance of the rights conferred on them by virtue of their status as citizens of the Union'.[117] This, read with the deprivation of genuine enjoyment, became the new test to determine the scope of Article 21 TFEU. However, seven paragraphs were not sufficient to clarify what this new test would entail, especially as regards fundamental rights protection. Commentators particularly criticised this in light of AG Sharpston's extensive discussion on fundamental rights in her Opinion.[118]

The short *Zambrano* judgment established crucial elements of the third age in terms of what judicial instrument the Court would apply in its citizenship judgments going forward. Dougan has noted that there has been 'unhelpful fragmentation in the range of legal tools by which the Court reasons through the impact of Union citizenship'[119] and this has resulted in confusion as to their relevance today. It was especially problematic for the purely internal situations rule. It was clear now that the Citizenship Directive exclusively governed situations where there was actual movement across borders. If there was no movement, the question fell under the interpretation of the much broader provisions under the Treaty in Articles 20–21 TFEU. The deprivation of genuine enjoyment test would be applied and the Court would consider whether the claimant was deprived of genuine enjoyment of their rights under EU citizenship law. If there was movement, then the citizen could have a right to the protection offered under EU citizenship, 'subject to the limitations and conditions laid down in the Treaties and by the measures adopted to give them effect'.[120] It was the Court that decided on what 'limitations and conditions' would be applicable to make room for fundamental rights protection.

The Court in *Zambrano* neither confirmed nor denied a potential fundamental rights influence when it established the deprivation of genuine enjoyment test, which stated that 'Article 20 TFEU precludes national measures which have the effect of depriving citizens of the Union of the genuine enjoyment of the substance of the rights conferred by virtue of their status as citizens of the Union'.[121]

[117] Judgment of 8 March 2011, *Zambrano* C-34/09, EU:C:2011:124 para 44.
[118] Wiesbrock (n 98) 2091; Sara Iglesias Sánchez, 'The Court and the Charter: The Impact of the Entry into Force of the Lisbon Treaty on the ECJ's Approach to Fundamental Rights' (2012) 49 *CML Rev* 1565, 1593.
[119] Dougan (n 84) 144.
[120] Article 21 TFEU.
[121] *Zambrano* (n 4) para 42.

It simply confirmed that if the Court perceived that an EU citizen has been deprived of the genuine enjoyment of their rights as citizens, they could rely on protection under the Treaty. The notion of rights conferred by virtue of being an EU citizen included the substantive orthodox rights under citizenship that were discussed in previous chapters, such as the right to residency and the right to non-discrimination.[122] However, more recent developments would indicate that it may also include fundamental rights. EU citizens had to first satisfy being deprived of the genuine enjoyment of their rights, and in the post-Lisbon atmosphere of the legally binding Charter, it is argued that the limitations and conditions in the Treaties subjected to EU citizenship status could refer to respect for family life from the Charter because of Article 6 TEU.

Arguably, making fundamental rights protection a permanent feature of the deprivation of genuine enjoyment test could have been what the Court intended to achieve in *Zambrano*.[123] Prior to this, there were three accepted limitations and conditions. The first was the requirement of comprehensive health insurance and sufficient resources from the 1990s Residency Directives.[124] The second was guaranteeing protection of the principle of non-discrimination under Article 18 TFEU after the *Sala* case.[125] Third, through the application of the judicial instruments, the Court created their own limitations and conditions by asking claimants to prove they had a genuine link with the host society,[126] and also by asking them to cross borders to ensure they were not in a purely internal situation.[127] Fundamental rights in the Charter were arguably now the most appropriate consideration because of the impact of its constitutionalised development, but also because of how it enhanced the status of EU citizenship. This was evident from the Court's increased interaction with these rights in cases at the end of the second age. AG Sharpston strongly supported this position as well.

However, there was a distinctly vague character in statements made by the Court in *Zambrano*, leading to the speculation surrounding exactly what amounted to genuine enjoyment and what rights it sought to protect.[128] The situation of the Zambrano family was unique. Sympathy may have played a role in the

[122] Judgment of 12 May 1998, *Martinez Sala* C-85/96, EU:C:1998:217; *Baumbast* (n 47).

[123] Michaela Hailbronner and Sara Iglesias Sánchez, 'The European Court of Justice and Citizenship of the European Union: New Developments towards a Truly Fundamental Status' (2011) 5 *Vienna Journal on International Constitutional Law* 498, 517.

[124] Council Directive (EEC) 90/364 of 28 June 1990 on the right of residence [1990] OJ L180/26; Council Directive (EEC) 90/365 of 28 June 1990 on the right of residence for employees and self-employed persons who have ceased their occupational activity [1990] OJ L180/28; Council Directive (EEC) 93/96 of 29 October 1993 on the right of residence for students [1990] OJ L180/59.

[125] *Martinez Sala* (n 122).

[126] Judgment of 11 July 2002, *D'hoop* C-224/98, EU:C:2002:432.

[127] Judgment of 5 June 1997, *Uecker and Jacquet* C-64/96 and C-65/96, EU:C:1997:285; *Garcia Avello* (n 72).

[128] Kay Hailbronner and Daniel Thym, 'Case C-34/09, *Gerardo Ruiz Zambrano v Office national de l'emploi* (ONEm), Judgment of the Court of Justice (Grand Chamber) of 8 March 2011' (2011) 48 *CML Rev* 1253, 1256.

ultimate decision of the Court, as well as the family's *non-refoulement* clause, which prohibited Belgium returning them to Colombia.[129] It added a further element of helplessness to the family's plea for residency. Thym notes that: 'The facts of *Ruiz Zambrano* are in essence about considerations of social justice.'[130] Most convincing would be the fact that without the parents' legal residency, the family would be separated. Reflecting sentiments of family life and inconveniences as expressed in *Carpenter*, the Court rectified the situation by arguing that this situation would amount to a genuine deprivation of the rights under EU citizenship in the most extreme sense – EU citizens would be forced to leave the EU's territory. However, the question remained as to what else would satisfy the deprivation of genuine enjoyment test, thus inciting criticism of the Court's reluctance in *Zambrano* to clarify the matter.[131]

The Court in *Zambrano* allowed the parents to derive rights to residence from their children, who would be deprived of their genuine enjoyment of rights as EU citizens. This suggested that the Court had considered protection of the fundamental right to private and family life in the case itself. However, the Court offered no further confirmation as to what else amounted to deprivation of genuine enjoyment, which was the determining judicial instrument for EU citizenship rights available to claimants in what were previously purely internal situations. Interpreted liberally, the deprivation of genuine enjoyment test could expand the scope of EU citizenship further, especially when compared to the cross-border test. Fundamental rights were becoming instrumental to these kinds of citizenship cases because of family life elements.[132] With such support for a fundamental rights discourse as the constitutional direction that EU citizenship follows, it would be logical if this were translated into the CJEU's judgments in future.[133] What *Zambrano* established is that the deprivation of genuine enjoyment test could consider rights to family life as a factor in conferring rights under Article 21 TFEU. What it did not confirm was whether the deprivation of genuine enjoyment test necessarily required a fundamental rights assessment.

There were signs pointing towards a fundamental rights direction for the CJEU in citizenship, not only because it was foreshadowed by earlier cases, but also because the Charter consolidated EU fundamental rights constitutionally in the Lisbon Treaty. Both politically and judicially, adopting a more prominent fundamental rights discourse would appear to be where the Court would next logically

[129] Loïc Azoulai, '"Euro-Bonds": The *Ruiz Zambrano* Judgment or the Real Invention of EU Citizenship' [2011] *Perspectives on Federalism* 31, 34.

[130] Daniel Thym, 'Towards "Real" Citizenship? The Judicial Construction of Union Citizenship and its Limits' in Maurice Adams et al (eds), *Judging Europe's Judges* (Hart Publishing, 2013) 166.

[131] Eleanor Spaventa, 'Striving for Equality: Who "Deserves" to Be a Union Citizen?' in Antonio Tizzano et al (eds), *Scritti in Onore di Giuseppe Tesauro* (Editoriale Scientifica, 2014) 5.

[132] As was evident in *Chen* and *Metock and Others*.

[133] See *Zambrano* (n 4); and Armin von Bogdandy et al, 'Reverse Solange: Protecting the Essence of Fundamental Rights against EU Member States' (2012) 49 *CML Rev* 489 for two different approaches.

proceed. It is argued that this direction would have substantiated and legitimised the fundamental status of being an EU citizen, confirming that it would guarantee fundamental rights protection.[134] There should have been an element of recognising a citizen's right to have rights.[135] The fundamental rights element in citizenship would create a greater platform of shared interests, and protecting these shared interests would increase solidarity between EU individuals.[136] It was thus unprecedented what the judgments instead interpreted as amounting to the deprivation of genuine enjoyment.

IV. Conclusion

Cygan has argued that citizenship is a fundamental right in itself.[137] This led to much speculation as the development entered its third age after Article 6 TEU in the Lisbon Treaty made the Charter binding. It is important to note that there are many benefits for the citizen, particularly when it came to applying and enjoying fundamental rights protection, but 'the Court has made a choice between legal certainty and the protection of fundamental rights, opting for the latter at the expense of the former'.[138] In order for fundamental rights and citizenship to be as meaningful as their legal expression suggest, the Court has often had to tailor its application of the rights to the factual scenarios presented to it, which raises the question of legal certainty.[139] In a broad constitutional context, legal uncertainty is undesirable. However, given the framework under which both EU citizenship and fundamental rights exist, it is difficult to find a solution which will suit Member States as much as it suits the EU and its individual citizens. As Dougan argues, 'logic can provide Union law with only so much legitimacy'.[140]

[134] See most recently, Sánchez (n 51).

[135] Hannah Arendt, *Totalitarianism: Part Three of the Origins of Totalitarianism* (Harcourt Brace Jovanovich, 1968). See further Samantha Besson, 'The Right to Have Rights: From Human Rights to Citizens' Rights and Back' in Marco Goldoni and Christopher McCorkindale (eds), *Hannah Arendt and the Law* (Hart Publishing, 2012); and Alison Kesby, *The Right to Have Rights: Citizenship, Humanity, and International Law* (Oxford University Press, 2012).

[136] It is also prudent to acknowledge that art 3(5) TEU provides the following guarantees: 'In its relations with the wider world, the Union shall uphold and promote its values and interests and contribute to the protection of its citizens. It shall contribute to peace, security, the sustainable development of the Earth, solidarity and mutual respect among peoples, free and fair trade, eradication of poverty and the protection of human rights.'

[137] Adam Cygan, 'Citizenship and Fundamental Rights' (2009) 58 *ICLQ* 1002, 1004.

[138] Siofra O'Leary, 'The Past, Present and Future of the Purely Internal Rule in EU Law' [2010] *Irish Jurist* 13, 41.

[139] See Thym (n 130) and his criticism on this.

[140] Dougan (n 84) 138.

4

The Constitutional Crisis of EU Citizenship and Fundamental Rights

I. Introduction

The previous chapters have focused on the rise of fundamental rights protection in EU citizenship case law. The proponent for this has been the Court itself, and its willingness to adapt its legal culture to the growing fundamental rights discourse. The development has spanned over a significant amount of time, beginning even before the formal introduction of EU citizenship status with workers' rights. The potential for it to expand was immense, given that the scope of the rights concerning the free movement of persons was initially limited only to those who worked. As explained in the previous chapters, there has been a shift towards accepting and protecting citizens by virtue of their status as EU citizens. Underlying this has been fundamental rights protection, becoming so pervasive that in *Zambrano* it was finally made clear that EU citizenship was an independent legal basis for rights – such as fundamental rights – to be enjoyed.

The literature on *Zambrano* after the judgment was handed down discusses the case's two broad themes: the independent legal basis of EU citizenship rights and the introduction of the deprivation of genuine enjoyment test. The former discussion is often more positive, for this revelation had been anticipated for many years.[1] For it to finally be recognised judicially was a constitutional achievement for EU citizenship status, especially considering the arduous process the Court initially faced in legitimising EU citizenship status. However, the discussion on the deprivation of genuine enjoyment test is less positive. There was no clarification by the Court in *Zambrano* as to what being deprived of one's genuine enjoyment of rights meant.[2] It was praised for its expansive and inclusive interpretation in the *Zambrano* case itself, but remained ambiguous on the matter of its scope. This was especially unhelpful towards establishing an integrated relationship between fundamental rights and EU citizenship.

[1] Dimitry Kochenov and Richard Plender, 'EU Citizenship: From an Incipient Form to an Incipient Substance? The Discovery of the Treaty Text' (2012) 37 *European Law Review* 369, 387.

[2] Niamh Nic Shuibhne, 'Seven Questions for Seven Paragraphs' (2011) 36 *European Law Review* 161, 162; Alicia Hinarejos, 'Extending Citizenship and the Scope of EU Law' (2011) 70 *CLJ* 309, 312.

The reaction of the commentary as to the cases after *Zambrano* is mixed. It was a long-awaited liberalisation of the EU citizenship status, but the solution proposed to replace the cross-border test was not the panacea to all of the misgivings relating to EU citizenship. These included its legitimacy issues,[3] as well as the fact that it did not address AG Sharpston's questions on fundamental rights. Although the commentary generally accepted that the independence of Article 20 TFEU was positive progress for EU citizenship,[4] the deprivation of genuine enjoyment test was heavily criticised because the Court also failed to explicate exactly what 'genuine enjoyment' amounted to. The cases after *Zambrano* that subsequently endeavoured to do so still left much to be desired, especially for fundamental rights and EU citizenship.[5]

Immediately succeeding the *Zambrano* judgment were two important cases decided the year after *Zambrano*. *McCarthy* and *Dereci* were the first two opportunities for the Court to apply and clarify its newly declared genuine enjoyment test. However, as this chapter will demonstrate, the Court's clarification was not necessarily consistent with what the previous chapters anticipated for an integrated fundamental rights relationship. Instead, the focus here will be on the recent case law, including *McCarthy* and *Dereci*, which demonstrate the starkly different approach applied by the Court regarding fundamental rights protection in light of EU citizenship. By examining these cases, the decline of fundamental rights protection is evident. Since *Zambrano*, instead of fundamental rights protection coming within the scope *ratione materiae* of EU citizenship rights, the Court has made efforts to ensure that only in very narrow situations would fundamental rights protection become relevant. It is now clear that the 'deprivation of genuine enjoyment' was not what it first seemed to be.

The case law in EU citizenship had been concerned with TCN family members' rights for some time before the *Zambrano* case was decided.[6] This pattern in the subject matter of the cases continued after *Zambrano* was decided. The analysis here recognises that in the third age of citizenship, the questions referred on

[3] Nic Shuibhne (n 2).

[4] Robin Morris, 'Case C-34/09-*Gerardo Ruiz Zambrano v Office National de l'Emploi* (ONEm), Judgment of the Court (Grand Chamber) of 8 March 2011, Not Yet Reported' (2011) 18 *Maastricht Journal of European and Comparative Law* 179, 188; Hanneke van Eijken and Sybe de Vries, 'A New Route into the Promised Land? Being a European Citizen after *Ruiz Zambrano*' (2011) 36 *European Law Review* 704, 710.

[5] Niamh Nic Shuibhne, '(Some of) the Kids are All Right' (2012) 49 *CML Rev* 349, 375.

[6] There were also several cases on the rights of free moving students, which were fairly straightforward. See Judgment of 13 April 2010, *Bressol* C-73/08, EU:C:2010:181; Judgment of 4 October 2012, *Commission v Austria* C-75/11, EU:C:2012:605; Judgment of 21 February 2013, *LN* C-46/12, EU:C:2013:97; Judgment of 18 July 2013, *Prinz and Seeberger* C-523/11, EU:C:2013:524; Judgment of 24 October 2013, *Thiele Meneses* C-220/12, EU:C:2013:683; Judgment of 24 October 2013, *Elrick* C-275/12, EU:C:2013:684. Some were also decided under the free movement of workers – see Judgment of 14 June 2012, *Commission v The Netherlands* C-542/09, EU:C:2012:346; Judgment of 25 October 2012, *Prete* C-367/11, EU:C:2012:668.

TCN family members' rights were either by claimants who had crossed borders (subject to Directive 2004/38) or claimants who had not (subject to the deprivation of genuine enjoyment test). Where there was clear cross-border movement, the Court protected rights under Directive 2004/38, as confirmed by the *Zambrano* case. This quickly became the orthodox standard.[7] There is a procedure under Directive 2004/38 in its conferral of residency rights for TCN family members,[8] so the clarification sought in this chapter is for the deprivation of genuine enjoyment test.

The chapter is structured as follows. First, the *McCarthy* and *Dereci* cases are discussed as the first cases after *Zambrano* to apply the deprivation of genuine enjoyment test. However, these cases are evidence of the scope of EU citizenship status becoming narrower and narrower by virtue of the Court. The further decline of fundamental rights protection will then be examined by looking at patterns in the case law to argue that since *Zambrano*, the developments have not followed the trend of the past that has been outlined in the previous chapters. The groups of cases that follow *McCarthy* and *Dereci* demonstrate this. The chapter will end by considering the most recent set of cases that also indicate a pattern, not unlike the cases after *McCarthy* and *Dereci*, that embody a more political element as the politics of the EU begins to pervade the Court's decision-making. In doing so, the chapter sets up the following chapter's discussion on the effect of the UK's vote to leave the EU and how this trend in the Court's decision-making on citizenship rights has failed to empower citizens.

II. The Aftermath of *Zambrano*

The *Zambrano* case introduced two concepts to the third age: the first was that EU citizenship status was now an independent legal basis for rights, while the second was the deprivation of genuine enjoyment test. By making EU citizenship an independent legal basis for rights, all EU citizens could now rely on their respective Treaty rights irrespective of movement. It was thought that after Lisbon, this should have included fundamental rights because of the Charter's now-binding nature. This has been what the previous chapters have alluded to. The Court in *Zambrano* made this independent legal basis for rights subject to the deprivation of genuine enjoyment. Family reunification cases have more often involved situations of TCNs, and it is this which is the underlying question of the chapter – whether an independent legal basis of EU citizenship rights means enjoying the fundamental right to have one's (TCN) family with you, subject to it being a deprivation

[7] This was true until the recent Judgment of 12 March 2014, *O and B; S and G* C-456/12 and C-457/12, EU:C:2014:135 case, where the exact rights sought were not under the Directive itself, and analogies had to be made to Judgment of 7 July 1992, *Singh* C-370/90, EU:C:1992:296 and C-291/05 *Eind* [2007] ECR I-0719 to confer rights instead.

[8] Judgment of 5 May 2011, *McCarthy* C-434/09, EU:C:2011:277, para 32.

of the genuine enjoyment of one's rights under Articles 20–21 TFEU. However, if confirmed, it would mean that the scope *ratione personae* would have expanded beyond the strict boundaries of the EU's territory.[9] If the Court intended to allow such rights to be conferred on TCN family members, it would have to present a constitutionally supported judicial approach, otherwise there would be questions raised in relation to its legitimacy and the boundaries of its competence.[10]

In the *Jia* case on the financial dependency of a TCN family member claiming rights upon an EU citizen, the Advocate General did not consider 'that the protection of family life can be used as a guideline for the interpretation of the scope and the content of the relevant provisions in Regulation 1612/68 and Directive 73/148'[11] on rights to residency for TCN family members. Delivered prior to the Lisbon Treaty coming into force, but late enough into the development that fundamental rights could have potentially influenced the Opinion, this statement demonstrates that fundamental rights as applied to citizenship were not without their limits.[12] The *Zambrano* case should have clarified what these were, but instead the situation remained inconclusive and open to interpretation. Whilst this was not uncommon for concepts in EU citizenship law, as the previous chapters demonstrated, the general ambiguity it suggested did no favours in terms of enhancing the legitimacy of the project for the EU or for solidarity between citizens. It was not long after *Zambrano* where the first opportunity arose for the Court to apply the deprivation of genuine enjoyment test in *McCarthy*.[13]

A. Restricting Scope in the *McCarthy* and *Dereci* Cases

In *McCarthy*, a British-Irish dual national living in the UK, economically inactive and static, married a Jamaican national, who then sought a residency permit as a spouse of an EU citizen. Rejecting Directive 2004/38's application first because of Ms McCarthy's lack of movement, the Court proceeded to also reject the premise that simply having dual nationality would trigger the movement required under the Directive.[14] This was different from *Garcia Avello*, where the children's dual nationality inherently suggested they would potentially want to cross borders in future, thereby triggering application of the Treaty. The scenario in *McCarthy* was not a purely internal situation falling outside the scope of the Treaty entirely,[15] so the

[9] See Judgment of 5 June 1997, *Uecker and Jacquet* C-64/96 and C-65/96, EU:C:1997:285 and art 5 TEU, the principle of conferral.

[10] Opinion of 30 September 2010, *Zambrano* C-34/09, EU:C:2011:560, para 162.

[11] Opinion of 27 April 2006, *Jia* C-1/05, EU:C:2006:258, para 72. Directive 73/148 has now been replaced by the Citizenship Directive 2004/38.

[12] Limits as to the application of the Charter are found in arts 51ff.

[13] *McCarthy* (n 8).

[14] ibid para 49.

[15] ibid para 46.

Court applied the genuine enjoyment test to determine whether Ms McCarthy could claim rights under citizenship, the first time that it applied the deprivation of genuine enjoyment test after *Zambrano*.

The Court in *McCarthy* began by focusing on the claimant's movements across borders, as was the norm prior to *Zambrano*. It considered whether the lack of movement meant that her situation was one of a purely internal situation. Because the Directive specified that 'all Union citizens who "move to" or reside in a Member State "other" than that of which they are a national are beneficiaries of that directive',[16] being static meant that Ms McCarthy was unable to rely on the Directive. Confirming that the Directive would be applicable only to citizens who crossed borders, but that non-moving citizens of the EU would have recourse to Treaty rights, the Court then considered whether Ms McCarthy's genuine enjoyment of citizenship rights were being deprived by it refusing to allow her husband residency rights in the Member State in question.

There appeared to be a chance that Ms McCarthy would be able to claim that she was being deprived of the genuine enjoyment of her rights by the fact that her husband was not allowed to reside with her. Her claim was bolstered by the Charter's protection of the fundamental right to private and family life. Ms McCarthy was being separated from her spouse, which could amount to a breach of family reunification.[17] However, in the Opinion, AG Kokott was decidedly less convinced that the approach offered by AG Sharpston in *Zambrano* applied to the facts in *McCarthy*.[18] Interpreting the questions referred narrowly, she argued that there were no rights to residency under Directive 2004/38 because of a lack of a cross-border element.[19] There was no mention of any other basis for rights, of the deprivation of genuine enjoyment test or of Charter rights because AG Kokott argued that 'Directive 2004/38 is consistent with the requirements of primary law'.[20] This was a significantly narrow approach compared to the Opinion and judgment in *Zambrano*.

It then transpired that the Court in *McCarthy* did compare the situation with *Zambrano*, only to determine that Ms McCarthy was not being deprived of the genuine enjoyment of her rights.[21] The claimant was not obliged to leave the territory of the EU if residency was denied, having never left her current home Member State. Furthermore, because she and her husband had not been separated (given they had not been physically together for long enough; he was only a visitor to the UK), she was not being burdened enough to be considered 'deprived' of the genuine enjoyment of her rights under citizenship. By doing so, the Court

[16] ibid para 32.

[17] As seen in Judgment of 11 July 2002, *Carpenter* C-60/00, EU:C:2002:434; Judgment of 19 October 2004, *Zhu and Chen* C-200/02, EU:C:2004:639; and Judgment of 8 March 2011, *Zambrano* C-34/09, EU:C:2011:124.

[18] Opinion of 25 November 2010, *McCarthy* C-434/09, EU:C:2010:718, para 41.

[19] ibid paras 31 and 56.

[20] ibid para 31.

[21] ibid para 49.

suggested that it would only consider the *Zambrano* situation where claimants had to be forced to exit the territory of the EU *completely*.[22] As this amounted to a violation of the most fundamental kind in terms of restriction on free movement, it would be a clear deprivation under the genuine enjoyment test. However, the standard set by this interpretation is extremely high, and the *McCarthy* case does not add any flexibility to the notion of being deprived of the genuine enjoyment of one's rights under citizenship.

Van Elsuwege argued that the judgment in *McCarthy* brings questions of the cross-border element back into the picture, after the Court in *Rottmann* seemed to put them to rest.[23] This behaviour could also reflect an increasingly wary attitude towards EU solidarity as to the effects of increasing political pressure on the economy.[24] The Opinion of AG Kokott focused heavily on this cross-border element, only to determine that there were no rights under Directive 2004/38 available because there was no crossing of borders, otherwise it would be considered 'cherry-picking' which situations fell within the scope of the Treaty or not.[25] The Opinion served the purpose of confirming that the purely internal situations rule still had weight before the Court. The principle of conferral, which underpinned the rule, was guaranteed by Article 5(1) TEU and could not be negotiated. However, this did not necessarily mean that the cross-border test was still relevant. If there was cross-border movement, the Court recognised that this granted claimants an additional basis for rights under the Directive.[26] If there was not, in order to determine whether the situation fell within the scope of the Treaty, the Court would use the deprivation of genuine enjoyment test as set out in *Zambrano*.

The evolution of the purely internal situations rule and the cross-border test in the third age of citizenship demonstrated the extent to which EU citizenship as a concept had been broadened. The expanding development of EU citizenship, especially when read with fundamental rights, prompted a different interpretation of how to conceive of the purely internal situations rule in the case law,[27]

[22] Chiara Raucea, 'Fundamental Rights: The Missing Pieces of European Citizenship' (2013) 14 *German Law Journal* 2021, 2034.

[23] Peter van Elsuwege, 'Court of Justice of the European Union: European Union Citizenship and the Purely Internal Rule Revisited Decision of 5 May 2011, Case C-434/09 *Shirley McCarthy v Secretary of State for the Home Department*' (2011) 7 *European Constitutional Law Review* 308, 313.

[24] In May 2011, Portugal was officially bailed out, becoming the third EU Member State to be bailed out after Greece and Ireland in 2010. See James G Neuger and Anabela Reis, 'Portugal Bailout Approved as EU Prods Greece to Sell Assets' *Bloomberg Business* (17 May 2011), www.bloomberg.com/news/articles/2011-05-16/portugal-bailout-approved-as-eu-prods-greece-to-sell-assets.

[25] *McCarthy* (n 18) para 56.

[26] See Judgment of 16 January 2014, *Onuekwere* C-378/12, EU:C:2014:13; Judgment of 16 January 2014, *MG* C-400/12, EU:C:2014:9; Judgment of 16 January 2014, *Reyes* C-423/12, EU:C:2014:16; Judgment of 10 July 2014, *Ogieriakhi* C-244/13, EU:C:2014:2068; Judgment of 27 March 2014, *Rüffer* C-322/13, EU:C:2014:189; Judgment of 18 December 2014, *McCarthy and Others* C-202/13, EU:C:2014:2450; Judgment of 11 November 2014, *Dano* C-333/13, EU:C:2014:2358; Judgment of 26 February 2015, *Martens* C-359/13, EU:C:2015:118, where the claimants had all crossed borders, thus triggering rights under Directive 2004/38.

[27] Hinarejos (n 2) 310.

leading to the redundancy of the cross-border test.[28] Importantly, the principle of excluding purely internal situations from the scope of EU law remained intact as it derived from the principle of conferral in the Treaty. Now that citizenship status was an independent legal basis for rights, in order to establish a link with EU law, the option existed to argue that one simply had to be an EU citizen under Article 20 TFEU. This was a liberal step compared to the relatively arbitrary threshold of previously having to move across borders. Providing an alternative to the cross-border test made it easier for citizens to claim rights under the Treaty.[29] This broadened the scope *ratione personae* of EU citizenship significantly. *McCarthy* was an opportunity after *Zambrano* to clarify what the boundaries of the application of the deprivation of genuine enjoyment test were in relation to the new scope *ratione personae* of citizenship. However, instead of confirming its expansion, *McCarthy* suggested that the standard in *Zambrano* regarding being forced to leave EU territory in order to be deprived of one's genuine enjoyment was becoming the general standard of the test itself.[30]

Although the lack of a cross-border element no longer prevented claimants from claiming rights under the Treaty for citizenship, allowing an individual more rights under Directive 2004/38 if they could demonstrate that there had been movement between Member States proved that this element still held some judicial weight in the Court's assessment of the EU citizenship provisions.[31] It would again reflect that the Court's legal culture still cleaved to old logic from the free movement principles in the internal market,[32] instead of embracing a new approach founded upon protection of one's fundamental rights as an EU citizen. The Court sent mixed messages by declaring that the cross-border element was no longer the determinant for rights, yet favoured those who could prove they had moved. This incited confusion as to the future interpretation of the deprivation of genuine enjoyment test and its relationship with fundamental rights protection.

As Kochenov put it, the Court in *McCarthy* 'failed to distinguish *Zambrano* in a convincing manner', leading to criticism.[33] Six months after the judgment in *McCarthy*, the *Dereci* case was decided. In *Dereci*, four TCNs sought residency with Austrian family members who had never exercised their free movement rights under the Treaty. Two claimants had entered the EU illegally, while two had not. Each of the EU citizens claiming a violation of their rights had not moved; therefore, none could rely on the Directive. The question thus fell to rights under the Treaty, governed by the deprivation of genuine enjoyment test. The outcome from *Dereci* was similar to *McCarthy* where the deprivation had to amount to

[28] See Anja Wiesbrock, 'Union Citizenship and the Redefinition of the "Internal Situations" Rule: The Implications of Zambrano' (2011) 12 *German Law Journal* 2077.

[29] See *Zambrano* (n 10) paras 77ff.

[30] *McCarthy* (n 8) para 56.

[31] Nic Shuibhne (n 5) 350. See also the discussion in ch 6.

[32] See Niamh Nic Shuibhne, 'The Resilience of EU Market Citizenship' (2010) 47 *CML Rev* 1597.

[33] Dimitry Kochenov, 'A Real European Citizenship; A New Jurisdiction Test; A Novel Chapter in the Development of the Union in Europe' (2011) 18 *Columbia Journal of European Law* 56, 88.

being forced to leave the EU. The Court reiterated that this could not simply be a mere inconvenience.[34] This is in contrast to the concept of serious inconvenience, as mentioned in the previous chapter, as it pertains to the right to private and family life. The *Dereci* case on its facts was a good opportunity for the Court to provide further clarification on how fundamental rights can play a part in the deprivation of genuine enjoyment test. This is especially the case given the fact that the notion of a serious inconvenience was usually left to the national authorities to determine, providing them with a significant amount of discretion. Yet again, though, the Court did not engage with this discussion on whether deprivation of genuine enjoyment included fundamental rights elements, and how something could amount to being more than a mere inconvenience.

Prior to the *Dereci* case being decided, it was only *Zambrano* and *McCarthy* that were decided based on the deprivation of genuine enjoyment test. Therefore, it was still possible for the Court to limit *McCarthy* to its facts, given its relative restrictiveness, especially as to a relationship between citizenship status and fundamental rights. However, what the Court in *Dereci* did instead was to limit *Zambrano* to its facts[35] and reaffirm the standards set in *McCarthy* for satisfying the deprivation of genuine enjoyment test. The Court confirmed that TCNs could not have rights to residency if their EU citizen family member were not deprived of the genuine enjoyment of their EU citizenship rights,[36] which was triggered by only the most extreme situation – being forced to the leave the territory of the EU. Deciding to limit *Zambrano* to its facts would potentially appease Member States that were concerned about infringements on their autonomy.[37] It emerged that this negative sentiment was actually becoming more pronounced at the time.

The Court left the national courts to determine whether there was a deprivation of genuine enjoyment to trigger rights under the Treaty in *Dereci*. However, it confirmed that the standard was whether the EU citizen would be forced to leave the EU. In a purely legalistic and formulaic sense, the Court's reasoning was justified because the judgment provided safeguards for both the EU and the Member States, thereby also adhering to the purely internal situations rule. Furthermore, it did not contradict the decision in *Zambrano*. Lenaerts argues that the Court's approach is one of 'judicial prudence' and does not believe that 'the ECJ decided to avoid answering difficult, complex and politically sensitive questions; on the contrary, it is simply that those questions would only be addressed when the cases at hand required it'.[38] However, an alternative interpretation of the independent legal basis for rights and the deprivation of one's genuine enjoyment raises the

[34] *McCarthy* (n 8) para 54.

[35] Judgment of 15 November 2011, *Dereci* C-256/11, EU:C:2011:734, para 66.

[36] ibid.

[37] See Koen Lenaerts, 'The Court's Outer and Inner Selves: Exploring the External and Internal Legitimacy of the European Court of Justice' in Maurice Adams et al (eds), *Judging Europe's Judges* (Hart Publishing, 2013).

[38] ibid 51.

claim that fundamental rights should have been applicable simply by virtue of being an EU citizen.

B. 'Genuine Enjoyment' and Fundamental Rights

It is difficult to assess objectively what amounts to 'deprivation'. A high standard as to what deprivation is interpreted to mean in the context of the genuine enjoyment of citizenship rights limits who can then claim to have satisfied this test. The Court has thus far only allowed deprivation of genuine enjoyment to be considered as the claimant having to leave the EU if there is no other option. The judgments have been criticised because in their assessments of the judicial instrument introduced by the Court in *Zambrano*, it appeared to overly favour the interests of the EU and the Member States at the expense of individual citizens' protection.[39] The Court's analysis of the facts in both cases is narrow, with it choosing not to undertake a fundamental rights assessment. The judgments appeared to diminish the normative effect of the Lisbon Treaty and the codification of the Charter of Fundamental Rights.

Refusing to engage with fundamental rights in *McCarthy* as the first case to apply the deprivation of genuine enjoyment test marks the beginning of a decline in the influence of fundamental rights in EU citizenship law. Nic Shuibhne described the *McCarthy* and *Dereci* decisions as 'cold comfort', especially '[g]iven what was at stake for the EU citizens actually involved'.[40] The claimant, an EU citizen, was being denied the right to reside with her husband of non-EU nationality for failing to meet the threshold of the deprivation of genuine enjoyment, which was interpreted by the Court as having to amount to forcing the EU citizen to leave the territory of the EU. Deporting or expelling an EU citizen from the EU is the most extreme of cases that would certainly be denying residence and free movement rights under EU citizenship. However, it would appear from the *McCarthy* case that the Court was rather inflexible in this regard, maintaining a high threshold where nothing less than forcing her to leave the EU would be a deprivation of genuine enjoyment.

In *McCarthy*, the Court considered that because Ms McCarthy had never exercised her rights to free movement, her husband not residing with her did not deprive her of her EU citizenship rights. It would seem that she could not prove her family life had ever been disrupted because she had remained static before and after being married, and her husband had only been a visitor to the UK. It was an

[39] See Nic Shuibhne (n 5); Stanislas Adam and Peter van Elsuwege, 'Citizenship Rights and the Federal Balance between the European Union and its Member States: Comment on *Dereci*' (2012) 37 *European Law Review* 176; Alicia Hinarejos, 'Citizenship of the EU: Clarifying "Genuine Enjoyment of the Substance" of Citizenship Rights' (2012) 71 *CLJ* 279.

[40] Niamh Nic Shuibhne, *The Coherence of EU Free Movement Law* (Oxford University Press, 2013) 153.

opposite effect to that envisaged after the liberation of the EU citizenship status as an independent source of rights. If the Court were a human rights court, there may have been greater weight to the argument that she had the right to have her husband with her and keep her family together. However, as many have noted, it is not,[41] so although the judgment is flawed in many ways, criticism cannot be on the lack of consideration for this human rights aspect. What can be noted is that there is clearly still legal uncertainty[42] and that *Zambrano* is to be treated as a 'narrow' decision.[43]

In *Dereci*, the Court does emphasise that failing to exercise the rights to free movement 'cannot, for that reason alone, be assimilated to a purely internal situation',[44] confirming that the cross-border test was no longer the sole determinant for whether one fell within the scope of the Treaty or not. However, citing *Zambrano*, it was held that though family reunification may 'appear desirable',[45] the economic reasons cited would not be enough to force the EU citizen to leave the territory of the EU and therefore was not a basis for rights to residency for the TCN family members. Though the Court dedicated four paragraphs of the judgment in *Dereci* to respect for the right to private and family life,[46] it then dismissed these rights, going on to state its decision matter-of-factly and reconfirming the standards of the *Zambrano* ruling to *Dereci*. Described as a '"minimalist" understanding of *Ruiz Zambrano*', it further confirmed that *Zambrano* 'was exceptional and did not entail the risk of a "Copernican" revolution of the traditional paradigms of free movement and EU citizenship'.[47] This case suggested that the Court was unlikely to exhibit as liberal an approach as it had in *Zambrano* and *Chen* towards TCN family members upon later interpretations of the deprivation of genuine enjoyment test.

The approach taken by AG Mengozzi in his Opinion on *Dereci* is particularly difficult to reconcile with the analysis thus far as to the rise of fundamental rights in citizenship. His focus was on clarifying the rules laid out by the judgments in *Zambrano* and *McCarthy*. In particular, he recognised that *Zambrano* had created confusion as to the rights available under Article 20 TFEU without crossing borders and, more confusingly in *McCarthy*, where it was held that the claimant's situation did not provide a sufficient link with EU law to confer rights under

[41] See Piet Eeckhout, 'The EU Charter of Fundamental Rights and the Federal Question' (2002) 39 *CML Rev* 945; Armin Von Bogdandy et al, 'Reverse Solange: Protecting the Essence of Fundamental Rights against EU Member States' (2012) 49 *CML Rev* 489; Philip Alston and Joseph Weiler, 'An "Ever Closer Union" in Need of a Human Rights Policy: The European Union and Human Rights' in Philip Alston (ed), *The EU and Human Rights* (Oxford University Press, 1999); Sionaidh Douglas-Scott, 'The European Union and Human Rights after the Treaty of Lisbon' (2011) 11 *Human Rights Law Review* 645; *Zambrano* (n 10) para 155.

[42] Peter van Elsuwege and Dimitry Kochenov, 'On the Limits of Judicial Intervention: EU Citizenship and Family Reunification Rights' (2011) 13 *European Journal of Migration and Law* 443, 453.

[43] Hinarejos (n 39) 281.

[44] *Dereci* (n 35) para 61.

[45] ibid para 68.

[46] ibid paras 70–74.

[47] Adam and van Elsuwege (n 39) 182.

Article 21 TFEU.[48] Drawing upon this, AG Mengozzi argued that the 'judgment in *Ruiz Zambrano* does not include the right to respect for family life enshrined in Article 7 of the Charter of Fundamental Rights of the European Union and in Article 8(1) of the ECHR'.[49] In fact, this fundamental right is 'insufficient'[50] to bring an individual within the protection afforded by the Treaty. In the absence of the cross-border test, therefore, the fact that a claimant is an EU citizen under Article 20 TFEU is not sufficient to protect their rights to private and family life. The argument that 'the protection afforded to [fundamental rights] by these three legal orders – national, Union and treaty law – proves to be complementary' has the effect of excluding the Charter, which is legally inconsistent, given that it was now binding because of the Lisbon Treaty, subject to finding a link with EU law.[51] It has been argued that this link to the Treaty was simply Article 20 TFEU, the status of EU citizenship.

The discussion in previous chapters as to the accrual of rights under EU citizenship consistent with fundamental rights protection, particularly in cases where it would otherwise appear that fundamental rights would not be the main focus of the judgment, are thus also inconsistent with the AG Opinion and judgment in *Dereci*. However, more surprising is that in relation to the binding nature of the Charter and the interpretation of its scope as to fundamental rights protection after Lisbon, a significant discrepancy emerges. The AG excludes the determination of Member State obligations under the ECHR, which seems understandable in the face of not yet having acceded to the Convention.[52] However, as far as the binding nature of the Charter is concerned, an unsatisfactory outcome is presented where both the AG and the Court do not consider fundamental rights under the deprivation of genuine enjoyment test. This is opposed to the prior constitutional direction indicated by the substantiation of the status of EU citizenship under Article 20 TFEU and its requisite rights.

It is argued that these situations are clearly of family reunification rights under the right to private and family life, which are far less ambiguous than some cases in the earlier chapters in terms of warranting protection under fundamental rights. For this reason, it would appear to be clear how the Court would approach the case by looking to its previous decisions, but also considering that citizenship status had evolved to encompass a normatively liberal interpretation as to which fundamental rights would play a key role. The fact that AG Mengozzi recognised that the outcome he suggested is not legally certain indicates that this is not an entirely satisfactory outcome.[53] However, this was nonetheless the approach adopted by the Court. For citizens in particular, the law thus becomes even less legally certain.

[48] Opinion of 29 September 2001, *Dereci* C-256/11, EU:C:2011:626, paras 17 and 30.
[49] ibid para 37.
[50] ibid para 38.
[51] Judgment of 26 February 2013, *Melloni* C-399/11, EU:C:2013:107 paras 18 and 19.
[52] On this, see Opinion of 18 December 2014, Opinion 2/13, EU:C:2014:2454.
[53] *Dereci* (n 48) para 49.

Therefore, it would appear that though the Lisbon Treaty provided a constitutional basis from which it would be acceptable normatively and legally for EU citizenship status and its rights to be clarified in terms of fundamental rights protection, the opposite occurred instead. The law concerning EU citizenship and fundamental rights in relation to the Charter's legally binding status had now been muddied by the technicalities of the deprivation of genuine enjoyment test.

At this point in the development, it was becoming incredibly clear that the scope of EU citizenship was regressing. This was especially as compared to when the Court in *Rottmann* and *Zambrano* treated citizenship as an independent legal basis for rights, thereby also hinting at a stronger fundamental rights rationale for the Court. The growing constitutional independence of the EU citizenship status and its increasing judicial fundamentality indicated the potential for fundamental rights to become integral to EU citizenship, for political and constitutional reasons. However, there is a link to be made between the Court's lack of enthusiasm for greater protection of citizens' rights and the worsening political crisis in the EU. It is argued that the Court appears to have found it difficult to ignore the pervading sense of dissatisfaction with the EU's project of integration,[54] which began to overshadow the gains made by the Treaty in protecting individual rights.[55]

III. EU Citizenship Cases after *Zambrano*

As this chapter has argued thus far, the protection of fundamental rights in EU citizenship case law has been steadily declining as a result of the Court's consistent and strict interpretation of the deprivation of genuine enjoyment test. It is thought that '[t]he omission of any reference to fundamental rights is anything but accidental'[56] in *McCarthy* and *Dereci*, though this observation is more easily noted in retrospect. This section will introduce the hypothesised underlying reason why the Court chose not to engage with fundamental rights, which is related to a growing dissatisfaction amongst Member States with the EU's free movement laws as a result of the growing dissatisfaction with the EU as a whole. To do so, it will look at the case law since *McCarthy* and *Dereci*. There are two identifiable strands of considerations made by the Court as to the claimants: the first is its treatment of TCNs, while the second is its treatment of citizens it considers 'deserving' of such rights.

[54] *Dano* (n 26); Judgment of 15 September 2015, *Alimanovic* C-67/14, EU:C:2015:597; Judgment of 25 February 2016, *Garcia-Nieto and Others* C-299/14, EU:C:2016:114.

[55] See Jay C Shambaugh, Ricardo Reis and Hélène Rey, 'The Euro's Three Crises' [2012] *Brookings Papers on Economic Activity* 157.

[56] Michaela Hailbronner and Sara Iglesias Sánchez, 'The European Court of Justice and Citizenship of the European Union: New Developments towards a Truly Fundamental Status' (2011) 5 *Vienna Journal on International Constitutional Law* 498, 529.

It is certainly interesting to note that there is a qualitative assessment of who 'deserves' what rights, especially given that the normative underlying quality of fundamental rights is that they are universal and therefore everyone deserves their protection.[57] Given that the Treaty emphasises equality and non-discrimination of all peoples as a matter of general principle, in the EU in particular, this would be even more pertinent. At this point, it is relevant to point out that if the Court seems to be adopting an assessment where it grants rights to citizens who are more 'deserving', then this would be a backwards step in the sense of not being able to move away from the approach of the first age, where being economically active was the determinant factor in rights conferral. This is important to raise here because it is somewhat of a prelude to the later discussion in this book, where the context of Brexit becomes relevant. As far as the negotiations for the UK's withdrawal from the EU are concerned, Brexit has raised more issues of this sort where the question of whether one truly 'deserves' rights post-Brexit becomes relevant. This will be discussed further in the next chapter.

The fundamental rights and EU citizenship relationship dynamic has been on the minds of many commentators, but none more so than AG Sharpston, as evidenced by her Opinion in *Zambrano*. In her subsequent Opinion on *O and B*, AG Sharpston simplified the analysis of the relationship to simply consider how a TCN family member attains a derived right to residency, thereby also upholding the right to private and family life. There was no consistency or clarity in terms of exactly how a TCN family member derived rights to residency. AG Sharpston noted that there was never any express denial of the influence of family reunification rights under Article 7 of the Charter or Article 8 ECHR in determining residency rights, nor had there been any confirmation, despite the Lisbon Treaty's guarantees. This created a 'puzzling' situation where three different bases for claiming rights to residency potentially existed.[58] This uncertainty has undermined judgments since *Zambrano*, so AG Sharpston again took it upon herself to offer a clarification of the situation.

When AG Sharpston raised the issue of competence to address fundamental rights in her Opinion in *Zambrano*, she cautioned that the 'desire to promote appropriate protection of fundamental rights must not lead to usurpation of competence'.[59] However, to come within the scope of EU law, she advanced a fairly broad test on the existence of material competence while remaining consistent with her (confined) liberalisation of fundamental rights.[60] However, the Court

[57] John Finnis, *Natural Law & Natural Rights*, 2nd edn (Oxford University Press, 2011).

[58] Opinion of 12 December 2013, *O and B; S and G* C-456/12 and C-457/12, EU:C:2013:842, para 57. These are art 7 of the Charter (right to private and family life), art 21(1) TFEU (free movement and residence under EU citizenship) and art 20 TFEU (deprivation of genuine enjoyment).

[59] *Zambrano* (n 10) para 162.

[60] ibid paras 164ff.

refused to engage with this element in its judgment on *Zambrano* and has since also avoided clarifying the situation. AG Sharpston has asked for the Court to address this in her Opinions in both *Zambrano* and *O and B*. However, in *O and B*, delivered three years after *Zambrano*, she presents a slightly revised perspective upon analysis of the case law since *Zambrano*.

Noting that 'it is clear that, at present at least, the Charter does not grant "free-standing" fundamental rights',[61] AG Sharpston continued to clarify that: 'Citizenship rights under Article 20 or 21 TFEU must thus be interpreted in a way that ensures that their substantive content is "Charter-compliant".'[62] This brought the EU citizenship and fundamental rights questions together as one single consideration, and did not require any radicalism on the part of the Court. Despite this element being somewhat tangential to the central preliminary reference, a gentle request for the Court to nonetheless engage with this issue was added in a postscript at the end of the Opinion.[63] However, this made it more surprising that the Court again decided against clarifying the situation.[64] Therefore, the general sentiment surrounding the judgment in *O and B* is sound in terms of the Court's application of judicial reasoning, but still lacking clarity in terms of fundamental rights protection.[65]

It is unclear why the Court did not engage with the fundamental rights question. Perhaps it was wary of overstepping boundaries, thereby choosing not to engage into a discussion on this sensitive topic, like it had done in the past on other sensitive matters.[66] Perhaps it was unable to agree on a clear direction or was uncertain about this, which would be the issue throughout the development that was evident early on.[67] However, it was a legal symptom of the Court's decision-making in citizenship evident from the previous chapters for it to be especially careful to base its claims on valid legal foundations when undertaking difficult assessments that would greatly affect a Member State's autonomy.[68] Therefore, this section will now consider the judgments in recent cases which reflect how cautious the Court can be, and will argue that this is exacerbated because of the growing discontent within the EU attributed to the period of crisis it was facing at the time.

[61] *O and B; S and G* (n 58) para 60.

[62] ibid para 62.

[63] ibid para 158.

[64] Eleanor Spaventa, 'Family Rights for Circular Migrants and Frontier Workers: *O and B, and S and G*' (2015) 52 *CML Rev* 753, 759. She argues that the Court 'cherry-picked from the Opinion'.

[65] Adrienne Yong, 'Opinion of AG Sharpston (12 December 2013) and Grand Chamber Judgment (12 March 2014) in Cases C-456/12 *O and B* and C-457/12 *S and G*' (2014) 25 *King's Law Journal* 155.

[66] On abortion, see Judgment of 4 October 1991, *SPUC v Grogan* C-159/90, EU:C:1991:378; on gambling, see Judgment of 8 September 2009, *Bwin* C-42/07, EU:C:2009:519; on drugs, see Judgment of 16 December 2010, *Josemans* C-137/09, EU:C:2010:774.

[67] The case law discussed in the previous chapters is indicative of this.

[68] For example, Judgment of 2 October 2003, *Garcia Avello* C-148/02, EU:C:2003:539; *Carpenter* (n 17); *Chen* (n 17); Judgment of 2 March 2010, *Rottmann* C-135/08, EU:C:2010:104; *Zambrano* (n 10).

A. 'Genuine Enjoyment' after *McCarthy* and *Dereci*

The previous section discussed three cases in the third age of citizenship – *Zambrano*, *McCarthy* and *Dereci* – and the deprivation of genuine enjoyment test as introduced by the Court. It highlighted that despite the potential set out by *Zambrano* inspired by the *Rottmann* case, the integrated fundamental rights and EU citizenship relationship has not materialised as expected. All three cases discussed were decided in 2011; therefore, there was still a possibility that the Court would turn the other way for fundamental rights and citizenship in later years. However, looking at the cases since 2011, it is more evident that the sole acceptable condition for being deprived of the genuine enjoyment of one's rights was that of being forced to leave the territory of the EU. This is contrary to arguments that with EU citizenship status now an independent legal basis for rights, it would be easier to trigger protection under Articles 20–21 TFEU as it was now 'released from the mobility condition'.[69]

It was in *Iida* in 2012 that the CJEU first emphasised that 'the Treaty provisions on citizenship of the Union do not confer any autonomous right on third-country nationals'.[70] This was interesting given that this principle had been inherent in EU citizenship provisions when the EU citizenship status emerged in Article 8 EC as dependent upon nationality. Clearly, the Court felt it was necessary to clarify this position after *Zambrano* in order to mitigate criticism that the scope of EU citizenship might begin to transcend even the EU's external borders as it became an independent source of rights. It was also well timed politically.[71] In *Iida*, the claimant was the TCN father of an EU citizen who lived with her German mother in Austria. The parents separated after living apart in Germany and Austria respectively for some time. The father sought a residency card as a family member of his German daughter living in Austria from Germany, where he had resided, previously with her and her mother, which was denied. Mr Iida had not moved, so there was no cross-border element to trigger Directive 2004/38 as a family member beneficiary occasionally could.[72] However, the deprivation of genuine enjoyment test was applied in relation to his daughter's right to have her father with reside with her, which yet again was interpreted strictly by the Court.

Because Mr Iida's daughter was not forced to leave the EU despite her father not being with her in Austria, the Court interpreted this as her not being deprived of the genuine enjoyment of her rights. His regular visits from Germany, as well as the fact that she had exercised her right to move by moving from Germany

[69] Loïc Azoulai, 'A Comment on the *Ruiz Zambrano* Judgment: A Genuine European Integration' [2011] European Union Democracy Observatory on Citizenship, http://globalcit.eu/a-comment-on-the-ruiz-zambrano-judgment-a-genuine-european-integration.

[70] Judgment of 8 November 2012, *Iida* C-40/11, EU:C:2012:691, para 66.

[71] Jose Ignacio Torreblanca and Mark Leonard, *The Continent Wide Rise of Euroscepticism* (European Council on Foreign Relations Policy Memo, 2013).

[72] *Iida* (n 70) paras 49ff.

to Austria with her mother, but without her father, was evidence that she was not being deprived. Furthermore, Mr Iida's daughter was not a minor dependant like baby Chen, the Garcia children or the Zambrano children. This notion of dependency raised fundamental rights arguments of family life. However, the Court held that there was no link to EU law to trigger the Charter because the conditions for conferral of a German residence card did not involve EU law and therefore also no Charter rights.[73] Mr Iida was thus denied protection under EU law and *Iida* confirmed the high standard for invoking the deprivation of genuine enjoyment test.

In light of *Zambrano*, this case is quite telling. *Iida* was not a situation where the dependant needed the care of her parents, unlike in *Zambrano*. However, it would suggest that there is a variable standard of how dependent one is to trigger rights under the Treaty. When the matter is simply one of the fundamental right to respect for private and family life, then it is should be applied consistently across the board. It would suggest that the *Zambrano* case actually did not concern itself with fundamental rights protection so much, but that it was rather about setting a new standard for triggering the Treaty, considering that the Court had made EU citizenship an independent legal basis for rights. Thus, as far as the fundamental rights discourse is concerned, it is consistent with the decline that has been evident in the aftermath of *Zambrano*. Nevertheless, it is troubling that the cases are often to do with family rights to reunification and dependency, which are often excellent opportunities to develop the fundamental rights discourse.

O, S and L presented another opportunity for the Court to demonstrate its commitment to fundamental rights, considering the degree of family reunification and dependency to attain rights to residency under EU citizenship law.[74] The cases concerned three TCN stepfathers and their EU citizen stepchildren's dependency to them. The stepfathers all sought residency from their stepchildren, and the extent to which they were needed by their stepchildren was the relevant factor. This was another case on TCN family members' rights, and could have further clarified how rights could be enjoyed by this increasingly common group of claimants, the inclusion of which would expand the scope of EU citizenship significantly. In particular, the family life element was also not as straightforward, given that the children were not biologically related to the parents. Indeed, consistent with the cases decided around the same time, the Court did not depart from the understanding it had established in previous judgments as to what amounted to a deprivation of genuine enjoyment.

The Court in *O, S and L* unsurprisingly remained firm as to the standard for deprivation of one's genuine enjoyment. Citing *Dereci* and the fact that rights could not be conferred simply for economic reasons of convenience,[75] it was held that the TCN claimants were not dependent enough to their stepchildren to force

[73] ibid para 81.
[74] Judgment of 6 December 2012, *O, S and L* C-356/11 and C-357/11, EU:C:2012:776.
[75] ibid para 52.

them to have to leave the EU. The Court recognised that 'while emphasising the importance for children of family life, [Articles 7 and 24 of the Charter][76] cannot be interpreted as depriving the Member States of their margin of appreciation when examining applications for family reunification'.[77] The referring court was left with the discretion to decide this. Yet again, the fundamental rights argument was impeded by the fact that the first hurdle – the deprivation of genuine enjoyment test – was not satisfied.

Both *Ymeraga*[78] and *Alokpa*[79] came after *O, S and L*, and were also not decided upon protection of the fundamental rights to private and family life. The Court in both cases denied the derived right to residency because there was no link with EU law to trigger such protection under the deprivation of genuine enjoyment test. Both cases confirmed that there could not be an autonomous right to fundamental rights, also citing provisions under the Charter which restricted its scope only to situations where EU law was being implemented.[80] In *Ymeraga*, the situation concerned the right to family reunification of individuals from Kosovo seeking residency in Luxembourg with family who were Luxembourg nationals. It was decided that the family links, namely that the Kosovo nationals were just the nephews of the Luxembourg citizen, did not amount to enough of a deprivation of genuine enjoyment. Their uncle would not be forced to leave the EU if they were denied rights to remain. In *Alokpa*, Luxembourg was also the Member State in question where the claimant, a national from Togo who had French twins with a French national, sought residency in Luxembourg upon this notion of dependency. It was decided here that she could derive a right to reside in France, where the children were from, but did not have a right to stay in Luxembourg. Unfortunately, these cases seek to confirm that unlike citizenship status, fundamental rights have never been declared an independent source of rights. However, consistent with AG Sharpston's Opinion in *Zambrano*, this book argues that a less 'partial and fragmented' fundamental rights discourse would be more consistent with the fundamental, and now independent, status of EU citizenship, thereby justifying her argument that they should be relied upon in situations where the EU has competence, rather than having to exercise this competence first.[81]

From these cases, the underlying problem between fundamental rights and EU citizenship begins to emerge. Fundamental rights, as the human rights of the EU, in theory warrant unrestricted protection at their core. However, in the EU's constitutional structure, the Court has to first establish a relevant link with EU law, meaning that in reality, fundamental rights in the EU were restricted. This book has argued that after the Court in *Zambrano* established an independent legal basis

[76] Article 7 protects the right to private and family life and art 24 protects the rights of a child.
[77] *O, S and L* (n 74) para 79.
[78] Judgment of 8 May 2013, *Ymeraga* C-87/12, EU:C:2013:291.
[79] Judgment of 10 October 2003, *Alokpa* C-86/12, EU:C:2013:645.
[80] Article 51 of the Charter.
[81] *Zambrano* (n 10) paras 163 and 170.

for EU citizenship rights, the link with EU law could come from simply being an EU citizen. It would bring the situation closer to the concept at the core of fundamental rights, namely universality. *Zambrano* demonstrated a potential solutión, especially in relation to residency rights for TCN family members of EU citizens. If the Court adopted this judicial approach in later cases, it would have brought the fundamental rights and EU citizenship discourse closer, for their objectives and scope would be more similar. They would be able to focus on the protection of the individual citizen over safeguarding the Member State's broader financial interests. However, as the case analysis has shown, this did not occur.

What this section has aimed to elucidate is what constitutional direction the Court was indicating in its case law, which emerged from the speculation and expectations raised by the *Zambrano* case. In the *Zambrano* Opinion, AG Sharpston asked the Court to clarify this relationship.[82] The cases analysed here attempted to do what AG Sharpston asked; however, what resulted did not accord with the prediction and intended outcome vis-a-vis fundamental rights and EU citizenship status. It should be noted that in most of the scenarios, the Court does not ignore family reunification rights outright, but rather simply cannot consider its relationship with EU citizenship because there is no legal basis for their protection. This left much to be desired in terms of their invocation and the reality of being able to judicially rely on them under future interpretations of Articles 20–21 TFEU.

It is clear from the above discussions that what emerged in the aftermath of *Zambrano* has limited the scope *ratione materiae* of EU citizenship. Although it would appear to broaden the scope *ratione personae* so that any EU citizen could claim rights irrespective of movement, it was equally restrictive because of the deprivation of genuine enjoyment test and the standard set to satisfy this. It was not that one simply had to be an EU citizen to establish a link with EU law that would trigger rights under the Charter to family reunification; rather, it was the opposite effect, where being an EU citizen no longer sufficed and a person had to prove that they would be forced to leave the EU if they were not granted protection by the Treaty. This was an unexpected shift in the Court's attitude towards integrating fundamental rights and EU citizenship status. Of late, this has not changed.

B. Patterns in Recent Case Law

The most recent cases on citizenship have largely been concerned with TCNs and their rights, mainly to residency, in the EU.[83] However, during this time,

[82] ibid para 177.

[83] Exceptions include criminal and asylum cases; see Judgment of 6 October 2015, *Delvigne* C-403/03, EU:C:2015:648; Judgment of 2 May 2018, *K (and allégations de crimes de guerre)* C-331/16, EU:C:2018:296; Judgment of 17 April 2018, *B* C-316/16 and C-424/16, EU:C:2018:256.

nationalism as a sentiment was growing amongst Member States' citizens. This presented a particular challenge to the EU's integration objectives.[84] It seems that in this period, the Court reacted to this challenge by beginning to exhibit more caution and less flexibility in cases where there was a sensitive issue like rights being claimed by non-EU citizens. This has often meant that it deferred to Member States' interests – usually their interest in protecting their national welfare and autonomy – rather than the citizens' enjoyment of rights. Though this behaviour was part of the Court's legal culture and is not unlike the behaviour it exhibited in the first age, it does contradict what had been the direction indicated since fundamental rights considerations became more explicit in the Court's reasoning for citizenship cases in the latter half of the second age. The recent cases broadly fall into the following groups: cases concerning '*Zambrano*-style' carers; cases on how a family is defined under Directive 2004/38; cases involving individuals with criminal convictions; cases on residency rights under Directive 2004/38 for TCN family members; and cases on welfare benefits. The analysis will look at these in turn. The cumulative pattern that the cases demonstrate is that of an increasingly hesitant approach being adopted by the Court in citizenship, and even less willingness to allow fundamental rights to influence the final decision. The analysis will also explain why this is a troubling development that is out of sync with what has been argued throughout this book so far.

The first group of cases that demonstrate a pattern in the Court's reasoning of late are those concerning *Zambrano* carers. They provide further discussion of the genuine enjoyment test. Given the relative dissatisfaction with the *Zambrano* judgment itself failing to provide clarity on what being 'deprived' of the genuine enjoyment of one's rights entailed, the Court seemed to be open to the idea of providing some clarity to the situation in future cases. Moreover, *Rendón Marín*[85] and *CS*[86] are two examples where the Court did find breaches of citizenship rights, yet nonetheless maintained a strict interpretation of what being 'deprived' of the genuine enjoyment of these rights entailed. Notably, cases that have dealt with *Zambrano* carers since the original judgment have seen the Court adhering to a strict interpretation of the test, leaving commentators to assume that deprivation is considered only to be akin to being forced out of the EU. Therefore, the clarity sought was that of more flexibility by way of considering how fundamental rights protection may play a role in the Court's understanding of 'deprivation'.

[84] This is seen in the rise of political support for many far-right parties in central EU Member States, such as the *Rassemblement National* (RN; previously the *Front National* in France) and the UK Independence Party (UKIP) in Britain. See Emmanuel Berretta, 'François Hollande démuni face au Front national' *Le Point* (6 March 2015), www.lepoint.fr/politique/emmanuel-berretta/francois-hollande-demuni-face-au-front-national-06-03-2015-1910490_1897.php; Alex Hunt, 'UKIP: The Story of the UK Independence Party's Rise' *BBC News* (21 November 2014), www.bbc.co.uk/news/uk-politics-21614073; 'Queen's Speech 2015: Bill-by-Bill' *BBC News* (27 May 2015), www.bbc.co.uk/news/uk-politics-32898443.

[85] Judgment of 13 September 2016, *Rendón Marín* C-165/14, EU:C:2016:675.

[86] Judgment of 13 September 2016, *CS* C-304/14, EU:C:2016:674.

This trouble with affording this kind of discretion to the Court, especially in the interpretation of deprivation, is that more often than not, it puts the claimant in an unfavourable position. It again highlights the inclination by the Court towards making a judgement call as to who deserves what rights, which, as mentioned, narrows the scope of EU citizenship rights to a position where it appears that those who economically contribute are the only ones who 'deserve' rights. Given that this has all occurred in the lead-up to the UK's withdrawal from the EU, the argument is that it is all symptomatic of the declining faith in the status of EU citizenship overall in the constituent Member States. It is also a clear prelude to the next chapter's discussion on the correlation between the Brexit vote and the decline in fundamental rights protection in EU citizenship case law. There is something to be said for the fact that there seems to be a quality assessment of the claimant and their situations before granting rights.

Both *Rendón Marín* and *CS* involved TCNs whose EU citizen children were dependent on them and were being denied residency because of criminal records.[87] The Court in *Rendón Marín* stated that 'a derived right of residence of a third-country national exists, in principle, only when it is necessary in order to ensure that a Union citizen can exercise effectively his rights to move and reside freely in the European Union'.[88] In this case and in *CS*, the Court determined that it was necessary for reasons relating to family life – a fundamental rights – to allow the claimant to remain. Both claimants were the sole carers of their children, so automatically refusing to allow them rights to remain would have deprived their EU citizen children of their rights under the Treaty. However, this meant ultimately that they would not be able to remain in the EU without their parent. In these cases, the Court allowed fundamental rights protection to be considered as part of its decision-making, but did not concede on its strict interpretation of the deprivation of genuine enjoyment. Fundamental rights did not play a particularly instrumental role in the final judgments, and instead seemed to be mentioned in a more cursory and symbolic manner.[89] Ultimately, the reliance was still upon whether the children would be forced out of the EU, which necessitated a consideration of elements of family life.

Later, in *Chavez-Vilchez*,[90] the *Rendón Marín* and *CS* reasoning was qualified, clarifying that even if the other parent is able and willing to assume sole responsibility of a child with EU citizenship in the territory of the EU, this did not automatically mean that TCN parents will not be able to derive a right to residency. It was especially if a relationship of dependency would nonetheless deprive the EU citizen of the genuine enjoyment of their rights and would force them to

[87] For cases on criminal law and citizenship, see Stephen Coutts, 'Union Citizenship as Probationary Citizenship: *Onuekwere*' (2015) 52 *CML Rev* 531.

[88] *Rendón Marín* (n 85) para 36.

[89] ibid para 66.

[90] Judgment of 10 May 2017, *Chavez-Vilchez* C-133/15, ECLI:EU:C:2017:354.

leave the territory of the EU. Therefore, whilst the interpretation of the deprivation of genuine enjoyment remained consistently strict, it seemed that the Court was willing to entertain a wider assessment of what it means to be forced to leave the territory of the EU before determining whether Treaty rights have been engaged. This is positive in light of the restrictive approach taken by the Court in the cases directly following *Zambrano*. However, the Court in *Chavez-Vilchez* was faced with quite specific and targeted questions, which may have forced its hand and into giving a more direct answer. Importantly, the Charter was also referenced in all three cases. Therefore, despite the limitations, the cases were decided in favour of the claimants and indirectly protected the right to private and family life.

It is perhaps for reasons of avoiding direct engagement with fundamental rights that the Court appears to prefer to apply existing alternative basis for rights conferral when deriving rights of residency for TCN family members instead of turning straight to Article 20 TFEU. It should be noted that relying upon alternative basis of rights, particularly those related to economic activity, has not amounted to as much deference to fundamental rights as compared to cases on citizenship. In the *NA* case, a TCN mother sought residency rights deriving from either her abusive ex-husband (an EU citizen) who had left the host Member State, or her children (also EU citizens) who remained with her. Because the ex-spouse had been a worker, workers' rights were chosen as the main source of derived residency rights for the claimant. Despite the situation involving clear elements of family life, especially concerning domestic violence and children, there was no mention of the Charter in the operative part of the judgment. The Court appeared to favour categorising individuals into workers or non-workers in order to clearly demarcate who should enjoy certain rights.[91] The focus was entirely on interpreting the Directive's provisions, and even clearly rejected Article 20 TFEU as a legal basis for rights because there was no crossing of borders.[92] This is an approach that the Court employed in the past and for which it was criticised because it appeared to favour economically active individuals and failed to appreciate a wider range of situations involving fundamental rights that were relevant to both non-economically active and economically active individuals.[93]

The contrast between the judgments in *Rendón Marín*, *CS* and *Chavez-Vilchez* against *NA* are striking. Understanding that all four cases involved family members and rights to residency, it is telling that when Directive 2004/38 is chosen by the Court as the preferred legal basis for rights that the situation is one characterised

[91] Judgment of 19 June 2014, *Saint Prix* C-507/12, EU:C:2014:2007; Judgment of 13 June 2013, *Hadj Ahmed* C-45/12, EU:C:2013:390.

[92] Judgment of 30 June 2016, *NA* C-115/15, EU:C:2016:487, para 80. Previously in *Hadj Ahmed* (n 91), it was made clear that a TCN family member with a residence permit did not have the same rights as EU citizens protected by the Treaty, referring mainly to rights to non-discrimination under art 18 TFEU; see para 39.

[93] See *Singh* (n 7).

by economic factors and analysing the rights of a worker. Unlike in the former three cases, the Court's refusal in *NA* to engage with the Charter rights holds some significance in general for the protection of fundamental rights and the situations in which the Court considers they are relevant. *NA* on its facts involved just as many elements of family life as the other three cases. Yet, in the former three cases, workers' rights were not relevant, and yet fundamental rights were. In *NA*, when workers' rights were relevant, fundamental rights were not. By appearing to choose either workers' rights or fundamental rights, the Court is demarcating boundaries for when it considers fundamental rights protection is and is not enforceable, which is difficult to justify normatively, especially considering the early struggles to get the Court to recognise rights of non-economically active individuals. Not only does it not align with the theory behind fundamental rights, but it is also ignorant of the rhetoric of non-discrimination as a general principle of the EU.

A second related trend in the recent case law sees the Court determining how it considers the family nucleus is defined, often under Directive 2004/38. *Despesme and Kerrou* involved claims for student financial aid that depended upon the worker status of the students' parents if they were not from the host Member State.[94] When situations concerning dependency upon stepfathers arose, the Court held that national courts had to make a factual assessment of the situation. Whether the child was biologically related to their stepfather was irrelevant, as was the reason for the dependency or amount. The situation, however, was less straightforward if TCNs and divorce were involved. In *Singh and Others*, TCNs seeking residency in Ireland after marrying EU citizens were subject to strict interpretations by the Court as to when the divorce proceedings had commenced and whether this would allow them residency rights or not.[95] If divorce proceedings commenced after the claimant had left the host Member State, they could not 'revive' the right of residence to be allowed to return.[96]

The Court appears to be attempting to strike a difficult balance between the interests of the family and also the interests of host Member States by interpreting Directive 2004/38 narrowly in *Despesme and Kerrou*. The *NA* case was similarly complicated as it involved TCN family members and divorce, but the Court was not particularly sympathetic to the plight of the claimant, despite elements of family life being blatantly clear. It can therefore be argued that excessive reliance on the Directive has often translated into a restrictive reading of the rights set out therein, and the Directive has already been noted as being less generous in terms of its scope than the Treaty provisions themselves.[97] In none of these cases does any mention of fundamental rights seem to play a decisive role. It is curious why the Court wants to diminish the role of fundamental rights when their status was so clearly upgraded when the Charter became binding in Article 6 TEU.

[94] Judgment of 15 December 2016, *Despesme and Kerrou* C-401/15, EU:C:2016:955.
[95] Judgment of 16 July 2015, *Singh and Others* C-218/14, EU:C:2015:476. See also *Reyes* (n 26).
[96] *Garcia-Nieto and Others* (n 54).
[97] See *McCarthy* (n 8); *Dereci* (n 35); *cf Zambrano* (n 10).

It is also troubling to note that this trend presented itself around the same time as the UK's vote in favour of Brexit. Even in the Court itself, fundamental rights protection was not interpreted as playing as much of a role as they were once considered to potentially be able to.[98] This has been clear from the preceding chapters. The more consistently that this became the case in the judgments by the Court, the more fundamental rights protection fades into the background. In addition, as previously mentioned, there have been some indications that the case law is beginning to resemble cases in the first age, where economic activity was the deciding factor in one's conferral of rights, and therefore the general atmosphere suggests that the Court is succumbing somewhat to the Euroscepticism in the political environment in which it finds itself deciding cases. This could arguably also have been a reason for the Brexit vote. This relationship will be discussed further, but it is a troubling consideration at this point as well.

In recent years, Directive 2004/38 has been cited in many cases that do not mention citizenship status and rights under Articles 20–21 TFEU. However, the trend that has unfolded sees the Court being more likely to interpret Directive 2004/38 narrowly, not in favour of the parties claiming rights under it. This is partially because of the way in which the Directive has been drafted and partially because the Court simply approaches the Directive provisions more strictly. The scope of rights under the Directive as compared to the Treaty is more limited, and there are fewer references to fundamental rights in cases involving the Directive because it does not directly refer to fundamental rights. It is often left in the hands of the Court, and the Court has not been as likely to reference fundamental rights lately, as seen above. Given that Directive 2004/38 was initially established to codify the case law under Articles 20–21 TFEU, questions of consistency are raised. As understood from recent case law, doing away with relying upon the cross-border test as a way of triggering the Treaty has instead meant that those who have crossed borders are to rely upon the Directive instead.[99] However, of late, interpretations by the Court of the provisions under the Directive have not been kind to certain claimants seeking rights. The Court has repeatedly scrutinised its provisions, often to clarify whether the Directive applies to individual situations that do not fall within the scope of Article 21 TFEU.

Another interesting trend that has emerged recently is cases on individuals with criminal convictions – both EU citizens and TCN family members – and their rights to remain.[100] Of particular interest to the Court is whether it could expel these individuals. In most of these cases, the claimants' rights to residency had to be balanced against the seriousness of their criminal convictions, considering whether it was proportionate to expel them. Often, a permanent residency status

[98] *Rottmann* (n 68).

[99] *McCarthy* (n 8) paras 30ff.

[100] *Onuekwere* (n 26); Judgment of 13 July 2017, *E* C-193/16, EU:C:2017:542; *Rendón Marín* (n 85); *CS* (n 86), Opinion of 24 October 2017, *B* C-316/16 and C-424/16, EU:C:2017:797. Because *Rendón Marin* and *CS* have already been discussed in the context of family life, the analysis here will focus on the other cases.

meant that the Court had less discretion and room for manoeuvre, and this factor determined the final decision. However, where the Court was given discretion to introduce other factors into its decision-making process, it did, and this was the case in *Onuekwere* and *E*.[101] In *Onuekwere*, a TCN family member of an EU citizen was imprisoned, and sought to count his time in prison as part of his period needed for permanent residency. This was rejected. In *E*, the EU citizen was in prison at the time that his expulsion decision was taken, and he argued that he did not present a genuine threat justifying expulsion because he was in prison at the time. This was also rejected. In the past, the approach was more in favour of improving the protection of citizens' rights rather than finding ways and reasons to restrict it.[102] Nowadays, to appease Member States, the opposite seems to be true.

Related to the cases on criminal convictions and residency rights is a pattern of the Court considering legal residency under the Directive itself for non-criminals. Importantly, this differs from legal residency as laid out by the Treaty under Article 21 TFEU. Again, despite questions of residency often involving delicate issues of family reunification, none of the cases to be discussed mention the Charter. Instead, the Court has stuck very methodically to a precise interpretation of provisions under the Directive, which has the effect of resulting in a specific outcome. It stated in *O and B* that: '[i]t follows from a literal, systematic and teleological interpretation of Directive 2004/38 that it does not establish a derived right of residence for third-country nationals who are family members of a Union citizen in the Member State of which that citizen is a national.'[103] Interestingly, in the *Chen* case, the Court had interpreted Article 21 TFEU as allowing a derived right of residence for TCN family members. Therefore, this confirms that when approached literally, systematically and teleologically, the Court finds Directive 2004/38 more restrictive than the Treaty.[104] It is concerning that this approach is also applied in the context of non-economically active citizens.

Ensuring strict compliance with the rules laid out in the Directive is a trend running throughout the recent case law. However, given that it is already more limited in terms of scope than the Treaty, strictly interpreting its provisions seeks to limit the scope of rights for citizens even further. For example, the residency requirements under Article 7(2) of the Directive were strictly upheld in *Alarape*, with emphasis placed on the condition of having sufficient resources.[105] This reinforces the notion that there is yet again a distinction between the non-economically active and economically active, which is also seen in the cases discussed above. The Court went on in *O and B* to emphasise that derived rights of residency for TCN family members were only available under the Directive if there

[101] *Onuekwere* (n 26) para 26; *E* (n 100) para 19.

[102] Jürgen Gerhards and Holger Lengfeld, *European Citizenship and Social Integration in the European Union* (Routledge, 2015) 168.

[103] *O and B; S and G* (n 7) para 37.

[104] Directive 2004/38 is also only available to individuals who have crossed borders.

[105] Judgment of 8 May 2013, *Alarape* C-529/11, EU:C:2013:290.

was movement.[106] This confirmed that whilst the cross-border test was no longer the determinant for whether the situation fell under the Treaty, elements of crossing borders were clearly still instrumental for the Court. In this regard, the Court appears to be placing restraints on what EU citizenship status as an independent legal basis for rights specifically entailed in terms of rights conferral. However, the effect of this is that it seems to be further limiting the scope of fundamental rights protection to influence the final decision of the Court.

Alongside the cases that are specific to citizenship in terms of Article 21 TFEU and the Directive, the cases related to the *Dano* decision and welfare benefits have attracted a lot of attention recently. Though they do not fall strictly under EU citizenship law, they do deal with citizenship and free movement principles. They are also indicative of trends in the Court's case law and have most relevance in the context of the political reality of the EU today. Most importantly in these cases on welfare benefits, the Court also considers the non-application of the Charter and other politically sensitive matters at a time of turmoil for the EU. Again, there is a lot of deference to interpretations under Directive 2004/38. The *Dano* case is one that commentators agreed was involved more with EU and Member States politics than the law.[107] This has drawn much attention of late, as it is evidence proving that the Court is unduly influenced by external factors, such as the EU's political situation, which has led to undesirable outcomes in certain cases.

A Romanian citizen and her young son moved to live in Germany with the claimant's sister. The claimant, who depended on her sister, was low skilled and unable to communicate in German. She entered with no intention to seek work, nor did she have any work experience in either Germany or Romania. When she sought a special non-contributory cash benefit for subsistence, her claim was rejected. The German court argued that she had moved for the sake of claiming benefits, which was precluded by national law. Upon analysis of the facts, the Court found that it appeared that this was true, thereby denying her claim to rights to equal treatment for welfare because the Preamble to the Directive also did not intend to allow this in her situation.[108]

It has been widely noted that the Court took a 'backseat' in *Dano* as a response to the increasing concern from national governments surrounding benefit tourism.[109] The case itself is also highly politicised because of its timing.[110]

[106] *O and B; S and G* (n 7).

[107] See Michael Blauberger and Susanne K Schmidt, 'Welfare Migration? Free Movement of EU Citizens and Access to Social Benefits' (2014) 1 *Research & Politics* 1, 3; Daniel Thym, 'The Elusive Limits of Solidarity: Residence Rights of and Social Benefits for Economically Inactive Union Citizens' (2015) 52 *CML Rev* 17, 20.

[108] *Dano* (n 26) para 71.

[109] Anne Pieter van der Mei, 'Overview of Recent Cases before the Court of Justice of the European Union (October–December 2014)' (2015) 17 *European Journal of Social Security* 103; see also Thym (n 107).

[110] 'EU "Benefit Tourism" Court Ruling is Common Sense, Says Cameron' *BBC News* (11 November 2014), www.bbc.co.uk/news/uk-politics-30002138.

Benefit tourism, which initially emerged during the EU enlargement of 2004, resurfaced as a concern and point of interest for Eurosceptic political parties as the crisis began to affect its EU citizens.[111] Though nowadays benefit tourism is considered a myth,[112] as Verschueren noted, *Dano* was 'an adequate answer to the problem of benefit tourism ... even without the adoption of Treaty amendments or amendments of secondary Union legislation'.[113] Therefore, despite it being debunked as a myth, the idea of benefit tourism still being a risk remains. It is this perception of the *Dano* case that strikes a chord. It is an example of the Court appeasing national Member States during a time of uncertainty for the EU by applying restrictions under the genuine link test.[114] This is not unlike what has been seen in the context of the *Zambrano* carer cases, especially those under the Directive. Moreover, in regards to fundamental rights, the Court was careful to exclude this consideration because the question itself was not one that implemented EU law, so fell outside the jurisdiction of the Court.[115]

The supposed 'exclusion' of the Charter is to be considered here, for the analysis thus far has been focused on the increasing wariness of the Court in allowing protection of EU fundamental rights to become part of the rights available to EU citizens under Article 20 TFEU, alongside Article 21 TFEU and the various interpretations of Article 18 TFEU from the case law. As seen from the recent cases on *Zambrano* carers, the Court has been less and less concerned with fundamental rights protection under the genuine enjoyment test and more with what constitutes being forced to exit the EU. If fundamental rights protection is mentioned, it is often tangential and its enforcement by the Court is always consistent with the notion of the deprivation of one's genuine enjoyment. Considering the constitutionalisation of the fundamental rights discourse in Article 6 TEU as well as the various developments in relation to clarifying the scope of fundamental rights,[116] there was growing support from the Court's behaviour itself for there to be a 'link' made with EU law through Article 20 TFEU – the status of one's EU citizenship and Member State nationality. Doing away with the cross-border test in *Zambrano* had the potential to make this a constitutional reality. However, as recent cases have demonstrated, it has not been the culture of the Court to embrace this

[111] In *Public Opinion in the European Union* (European Commission, Standard Eurobarometer 82, 2014) 7, it was noted that: 'Concerns about immigration continue to rise, both nationally and at [the] European level.'

[112] T Coles, PM Burns and M Novelli, 'Telling Tales of Tourism: Mobility, Media and Citizenship in the 2004 EU Enlargement' in PM Burns and M Novelli (eds), *Tourism and Mobilities* (CABI, 2008) 74.

[113] Herwig Verschueren, 'Preventing "Benefit Tourism" in the EU: A Narrow or Broad Interpretation of the Possibilities Offered by the ECJ in *Dano*?' (2015) 52 *CML Rev* 363, 370.

[114] Although restrictions were applied under the genuine link test for claimants like Ms Dano who had moved solely to claim benefits, there was no mention of the effects of this decision on other kinds of claimants, such as those who moved to exercise their rights under the Treaty – students, job-seekers and workers. Therefore, *Dano* can be limited to situations only where the claimant appears to be moving only to claim benefits and does not substantially affect broader EU citizenship rights.

[115] *Dano* (n 26) paras 91–92.

[116] Judgment of 26 February 2013, *Fransson* C-617/10, EU:C:2013:105.

rights-based approach. It is strongly questioned whether this is truly convincing in a legal but also normative sense.

The Court has remained consistent in its cases after *Dano* on welfare benefits. In *Alimanovic*, the claimant and her daughter, Swedish nationals living in Germany, did not have work-seeker status at the time of claiming benefits. The Court relied upon Directive 2004/38 and Article 24(2) to deny the claimants social assistance unless they were considered work-seekers. At the time of seeking benefits, they were not. The Court chose not to engage with fundamental rights protection and individual assessments, but rather applied a blanket approach that was established by its decision in *Dano*.[117] What appeared to be important to its final decision was the economically active status of non-nationals. This was the claimants' ultimate undoing. Again, the re-emergence of the weight of the economically active status is concerning for the future of citizenship and fundamental rights protection. Many individuals claiming rights under citizenship and fundamental rights protection are not economically active.[118] To limit the rights of certain EU citizens to these strict categories again is to create regression in the progress made towards liberating the status of EU citizenship.

The *Garcia-Nieto* case confirms the rationale behind the Court's decision-making in *Alimanovic* and *Dano*. AG Wathelet, who delivered the Opinions in *Dano*, *Alimanovic* and *Garcia-Nieto*, re-emphasised that Article 20(2) TFEU requires that citizenship status is subject to the limitations and conditions laid out in the Treaty, which has been interpreted by the Court as referring to a narrow reading of Article 52(1) of the Charter.[119] Whilst for a time there was a possibility that Article 20(2) TFEU would be interpreted favourably in terms of fundamental rights protection, as argued in the previous chapters, the trend clearly indicates the opposite, alongside an equally narrow interpretation of citizenship rights and Directive 2004/38. In *Garcia-Nieto*, again, the claimant's undoing was the fact that he was not a worker and therefore could be denied benefits under Article 24(2) of the Directive. The judgment was devoid of any reference to fundamental rights; it was a straightforward application of the *Dano* case. Like the line of case law concerning the deprivation of genuine enjoyment, the Court's message on welfare benefits is clear as far as non-economically active citizens are concerned. This represents a significant regression in the progress made towards empowering the citizen as a citizen and towards making fundamental rights protection the centre of considerations before the Court.

The Charter and its requisite fundamental rights given legal traction by Article 6 TEU should be considered as rights available to an EU citizen, given the discussion in the previous chapters leading up to this point as to the Court's decisions. However, a narrow reading of the scope of the Charter under

[117] Adrienne Yong, 'Driving a Wedge between Friends? The Court of Justice of the EU and its Citizens in the Case of Welfare Benefits' (2016) 6 *European Human Rights Law Review* 664.

[118] See n 83.

[119] *Despesme and Kerrou* (n 94) para 63.

Article 51(1) and (2) has led to an exclusion of EU fundamental rights protection entirely from several recent cases.[120] This is particularly difficult to reconcile with the previous case law, considering the Court's persuasiveness early on in *Garcia Avello* and *Grunkin and Paul* as to the scope *ratione materiae* of Article 21 TFEU. Though certain competences may be exclusive to Member States, they 'must none the less, when exercising that competence, comply with Community law'.[121] In *Garcia Avello* and *Grunkin and Paul*, fundamental rights in the Charter were not yet binding. Therefore, when it was raised in equal status to the Treaty, the logical assumption would be that fundamental rights, on a legally binding foundation in the Charter, would become more efficacious as protection for individual citizens under Article 20 TFEU. However, the Court decided instead that it did not have jurisdiction over this question of fundamental rights protection, which confirmed that fundamental rights in EU citizenship law were indeed on the decline.[122]

To the politicians of Eurosceptic Member States and, to an extent, also to the Eurosceptic public, this curtailment on further 'intrusion' into Member States' authorities appears to be a relatively satisfactory solution to the EU's encroachment on their national autonomy. This is perhaps why the trend has been continuing. However, it does not seem particularly convincing in light of the Lisbon Treaty. In this particular analysis, the Court's decisions sit uncomfortably with the potential direction identified as to constitutional rights protection under EU citizenship status. However, the political atmosphere surrounding these cases, particularly those on welfare, speak volumes towards deciphering the reasons behind the ultimate judgment of the Court. It is argued that the Court acted to allay concerns from its Member States on sensitive issues like the rights of TCN family members and the risk of benefit tourism, confirming how 'reactionary' it could be.[123] However, the reaction has not been a positive one for those who are seeking rights. The Court has limited the scope of its decisions on citizenship rights to the detriment of many claimants, particularly those with claims under the protection of fundamental rights related to citizenship.

It is clear from the assessment of the recent case law from the Court that a reactionary phenomenon was occurring in the remit of EU citizenship as it pertained to rights conferral.[124] This was especially also the case when it concerned fundamental rights protection. At this point, it is important to bring the Court's judgments

[120] *Melloni* (n 51).

[121] Judgment of 14 October 2008, *Grunkin and Paul* C-353/06, EU:C:2008:559 para 16; *Garcia Avello* (n 68) para 25.

[122] *Dano* (n 26) para 91; *cf* Judgment of 2 June 2016, *Bogendorff von Wolffersdorff* C-438/14, EU:C:2016:401.

[123] Eleanor Spaventa, 'Earned Citizenship: Understanding Union Citizenship through its Scope' in Dimitry Kochenov (ed), *EU Citizenship and Federalism: the Role of Rights* (Cambridge University Press, 2017).

[124] Niamh Nic Shuibhne, 'Limits Rising, Duties Ascending: The Changing Legal Shape of Union Citizenship' (2015) 52 *CML Rev* 889, 916 describes the jurisprudence of the Court as 'distorted and unconvincing'.

into a different political setting. The Court's increasingly restrictive behaviour is not welcomed on two levels. The first, which has been discussed throughout this book, considers its history. There appeared to be an established expectation set by the Court itself that there was going to be a relationship fostered between fundamental rights and EU citizenship to the extent that fundamental rights were inherent and necessary in any matter concerning citizens' rights. These expectations were raised when the Court made EU citizenship an independent legal basis for rights and did away with reliance on the heavily criticised cross-border test for engaging the Treaty. However, this relationship has not manifested. This is undesirable for normative reasons and for the impact it has had on claimants.

The second reason why the Court's behaviour is not welcomed is related to the first. There is a clear indication from several years of case law since the seminal *Zambrano* case that the Court seeks to limit the scope of the independent legal basis for rights under citizenship. As above, this has been criticised. However, it has been argued that this is a reaction to the political situation in the EU that has persisted until today. Herein lies the problem. Whilst it is understandable that the Court does not exist in a vacuum and is therefore going to inherently reflect and react to external pressures, the way that this has manifested itself is excessively deferential to the Member States' interests. It is argued that this may simply be a way for the Court to appease them, because the political situation in the EU has become increasingly difficult in the last decade.[125] However, whilst the Court treads a fine line as a political entity of the EU, its recent behaviour is not to be welcomed. Its activist legal culture early on is what substantiated citizenship status to begin with, and to retreat to a position that does not adequately protect the reputation and expectations set from the past in terms of rights of EU citizens is to diminish the value of the individuals at the heart of the EU.

The individuals at the heart of the EU – its citizens, nationals of all Member State of the EU under Article 20 TFEU – are those who dictate the sentiment of trust and faith in the EU as a democratic project of integration. The task of fostering an integrated EU of 28 Member States, each with a different culture, history and background, is a mammoth task in itself. In its years of working towards this goal, there have been challenges. However, none are perhaps more intriguing than navigating the UK's decision to leave the EU. The politics that have plagued the Court's decisions of late in citizenship cases have been evident and, to an extent, unwelcome. It is argued in this book that the indirect knock-on effect of the Court's less generous interpretation of citizenship provisions, especially as they pertain to fundamental rights, is that of a sentiment of discontent and dissatisfaction with the rights under EU law. Because the Court has made it a point to continually restrict the scope of citizenship rights and fundamental rights protection, the status and

[125] Gregor Aisch, Adam Pearce and Rousseau Bryant, 'How Far is Europe Swinging to the Right?' *New York Times* (23 October 2017), https://www.nytimes.com/interactive/2016/05/22/world/europe/europe-right-wing-austria-hungary.html.

value of EU citizenship has diminished accordingly. Alongside the increasingly extreme right-wing sentiment pervading national politics, EU citizens now find themselves unable to trust or rely upon EU law for protection that previously appeared to be a given.

IV. Conclusion

In the wake of the *Zambrano* and *McCarthy* cases, Kochenov argued that EU citizenship had 'acquired a life of its own'.[126] Making EU citizenship status an independent legal basis for rights could have presented many opportunities for rights to be conferred under the Treaty, mostly by expanding the scope of citizenship's protection.[127] However, most recently, there has been a different approach adopted by the Court in regards to the deprivation of genuine enjoyment test. As Wiesbrock puts it, 'the question is thus not whether Union citizenship serves any but a symbolic purpose, but where exactly the limits to its expanding reach have to be drawn'.[128] The Court has slowly but surely applied this test, not to liberalise the status of EU citizenship, but rather to add greater restrictions on whether individuals can fall under the Treaty's scope of protection.

Originally, a relationship between EU citizenship and fundamental rights was considered 'little more than a cynical exercise in public relations on the part of the High Contracting Parties'.[129] However, as this book has argued, the relationship became more of a tangible reality because of the way in which the Court interpreted fundamental rights in EU citizenship law. Both concepts, when applied together, had proven effective in enhancing protection of individual rights[130] and, by linking the two, it was thought that this could also help to improve the sense of solidarity and legitimacy in the EU.[131] However, it became increasingly evident in the third age that although this was one direction that the EU citizenship development could have followed, the Court had a different intention in mind that opposed the hypothesis of this book at the outset that there was potential for a relationship between fundamental rights and citizenship because of their similar objectives and focus.

[126] Dimitry Kochenov, 'The Right to Have What Rights? EU Citizenship in Need of Clarification' (2013) 19 *European Law Journal* 502, 508.

[127] This refers to the fact that there was a chance that TCNs could potentially be brought within the scope of the Treaty by means of fundamental rights protection.

[128] Anja Wiesbrock, 'Disentangling the "Union Citizenship Puzzle"? The *McCarthy* Case' (2011) 36 *European Law Review* 861, 862.

[129] Joseph Weiler, 'Citizenship and Human Rights' in Jan A Winter et al (eds), *Reforming the Treaty on the European Union* (Kluwer Law International, 1996) 57.

[130] See *Chen* (n 17); *Carpenter* (n 17).

[131] See Michael Dougan, 'The Spatial Restructuring of National Welfare States within the European Union: The Contribution of Union Citizenship and the Relevance of the Treaty of Lisbon' in Ruth Nielsen, Ulla Neergaard and Lynn Roseberry (eds), *Integrating Welfare Functions into EU Law: From Rome to Lisbon* (DJØF Publishing, 2009).

EU citizens are facing a crisis of faith in the EU. It is argued that the Court's deferential behaviour seen in the most recent citizenship cases does not help to reassure citizens that there is value and worth in supporting an 'ever closer Union'.[132] This is especially when it purports to exclude fundamental rights protection. The most poignant example of this crisis manifesting in a Member State is the vote in favour of leaving the EU by the British electorate in June 2016. Whilst the exact reasons for the outcome of the EU referendum cannot be pinpointed, the rhetoric that ran throughout many of the campaigns in favour of leaving the EU related to concerns about immigration.[133] Many recent cases on citizenship rights involve TCN family members and their rights to remain, and as mentioned previously, the Court has not been particularly generous when handling these claims. Therefore, the argument is that the CJEU refusing to empower citizens of the EU with their rights under the Treaty has not helped to minimise the effect of the increasingly Eurosceptic sentiment that has been slowly increasing over the years.[134]

It is for this reason that fundamental rights protection was the supported route, because the Court had the scope to confer greater rights upon citizens using this as a legal basis. However, it chose to turn away from this line of reasoning and instead towards greater limitations to appease Member States. The next chapter will discuss how this choice relates to the vote in favour of leaving the EU for the UK and how troubling it is that the Court is shying away from fundamental rights at a time when they are ever more necessary. Compounded by the fact that there was an expectation set by the Court in the past concerning the relationship between fundamental rights and EU citizenship status, it seems that this problem is only the beginning in the saga concerning EU Member States and the EU in the context of protection of individual rights.

[132] Preamble to the TEU.

[133] Heather Stewart and Rowena Mason, 'Nigel Farage's Anti-migrant Poster Reported to Police' *The Guardian* (16 June 2016), https://www.theguardian.com/politics/2016/jun/16/nigel-farage-defends-ukip-breaking-point-poster-queue-of-migrants.

[134] In *European Citizenship* (European Commission, Standard Eurobarometer 89, 2018), it states that: 'Since autumn 2017 the sense of European citizenship has gained ground in 15 EU Member States … However, it has lost ground in ten countries.'

5

Fundamental Rights and EU Citizenship in a Eurosceptic EU

I. Introduction

This book has identified three ages of EU citizenship, with the triggers for each new age of citizenship identified as the constitutional landmarks in the development. The first landmark was the introduction of citizenship in Article 8 EEC in the Maastricht Treaty. The second was the *Sala* case, which marked the end of citizenship being perceived as merely a cosmetic exercise, and the beginning of the Court's interaction with fundamental rights protection under the guise of non-discrimination. The third was the introduction of the Lisbon Treaty, after which the Court made EU citizenship an independent legal basis for rights. Article 6 TEU also strengthened the legal enforcement of fundamental rights. However, it has become clear now that the constitutionalisation of fundamental rights in the Treaty has not encouraged the Court to integrate fundamental rights into citizenship law. For this reason, the development has regressed in terms of the scope *ratione personae* and *ratione materiae* of EU citizenship rights, diminishing the value of fundamental rights protection as part of the protection afforded to citizens.

Initially, the shift from the first to the second age of citizenship saw the Court broadening the scope of EU citizenship rights as they pertained to non-economically active citizens. It has been argued that fundamental rights were instrumental to this, albeit indirectly at first, through the principle of non-discrimination. The second age then saw the Court dedicated to expanding the scope *ratione personae* and *ratione materiae* of citizenship further, so that fundamental rights protection had potential to significantly influence the Court's ultimate decisions on EU citizenship cases. This developed more explicitly in cases on the right to family life, the right to identity and occasionally with cases that only indirectly involved EU citizenship rights.[1] However, the developments of the third

[1] Judgment of 2 October 2003, *Garcia Avello* C-148/02, EU:C:2003:539; Judgment of 19 October 2004, *Zhu and Chen* C-200/02, EU:C:2004:639; Judgment of 11 July 2002, *Carpenter* C-60/00, EU:C:2002:434; Judgment of 25 July 2002, *MRAX* C-459/99, EU:C:2002:461; Judgment of 14 October 2008, *Grunkin and Paul* C-353/06, EU:C:2008:559; Judgment of 25 July 2008, *Metock and Others* C-127/08, EU:C:2008:449; Judgment of 12 July 2001, *Peerbooms* C-157/99, EU:C:2001:404.

age of citizenship after Lisbon saw a departure from this generous rights-based approach, as the previous chapter has shown. This chapter therefore purports to explain the reasons for this in political terms.

This book has demonstrated thus far that there was an early rise in fundamental rights protection before the Court, and now an obvious decline. There seems to be little appetite in effecting change in the current relationship between fundamental rights and EU citizenship as it continues to decline. This chapter argues that there are highly politicised reasons for these choices. Though unrelated to the specific substance of EU citizenship matters, the EU is facing a crisis and this has had a notable effect on its citizens.[2] It is argued that the Court's reaction to this has been to restrict the application of fundamental rights under citizenship status. This has the effect of deferring to its Member States in the interests of striking a balance between protecting individual rights and protecting national autonomy. Whilst this may provide something of an explanation, this cannot be an excuse.

A relationship between fundamental rights and EU citizenship has been the main hypothesis underlying the analysis in this book. A fuller explanation for how this relationship can be imagined is established here. The focus is on the wider human rights implications of this relationship, and the justifications for supporting more integration of fundamental rights protection when interpreting rights under citizenship status. These are mainly in terms of the enforcement and strength of the ECHR as a human rights treaty, and the commitment that has been clear from the EU in terms of fundamental rights protection.[3] However, there are difficulties and clear limitations that need to be laid out to protect the integrity of Member States' autonomy, because introducing the ECHR to situations where the EU itself has established its own constitutional limits presents a problem. AG Sharpston's Opinion in *Zambrano* is analysed here as it is a good exposition of the considerations necessary in striking a balance when fundamental rights are involved. However, there are some constitutional limits that even enforcement of the ECHR cannot overcome. This may prove to be the Achilles' heel for citizenship and fundamental rights.

The chapter begins with an introduction to the crisis in the EU and how it has affected citizens in the context of citizenship and fundamental rights rather than economically. The concept of Euroscepticism and rising nationalism is contextualised in the case law of the Court to draw the conclusion that the Court is reacting to appease Member States in light of their increasing dissatisfaction with the EU project. Then there is a broader discussion on the value of linking fundamental rights with EU citizenship, which brings the ECHR into focus. The ECHR being outside the EU framework is a more targeted source of rights protection that has

[2] *European Citizenship* (European Commission, Standard Eurobarometer 89, 2018).

[3] Opinion of 28 March 1996, Opinion 2/94, EU:C:1996:140, Opinion of 18 December 2014, Opinion 2/13, EU:C:2014:2454, Judgment of 18 June 1991, *ERT* C-260/89, EU:C:1991:254, Judgment of 18 July 2013, *Kadi II* C-584/10, EU:C:2013:518.

the potential to liberalise the relationship between EU citizenship and fundamental rights. However, this assertion is not boundless and limitations are acknowledged here as well. The chapter concludes by considering the struggle of aligning the ECHR with rights under EU citizenship status in both constitutional and political terms. All this discussion is intended to provide a prelude to the next chapter, which considers the conclusions made as to the relationship between fundamental rights and citizenship in the context of the crisis now facing the UK – that of its withdrawal from the EU.

II. The Effect of Europe's Crisis on its Citizens

The late 2000s marked the beginning of the eurozone debt crisis.[4] It was widely known as the 'Eurocrisis' and this term was pertinent for its substance (concerning the monetary and financial situation) as well as scope in terms of encompassing the problems facing Europe. The negativity that such problems generated is known as Euroscepticism. This refers to the general sentiment of uncertainty and criticism surrounding the benefits of the EU as an economic, political and social entity, mostly related to integration.[5] It is the notion that individuals in the EU do not feel they benefit from its existence, and the impact on the feeling of solidarity within individuals in the community as well as the legitimacy of the EU's provisions and governance.

EU citizenship was a product of the Maastricht Treaty, and Taggart argues that Maastricht 'seemed to act as a spur to dissent' for Euroscepticism as well.[6] For this reason, there is a correlation between the poor initial reception of EU citizenship amongst its citizens and the general feeling of Euroscepticism from Maastricht around the same time. Many of the sentiments that existed then have yet to subside today, as Eurobarometer polls demonstrate.[7] These negative sentiments have been exacerbated by the crisis that the EU is currently facing, the effects of which are felt beyond the financial realm.[8] When the eurozone entered its debt crisis,

[4] Alicia Hinarejos, 'Fiscal Federalism in the European Union: Evolution and Future Choices for EMU' (2013) 50 *CML Rev* 1621, 1627. See also 'Greece's Debt Reaches 300bn Euros' *BBC News* (10 December 2009), http://news.bbc.co.uk/1/hi/business/8406665.stm.

[5] Paul Taggart, 'A Touchstone of Dissent: Euroscepticism in Contemporary Western European Party Systems' (1998) 33 *European Journal of Political Research* 363, 365.

[6] ibid 363.

[7] See *Public Opinion in the European Union* (European Commission, Standard Eurobarometer 89, 2018): 'While levels of trust in the European Parliament and the European Commission have improved considerably, the recovery of trust in the European Union in general is less perceptible. Trust has increased only slightly since autumn 2017 (+1 percentage point) and a majority of respondents, with an unchanged score, continue to distrust the European Union.'

[8] Simon Usherwood and Nick Startin, 'Euroscepticism as a Persistent Phenomenon' (2013) 51 *Journal of Common Market Studies* 1, 4.

satisfaction plummeted further,[9] hence the increasing nationalism and backlash towards the EU institutions.[10] Nowadays, the legitimacy crisis facing the EU is that of its Member States' growing dissatisfaction with the laws operating within their own national authorities, most recently in relation to the free movement of persons and equal treatment to social welfare benefits.[11] At its core, the matter was a question of a lack of solidarity between the EU and its Member States.[12] This had been noted by the Court and fed into its decision-making process with an impact on EU citizenship that was particularly evident in the cases of the third age. The outcome has been the opposite of what was initially proposed as to fundamental rights integration.

The problems of Euroscepticism, especially as they relate to the relationship between citizenship and fundamental rights, were unsurprising when considering the nature of fundamental rights protection itself within the framework of a supranational EU. As Muir notes, 'systems for the protection of fundamental rights inevitably constitute a challenge to the authority of decision-makers',[13] causing tension at the very outset. The challenge she refers to is the tension between fundamental rights as human rights intended to be a universal means of protection, and the EU as a supranational entity operating within territorial boundaries. These problems are the same problems seen in the context of fundamental rights and the relationship between these and EU citizenship, attributable to EU citizenship's problems as a concept defined by its exclusivity within the EU. It is argued that the introduction of social and political elements like less implicit fundamental rights protection and the creation of a citizenship of the EU caused some controversy when they were introduced. Such non-economic concepts were not originally envisaged to be part of the EU when it was first established in the 1950s.[14]

[9] *The Euro Area, 2009, Public Attitudes and Perceptions, Analytical Report* (European Commission, Flash Eurobarometer 279, 2018) 66 states that 'the level of optimism is still lower than two years ago, before the outbreak of the financial and economic crisis in the euro area.'

[10] Daniela Braun and Markus Tausendpfund, 'The Impact of the Euro Crisis on Citizens' Support for the European Union' (2014) 36 *Journal of European Integration* 231.

[11] See the uproar surrounding the Judgment of 11 November 2014, *Dano* C-333/13, EU:C:2014:2358 on benefit tourism in the British media particularly; 'EU "Benefit Tourism" Court Ruling is Common Sense, Says Cameron' *BBC News* (11 November 2014), www.bbc.co.uk/news/uk-politics-30002138; Nicholas Watt and Kate Connolly, 'Merkel Suggests a Deal Can Be Reached over Cameron's EU Demands' *The Guardian* (29 May 2015), http://www.theguardian.com/world/2015/may/29/angela-merkel-hints-revising-lisbon-treaty-accommodate-david-cameron-demands; see also Ben Riley-Smith, 'Labour Says EU Immigrants Should Be Banned for Two Years from Getting Jobless Benefits' *The Telegraph* (18 November 2014), www.telegraph.co.uk/news/politics/labour/11238587/Labour-says-EU-immigrants-should-be-banned-for-two-years-from-getting-jobless-benefits.html.

[12] On models of solidarity, see Catherine Barnard, 'EU Citizenship and the Principle of Solidarity' in Michael Dougan and Eleanor Spaventa (eds), *Social Welfare and EU Law* (Hart Publishing, 2005). On Euroscepticism more generally, see Taggart (n 5).

[13] Elise Muir, 'Fundamental Rights: An Unsettling EU Competence' (2014) 15 *Human Rights Review* 25, 29.

[14] The text of the ECSC, Euratom and EEC Treaties all do not mention human rights protection.

Groenendijk also highlights the problem facing the Court in EU citizenship law as it entered the third age, which was that the Eurocrisis was unlikely to 'create a fertile environment for such radical changes'.[15] Changes such as introducing an integrated fundamental rights *acquis* to the Court's interpretation of EU citizenship law would be made more difficult as a result. Furthermore, the Court had already faced obstacles for over 15 years to reach its current position where it would be potentially justifiable to integrate fundamental rights and citizenship.[16] Because 'the Treaties establish a transnational paradigm of EU citizenship based on Member State territoriality',[17] it had been difficult from the outset to generate common EU solidarity between its citizens. Therefore, this normative dilemma presented the Court with yet more obstacles, and growing dissatisfaction with the EU leading to its political crisis has added to the tense political atmosphere. This has clearly overshadowed the constitutional indicators in the case law (such as *Rottmann* and *Zambrano* broadening the scope of EU citizenship status) and the Treaties (such as Article 6 TEU) that, if interpreted differently, could have mitigated the political effects of the crisis and influenced the Court's judicial reasoning in a more favourable light towards its citizens. However, trying to resolve the problems faced by citizenship in the EU in this context is a difficult task. There is not a straightforward way to balance interests and there is a fine line to tread to avoid stepping on Member States' toes.

Leconte has noted that 'hostility toward the [EU fundamental rights policy] may be analyzed as a form of Euroscepticism'.[18] She argues that what she terms 'value-based Euroscepticism' is the idea that more integration will amount to more interference with the protection of values such as fundamental rights. The argument advanced in this chapter is consistent with this – that the reason for the Court's hesitance of late is the fact that it is cognisant of the rising Euroscepticism in Member States and is therefore acting to mitigate judicial interference that could potentially worsen the sentiment. There is a correlation between the emergence of Euroscepticism and the introduction of greater fundamental rights policies and protection in the mid-1990s. This is both at a judicial level in the Court with the *ERT* case,[19] and institutionally with the establishment in 1994 of the European Monitoring Centre for Racism and Xenophobia (EUMC), later the European Union Agency for Fundamental Rights.[20] Drawing upon Leconte's point, then, it is

[15] Kees Groenendijk, 'Reverse Discrimination, Family Reunification and Union Citizens of Immigrant Origin' in Elspeth Guild, Cristina Gortázar and Dora Kostakopoulou (eds), *The Reconceptualization of European Union Citizenship* (Martinus Nijhoff, 2014) 463.

[16] As evident in the case law in the second age, where fundamental rights became more of a factor in the ultimate decision-making process – see *Carpenter* (n 1); *Garcia Avello* (n 1); *Chen* (n 1).

[17] Loïc Azoulai, 'The (Mis)Construction of the European Individual: Two Essays on Union Citizenship Law' [2014] *EUI Department of Law Research Paper 2014/14*, 2.

[18] Cécile Leconte, 'The EU Fundamental Rights Policy as a Source of Euroscepticism' (2014) 15 *Human Rights Review* 83, 84.

[19] *ERT* (n 3).

[20] Or the Fundamental Rights Agency (FRA).

argued that greater fundamental rights protection that could incite more 'interference' into national autonomy and that this would also incite negativity towards the body that is the vehicle for such 'interference' – the CJEU.

It is perhaps for this reason that a fundamental rights and EU citizenship relationship was less well received when it was realised as a potential reality after the *Zambrano* judgment due to the liberalisation of the status of EU citizenship. Despite the incremental development of fundamental rights protection and EU citizenship status before the Court in the past, the current reality of the political situation in the EU and in EU Member States could not be ignored. It appears especially difficult to reconcile greater rights protection in cases where the issue is so politically sensitive and imposes a greater burden on national interests, such as welfare. The competing strands of reasoning – one from EU law that supports greater conferral of individual rights and the other on a national level that is more protectionist – raises difficult questions for the Court. It is increasingly evident that its response of late has mainly been to appease Member States. Whilst this is not necessarily outside the Court's prerogative, it is nonetheless argued that the trend is not consistent with the constitutional discourse that promoted fundamental rights protection. To side with Member States for such politicised reasons perpetuates the notion that the Court is too easily influenced by its political atmosphere to the detriment of legal certainty for its subjects. This has been an underlying problem for EU citizenship status for many years.

A. Struggles of the Status of EU Citizenship

As this book has outlined thus far, the Court struggled early on balancing interests under the guise of the status of EU citizenship, particularly when the status was interpreted alongside other economic EU concepts.[21] Problems have mainly arisen because EU citizenship case law involves non-economically active individuals as well as TCN family members, and these categories of individuals have not historically been treated favourably. This has affected the EU's objective of fostering legitimacy and solidarity with the EU, which is an ongoing project.[22] It is still difficult to depart entirely from the EU's original economic origins and from adopting a partially 'market-based' approach to any social or political concept, especially one like EU citizenship status. However, during the second age, it is argued that the Court successfully overcame these obstacles by means of promoting the protection

[21] See Judgment of 12 May 1998, *Martinez Sala* C-85/96, EU:C:1998:217; Judgment of 15 March 2005, *Bidar* C-209/03, EU:C:2005:169; Judgment of 7 September 2004, *Trojani* C-456/02, EU:C:2004:488; Judgment of 11 July 2002, *D'hoop* C-224/98, EU:C:2002:432.

[22] Koen Lenaerts, 'European Union Citizenship, National Welfare Systems and Social Solidarity' (2011) 2 *Jurisprudencija* 397, 418. See also the discussion in Craig Calhoun, 'Imagining Solidarity: Cosmopolitanism, Constitutional Patriotism, and the Public Sphere' (2002) 14 *Public Culture* 147.

of fundamental rights. Unfortunately, of late, the Court has distanced itself from continuing to adopt this rights-based approach. This is what is criticised in this book and what this chapter seeks to clarify the reasons for.

Criticism in the literature of the legal concept of EU citizenship is mainly in regards to its lack of clarity as to scope.[23] There is a link between this and EU citizenship's dependence upon nationality. EU citizenship relies on this national status, and the CJEU must defer to Member State's prerogatives in terms of determining whether an individual is a national and therefore whether they are also an EU citizen.[24] Though the *Rottmann* decision allegedly calls this principle into question, it is still the premise upon which EU citizenship was based at the outset. In legal terms, this is retained in Article 20 TFEU. It is unlikely that this will change in the foreseeable future.[25] As a political statement, it is also unlikely to be wise to detach EU citizenship status from nationality. The nationality prerequisite affords a level of autonomy to national authorities that is likely to be something the Member States would value the preservation of.[26]

However, having to be a national of an EU Member State as a prerequisite to attaining EU citizenship status has emphasised the distinctions that territorial borders represent, thereby also seemingly undermining the status of a transnational identity like citizenship of the EU. This safeguarding of territorial borders has added to the struggles faced by the Court in EU citizenship towards fostering legitimacy amongst its subjects, for without this legitimacy, there cannot be solidarity.[27] It was thought that the influence of the fundamental rights discourse would overcome such barriers given its own universality, with the Court able to put less emphasis on the strict conditions of the scope *ratione personae* of citizenship. The more citizens felt that they were protected by the rights afforded to them by virtue of Article 20 TFEU, the more likely it would be that they would feel solidarity with the EU. Fundamental rights could have also encouraged a broader set of rights available under the scope *ratione materiae* of citizenship. However, the reality is that the Court has been unwilling to transcend such boundaries to the detriment of greater individual fundamental rights protection through the status of EU citizenship.

The political atmosphere in which the Court finds itself deciding cases has decidedly influenced its legal culture. The Court has seen shifts in this culture

[23] Eleanor Spaventa, 'Seeing the Wood Despite the Trees? On the Scope of Union Citizenship and its Constitutional Effects' (2008) 45 *CML Rev* 13, 44; Niamh Nic Shuibhne, 'Seven Questions for Seven Paragraphs' (2011) 36 *European Law Review* 161, 162; Anja Wiesbrock, 'Disentangling the "Union Citizenship Puzzle"? The *McCarthy* Case' (2011) 36 *European Law Review* 861, 2091.

[24] Judgment of 7 July 1992, *Micheletti* C-369/90, EU:C:1992:295; Judgment of 20 February 2001, *Kaur* C-192/99, EU:C:2001:106.

[25] Article 48 TEU.

[26] See Paul Magnette, *Citizenship: The History of An Idea* (ECPR, 2005); Derek Heater, *What is Citizenship?* (Polity Press, 1999); David Miller, *On Nationality* (Clarendon Press, 1995).

[27] Takis Tridimas, *The General Principles of EU Law*, 2nd edn (Oxford University Press, 2006) 298.

throughout the development of EU citizenship, from taking an economic approach to free movement and rights, to stringent application of judicial instruments and their relevant tests, to now applying and interpreting the independent legal basis of EU citizenship rights restrictively. However, these changes have not only made the application of the law legally uncertain, but have also resulted in unforeseeable outcomes, especially as they relate to protection of the individual in the EU as a citizen. Because the EU institutions are wary of the problems they face as a result of its political crisis,[28] there is a link to be made between this and the increasingly cautious behaviour by the Court in its citizenship case law when applying fundamental rights protection. This has resulted in increasingly regressive decisions as to the scope *ratione personae* and *ratione materiae* in the third age of EU citizenship.

In a supranational construct like the EU, it is more understandable that the judicial institution's legal culture is influenced by external political factors because the structure lends itself to such considerations. Driven by the constitutionalisation of the fundamental rights discourse and growing commitment to values outside those of the EU's internal market, the legal culture of the Court in EU citizenship cases did shift somewhat, which helped to substantiate the concept of EU citizenship by focusing less on economic rights of consumers and more on individual fundamental rights of citizens. The Court demonstrated both an interest in deferring to Member States and at the same time a willingness to broaden the scope *ratione personae* and *ratione materiae* to better protect its individual citizens.[29] It increasingly utilised fundamental rights as the justification for this, as the previous chapters have argued.

The argument here, however, is that there is a correlation in time between the Eurocrisis, the EU's most widely recognised and public time of crisis, and the Lisbon Treaty coming into force. Both occurred within a week of each other.[30] The Lisbon Treaty itself had come under fire in its previous form as the draft Treaty establishing a Constitution for Europe. Arguably, there was still scepticism even when it evolved into the Lisbon Treaty because, after all, it was noted that 'the innovations of the Constitutional Treaty have to a very large extent been preserved'.[31] Early rejections of this Treaty pre-ratification by the Dutch and French were followed by the Irish rejection, with the protection of national identity given as the reason for the 'no' vote.[32] It is argued that this sentiment has possibly trickled down into

[28] Mark Dawson and Floris de Witte, 'Constitutional Balance in the EU after the Euro-Crisis' (2013) 76 *MLR* 817, 824.

[29] As per the development in cases outlined in ch 2.

[30] The beginning of the eurozone crisis is accredited to Greece's declaration that its debt had reached 'the highest level in its modern history'. See 'Greece's Debt Reaches 300bn Euros' (n 4).

[31] Sebastian Kurpas, *The Treaty of Lisbon: How Much 'Constitution' is Left?* (CEPS Policy Brief No 147, 2007). See also Espen DH Olsen, *Transnational Citizenship in the European Union* (Bloomsbury, 2012) 112 for his take on the effects of the Draft Constitution's rejection on citizenship.

[32] 'Les résultats département par département' *Le Monde* (27 May 2005), www.lemonde.fr/societe/infographie/2005/05/27/les-resultats-departement-par-departement_655042_3224.html; 'Dutch Say

the interpretations of the citizenship provisions, especially as citizenship status is one most closely related to identity. It was poor timing for the citizenship concept, given that prior to this there had already been speculation about an independent legal basis for the conferral of citizenship rights through Article 20 TFEU, which had been anticipated for some time.[33] Therefore, it would appear that the Court had to balance, on the one hand, acceptance of the constitutionalisation of citizenship and fundamental rights as the development indicated, but, on the other hand, ensure there were not more reasons for Member States to be sceptical of the EU and its institutions.

The correlation between the timing of the EU's political crisis and the CJEU's regression in terms of expanding the scope of EU citizenship to accommodate fundamental rights protection may be a reason why the judgments under Article 20 TFEU set such a high threshold for the new deprivation of genuine enjoyment test. The case of *Zambrano* itself has been declared an exception on several occasions,[34] which downplayed the effects of its decision in terms of the guarantees of protection it could have offered. For the fundamental right to family life, the fundamental status of EU citizenship and Article 20 TFEU as an independent source of citizenship rights, the *Zambrano* case was welcomed. However, upon realising that this would actually amount to a significant level of compromise from the Member States in terms of their autonomy, especially as to greater protection of fundamental rights, the CJEU began to exhibit signs of worry as the EU came under more political, economic and social pressure.[35]

It was telling that in a time of austerity in Europe where even its citizens did not feel solidarity between themselves (and Member States even less so), certain types of citizen trying to claim rights would prompt the CJEU to display a greater degree of caution when conferring such rights.[36] The Court's willingness to protect

"No" to EU Constitution' *BBC News* (2 June 2005), http://news.bbc.co.uk/1/hi/4601439.stm; *Post-referendum Survey in Ireland* (European Commission, Flash Eurobarometer No 245, 2008) 7. See Paul O'Neill and Susan R Sandler, 'The EU Citizenship Acquis and the Court of Justice: Citizenship Vigilante or Merely Vigilant Treaty Guardian' (2008) 7 *Richmond Journal of Global Law and Business* 205, 208.

[33] See Francis G Jacobs, 'Citizenship of the European Union: A Legal Analysis' (2007) 13 *European Law Journal* 591; Dora Kostakopoulou, 'Ideas, Norms and European Citizenship: Explaining Institutional Change' (2005) 68 *MLR* 233.

[34] See Judgment of 5 May 2011, *McCarthy* C-434/09, EU:C:2011:277; Judgment of 15 November 2011, *Dereci* C-256/11, EU:C:2011:734; and commentary by Alicia Hinarejos, 'Citizenship of the EU: Clarifying 'Genuine Enjoyment of the Substance' of Citizenship Rights' (2012) 71 *CLJ* 279, 280; Chiara Raucea, 'Fundamental Rights: The Missing Pieces of European Citizenship' (2013) 14 *German Law Journal* 2021, 2031; James McConnon, '*Dereci*: An Analysis of the Genuine Enjoyment Test and European Union Citizenship under Articles 20 and 21 TFEU' (2012) 15 *Trinity College Law Review* 119, 125.

[35] Arguably the reason for its decisions after *Zambrano* until today.

[36] This is directly comparable to the cases decided on the free movement of students and the exportability of student benefits around the same time, which were more generous and less controversial because they only concerned EU citizens. See Judgment of 18 July 2013, *Prinz and Seeberger* C-523/11, EU:C:2013:524; Judgment of 24 October 2013, *Thiele Meneses* C-220/12, EU:C:2013:683; Judgment of 21 February 2013, *LN* C-46/12, EU:C:2013:97; Judgment of 4 October 2012,

these EU citizens, as compared to either static EU citizens, TCN family members or those who did not display 'good' behaviour, is more evident. However, even this was not always consistent and depended entirely on the legal basis the Court decided to adopt at the time – this changed depending on the economic activity of the individual.[37] It is this lack of legal certainty which the introduction of a fundamental rights discourse could have mitigated, because of its less discriminate nature as compared to EU citizenship status and the various categories of economically active citizen. However, it is clear now that the Court intends to continue to scrutinise claims to citizenship rights in a manner that seems to mimic how it decided cases in the first age of citizenship, in lieu of considering fundamental rights protection.

Schrauwen recognised that the heading 'Fundamental Rights and Citizenship of the Union' did not make the final Lisbon Treaty text because of the 'mandate to abandon the constitutional concept'.[38] However, she noted that this constitutional concept was nonetheless present in EU citizenship itself as it existed in the Treaty. This book has recognised that there was an intention for fundamental rights to become more constitutionally relevant in the Lisbon Treaty, but has come up against an unexpected political crisis.[39] Though it has elaborated the role that fundamental rights has played throughout the development of EU citizenship law since its inception, it recognised that despite having built up so much anticipation, a predicted relationship between the two concepts of rights is unlikely to materialise as expected. Though the trajectory towards this has not been unjustified, it is clear that in today's political atmosphere of crisis, the increasing dominance of Eurosceptics and nationalists has all but forced the Court to allay their concerns by issuing conservative judgments that encourage a narrower interpretation of scope.

Von Bogdandy argues that fundamental rights and EU citizenship emerged 'in reaction to the pressing legitimacy question'. He further argues that they are 'two mutually strengthening concepts which essentially pursue the very same objective, i.e. to bring the Union closer to the individual'.[40] For this reason, the effects

Commission v Austria C-75/11, EU:C:2012:605; Judgment of 14 June 2012, *Commission v The Netherlands* C-542/09, EU:C:2012:346; Judgment of 26 February 2015, *Martens* C-359/13, EU:C:2015:118. On language, see also Judgment of 27 March 2014, *Rüffer* C-322/13, EU:C:2014:189. *cf* cases on criminals – see Judgment of 16 January 2014, *Onuekwere* C-378/12, EU:C:2014:13; Judgment of 10 July 2014, *Ogieriakhi* C-244/13, EU:C:2014:2068; Judgment of 13 September 2016, *Rendón Marín* C-165/14, EU:C:2016:675; Judgment of 13 September 2016, *CS* C-304/14, EU:C:2016:674.

[37] See Judgment of 23 March 2004, *Collins* C-138/02, EU:C:2004:172; Judgment of 4 June 2009, *Vatsouras* C-22/08, EU:C:2009:344; *Carpenter* (n 1).

[38] Annette Schrauwen, 'European Union Citizenship in the Treaty of Lisbon: Any Change at All' (2008) 15 *Maastricht Journal of European and Comparative Law* 55, 57.

[39] Fundamental rights have not even been relevant in the context of the Eurocrisis; see Sionaidh Douglas-Scott, 'Fundamental Rights Not Euroscepticism: Why the UK Should Embrace the EU Charter' [2014] *Legal Research Paper Series* 1, 10.

[40] Armin von Bogdandy et al, 'Reverse *Solange*: Protecting the Essence of Fundamental Rights against EU Member States' (2012) 49 *CML Rev* 489, 506.

on EU legitimacy and solidarity are more obvious when considering that the relationship between fundamental rights and EU citizenship has not materialised as expected. This unforeseen constitutional crisis in the EU has had a knock-on effect on the EU's overarching goal since 1957 of achieving an 'ever-closer Union'.[41] For this reason as well, McCauliff argues that 'the Court is at a crossroads because it has the Charter of Rights dangling before it as both the sword of Damocles and a siren call'.[42] The difficulties that the Court faces when balancing fundamental rights protection with adequate reactions to the political atmosphere in which it finds itself are not easily reconciled, and politics has prevailed more often than not. This is not a supported approach, especially when there has been such a strong constitutionally driven push towards greater fundamental rights protection by way of making the Charter of Fundamental Rights binding.

B. The Effect of the Charter of Fundamental Rights

This book has presented its intention at the outset of demonstrating that EU citizenship law under Article 20 TFEU and fundamental rights as recognised by the EU were inherently linked and that, having recognised this, the Court would eventually come to integrate the two concepts as part of its normative reasoning. It has been argued that both concepts converged because EU citizenship and fundamental rights law appeared to be directed towards the same goal – the empowerment of the citizen as a citizen. The fundamental rights rhetoric was particularly influenced by the constitutional changes in the Treaties,[43] and this was seen to be especially influential in the evolution of EU citizenship law. However, because the Court has chosen to opt instead for a conservative approach influenced by the Eurosceptical political discourse in its Member States, this argument now bears less conviction.

Article 6(1) TEU raises the Charter of Fundamental Rights to equal status with that of the Treaties. In the 2014 Report on the Application of the EU Charter of Fundamental Rights,[44] statistics showed that the Charter had been increasingly referred to by the EU Courts since 2011,[45] with a particular noted rise in references to the Charter as they pertained to citizens' rights in 2014. This painted a rather more positive picture and is at odds with the interim conclusion reached earlier as to the declining fundamental rights influence in recent cases on citizenship.

[41] Treaty of Rome (Treaty Establishing the European Economic Community), Preamble; art 1 TEU.

[42] CMA McCauliff, 'EU Citizenship: Why Can't the Advocates General Keep Sheila McCarthy's Family Together' (2013) 36 *Fordham International Law Journal* 1372, 1378.

[43] Article 6 TEU.

[44] Vera Jourova, *2014 Report on the Application of the EU Charter of Fundamental Rights* (DG Justice, Consumers and Gender Equality, 2014).

[45] This includes all three Courts: the General Court, the Court of First Instance and the Court of Justice.

However, it is argued here that the reason for this disparity is that referencing the Charter is not the same as considering Charter rights in the operative parts of the judgment.[46] Therefore, these numbers cannot be entirely relied upon to prove that the Charter has been more effective since coming into binding force, especially not in EU citizenship law.[47] In the more recent 2017 report as well, the focus was rather more on the different initiatives that the Charter inspired and on emphasising that in the testing times: 'It has never been more important to highlight that respect for the Charter of Fundamental Rights is not an option but an obligation for EU institutions and the Member States when implementing EU law.'[48]

This is not to say that the Charter had no impact after the Lisbon Treaty. It is simply demonstrative of a more recent decline in its consideration by the Court for EU citizenship in particular. There are examples of the Charter itself becoming more effective after the Lisbon Treaty, which added to the discussion around the constitutionalisation of fundamental rights.[49] Cases have been decided which appeared to broaden the scope of the Charter too, as well as its horizontal effects.[50] Muir argues that '[t]he expansion of EU fundamental rights law stretches to the limits the doctrine that carefully circumscribes the process of European integration',[51] given that these rights would demand greater attention as a result of deeper EU integration. This is also the premise behind the initial argument that making EU citizenship status an independent legal basis for rights would require the Court to also protect EU fundamental rights, thereby also deepening EU integration.

However, Kokott and Sobotta note generally that with the introduction of the Lisbon Treaty, fundamental rights have not changed in scope, as they are constrained to only applying when EU law applies. Rights protection is therefore 'rooted in the constitutional traditions of the Member States'.[52] This obstacle is a common one faced by the Court when interpreting concepts within the confines

[46] Upon further analysis, it was noted that the Charter may have been raised as part of the parties' claims, but the Court did not always engage with them.

[47] There is also an argument that 'citizens' rights' included a wider range of rights than those considered in this book – for example, workers' rights have been seen to fall under this category as per the categorisation of the CJEU's website. This is an area this book believes is separate to pure citizenship rights.

[48] Commission, '2017 Annual Report on the Application of the EU Charter of Fundamental Rights' COM (2018) 396 final.

[49] Judgment of 6 September 2012, *Deutsches Weintor* C-544/10, EU:C:2012:526; *Kadi II*; Judgment of 8 April 2014, *Digital Rights Ireland* C-293/12, EU:C:2014:238; Judgment of 13 May 2014, *Google Spain* C-131/12, EU:C:2014:317. See Eleni Frantziou, 'The Horizontal Effect of the Charter of Fundamental Rights of the EU: Rediscovering the Reasons for Horizontality' (2015) 21 *European Law Journal* 657.

[50] Judgment of 26 February 2013, *Melloni* C-399/11, EU:C:2013:107; Judgment of 26 February 2013, *Fransson* C-617/10, EU:C:2013:105; Judgment of 15 January 2014, *Association de Médiation Sociale* C-176/12, EU:C:2014:2.

[51] Muir (n 13) 27.

[52] Juliane Kokott and Christoph Sobotta, 'The Charter of Fundamental Rights of the European Union after Lisbon' [2010] *EUI Working Papers, Academy of European Law 2010/6* 11.

of EU law, but has been an especial problem in citizenship.[53] There are still conceptual difficulties surrounding the reconciliation of fundamental rights operating within the restricted remit of the application of the EU citizenship provisions. EU citizenship status is characterised by its exclusive nature; it was not always the case that any citizen could rely on these rights. EU fundamental rights protection did not influence the Court's interpretation of what it meant to be deprived of the genuine enjoyment of one's rights; therefore, if an individual did not satisfy this test, they also had no recourse to fundamental rights protection.

Above all, the EU still struggles to establish legitimacy and solidarity with its citizens, despite over two decades of the existence of EU citizenship status.[54] The negativity surrounding the Euroscepticism exhibited by so many of the EU Member States contributed to its lack of political legitimacy and solidarity with its citizens.[55] There are thus two potential solutions. First, the CJEU could mitigate the effects of poor legitimacy and solidarity by offering short-term resolutions in case-by-case analyses of different situations. This is less desirable simply for its legal uncertainty and lack of clear guidance as to what the provisions truly amount to.[56] Furthermore, it also assumes that greater activism on the part of the Court in terms of rights protection would improve solidarity. However, it is conceivable that this could be interpreted negatively as further judicial activism on the part of the Court and could actually exacerbate the feelings of Euroscepticism for instigating greater intrusion into the autonomy of national Member States.[57] The alternative was to frame the entire concept differently so as to change overall perspectives on a longer-term basis. It seems the latter would be a more effective way to resolve the EU's problems than to simply downplay the effects of inherent troubles in a citizenship regime created by the EU. Because currently 'there is no 'real' citizenship, since every usage requires qualification',[58] there was potential to reinterpret its meaning. This is arguably what the intention was when the Court initially began to integrate fundamental rights considerations into its judicial reasoning, although as the most recent analysis has shown, this approach has shifted to a more restrictive one.

This restrictive approach recently adopted has done no favours for the fact that the EU and the UK are now facing a difficult situation of their own in terms of

[53] Editorial, 'Two-Speed European Citizenship? Can the Lisbon Treaty Help Close the Gap?' (2008) 45 *CML Rev* 1.

[54] Michael Dougan, 'The Bubble That Burst: Exploring the Legitimacy of the Case Law on the Free Movement of Union Citizens' in Maurice Adams et al (eds), *Judging Europe's Judges* (Hart Publishing, 2013) 153.

[55] See *Public Opinion in the European Union* (European Commission, Standard Eurobarometer 83, 2015) for statistics on this.

[56] Siofra O'Leary, 'The Past, Present and Future of the Purely Internal Rule in EU Law' [2010] *Irish Jurist* 13, 41.

[57] Muir (n 13) 30.

[58] Daniel Thym, 'Towards "Real" Citizenship? The Judicial Construction of Union Citizenship and its Limits' in Maurice Adams et al (eds), *Judging Europe's Judges* (Hart Publishing, 2013) 172.

negotiating a deal for the UK's withdrawal as a Member State. As the next chapter will discuss in more detail, there is a correlation in time between the Brexit vote and the Court's increasingly restrictive approach, though it cannot be proven that they are intrinsically linked. However, it is not the intention of this book to try and prove a conclusive link. Instead, what the analysis will highlight is that the pattern of decision-making by the Court – in particular, its decision against integrating fundamental rights into citizenship – has been especially difficult to swallow in light of the difficulties that EU citizens in the UK and British citizens in the EU are facing because of Brexit. The weaker the rights under citizenship appear, the more difficult it becomes to argue that there is significant value and worth in fighting for the maintenance of the status quo of these rights after Brexit occurs.

However, it is evidently difficult to convince an entire community who are not united at the outset to believe in a potentially novel conceptual framework, such as that presented by the Maastricht Treaty.[59] The Court struggles between whether to act positively to protect rights or whether to remain cautious to avoid criticism for excessive judicial activism. This was a problem from the outset of the introduction of citizenship. Member State nationality created inherent solidarity with its nationals in its territory such that the introduction of EU citizenship status found itself in competition with these longer-established values, and paling in comparison.[60] The ideal situation would be for the legislator and the governing body to instil a political sentiment of trust and legitimacy into the regime being introduced, which must not 'compete' per se with non-comparable concepts like nationality.[61] Though it is the most closely related to EU citizenship, nationality is in reality very different. Therefore, in order to escape these inherent problems, focus had to be on other areas that did not affect nationality and were exclusive to citizenship, such as rights in the EU.

The constitutional acknowledgement of the fundamental rights *acquis* in the Lisbon Treaty indicated that there was now a normative acceptance of such non-economic values, despite the EU's historically economic origins. With this in mind, this book has hypothesised that a fundamental rights discourse would be less intrusive as part of the general normative framework in enhancing the status of EU citizenship for its citizens. The hope was that fundamental rights would help augment overall solidarity and legitimacy by substantiating EU citizenship status. An understanding of human rights compared to the more restricted idea of EU fundamental rights would help to distinguish EU citizenship from Member State nationality. The next section will discuss these rights-based EU-centric problems against a belief that human rights stem from being part of a political community rather than as a general indiscriminate right of all individuals.[62] The issues of

[59] Joseph Weiler, 'Citizenship and Human Rights' in Jan A Winter et al (eds), *Reforming the Treaty on the European Union* (Kluwer Law International, 1996) 62.

[60] See the works by civic nationalists like Miller (n 26).

[61] Alison Kesby, *The Right to Have Rights: Citizenship, Humanity, and International Law* (Oxford University Press, 2012) 40.

[62] This is the notion of the 'right to have rights'; see Hannah Arendt, *Totalitarianism: Part Three of the Origins of Totalitarianism* (Harcourt Brace Jovanovich, 1968).

territory concerning Member States will be attributed to EU citizenship's poor reception into the legislative framework of certain Member States from the outset, and the EU institutions being wary of linking EU citizenship too closely to fundamental rights throughout the development until today.

III. Linking EU Fundamental Rights with EU Citizenship

It is important to understand the intricacies of the relationship between human rights and EU fundamental rights for two reasons. First, it sets the EU framework and its fundamental rights apart from the more common framework of human rights, which do not necessarily derive from being part of a political community. Second, the differences between a truly universal human rights regime and a limited EU one adds to the legitimacy problems that EU citizenship faces. This section aims to consider this, which is the source of the problems faced by EU citizenship and contributed to the concept's tense relationship with fundamental rights. It will also be contextualised amongst the growing political difficulties faced by the EU, which, it is argued, play a significant role in how the Court treats citizenship status and fundamental rights.

Nationality is the determinant of EU citizenship status in the EU; without this, individuals have no claim to their relevant rights, including fundamental rights.[63] However, Mantouvalou argues that 'full citizenship requires the protection of all groups of rights'.[64] Human rights themselves are perceived to be natural as part of humanity,[65] and this underpins the protection of fundamental rights in the EU. This idea is what made it difficult to reconcile the Court's choice not to integrate fundamental rights with EU citizenship status. Being deprived of the genuine enjoyment of one's fundamental rights is not part of being deprived of the genuine enjoyment of one's citizenship rights according to the Court after *Zambrano*, although the nature of EU fundamental rights and the constitutionalisation of this concept in Article 6 TEU appeared to encourage this. The scope of both EU fundamental rights and EU citizenship would have become extremely wide-ranging if this had materialised. With immigration such an important issue for the EU in the minds of EU citizens, it is unlikely to have been received well by national Member States.[66] The correlation between this and the EU's political situation is striking.

[63] Judgment of 2 March 2010, *Rottmann* C-135/08, EU:C:2010:104.

[64] Virginia Mantouvalou, 'Workers without Rights as Citizens at the Margins' (2013) 16 *Critical Review of International Social and Political Philosophy* 366, 369.

[65] John Locke, *Two Treatises of Government* (Cambridge University Press, 1963). This is a debate that is outside the scope of this book.

[66] Gregor Aisch, Adam Pearce and Rousseau Bryant, 'How Far is Europe Swinging to the Right?' *New York Times* (23 October 2017), https://www.nytimes.com/interactive/2016/05/22/world/europe/europe-right-wing-austria-hungary.html.

The relationship is thus as follows: as a national of an EU Member State, Article 20 TFEU states that individuals all automatically have the right to EU citizenship status. This status grants rights under Article 21 TFEU and, as the case law has demonstrated, a broader right to non-discrimination under Article 18 TFEU,[67] to fundamental rights now protected by the Charter of Fundamental Rights[68] and to rights under Directive 2004/38.[69] Fundamental rights, before the Charter became legally binding in Article 6 TEU, were applicable if the situation involved fundamental rights considerations.[70] This suggested that they were more free-standing because of their moral nature. However, after Article 6 TEU, the scope of fundamental rights in the Charter was applicable only when the situation was implementing EU law. Though this has been broadly interpreted,[71] it is still clear that if there is no link with EU law, there is no protection under the Charter. However, where this link can be purported to be found is through an individual's status as an EU citizen.

An independent legal basis of EU citizenship rights, as established by the Court in *Zambrano*, would have been more constitutionally significant if the link with EU law that was needed to trigger protection of fundamental rights was accepted to be citizenship status. Previously, in order to trigger rights under EU citizenship, a citizen had to move across borders. Now, by simply being an EU citizen, the individual should be able to enjoy the full array of EU citizenship rights, which includes protection under fundamental rights.[72] Because the EU is a political entity, it required a legitimate procedure; therefore, by linking EU citizenship status to the conferral of fundamental rights, it was imagined that this should have led smoothly to a seamless integration of EU citizenship and fundamental rights. The obstacle in the way of this was the deprivation of genuine enjoyment test, which emerged to restrict such a broad interpretation of the independent EU citizenship status. Furthermore, in *Zambrano* itself, the fact that there was a TCN family member involved was arguably also a factor in the ultimate decision to restrict citizenship and fundamental rights protection.

TCN family members have featured as beneficiaries in almost all the cases in the third age.[73] For this reason as well, 'it is not surprising that the legal status of third-country national family members has become the new battleground, since it raises formidable challenges for the ECJ'.[74] These challenges are also related to

[67] *Sala* (n 21).
[68] In the context of citizenship, see *Garcia Avello* (n 1); *Chen* (n 1); *Carpenter* (n 1).
[69] Subject, of course, to art 7(1) demonstrating sufficient resources and comprehensive health insurance.
[70] *ERT* (n 19).
[71] *Fransson* (n 50).
[72] Judgment of 8 March 2011, *Zambrano* C-34/09, EU:C:2011:124, para 40. Notably this is subject to the genuine enjoyment test.
[73] Apart from Judgment of 16 January 2014, *MG* C-400/12, EU:C:2014:9; and *Dano* (n 11).
[74] Thym (n 58) 165.

the fact that in *Chen*, the Court adopted a liberal approach to derived rights to residency for an EU citizen dependent on a TCN family member,[75] which was later consolidated by the *Zambrano* ruling. If fundamental rights protection then became an integrated part of one's independent legal status of EU citizenship, claims to rights of TCNs would be strengthened significantly. The extent to which TCN family members could be brought under the remit of the Treaty through greater protection of constitutionalised fundamental rights and an independent legal basis for EU citizenship status seemed to be a common underlying question in many of the recent cases. It appears now that the potential constitutional implications of bringing TCNs under the scope of the Treaty have overshadowed the importance of making fundamental rights an inherent part of the EU citizenship analysis.[76]

It was thought that because human rights are universal, fundamental rights would also embody an element of this character. However, under the EU's framework, this is impossible because the concept had to be subject to restrictions set by the boundaries in the Treaty, thereby justifying such rights from only being protected within the EU's domain and only being triggered when implementing EU law.[77] These limitations have changed the nature of EU fundamental rights, so they differ starkly from human rights. Thus, by linking fundamental rights to EU citizenship status, the required link with EU law is established, thereby allowing a broader application of fundamental rights that is more consistent with its originally universal nature. This has not occurred because of the political pressures on the Court not to expand into areas that would bring further dissatisfaction from its citizens, as 'Europeans feel that immigration remains the main issue facing the EU', according to most recent Eurobarometer polls.[78] The next section will consider one of the potentially relevant factors affecting this: the standards of human rights protection under the ECHR.

A. Implications of Human Rights Protection under the ECHR

EU citizenship status as it was understood vis-a-vis fundamental rights was a delicate issue because of its effect on the perceived legitimacy of the EU by its citizens. However, this changed the understanding of two sets of rights-based concepts.

[75] *Chen* (n 1).

[76] See Anja Wiesbrock, 'Granting Citizenship-Related Rights to Third-Country Nationals: An Alternative to the Full Extension of European Union Citizenship' (2012) 14 *European Journal of Migration and Law* 63.

[77] Article 51(1) of the Charter of Fundamental Rights of the European Union 83/02 [2010] OJ C83/389.

[78] *Public Opinion in the European Union* (n 7) 15.

The legal basis of EU citizenship was that individuals only have rights if they are members of the community of EU citizens, whilst the (original) foundation of EU fundamental rights – universal human rights – was that individuals deserve these rights because they are human.[79] EU fundamental rights apply to all EU citizens. However, they were restricted to also applying only within the remit of EU law in line with the EU framework, and this had the effect of presenting something of an obstacle to the protection of such rights.[80] Therefore, Kesby is correct to say that: '[i]f human rights flow from membership of a political community, the one true human right is the right to belong to such a community'.[81] If fundamental rights protection was only relevant when EU law was being implemented, then citizenship status becoming an independent legal basis for rights was the opportunity for the Court to integrate fundamental rights to the analysis so that it could become an inherent part of being a citizen of the EU.

It is the question of rights of TCNs that raises the notion of universality of human rights and how the CJEU should best afford these individuals protection when they deserve it. The problem that TCNs are currently facing is their exclusion from the scope of the Treaty, which, it is argued, is unjustifiable in certain circumstances and particularly in the constitutional legal atmosphere of rights protection today after Lisbon. Some inconsistencies have been presented criticising this approach by the Court in recent cases.[82] However, most important to this criticism in the context of TCNs are the universal standards of human rights, which derive from the ECHR and its jurisdiction, which differs from that of the EU institutions and instruments. It is this difference which formed the basis of much debate before Article 6(2) TEU came into being in the Lisbon Treaty[83] and this human rights standard which is still the centre of debate today, as it differs in scope and breadth from the Charter and other EU-derived standards of human rights.

Under Article 1 ECHR, human rights protection extends to all individuals within the jurisdiction of the relevant Member States. Therefore, if a TCN should find themselves within the scope of a Member State's jurisdiction, protection is to be afforded to them by virtue of the ECHR. As Gaja notes, the ECHR imparts positive obligations on its Member States,[84] again demonstrative of a stronger and more convincing hand the European Court of Human Rights has as regards human rights protection. Article 6(2) TEU and its required accession to the ECHR brings this concern regarding protection of TCN rights to the forefront. The greatest risk in this is that by excluding TCNs from the scope of fundamental rights

[79] This is in reference to EU fundamental rights being a branch of human rights more generally.
[80] *Melloni* (n 50).
[81] Kesby (n 61) 3.
[82] *Dano* (n 11).
[83] Opinion of 28 March 1996, Opinion 2/94, EU:C:1996:140.
[84] Giorgio Gaja, 'Accession to the ECHR' in Andrea Biondi, Piet Eeckhout and Stefanie Ripley (eds), *EU Law after Lisbon* (Oxford University Press, 2012) 184.

protection, the standards guaranteed by the ECHR will be affected. This would be attributed to the Court interpreting the Charter and its requisite fundamental rights in a manner inconsistent with the normative trajectory indicated, leading into the third age of citizenship.

Two provisions of the ECHR are especially relevant in terms of increasing judicial protection through the European Court of Human Rights – Article 8 ECHR, the right to private and family life, and also Article 14 ECHR, the right to non-discrimination. The scope of the protection of Article 8 ECHR has been broad, particularly regarding situations of family reunification, and has also manifested itself in terms of identity rights. Though the effect of Article 14 ECHR is not unlike that of EU citizenship status initially in terms of its cosmetic nature,[85] criticism has often been in the context of Article 14 ECHR being invoked only when concurrently with another provision in the Convention. Gerards argues that: '[t]o provide for a high level of protection against discrimination, the ECtHR would need to bring the protection offered by Article 14 in line with the sophisticated case law of the CJEU.'[86] However, given that the identified trend in citizenship case law has tended towards rights to family life, this appears less problematic.[87] Therefore, reading both Article 8 ECHR and Article 14 ECHR concurrently has the potential to strengthen the support for upholding TCN rights as an extension of EU citizenship status and fundamental rights protection.

From its decisions on welfare benefits particularly, there appears to be a standard that has emerged whereby the Court appears to discriminate when considering standards related to rights under the ECHR. The cumulative reading of the rights accrued by EU citizens and their dependants, whether TCNs or not, in terms of rights to family life, rights to identity and even more broadly at the level of rights to non-discrimination has now been constitutionally ingrained. This book has noted that the Court's legal culture is inclined to succumb to the political pressure exerted by Member State authorities. However, given that the Lisbon Treaty was ratified and signed after some years of disagreement, there is less argument for the Court now retreating to a position whereby fundamental rights, as highlighted by the changes in the Treaty, are not adequately protected by constitutional means which had been agreed upon by the constituent Member States.

The EU's increasingly liberal nature has been both criticised and applauded. Those who criticise this direction argue for less intervention by the supranational entity,[88] and this sentiment is arguably even more prominent in today's

[85] Janneke Gerards, 'The Discrimination Grounds of Article 14 of the European Convention on Human Rights' [2013] *Human Rights Law Review* 99, 100.

[86] ibid 102.

[87] Aaron Baker, 'Article 14 ECHR: A Protector, Not a Prosecutor' (2006) 69 *MLR* 714, 716.

[88] Andrew Moravcsik, 'Liberal Intergovernmentalism and Integration: A Rejoinder' (1995) 33 *Journal of Common Market Studies* 611; Daniel Wincott, 'Institutional Interaction and European Integration: Towards an Everyday Critique of Liberal Inter-governmentalism' (1995) 33 *Journal of Common Market Studies* 597.

Eurosceptic era. Those in favour support the greater protection and rights afforded to citizens,[89] and this element is what has driven this book's argument for the model of citizenship and fundamental rights protection as proposed above. The argument derives, in part, from the standards of human rights protection under the ECHR which informs the Court's interpretation of fundamental rights protection in the EU. Therefore, particularly in relation to TCN family members of EU citizens, further human rights implications under the ECHR warrant more serious consideration by the Court.

This book has supported a pragmatic attribution of rights such as fundamental rights and citizenship to the individual through established processes. Such processes include recourse to the rights under EU citizenship, the now-binding Charter of Fundamental Rights and, to an extent, the ECHR. It is only in this manner that granting more rights under the EU provisions will be amenable to Member States' interests in preserving their authority.[90] Because of the *Zambrano* case and the independent legal basis of rights under EU citizenship, the right to fundamental rights through EU citizenship status became more direct, facilitating a stronger normative relationship between the two concepts. However, the Court has implemented differentiated interpretations of who deserves the right to which fundamental rights, which contradicts the idea of human rights protection to begin with. The hesitation in linking fundamental rights and EU citizenship appears to be connected to the Eurosceptic atmosphere of the time, and this has not been helped by an underlying lack of solidarity and poorly perceived EU legitimacy prior to these judicial changes.

This has been to no one's benefit and particularly not in the political climate of Brexit. It is for this reason that the analysis in this book leading up to the last few chapters has emphasised how and why this should have become more prominent. This helps to explain the disappointment that this is not the situation at present and that it does not appear likely that this will change given the recent case law. It is also serves to demonstrate that there are a significant number of political statements made that seemed to appease individuals at the time (such as in *Zambrano*), but the true intention of the Court was to avoid upsetting Member States further and to defer to their interests and wishes instead. Whilst this is not necessarily undesirable, when it is to the detriment of claimants and to fundamental rights protection, then there is a bigger problem.

EU citizenship status has not liberalised claims to fundamental rights protection, despite normative arguments that allowed citizens to claim protection of these rights simply by virtue of being an EU citizen. The responsibility for this lies with the Court and the EU institutions, who seemed wary of the effects of an

[89] Elspeth Guild, Cornelis Arnoldus Groenendijk and Sergio Carrera, *Illiberal Liberal States: Immigration, Citizenship and Integration in the EU* (Ashgate, 2009).

[90] See Erik Oddvar Eriksen and John Erik Fossum, 'Europe in Search of Legitimacy: Strategies of Legitimation Assessed' (2004) 25 *International Political Science Review* 435.

integrated EU citizenship and fundamental rights regime in the EU. This argument explains why the genuine enjoyment test was employed to limit the effects of *Zambrano* when it made EU citizenship an independent legal basis for invoking rights. It would also explain the Court's increasing need to distinguish between citizens whom they deemed deserving of the full protection of citizenship rights to the detriment of the application of its judicial instruments, such as the principle of non-discrimination. However, there are necessary limits to be placed on such a liberal approach because of potential political backlash, and these limits will be considered next.

B. Limits on Linking EU Fundamental Rights with EU Citizenship Status

Having outlined the proposed model of integration for EU fundamental rights and EU citizenship status, it is important to also acknowledge that there must be limitations to this approach. Noting the difficulties faced at the outset for the EU citizenship project, but also the worsening political situation, boundaries become necessary to ensure that the perceived legitimacy of the EU by increasingly Eurosceptic Member States is not compromised excessively. Recognising the broad-brush nature of this approach, questions arise as to whether the previously established constitutional limits – such as the purely internal situations rule – would still apply. It is argued that given the diminishing role of crossing borders to trigger the Treaty, this is no longer an appropriate restriction. This discussion warrants a fuller consideration of AG Sharpston's Opinion in *Ruiz Zambrano*, for she presents some limits to this potential integration of the two sets of rights, and these are supported here.

AG Sharpston puts it most aptly in her Opinion that bringing EU fundamental rights within the scope of the Treaty puts these rights 'into the sphere of each Member State, where it coexists with the standards of fundamental rights protection enshrined in domestic law or in the ECHR'.[91] These rights are inherently sensitive, and her suggested approach might have brought various differential standards of human rights protection together under one roof. Therefore, and quite rightly, AG Sharpston advances a warning against her model without any limits because a 'change of that kind would alter, in legal and political terms, the very nature of fundamental rights under EU law'.[92] Acknowledging the reasonableness of AG Sharpston's argument that fundamental rights cannot be a free-standing right on their own, the model in this chapter has proposed the link to EU law to be EU citizenship status. However, the practicalities of allowing EU fundamental

[91] Opinion of 30 September 2010, *Zambrano* C-34/09, EU:C:2011:560, para 156.
[92] ibid para 173.

rights to apply to all situations involving individuals in the EU simply by virtue of their status as EU citizens would be difficult to reconcile with the standards of protection established in national law and indeed, to a greater extent, also ECHR law.

The proposed model here is noted in reality to be likely to lead to most, if not all, domestic situations falling within the scope of the Treaty, thereby always requiring recourse to rights in the EU. Whilst this supports the liberalism exhibited by some of the Court's case law thus far, boundaries must be clarified. This is particularly so when considering that the EU's supranational relationship with its Member States is premised upon the principles of conferral and subsidiarity.[93] However, the established limits as recognised prior to the third age are argued not to be suitable in the context of this model. The reasons for this have been outlined and include the arbitrary and tenuous nature of requiring a cross-border element to trigger the Treaty. Instead, AG Sharpston's suggestion on only allowing Charter rights to apply when there is an established EU competence – whether exercised or not – is the supported avenue for the clarified scope of integration for fundamental rights and EU citizenship. Considering the notion of perceived EU legitimacy and solidarity amongst its citizens, there must be a compromise in limiting the scope *ratione personae* of citizenship to make way for an expanded scope *ratione materiae*, which will include fundamental rights protection.

Article 51(1) of the Charter requires Member States to implement EU law before the Charter can apply. This provision ensures that there are no conflicts between different standards of rights protection, especially as the Charter cannot extend or change any EU powers as per Article 51(2). Therefore, in order for this model to operate effectively, any limits must ensure that the scenario will fall within the scope of the Treaty legally. It was argued that from considering the more recent cases on welfare benefits especially, the Court was unduly restrictive, narrowly interpreting what it considered to amount to an implementation of EU law, despite *Fransson*, where a broader notion of the scope of the Charter was initially accepted by the Court itself.[94] Whilst the ideal is that all EU citizens should be able to claim rights under the Charter simply by virtue of their citizenship, this is clearly unworkable if left to apply unrestricted in all situations. It would be especially politically unsound in the atmosphere of rising Euroscepticism and would encroach on national autonomy into areas where competence had not been conferred, expanding the scope *ratione personae* so that only when the matter concerns a legally conferred EU competence is a solution more consistent with the universality of human rights as well as the underlying principles of EU law and its operation amongst its Member States. It should also be noted that this removes the need to rely upon the purely internal situations rule as a demarcation of boundaries, thereby adding legal certainty for the beneficiaries of citizenship status and rights.

[93] Article 5 TEU.
[94] *Fransson* (n 50).

The *Zambrano* case itself already addressed the point regarding the purely internal situations rule by making EU citizenship status an independent legal basis for rights. As already noted, this had the potential for it to become a justified legal basis from which further rights may derive, especially given the constitutional direction of EU fundamental rights protection, but also in view of the comments made by AG Sharpston as to EU fundamental rights lacking this similar free-standing nature. Limiting the scope of the Charter to applying only to situations where the EU has legally conferred competences is most defensible in terms of the Court thus respecting the boundaries of the EU's framework. However, and more importantly, it also establishes a legal basis for which further expansion of the scope *ratione materiae* of the Treaty in terms of better integration of citizenship and fundamental rights can occur. It is this which this book has argued for throughout. The model in which citizenship status is the link needed to trigger the Treaty for fundamental rights should sit within a conceivable practical framework. Expanding the scope of EU citizenship by simply being an EU citizen would not be politically or legally practical, despite being consistent with the trends highlighted in the previous chapters. However, the reality reveals a different picture and, on the other hand, trends in the case law of the third age after the *Zambrano* case appear to demonstrate that the integrated fundamental rights and EU citizenship relationship is nonetheless unlikely to materialise as originally hypothesised at the outset of this book.

There is much to be said in terms of expanding interpretation of the fundamental rights discourse in the EU to be more consistent with the broader European framework of human rights under the ECHR. Now that Article 6(2) TEU has stated that the EU must accede to the ECHR, there is a legal basis for the EU to become a Contracting State to the ECHR. However, there have been difficulties in this accession process, which point to greater underlying problems with the ECHR's relationship with the EU. As outlined above, there is some difficulty in reconciling the application of the broad scope of the ECHR within the limited framework of EU fundamental rights under the Charter. Coupled with the struggles faced by the Court in its balancing act between EU citizenship rights and respecting Member State autonomy, it is clear that the protection of fundamental rights in citizenship case law has not been straightforward. It will be argued in the next section that the relationship between the ECHR and EU citizenship status is due to encounter more difficulties in light of the worsening political situation in the EU, but also simply because of the nature of the ECHR's application in the context of the EU.

C. The ECHR and EU Citizenship Going Forward

The evolution of fundamental rights protection in the EU has already been discussed in the previous chapters. This section will focus on the enforcement of the ECHR in the EU's framework, which had a significant role to play in the development of EU fundamental rights protection early on, especially in citizenship case law. The argument now is that the ECHR can provide further legal justification for the protection of fundamental rights. However, because it is a treaty that exists outside the framework of the EU, there are inherent constitutional obstacles in relation to its enforcement before the CJEU. It is even more complicated now that the Charter has been made binding and already replicates the ECHR provisions. Nevertheless, there is value in raising awareness of the potential value of these rights, especially in the current political climate. This not only refers to the politics rife in Member States themselves as to their attitudes towards the EU, but also to the political climate in which the Court has found itself in terms of its highly politicised decision-making process.

Because there has been so little appetite for applying the Charter in citizenship case law where there are clearly situations that involve fundamental rights, it is logical to turn to the ECHR as an alternative and more focused source of rights protection. However, the application of rights under the ECHR before the CJEU has not been a straightforward process, and it is this which is perhaps the difficulty going forward for the ECHR's enforcement in citizenship case law. It was clearly stated in Opinion 2/94 that the EU could not, in its constitutional form prior to the Lisbon Treaty, accede to the ECHR.[95] This was addressed in the Lisbon Treaty by the inclusion of Article 6(2) TEU. It made accession a legal obligation, which then led to the Draft Accession Agreement being drawn up by the Council.[96] However, when the Court sought to consider its legality, it became clear that the process of accession was not as simple a project as was once imagined. In Opinion 2/13, the Court criticised the Draft Accession Agreement for being contrary to EU law, therefore halting the process of accession indefinitely.[97] As a source of rights protection supposedly available to EU citizens, this complication does not bode well.

As outlined previously, the ECHR has been available as a further legal foundation for human rights arguments under the Treaty, alongside the Charter. It has been particularly important for TCNs who enjoy rights by virtue of their dependency or relationships with EU citizens. In light of the Charter's lukewarm reception in the jurisprudence of the Court in cases on citizenship, it was thought that the ECHR could in fact be the legal basis needed to add to the support in favour of protecting fundamental rights as a matter of protecting constitutional values. However, going forward, there are significant difficulties for the ECHR as it pertains to EU citizenship. The main problems relate to the constitutional

[95] Opinion 2/94 (n 3) para 36.

[96] The Draft Accession Agreement has since been removed from the Council of Europe website; however, for a summary, see Antoine Buyse, 'Accession of EU to ECHR Draft Agreement: Finally Finalised' *ECHR Blog* (8 April 2013), http://echrblog.blogspot.co.uk/2013/04/accession-of-eu-to-echr-draft-agreement.html.

[97] Opinion 2/13 (n 3).

obstacles to accession.[98] Whilst it was known that the EU was founded on respect for human rights[99] and that the ECHR has 'special significance',[100] there were questions raised as to the EU's non-state nature and the fact that the Contracting States to the ECHR are primarily Member States, not supranational non-state entities like the EU.

It was not enough for the Treaty drafters to simply insert a provision allowing for the EU to formally accede to the ECHR. Hence, an agreement on accession to the ECHR was drafted in 2013 and, as per EU law, an Opinion of the Court had to be delivered before any further progress could be made. However, as already mentioned, the Court determined in Opinion 2/13 that the draft accession agreement was incompatible with EU law. Of most concern was the fact that accession would interfere with the autonomy of the EU's legal order and the fact that it was not a state.[101] Therefore, whilst being a legal obligation under the Lisbon Treaty, accession was found to be conditional.[102] At present, the EU does not satisfy the necessary conditions and ECHR accession is at a stalemate. What the accession provision in the Lisbon Treaty thus represents is more of a political statement as to the general acceptance of a discourse of fundamental rights in the constitution of the EU, but less substance to this claim in reality. The Court seems to have mirrored this political 'hands-off' approach in its case law, to the detriment of the individuals claiming rights where rights protection would have previously been paramount.

The ECHR's status of special significance has thus far proven to be effective for claimants seeking rights under EU citizenship status before the Court. This is particularly the case for rights to private and family life, as mentioned in the previous chapters. Before the Charter was made binding, there was already an influence of fundamental rights in the Court's jurisprudence simply because it could not be ignored in certain situations – such as *Chen*, *Carpenter* and *MRAX*.[103] All three cases relied on the ECHR to strengthen their claim to rights under the Treaty successfully. As explained throughout this book thus far, this has been the underlying factor supporting an integrated relationship between fundamental rights and EU citizenship. When both the Charter was made binding and accession to the ECHR was established in the Lisbon Treaty, it appeared that there was a clear commitment to fundamental rights protection within the EU framework.

[98] See Piet Eeckhout, 'Opinion 2/13 on EU Accession to the ECHR and Judicial Dialogue: Autonomy or Autarky?' (2015) *Jean Monnet Working Paper 01/15*.

[99] Article 2 TEU.

[100] *ERT* (n 3) para 41; Judgment of 3 September 2008, *Kadi I* C-402/05 P and C-415/05 P, EU:C:2008:461, para 283.

[101] Opinion 2/94 (n 3) paras 156ff.

[102] Catherine Barnard, 'Opinion 2/13 on EU Accession to the ECHR: Looking for the Silver Lining' *EU Law Analysis Blog* (16 February 2015), http://eulawanalysis.blogspot.co.uk/2015/02/opinion-213-on-eu-accession-to-echr.html.

[103] See ch 2.

However, this too has been an empty promise on the part of the Court and its interpretations of citizens' rights.

Since the Charter has become binding, the Court has sought to apply Charter rights over ECHR rights where it can. While this is not always possible,[104] for the most part, the Charter is a sufficient source of rights protection, especially in the context of citizenship. Most cases are concerned with Article 8 ECHR and Article 7 of the Charter, the right to private and family life. In this manner, the Article 8 ECHR cases serve as indications of how the right can be legitimately protected in the context of a purely human rights jurisdiction. The Court had opportunities to draw inspiration from the jurisprudence of the European Court of Human Rights and apply it in the context of its own decision-making. In this way, it would be better equipped to draw out the fundamental rights aspects of case law and provide adequate protection. Indeed, this was the expectation it set for itself when the social and political rights were fundamental rights accepted as a general principle of EU law that needed to be given full consideration where relevant.[105]

Given that the Charter has not been favoured by the Court in its case law of late, the idea was that perhaps the ECHR could be the alternative source of rights protection as a safeguard. This would have been especially convincing in light of mandated accession of the EU to the ECHR in Article 6(2) TEU. However, noting the significant constitutional limitations of not only accession to the ECHR but also the application and scope of ECHR rights in the framework of EU law, there are difficulties in terms of trying to establish a consistent approach to rights under the ECHR when applied by two very different courts. This is especially so because the CJEU is not a human rights court and has never set out to become one. However, because there is an understanding that the Court considers fundamental rights to be of constitutional importance, it would not be unreasonable to seek some consistency and clarity in the application of fundamental rights protection when it does become relevant before the Court. This becomes especially so in cases on citizenship, because the situation often involved delicate matters relating to private and family life that would have significant consequences if ignored.

This argument is crucial in the political atmosphere that currently underlies much of the EU's decision-making. This is in reference particularly to the UK's process of withdrawal from the EU as a Member State. The conclusion made above regarding the ECHR will be applied to post-Brexit Britain in the context of human rights protection for EU citizens in the UK and British citizens in the EU.

[104] The Charter has some rights which are exclusive to the EU, such as data protection (art 8), the right to non-discrimination on the grounds of sexual orientation (art 21) and rights to conduct a business and property (arts 16 and 17). See Adrienne Yong, 'Forgetting Human Rights: The Brexit Debate' (2017) 5 *European Human Rights Law Review* 469.

[105] Judgment of 12 November 1969, *Stauder v Ulm* C-29/69, EU:C:1969:57, para 7; Judgment of 17 December 1970, *Internationale Handelsgesellschaft* C-11/70, EU:C:1970:114, para 14.

In particular, there will be no choice but to relinquish reliance on the Charter after Brexit and instead rely upon the ECHR as the main source of human rights in Europe that will remain binding on the UK after its withdrawal.[106] This much is clear. However, the weaknesses and issues outlined above in relation to the ECHR as the main enforcement mechanism for human rights are even more prevalent in the context of Brexit. The analysis will later focus on the implications of this in a different context. It is important to highlight here that there are issues that foreshadow difficulties in the future with Brexit that are indirectly related to EU citizenship status.

Understanding that the CJEU is not a human rights court justifies the claims that it should rely upon the case law of the European Court of Human Rights when dealing with matters such as fundamental rights protection. However, the future of EU citizenship status supported by the ECHR is not promising, given that ECHR enforcement within the framework of EU law is complicated. Whilst successful when relied upon in the past, it appears that the overall political appetite for a greater level of fundamental rights protection has been weak and that even though it helped to substantiate the status of EU citizenship, in today's day and age, this is not a priority. Instead, the priority has shifted towards ensuring that there is as little intrusion into Member States' autonomy as possible, which has been to the detriment of individual rights protection. Therefore, it is clear that the ECHR applied in EU citizenship case law is not the answer going forward.

The reason why the ECHR has become a focus here despite it being outside the EU framework is due to the way that the Court has decided to exclude the enforcement and application of the Charter because it considered the cases to fall outside the scope of the Charter under Article 51(2). As a broader instrument of rights protection, the rights under the ECHR had potential to fill these gaps, and enforcement of the ECHR could bring to fundamental rights protection back to centre stage. However, the Court exercised its prerogative not to defer to rights under the ECHR, for fairly legitimate constitutional reasons. However, it has also limited its application of the Charter, thereby undermining the scope of fundamental rights protection entirely. As also mentioned in the previous section, there are some limitations that simply must exist to protect the integrity of national authorities in an international or supranational setting. Whilst not supporting eliminating such necessary limitations, it is clear that the Court has decided to interpret the limits strictly as a politically charged decision. The excessive influence of politics when interpreting rights that are so central to EU citizens' lives is troubling.

As explained in the previous chapter, there have been recent cases that disappoint in terms of the scope of fundamental rights protection under the guise of EU citizenship status. The problems are down to the fact that the Court does not

[106] Department for Exiting the European Union, *Legislating for the United Kingdom's Withdrawal from the European Union* (Cmd 9946, 2017) para 2.22.

entertain any arguments pertaining to fundamental rights in the cases, finding that they fall outside the scope of its remit. The argument that has been alluded to thus far is that this is too closely associated with a hands-off approach by the Court that seeks to avoid excessive intrusion in national autonomy. However, in doing so, the Court has compromised rights protection and undermined fundamental rights protection and the status of being an EU citizen. The ECHR, whilst appearing to be a valid alternative source of rights in theory, has faced difficulties in practice before the Court. It has been argued that a worsening political situation, particularly one which has now resulted in the UK's vote to leave the EU, was not a good reason to pander to Member States' interests in lieu of protecting the rights of EU citizens. Indeed, it will be argued in the next chapter that the Court's failing to link fundamental rights protection with EU citizenship status has not helped to develop greater feelings of solidarity amongst EU citizens, thereby leading to disillusionment amongst the citizens as to the project of EU integration in a time of crisis, where the project of the EU is losing support amongst its constituents.[107]

IV. Conclusion

It is pertinent here to recall AG Jacobs' declaration, *civis europeus sum*, which emphasised the value of recognising individuals in the EU as more than simply consumers from the outset. The Court did not ignore this and sought to substantiate this idea through supporting the fundamental status of being an EU citizen. It has been argued that this was done through the lens of fundamental rights protection, which emerged modestly at the outset and gained momentum as the EU itself began to accept this discourse constitutionally. The effectiveness of linking fundamental rights and citizenship arguably paved the way for the highly anticipated and hypothesised integrated relationship of fundamental rights into EU citizenship law. Though this was how the third age began, it was not how it developed, and from 2009 until today, the fundamental rights and EU citizenship relationship has not developed as was initially hypothesised.

A clearer direction for EU citizenship status was formed by the Court when it judicially constitutionalised the status of EU citizenship and the rights conferred therein. Without this, EU citizenship would still be criticised as an empty promise. Though its beginnings were conservative and traditional to the foundations of the EU in the internal market, the Court was able to demonstrate great initiative when bringing fundamental rights protection under its remit. Taken to its logical conclusions, this should have amounted to fundamental rights becoming firmly rooted within the constitution of EU citizenship law. However, this

[107] *European Citizenship* (n 2).

chapter has shown that in most recent cases, this is no longer the intention of the Court, if ever it was. It was for this reason that the analysis turned to an alternative source of European human rights protection by considering rights under the ECHR. However, as demonstrated, this too has faced obstacles, mainly pertaining to constitutional limitations related to accession that impede the full effective of the ECHR's enforcement. Though it bore significant potential in theory as a dedicated human rights treaty with binding force within the EU's framework, in practice the Court has not capitalised on this opportunity, to the detriment of its citizens.

It is thus concluded at this point that a more optimistic outlook for fundamental rights and citizenship is unlikely to arise, if at all, until the general Eurosceptic sentiment subsides. It is concerning that the Court has chosen to interpret the scope of the Charter so narrowly. There are evidently some definitive limits that must be respected in relation to the ECHR's application, and therefore reliance must be on the Charter instead. However, this is restricted by its scope as interpreted by the Court. This chapter has aimed to introduce the idea that the Court is unduly burdened by the politics of its Member States and their tumultuous relationship today with the EU. This seems to have affected the Court's approach to cases under EU citizenship, to the effect that the Court seems oblivious to effects that its decisions have on claimants and their families' lives. Whilst attempting to appease Member State authorities by adopting a less activist stance in its judgments, the Court is doing itself no favours as a source of reliable judicial protection that should have its citizens' interests at heart.

Upon analysis of the Court's recent decision-making, the conclusion reached is that it has appeared to have taken a restrictive stance in its interpretation of the scope of EU citizenship and consequently, also limited the scope of fundamental rights protection. There is a correlation between this change in judicial attitudes and the increasingly sceptical political atmosphere in the EU amongst its Member States. This has been exacerbated by the various crises and difficulties that have dominated the attention of the EU institutions, taking the focus away from enhancing protection of its citizens and instead towards addressing the various crises. The next chapter will discuss how this increasingly restrictive interpretation of EU citizenship status bears some correlation with the increasingly hostile attitude of the British electorate. An argument is to be made in favour of greater activism on the part of the Court to make the claim that had the Court been able to truly empower EU citizens and offer a broader scope of protection of their fundamental rights, then perhaps there would be more faith in the concept of EU citizenship status and more faith in the EU's integrationist agenda.

6

The Unfolding Story of EU Citizenship and Fundamental Rights in Brexit Britain

I. Introduction

It is difficult to discuss the rise and decline of fundamental rights protection in EU citizenship law without also discussing the current political climate in the EU, which is dominated by the negotiations concerning the UK's withdrawal from the EU. As the previous chapter has alluded to, there are some correlations to be made between the political trends of the Court's declining interest in supporting a fundamental rights discourse and the increasing scepticism of EU citizens in the integrationist project of the EU. The notion of a crisis of faith in the EU as experienced by its citizens will be clarified here in the context of the UK's withdrawal from the EU. It is the basis for the argument that the Court could have added more value to citizenship rights when it was presented with the opportunity to do so through integration of fundamental rights protection. Refusing to do so suggested that the Court wanted to adopt a more restrictive judicial approach to fundamental rights protection, to the detriment of the individuals who not only benefited from a broader approach, but who valued these rights on an individual level.[1]

The previous chapter in particular slowly introduced the idea that much of the lead-up to the referendum and its outcome was foreshadowed by the Court's narrowing of the scope of EU citizenship rights. This has had the effect of diminishing the value of the status of having EU citizenship. The aim of this chapter is to consider the parallels between the Court's lack of enthusiasm in protecting and giving effect to a broader scope of fundamental rights protection through EU citizenship, and the vote in favour of withdrawal from the EU. It has been noted that 51 per cent of individuals who cited immigration as their biggest concern for the UK also voted to leave the EU.[2] Immigration has been a particular focal point for discussion of many far-right political parties in Europe that have of

[1] Merris Amos, 'Problems with the Human Rights Act 1998 and How to Remedy Them: Is a Bill of Rights the Answer?' (2009) 72 *MLR* 883.

[2] Geoffrey Evans and Anand Menon, *Brexit and British Politics* (John Wiley & Sons, 2017).

late gained traction in many Member States.[3] What this suggests is that the EU's quest to make EU citizenship the fundamental status has not entirely succeeded. The EU project has yet to achieve its intention of unifying the community of disparate citizens from 28 different Member States. Most disappointingly, this failure has given Eurosceptics in the UK additional support in their arguments against remaining in the EU.[4] There are simply fewer tangible benefits that could convince a community of people who primarily identify with their nationalities of the worth of an additional EU citizenship status.[5] In its negotiations with the EU, the UK government have appeared to attempt to use EU citizens as 'bargaining chips'[6] and this represents a serious problem in terms of the recognised normative value of human rights. However, it is also indicative of a lack of understanding of the core of the fundamental freedoms that are the foundations of the EU.

As mentioned in the previous chapter, there is much to be said for a value-added citizenship status, which had it truly been destined to be the fundamental status of all EU citizens should, in theory, tangibly add value to the lives of all individuals who enjoyed the right to EU citizenship under Article 20 TFEU. This, it has been argued, could have been done by greater integration of fundamental rights into the jurisprudence of citizens' rights. Many opportunities were presented in terms of the protecting the right to private and family life. Whilst a direct correlation between the Court's behaviour and the Brexit vote cannot be proven, the argument to be made here is that the crisis of faith in the EU experienced by its citizens may have made less impact if the Court had not been so deferential to its Member States' interests in lieu of its citizens. Indeed, its choice to defer to Member State interests does not seem to have dissuaded disillusioned EU citizens from voting in favour of leaving membership of the entity which has conferred additional rights to be enjoyed by these individuals. It is therefore argued that the Brexit vote represents a failure on the part of the Court in convincing its subjects of the true value and meaning of having EU citizenship status. To this end, a potential correlation will be made between the decline of fundamental rights and the lack of interest in safeguarding European human rights protection in the UK.

The normative value of human rights as it pertains to the arguments in favour of protecting citizens' rights in the Brexit negotiations will also be discussed in this chapter. This will be done by looking specifically at how justice is sought in the context of human rights protection. The dynamic process of withdrawal from the EU by the UK has been fraught with difficulties, and at the centre of the negotiations

[3] Gregor Aisch, Adam Pearce and Rousseau Bryant, 'How Far is Europe Swinging to the Right?' *New York Times* (23 October 2017), https://www.nytimes.com/interactive/2016/05/22/world/europe/europe-right-wing-austria-hungary.html.

[4] Heather Stewart and Rowena Mason, 'Nigel Farage's Anti-migrant Poster Reported to Police' *The Guardian* (16 June 2016), https://www.theguardian.com/politics/2016/jun/16/nigel-farage-defends-ukip-breaking-point-poster-queue-of-migrants.

[5] Hans-Ulrich d'Oliveira, *European Citizenship: Pie in the Sky* (Sage Publications, 1995).

[6] Virginia Mantouvalou, 'EU Citizens as Bargaining Chips' *UK Constitutional Law Association Blog* (14 July 2016), https://ukconstitutionallaw.org/2016/07/14/virginia-mantouvalou-eu-citizens-as-bargaining-chips.

have been EU citizens' rights. The message was clear from the side of the EU negotiators: before talks could progress past the first stage, an appropriate deal for EU citizens had to be confirmed.[7] The hesitance on the part of the UK government to preserve rights of these individuals in its territory was particularly noticeable for a time.[8] If there had been a greater push towards fundamental rights protection in the Court's jurisprudence when the Lisbon Treaty came about, it would be easier to identify where the Court had made a difference in the protection of citizens' rights. However, because the Court began to consistently limit the remit of fundamental rights protection in EU citizenship case law,[9] there appeared to be less appetite on its part to substantiate the fundamental status of EU citizenship. The Court choosing not to integrate fundamental rights into the rhetoric left few opportunities for citizens to appreciate the substantive benefits of having EU citizenship status.

It remains the case that the greatest challenge of Brexit for commentators is that it is difficult to predict what the outcome of the negotiations will look like. There is great uncertainty despite the preliminary agreements reached; after all, 'nothing is agreed until everything is agreed'.[10] One of the ways to mitigate the risks of the uncertainties of Brexit is for the analysis here to draw upon static rights which are current obligations for the UK and will remain as such – these are the rights under the ECHR. In particular, as mentioned previously, the right to private and family life in Article 8 ECHR will be important as this is likely to be most affected by any citizens' rights agreement after Brexit. There is a specific need to ensure that EU citizens in the UK and British citizens in the EU do not find themselves in precarious positions as to the protection of their rights once the withdrawal process is complete. The legal arguments for ensuring that this is the case are argued to be particularly pertinent because of the various different obligations that will need to be considered in the messy process of withdrawal in which the UK now finds itself.

It is the intention of this chapter to highlight the struggles that are present, and are likely to remain, as negotiations progress between the UK and the EU. Of most importance is the fact that there are obligations that exist under both the Charter and the ECHR that are still binding at this stage. Under the current framework, there are some specific risks that the UK will need to be aware of concerning the rights of EU citizens. Without proper consideration of these risks, there is a serious question raised about whether the obligations pertaining to citizens' rights are

[7] European Commission, 'Brexit: European Commission Recommends Sufficient Progress to the European Council (Article 50)', press release, 2017, http://europa.eu/rapid/press-release_IP-17-5173_en.htm.

[8] HC Deb 3 July 2017, vol 626; HL Deb 14 July 2016, vol 774.

[9] Judgment of 5 May 2011, *McCarthy* C-434/09, EU:C:2011:277; Judgment of 15 November 2011, *Dereci* C-256/11, EU:C:2011:734; Judgment of 11 November 2014, *Dano* C-333/13, EU:C:2014:2358; Judgment of 15 Sept 2015, *Alimanovic* C-67/14, EU:C:2015:597; Judgment of 25 February 2016, *Garcia-Nieto and Others* C-299/14, EU:C:2016:114.

[10] *On Progress during Phase 1 of Negotiations under Article 50 TEU on the United Kingdom's Orderly Withdrawal from the European Union* (Joint Report from the Negotiators of the European Union and the United Kingdom Government, 8 December 2017) para 5.

being adhered to throughout the process of withdrawal or not. Given the complexity and unique nature of the negotiations, the concern at present is that the UK is forgetting the human rights of EU citizens because of the many other areas that require attention in withdrawal and have dominated the attention of UK negotiators thus far.[11] This chapter will emphasise why it is so crucial that EU citizens' rights constantly remain at the forefront of considerations under the framework of the rights and obligations to which the UK is bound, and will remain bound, whether it is an EU Member State or not.

It is accepted that the ECHR is a static right that will remain after Brexit[12] and, as such, will potentially be a source of rights protection for affected individuals. The ECHR's main value to individuals is that it is an international instrument that has human rights as its sole focus. It was a political commitment to human rights. The existence of a European Court of Human Rights dedicated to the enforcement of the ECHR also appeared to ensure greater protection and has been heralded as a success for this reason.[13] However, for some time after the ECHR's establishment, it and its Court came under some fire. The relationship between the ECtHR and domestic legal systems is tense because the ECHR is an international human rights instrument that has to be accepted into the national legal order of Contracting States. In this manner, whilst it provides some certainty and protection in cases of human rights breaches, the ultimate value of the rights is undermined by the fact that sometimes ECtHR rulings appear to be declaratory in nature rather than substantively instigating change. Furthermore, there are practical barriers that diminish its effectiveness that will be discussed here in the context of Brexit.

This chapter will evaluate the effectiveness of the ECHR as a means of protection and enforcement and as a rights protection mechanism after Brexit. This is in order to demonstrate whether as a matter of achieving a 'just' Brexit, the subjects of the human rights obligations are being given fair consideration or not. As it currently stands, the UK will remain a member of the Council of Europe and therefore will remain subject to the obligations under the ECHR. However, what is also important to note is that there are other sources of human rights protection that have to be taken into consideration and are still relevant prior to the UK's exit from the EU. The argument here is that human rights regimes should offer a significant amount of protection for individuals during this negotiation process and that the UK needs to be more cognisant of the risks it runs by refusing to consider its obligations and achieve an adequate level of human rights protection. Adequate human rights protection is realised most effectively by the Charter and the ECHR as the original source of its rights.

[11] *Topics for Discussions on the Future Framework at Forthcoming Meetings* (European Commission, Task Force for the Preparation and Conduct of the Negotiations with the United Kingdom under Article 50 TEU, 4 May 2018).

[12] Department for Exiting the European Union, *Legislating for the United Kingdom's Withdrawal from the European Union* (Cmd 9946, 2017, 2017) para 2.22.

[13] George Letsas, *A Theory of Interpretation of the European Convention on Human Rights* (Oxford University Press, 2009) 2.

The notion of achieving a 'just' Brexit for EU citizens is a term used in this chapter to highlight how rights conferral fits into the equation in the context of the Brexit negotiations. In particular, there are discussions on retaining the status quo as per the guarantees of fundamental rights protection that derive from currently existing human rights instruments and the theory behind the enforcement of these mechanisms. A framework for achieving a 'just' Brexit focused on the protection of human rights will be clarified. This will provide a justification for the arguments presented in this chapter pertaining to EU citizens' rights after Brexit and will explain why the current process of negotiations has been lacking. In particular, since EU citizens before the Court were denied the right to enjoy rights under citizenship status, it begs the question of why and how this would be any different in considerations on EU citizens' rights post-Brexit. There is greater flexibility in differentiating the conferral of rights in a situation where the Member State in question seeks to leave the jurisdiction of the entity from which the rights emanate.

This chapter will be structured as follows. First, it contextualises the UK's withdrawal from the EU in the political atmosphere of crisis faced by the EU. In particular, it focuses on how the CJEU's increasingly narrow scope of interpretation of EU citizenship rights has correlated in time with the declining faith in the EU project by its citizens, a lead-up to the eventual vote in favour of withdrawal from the EU by the UK. It also highlights the key points in the negotiations on EU citizens' rights thus far in order to emphasise where the gaps are in the negotiations and draft agreements. In particular, the lack of protection for human rights is evident. Second, it turns to analyse how to achieve a 'just' Brexit for EU citizens. The benchmark used are rights under the ECHR, the reason for this being that it is an international standard where human rights protection finds its best expression. Sample sets of post-Brexit scenarios are identified in light of application of the ECHR, particularly Article 8. Whilst there is some potential for effective protection by the ECHR as applied by the ECtHR, there are also grave flaws in its enforcement. The conclusion is that the situation for EU citizens in the UK post-Brexit is not particularly promising because the loss of rights that will occur as a result of Brexit cannot be adequately remedied by the ECHR's provisions. Therefore, before the Brexit process is complete, there needs to be more attention dedicated to addressing the potential breaches of rights, as identified here.

II. The Crisis of British Withdrawal from the EU

The EU has faced a wide range of problems since the Eurocrisis began in 2009. From migration and refugees to bailouts and referendums,[14] politics in Europe

[14] 'Migrant Crisis: Migration to Europe Explained in Seven Charts' *BBC News* (4 March 2016), https://www.bbc.com/news/world-europe-34131911; 'Acropolis Now' *The Economist* (29 April 2010), https://www.economist.com/leaders/2010/04/29/acropolis-now; 'EU Referendum: Cameron Sets June Date for UK Vote' *BBC News* (20 February 2016), https://www.bbc.co.uk/news/uk-politics-35621079.

has been ever present in all facets of the enforcement and application of EU law. This book has already highlighted how the legal culture of the Court is heavily influenced by the political atmosphere in which it finds itself. This is how both fundamental rights protection and citizenship status initially gained traction. This section will outline how this has come to light in the context of the UK's decision to leave the EU and the necessary considerations of protecting citizens' rights post-Brexit. In particular, it will focus on the difficulties of the UK in negotiating a settlement on EU citizens' rights, the normative reasoning for insisting on citizens' rights before the second round of talks continued on the EU's side, and how fundamental rights in the EU could and should affect the negotiations going forward.

The struggle to ensure a certain level of protection for affected EU citizens in the UK and the British citizens in the EU once the UK leaves the EU has dominated the concerns of not only the negotiators on the EU's side, but of the approximately five million affected individuals.[15] Importantly, more than half of these individuals were unable to vote in the EU referendum on a decision that determined many of their futures. There are legal arguments for maintaining the status quo for protection of the rights of EU citizens in the UK, which derive from the underlying justifications for human rights protection, namely the universality of human rights protection.[16] The question itself is a straightforward one and there are normative arguments to be made in favour of ensuring that these individuals have their rights protected, as the international human rights framework was intended to guarantee this.[17] However, what has transpired so far is not so straightforward and, as such, demands greater analysis.

Whilst there is no direct evidence to suggest that the Court's empathy and lack of interest in protecting citizens' rights contributed to the UK electorate voting in favour of leaving the EU, it is nonetheless worth investigating the similarities of the trends of rights declining in both jurisdictions. The previous chapters have extensively covered the increasingly deferential decisions made by the Court. In the area of EU citizenship and fundamental rights protection, the Court has tended towards protecting Member State interests' in lieu of protecting fundamental rights, despite EU citizenship status supposedly being the fundamental status of all Member State citizens. Although they may seem unrelated, it is argued that there is more of a correlation between the decline in fundamental rights protection and the increased Euroscepticism in the UK by its citizens than it might appear.

A. An Increasingly Eurosceptic UK and Deferential CJEU

The previous chapters have already examined how Euroscepticism has been on the rise and how this is correlated timewise to the CJEU's increasing deferential

[15] There are approximately 3.5 million EU citizens in the UK and 1.2 million UK citizens in the EU.

[16] John Finnis, *Natural Law & Natural Rights*, 2nd edn (Oxford University Press, 2011).

[17] Preamble to the Convention for the Protection of Human Rights and Fundamental Freedoms (European Convention on Human Rights, as amended).

decisions in citizenship towards Member State interests. This has had a negative effect on fundamental rights protection and has narrowed the scope of EU citizenship. Here, the intention is to assess the patterns in the Court's jurisprudence on citizenship within the Eurosceptic atmosphere in the EU and to compare it to the sentiment of Euro-distrust that was building in the lead-up to the UK's EU referendum. In particular, focus will be on what the outcome of the vote implies for the perception of legitimacy and value of the EU by the British electorate, and an argument is offered of the role that the Court's case law could have implicitly had in this.

When the UK voted in favour of leaving the EU on 23 June 2016, it could be implied that some did not consider that there were enough benefits of being a part of the EU as compared to the weaknesses of the EU. It has been understood for some time that the EU suffers from a democratic deficit, which has left something to be desired in the wider project of integration itself.[18] Furthermore, the EU has always struggled with its position as a supranational entity on an international playing field as well as amongst its domestic constituent Member States.[19] Arguably, another way to increase a feeling of solidarity, belief and trust in the EU is to make a significant difference in the lives of the individuals' subject to EU law, and this is best achieved through widening the scope of the rights available before the Court. This had already been demonstrated in the case law on EU citizenship status and fundamental rights protection; there was little to suggest that this should not have continued, especially given how tangible the benefits were in terms of the effects of individuals' livelihoods.

As noted above, a recent trend of the Court's jurisprudence lately was integrating EU fundamental rights in cases concerning EU citizenship status. It seemed there was a possibility that it would eventually become an integral part of the discourse because of the way in which the Court has interpreted it in the past. This was not only because there were inherent links connecting the two sets of rights, but also because the Court itself had consistently been the driver behind an expanded scope of rights for citizens. This had the effect of substantiating EU citizenship status.[20] It is important to recognise at this juncture that substantiating EU citizenship status was more than just a quantitative exercise; it also had the potential to qualitatively change the lives of Member States in the EU. This became clear when the Court chose to expand the scope *ratione materiae* of rights, to strengthen claims to protection of EU fundamental rights like the

[18] Brigitte Boyce, 'The Democratic Deficit of the European Community' (1993) 46 *Parliamentary Affairs* 458.

[19] Editorial, 'Two-Speed European Citizenship? Can the Lisbon Treaty Help Close the Gap?' (2008) 45 *CML Rev* 1.

[20] Opinion of 18 December 2014, Opinion 2/13, EU:C:2014:2454; Opinion 2/94 Opinion of 28 March 1996, Opinion 2/94, EU:C:1996:140; Judgment of 17 December 1970, *Internationale Handelsgesellschaft* C-11/70, EU:C:1970:114; and Judgment of 12 April 1984, *Wünsche Handelsgesellschaft* C-345/82, EU:C:1983:349.

right to private and family life, as the previous chapters have thus far indicated.[21] Because the benefits of the EU citizenship regime were now something that individuals enjoyed as part of simply having EU citizenship status,[22] there was reason to believe that this increasingly positive sentiment could also contribute to combating the Euroscepticism that was surfacing because of the Eurozone crisis and negative experiences of citizens in Member States affected.[23] It was especially important during this politically sensitive time.

It is here where the UK's vote to leave the EU becomes relevant. As mentioned, it cannot be conclusively proven that the Brexit vote is a result of the Court's actions. However, the argument is that the intended direction that the Court consistently suggested in its decision-making and the subsequent actuality of the decline in protecting fundamental rights in its jurisprudence related to EU citizenship did not help to support arguments in favour of remaining in the EU. The fact that there was a decline in fundamental rights protection in the Court's case law on citizenship and a subsequent vote in favour of leaving the EU by the British electorate thus warrants a deeper, more nuanced examination. The increasing deference to Member State interests by the Court could be seen to be a result of the Eurocrisis. However, the fact that a Member State of the EU still voted in favour of withdrawal from the EU is linked to, though is not necessarily directly a result of, the Court's decision not to empower the citizen by broadening its scope of rights. Furthermore, there has also been a significant increase in right-wing Eurosceptic populism that has yet to subside so many years after the Eurocrisis began.[24] This in itself suggests that the Court's deferential attitude towards Member State interests does not seem to be having the intended effect of appeasing Member States and rebuilding faith in the benefits of its membership.

Since the *Zambrano* case was decided in 2011 and EU citizenship status was finally made an independent legal basis for rights, EU citizenship and fundamental rights have not been a top priority of the Court's jurisprudence.[25] Despite attempts to remarket the notion of EU citizenship status and citizenship rights,[26] focus has primarily been on the eurozone crisis,[27] the refugee crisis[28] and now negotiating

[21] See Judgment of 19 October 2004, *Zhu and Chen* C-200/02, EU:C:2004:639, Judgment of 25 July 2008, *Metock and Others* C-127/08, EU:C:2008:449, Judgment of 2 October 2003, *Garcia Avello* C-148/02, EU:C:2003:539.

[22] This is particularly distinct from having to be an economically active individual and also benefiting from the free movement of workers.

[23] *Public Opinion in the European Union* (European Commission, Standard Eurobarometer 89, 2018).

[24] Aisch, Pearce and Bryant (n 3).

[25] *McCarthy* (n 9); *Dereci* (n 9).

[26] The EU declared 2013 to be the 'European Year of the Citizens'.

[27] Alicia Hinarejos, 'Fiscal Federalism in the European Union: Evolution and Future Choices for EMU' (2013) 50 *CML Rev* 1621.

[28] Mike Berry, Inaki Garcia-Blanco and Kerry Moore, *Press Coverage of the Refugee and Migrant Crisis in the EU: A Content Analysis of Five European Countries* (United Nations High Commission for Refugees, 2015).

the UK's withdrawal from the EU.[29] This is certainly in contrast to when EU citizenship rights and status were gaining ground as the fundamental status of all EU Member State citizens in the mid- to late 2000s. It is not the trend that was predicted leading up to the discussions prior to the *Zambrano* case.[30] Whether the effect of declaring EU citizenship an independent legal basis for rights in *Zambrano* was overshadowed by the other crises affecting the EU or whether the declaration was an empty gesture, the argument is that it has not been to anyone's advantage for the Court to take such a passive role in shaping the future of fundamental rights in EU citizenship. If the Court had been less passive, there would be more reason for individual citizens to believe in the project of EU integration and less reason to support withdrawal.

Debate in the literature regarding the Court's jurisprudence has often been on its excessive judicial activism and a need for it to be more passive. It is framed as a problem of democracy.[31] However, concerning EU citizenship and fundamental rights, since *Zambrano*, the Court has been criticised for failing to clarify concepts concerning the scope of EU citizenship.[32] This left much room for flexibility, which could have gone either way in terms of EU fundamental rights protection. Whilst it is the Court's prerogative to interpret the law and adapt it to the changing legal culture, the timing of these decisions suggests a lack of empathy towards individual interests and an even more troubling lack of value attributed to the influence of EU fundamental rights. It adds to the argument that EU citizenship status as a concept on its own was losing support, even by the institutions tasked with conferring rights that fall within its remit.[33] However, the response to this should not have been to restrict the scope further in an apparent attempt to allay criticism of EU citizenship's declining status. If this was indeed the intention, it seems clear that it has not been successful. The Eurosceptic sentiments have not necessarily subsided.[34]

The trouble with the Court's decision against integrating fundamental rights into EU citizenship and the high standard set by the deprivation of genuine enjoyment test is not so much the fact that it has significantly narrowed the scope of citizenship; rather, it is that the trend seems to be against granting TCNs rights deriving from their EU citizen family members, giving rise to a right to family and private life. It is this lack of value attributed to EU fundamental rights that

[29] Admittedly, this is quite a UK-centric attitude. See 'Taking European Views on Brexit in Account' *Financial Times* (31 October 2017), https://www.ft.com/content/931c512e-be33-11e7-b8a3-38a6e068f464.

[30] Judgment of 2 March 2010, *Rottmann* C-135/08, EU:C:2010:104.

[31] Andreas Follesdal and Simon Hix, 'Why There is a Democratic Deficit in the EU: A Response to Majone and Moravcsik' (2006) 44 *Journal of Common Market Studies* 533.

[32] Niamh Nic Shuibhne, 'Seven Questions for Seven Paragraphs' (2011) 36 *European Law Review* 161.

[33] Eleanor Spaventa, 'Earned Citizenship: Understanding Union Citizenship through its Scope' in Dimitry Kochenov (ed), *EU Citizenship and Federalism: the Role of Rights* (Cambridge University Press, 2017).

[34] *Public Opinion in the European Union* (n 23).

is troubling. The majority of the recent case law concerns family members from third countries,[35] and this is where the Court's generosity ends. The reason why this is so relevant to the UK's negotiations is because before the current settlement scheme was announced for EU citizens in the UK after Brexit, the fear was that they would be treated as if they were TCNs. This was rather than maintaining the status quo that exists currently as to their special status as EU citizens. However, despite the settlement scheme, the UK government is still adamant that there will be no special status for EU citizens after Brexit.[36] However, choosing to discriminate against non-nationals seems to be consistent with the sentiments expressed by the CJEU in its recent citizenship case law. Recent judgments have shown an increasing reluctance to protect family members of EU citizens if they themselves do not have nationality of a Member State of the EU.[37] This has been more pronounced for individuals who do not contribute economically.

The Court's repeated hesitance to afford adequate consideration to fundamental rights in its case law on citizenship proves that there is some interest in keeping TCNs at bay and a deference to Member States' interests in this area. It also seems to demonstrate a preference for those who are economically active.[38] The key cases that demonstrate this are those that follow from the *Dano* case, including *Alimanovic* and *Garcia Nieto*.[39] In these judgments, the Member State's protectionist and non-integrationist intentions are seemingly deferred to by the Court, which instead of garnering favour from EU citizens (like the British electorate) did not seem to have swayed them to consider the true benefits of EU citizenship status. Given that the Court supported a different message in the second age as to protecting TCN family members as part of EU citizenship rights – *Metock* being a good example[40] – there is a stronger argument that EU citizens have reason to believe that their rights would have been maintained in this way. Indeed, many may also have benefited from this generous interpretation of rights and would therefore be able to experience the benefits of having EU citizenship status. To move away from this reasoning, especially now that EU citizenship status is an independent legal basis for rights conferral, does not help matters. It is ever more difficult in the circumstances of British negotiations on withdrawing from the EU.

The argument to be offered here is that the Court's ambivalence towards citizenship status and fundamental rights has not helped foster a positive view of the benefits of EU citizenship status, in particular for family members. It is ironic that these rights have now become a central focus of the negotiations on a post-Brexit Britain for EU citizens in the UK and British citizens in the EU. It does not

[35] See the cases discussed in ch 4.

[36] 'Brexit: May Won't Rule out Special Rights for EU Citizens' *BBC News* (7 July 2018), https://www.bbc.co.uk/news/uk-politics-44752273.

[37] See the cases discussed in ch 4.

[38] *Dano* (n 9).

[39] Adrienne Yong, 'Driving a Wedge between Friends? The Court of Justice of the EU and its Citizens in the Case of Welfare Benefits' (2016) 6 *European Human Rights Law Review* 664.

[40] *Metock and Others* (n 21).

inspire hope for EU citizens' rights protection in future. It is thus worth briefly contextualising the UK's referendum on EU membership to analyse how the electorate may have been feeling about the EU in order to examine how, if at all, the Court's jurisprudence correlates with the UK's decision to leave the EU. In particular, it is important to identify the seeds of Euroscepticism that were planted at the outset and how and where they began to bloom prior to the Brexit vote. The reason for this is that it will provide more of a justification for the parallel to be made between the timing of the Court's narrowing of the scope of EU citizenship and the UK's decision to leave the EU, because similar sentiments seem to the underlie both decisions.

B. Negotiating Citizens' Rights

The process of negotiating EU citizens' rights as part of the process of Brexit has, like much of the rest of Brexit, come under some scrutiny. In particular, there is a fierce debate between the stakeholders and the UK government because discussions and beliefs do not seem to align.[41] For some time, this left discussions and negotiations in a deadlock.[42] It is interesting to compare the UK's and the EU's negotiating positions, for this is where the divergence in thinking becomes obvious. However, whilst the EU Commission may be presenting this position during negotiations to the UK government, its judicial body, the Court, tells a different story in the context of protecting citizens' rights. The dichotomy between the Court and the Commission is not something that is discussed in this book. However, the interplay between the UK and the EU is more relevant. In particular, there are some differing perspectives on citizens' rights and understanding of the free movement principles, especially relating to persons. This has affected the negotiations thus far on post-Brexit scenarios for EU citizens in the UK and British citizens outside the UK.

From the negotiations thus far on Brexit, it has become clear that the UK's perception of the importance of protecting rights of EU citizens and the EU's fundamental values of free movement and equal treatment differ somewhat. More often than not, when the UK government can restrict citizens' rights, it has sought to do so. This has been evident by the difficulties faced by EU citizens to have their rights guaranteed, and even one and a half years later not all issues have been resolved. It began with former Prime Minister David Cameron attempting to negotiate a bespoke EU deal in early 2016 with Council President Donald Tusk as part of his campaign to convince the British electorate to remain in the EU.[43]

[41] Most prominent campaign groups are The3Million & British in Europe.

[42] 'Deadlock over UK's Brexit Bill, Says EU's Michel Barnier' *BBC News* (12 October 2017), https://www.bbc.co.uk/news/uk-politics-41585430.

[43] 'European Council Conclusions on Migration (18 February 2016)', https://www.consilium.europa.eu/en/press/press-releases/2016/02/19/euco-conclusions.

The feature of most of the concessions negotiated were limits on the free movement of persons and non-discrimination on the grounds of nationality concerning welfare benefits. It also intended to prevent greater commitment on the UK's part to an 'ever closer Union'. Overall, the Cameron deal appeared to want to downplay or do away with any effects of foundational principles of the EU, namely integration and harmonisation. Interestingly, those in favour of exiting the EU did not think these concessions went far enough, hence the vote in favour of leaving the EU. However, from an EU law lens, the concessions suggested an incredible undermining of the general principles underpinning the fundamental freedoms and EU project.[44] The now-defunct deal is helpful to analyse here as it is indicative of the changing attitudes towards the EU in the UK.

The UK's perception of the EU is a relevant factor in this discussion on the current negotiations on citizens' rights because it is a good example of the significant disparities between how the EU perceives EU citizens' rights versus how the UK perceives citizens' rights. It can also explain why there has been such difficulty in reaching a valid agreement on citizens' rights today and also somewhat explains the missing parts that still exist in terms of the protection of EU citizens' rights.[45] When the Cameron deal was legally analysed, there were questions raised as to whether it would be upheld before the CJEU, highlighting the fact that it was an affront in many ways to the core of the EU's fundamental freedoms. However, given the fact that it was clearly rejected as a valid concession by the British electorate when they decided in favour of leaving the EU, the gap between the EU's perception of rights and the UK's perception of rights grows even wider. The deal clearly did not sufficiently convince the voting electorate in the UK that the EU was worth remaining a part of. It also highlights how little value was placed in the rights to free movement under EU law, which has now come to the fore in the light of Brexit. The fact that there will be such a loss of rights is only something considered now, after the fact. It demonstrates a lack of awareness of the true value of EU citizenship status.

Since the *Factortame* decision,[46] it has been clear that the UK has found its relationship with the EU a difficult one to reconcile with its doctrine of parliamentary sovereignty. However, in view of its interest in maintaining parliamentary sovereignty, it also appears that the UK has failed to prioritise human rights protection. Human rights are difficult for the UK because most of the standards that it adheres to derive in some way from external European standards, such as the ECHR or the Charter. The UK is not a Contracting State criticised for its human rights record generally, especially as compared to some of its counterparts in the

[44] Steve Peers, 'The Final UK Renegotiation Deal: Immigration Issues' *EU Law Analysis Blog* (20 February 2016), https://eulawanalysis.blogspot.com/2016/02/the-final-uk-renegotiation-deal.html.

[45] These mainly include deportation protection, criminality checks and *Zambrano* carers. See Adrienne Yong, 'EU Citizens: What Settled Status after Brexit Really Means – A Legal Expert Explains' *The Conversation* (22 June 2018), https://theconversation.com/eu-citizens-what-settled-status-after-brexit-really-means-a-legal-expert-explains-97810.

[46] *R v Secreatry of State for Transport ex parte Factortame (No 2)* [1991] 1 AC 603.

Council of Europe.[47] However, in light of the guarantees of protection concerning human rights that derive from the EU in particular, it has come under some fire. Most notably, the UK refused to agree to the Charter of Fundamental Rights unless it was offered an opt-out[48] and has refused to sign up to Protocol 12 ECHR on non-discrimination.[49] The debate about a British Bill of Rights[50] also adds to the argument that perhaps the UK is not as serious about EU fundamental rights as its membership of the EU requires. However, for the most part, the legal effect of this apathy has not been too problematic. As ever, it is more about the political perception of the UK and the notion that it has relinquished control over its sovereignty to the supranational democratically deficient EU.

It is disappointing that the status of EU citizenship became less of a priority for the Court as compared to during the second age, where the focus was more towards proving that EU citizenship was indeed the fundamental status for all Member State citizens.[51] This has given EU citizens less reason to declare *civis europeus sum* or declare solidarity with a body which is unlikely to grant them protection or offer any tangible benefits. Indeed, the problems of a status that meant little and added little to its subjects' lives has been the centre of debate in the past.[52] Therefore, it is clear that it is a step backwards for individual rights protection that the debate on this same issue seems to have come full circle. It is for this reason that the notion of a 'just' Brexit must be clear from the outset before making any claims as to supposed injustices on the parts of the EU citizens in the UK or British citizens in the EU. Here it is understood in terms of the human rights protection available and the international set of standards established under its guises.

On 19 March 2018, the Draft Withdrawal Agreement (DWA) for the UK's exit from the EU was provisionally agreed. This included a confirmed section on citizens' rights. Many described it as a concession from the UK government as to a number of its 'hardline' stances on provisions as to the protection of EU citizens.[53] On a positive note, the DWA does not allow EU citizens in the UK or British citizens in the UK to be treated as total aliens with no rights to remain in the territories in which they had previously been welcome. However, it is still silent on the situation of certain groups of individuals, who can be identified in particular by their vulnerability. EU citizens in the UK or British citizens in the EU who intend to return to their home Member State after the transition period were

[47] Nils Muižnieks, 'Human Rights in Turkey: The Urgent Need for a New Beginning' *Euronews* (10 March 2017), www.euronews.com/2017/03/10/view-human-rights-in-turkey-the-urgent-need-for-a-new-beginning.

[48] Protocol (No 30) on the Application of the Charter of Fundamental Rights of the European Union to Poland and to the United Kingdom. *cf NS* C-411/10, EU:C:2011:865.

[49] ECHR, Protocol 12.

[50] Amos (n 1).

[51] This has been desired for some time, but not necessarily achieved.

[52] Siofra O'Leary, 'Putting Flesh on the Bones of European Union Citizenship' (1999) 24 *European Law Review* 68.

[53] David Allen Green, 'The Emerging Mismatch of Brexit Detail and UK Rhetoric' *Financial Times* (5 March 2018), https://www.ft.com/content/a9cbe89e-2067-11e8-a895-1ba1f72c2c11.

not protected (from the *Singh* case), and non-EU citizens who are the primary carers for EU-citizen children (from the *Zambrano* case) are also excluded from the DWA.[54] These omissions suggest that the EU did not consider these vulnerable individual situations to be a priority. As a result, the EU conceded to the UK government for protection of these rights. This is interesting to note, given that the Court already downplayed the rights of these same groups, particularly in the cases after *Zambrano* regarding carers.[55]

Since then, the Home Office has published its guidance on EU settlement to clarify some of the questions raised by the DWA's provisions on citizens' rights post-Brexit.[56] A number of clarifications were made concerning *Singh* returners and future children or spouses of EU citizens in the UK after Brexit.[57] It seems that these parties have been granted rights to remain and be protected under the settlement scheme. Looking closely at this decision, it would appear that there are two aspects that stand out. First, logically, future children and spouses will always satisfy the test of being part of family life,[58] as children and partners are often the core of how family life is defined. It would clearly be a breach of Article 8 ECHR not to allow these future family members to settle with EU citizens in their place of residency. Second, in the same logical vein, *Singh* returners would be protected as these are likely to be individuals who are linked to British nationals, individuals whom the UK would not be turning away. However, more troubling is that *Zambrano* carers are still not protected, and nor is there much discussion about protecting EU citizens from deportation after Brexit or subjecting EU citizens to criminality checks in order to qualify them for settled status.[59] These issues will be analysed in more detail later.

If this exclusionary attitude is indeed the message being sent to EU citizens in the UK and British citizens in the EU, whether intentional or not, then it is highly problematic. It is especially problematic because it appears to fail to realise that human rights protection exists to protect these individuals. However, it is not simply the UK's fault. The argument is that there also seems to be little appetite for fighting for these rights to be protected by the EU, given that the case law precedence suggests that there is a narrowing of the scope of rights to family life in the context of EU citizenship law. This occurred prior to the Brexit vote and is therefore not influenced by the increasingly sceptical attitude towards the EU by

[54] 'Analysis of Draft Withdrawal Agreement Published by the Commission on 28 February 2018' *British in Europe*, https://britishineurope.org/wp-content/uploads/2018/03/18-03-06_Review-of-draft-WA_FINAL.pdf.

[55] See ch 4.

[56] Home Office, 'EU Settlement Scheme: Statement of Intent' (21 June 2018), https://assets.publishing.service.gov.uk/government/uploads/system/uploads/attachment_data/file/718237/EU_Settlement_Scheme_SOI_June_2018.pdf.

[57] ibid, paras 6.12 and 7.4.

[58] *Uner v The Netherlands* (2002) 35 EHRR 1.

[59] Home Office (n 56) para 1.14.

the UK. The underlying suggestion is that as sceptical as the UK has become of the EU so as to want to withdraw its membership, the EU seems to be equally concerned about not acting radically as to upset the delicate balance in its relationship with its Member States.

As it stands, the negotiations on the EU citizens' rights are largely agreed upon at the negotiators' level, which is a positive step forward in the whole round of discussions that the EU is undergoing with the UK. However, there is still some way to go, which gives EU citizens in the UK and British citizens in the EU some room for movement. In particular, because all agreements are subject to final ratification by both negotiating sides, there is still value in analysing the deal offered to highlight where improvements could be made and why. It is important to recognise that there are underlying issues that need to be addressed concerning the protection of citizens' rights and the protection of EU fundamental rights. The argument posited here is that the process of Brexit has potential to be just for affected individuals, as long as the relevant rights are protected in a satisfactory way. However, what is considered satisfactory is unclear. With the underpinning notion of a 'just' Brexit considering rights protection, there is a greater possibility that it is not about the UK's or the EU's perspective. Instead, the hope is that the focus will return to the citizen and their rights.

III. A 'Just' Brexit?

If the concept of justice and a 'just' Brexit is understood within in the context of rights protection, then there are many avenues by which justice or injustice may manifest in light of citizens' rights. This covers both EU citizens in the UK and British citizens in the EU.[60] Difficulties have arisen thus far because there was a stark difference between the position of the UK government as to citizens' rights as compared to that of the EU at the outset of the negotiations. This disparity became most obvious when the UK government repeatedly refused to provide guarantees for citizens' rights in the European Union (Withdrawal) Bill (now Act) as it went through the Houses of Parliament.[61] Indeed, it is still the case that it could all be for naught as a 'no deal' scenario looms large.[62] Nonetheless, the difficulties internally

[60] There are three times the number of EU citizens in the UK and therefore much of the discussion especially here is focused on them.

[61] UK Parliament, 'Bill Documents – European Union (Withdrawal) Act 2018', https://services.parliament.uk/Bills/2017-19/europeanunionwithdrawal/documents.html.

[62] Daniel Boffey, 'Brexit: EU is Getting Ready for No-Deal, Says Jean-Claude Juncker' *The Guardian* (21 June 2018), https://www.theguardian.com/politics/2018/jun/21/eu-is-getting-ready-for-no-deal-brexit-says-jean-claude-juncker; Jon Stone, 'Brexit Talks Should Be Extended if No Deal Agreed, EU Council Chair Says' *The Independent* (5 July 2018), https://www.independent.co.uk/news/uk/politics/brexit-talks-extended-march-2019-avoid-no-deal-uk-sebastian-kurz-european-council-chair-a8432736.html; HM Government, 'How to Prepare if the UK Leaves the EU with No Deal', https://www.gov.uk/government/collections/how-to-prepare-if-the-uk-leaves-the-eu-with-no-deal.

amongst the UK government officials signify that there are normative disparities between the EU's perception of citizens' rights compared to that of the UK. However, whilst this attitude may explain the slow Brexit negotiations, it does not justify the Court's lack of enthusiasm in protecting fundamental rights by means of empowering EU citizenship status early on.

However, now that a partially agreed agreement has been drafted, the tone has shifted somewhat to that of confusion as to why there is still not the full set of guarantees for all individuals. There are also questions as to why there is still so much uncertainty as to the status of some individuals that are more at the margins of society and, worse, if they are also not British. There are normative questions to be considered regarding the shift in the Court's legal culture away from integration of fundamental rights. This has no doubt been perpetuated by the UK's increasingly Eurosceptic attitude and eventual vote in favour of leaving the EU. Negotiations on citizens' rights were always going to be a fraught process given that the debate about immigration from the EU became so dominant early on for the UK.[63] However, the argument here is that it does not have to be such a fraught process and that there is certainly room for there to be a 'just' Brexit for EU citizens in the UK and British citizens in the EU.

A theory of justice will not be proposed here in the context of determining whether Brexit can be just for affected individuals. This would involve understanding the complexities behind the constitution of the UK as a Member State on its own, as well as the EU community as a supranational entity. Rather, the question of whether Brexit can be just for affected individuals will be addressed through a legal analysis of the framework of standards of protection of human rights that exist on the international, domestic and European stage. As Fraser states, overcoming injustice is about preventing people from participating at different levels from each other and encouraging more social interaction.[64] She supports public discussion, and it is this which is one of the most crucial aspects of achieving a just Brexit. The current DWA puts a particular emphasis on maintaining a distinction between UK nationals and non-UK nationals, when really EU citizens have enjoyed a privileged status because of their EU citizenship status. The argument for maintaining the status quo for EU citizens in the UK and British citizens in the EU stems from this notion; it would be a breach of human rights – particularly to private and family life – if there was undue disruption to individuals' lives in the respective Member States affected by the UK's withdrawal.

Therefore, the argument made here is that a 'just' Brexit can be achieved for individuals affected by Brexit, as long as their human rights are adequately protected. It is important to emphasise that human rights are meant to provide protection from authority,[65] or otherwise ensure the individual and their rights are

[63] Stewart and Mason (n 4).
[64] Nancy Fraser, 'Abnormal Justice' (2008) 34 *Critical Inquiry* 393, 405.
[65] Joseph Weiler, 'Eurocracy and Mistrust' [1986] 61 *Washington Law Review* 1103.

at the centre of judicial and executive considerations. This is best realised through effective legislation and standards. The ECHR is a piece of legislation that focuses purely on protection of human rights and is ratified by a large number of states. This is the reason for choosing it as the benchmark in this context. The long history of the ECHR as the main overarching human rights treaty in Europe with a sole focus on protecting traditional human rights (as opposed to social, civil and political rights) exists as a safeguard for individual rights, where perhaps a Member State has gaps in its domestic human rights protection. Indeed, the concern is that the gap that will be created by Brexit in terms of rights protection is likely to be significant, and there needs to be some legislative mechanism to fill this gap; otherwise, individuals' rights are at risk.

A. Human Rights as Realised by International Standards

The system of European human rights under the ECHR and its Court of Human Rights has been widely hailed as a success in terms of international human rights protection, a 'model of effectiveness'[66] proven successful by its influence on domestic law.[67] The opportunities to entrench rights protection as part of the domestic constitution should therefore have become a critical part of the legal discourse for any individual who enjoys these rights as part of a just democratic society. In particular, for those states whose constitution values human rights, this assimilation of external European standards of rights should not be too far removed from its already-existing standards of domestic human rights. This is especially so if that particular society has accepted the ECHR as part of its obligations under international law. The UK is an example of such a state. On the face of it, its commitment to the ECHR should provide a level of protection for EU citizens' rights so that their positions are secure once Brexit becomes a reality. It is for this reason that the ECHR is analysed in here in the context of protecting potentially affected individuals post-Brexit. It is also the reason why it is so heavily relied upon as a measure for a 'just' Brexit, because the argument here is that human rights find their best expression in such an international provision.

This section is a follow-up on the analysis in the previous chapter, where the value of the Charter was considered in light of the Court deciding against invoking its fundamental rights in certain situations that it did not deem necessary. The suggestion being offered was that perhaps this meant there had to be a greater focus on the obligations under the ECHR, given that it was the original source of

[66] R Bernhard, 'The Convention and Domestic Law' in R Macdonald, F Matscher and H Petzold (eds), *The European System for the Protection of Human Rights* (Kluwer, 1993) 25.

[67] Helen Keller and Alec Stone Sweet, 'The ECHR and National Legal Orders' in Helen Keller and Alec Stone Sweet (eds), *A Europe of Rights: The Impact of the ECHR on National Legal Systems* (Oxford University Press, 2008).

many of the Charter rights. This becomes very pertinent in light of the Charter having been dropped as a binding treaty in the UK after Brexit. In light of this, the analysis here focuses on the roots of the ECHR, its enforcement, and whether and how it will be able to replace the Charter. In the previous chapter, it has already been concluded that there are some well-known problems with the ECHR, and these will be analysed in the context of Brexit.

The mere existence of a system of human rights protection like the ECHR is indicative of the strides made in human rights protection in the Western world. In particular, the consolidation of a document that has the protection of human rights as its sole focus,[68] as well as an enforcement mechanism in the form of the European Court of Human Rights, is a statement of political commitment to human rights protection. Importantly as well, the ECHR system exists entirely outside the EU framework. Therefore, in the context of the UK's withdrawal from the EU and the rights that individuals will have at their disposal after this, the ECHR remains unaffected. On the face of it, this should provide some relief for individuals worried about their precarious position after Brexit takes place. As such, it would seem that the ECHR is serving its purpose as the safeguard for rights protection in cases where the state itself may otherwise be lacking in such protection. In the case of the UK, it is not so much the lack of domestic human rights, but rather the loss of EU fundamental rights instruments that are currently binding and directly effective.

The instrument most pertinent to this discussion is the Charter of Fundamental Rights. The Charter, an EU instrument that has a much shorter history than the ECHR, is an EU-specific instrument that was created somewhat out of necessity when the competences of the EU institutions under the Treaties became so extensive as to transcend just the economic realm.[69] As the previous chapters have discussed extensively, as a general principle of EU law, fundamental rights were valued by the Court in various cases where the central focus was not always traditional human rights issues.[70] It therefore gained traction because there were simply too many cases that required such considerations, particularly in the context of EU citizenship. The Charter was not a hugely controversial addition to the EU legal order, given that it was primarily a replication of the provisions under the ECHR with some EU-specific additions. This would raise the question why it has garnered so much attention as to its loss after Brexit.[71]

The enforcement of the Charter of Fundamental Rights is the loss that will be felt most from Brexit in the context of human rights protection. Currently, the Charter is enforced by the Court. The Court's competence is significantly

[68] ECHR, 5.

[69] Treaty of Maastricht on the European Union [1992] OJ C191/01.

[70] Judgment of 12 November 1969, *Stauder v Ulm* C-29/69, EU:C:1969:57; Judgment of 13 July 1989, *Wachauf* C-5/88, EU:C:1989:321; *Internationale Handelsgesellschaft* (n 20).

[71] Tobias Lock, 'Human Rights Law in the UK after Brexit' [2017] *Public Law* 117; Adrienne Yong, 'Forgetting Human Rights: The Brexit Debate' (2017) 5 *European Human Rights Law Review* 469.

wider in scope than the ECtHR. Constitutionally as well, they are very different entities. Under the EU framework, there are substantially more rights. The obligations under the EU Treaties mean that the CJEU has more legal effect in many more areas. This has importantly also included fundamental rights. As has been discussed, the Charter also has a wider scope than the ECHR because it is more modern and is thus able to adapt to changes that affect law. However, it is really the fact that the CJEU is the ultimate arbiter of EU law that makes the Charter so effective in terms of enforcement. Whilst transitionary arrangements in the DWA are not agreed upon yet regarding the CJEU's role after the official date of withdrawal,[72] the potential loss of this enforcement in the long term does not bode well for the future of human rights in the UK post-Brexit.

The claim to be made here is that the ECHR should in theory be able to fill this gap in the law that will exist after the Charter is no longer binding, and this will provide a just Brexit for the affected individuals (mostly EU citizens). For the reasons outlined above, human rights are best realised by these international standards of human rights protection. The ECHR, after all, is the backbone of most of the current legislation on human rights that exists in the UK domestic legal order – the Human Rights Act (HRA) 1998 gives effect to the ECHR, and the EU Charter of Fundamental Rights has direct effect and has replicated most of its rights. It has been relied upon in this way because it has arguably set the standard of human rights for 47 Contracting States and indirectly as well for those who are not part of the Council of Europe.[73] The scope of the ECHR is wide-reaching, and the ECtHR and its judges have expertise and experience in handling issues concerning human rights. Its jurisprudence and decision making are focused primarily on the protection of rights under the ECHR.

The ability of the ECtHR to focus solely on human rights issues without having to balance the interests of the internal market immediately elevates its value in establishing a clear human rights discourse.[74] It is for this reason that the analysis here turns to the precedence established before the ECtHR in judgments, and also those later adopted and applied in domestic UK case law. These will be considered carefully, with the intention being to shed light on the cases with similar situations in which individuals may find themselves after Brexit and what protection may exist for them. It highlights that it is worth placing faith in the ECHR and its standards, because whilst there are very few similar situations of withdrawal from the EU as a Member State, there are nonetheless potentially comparable situations which will be liable to affect individual rights in the same way, particularly respect for private and family life. Alternatively, there is precedent for situations that may arise out of the withdrawal process but are not specific to it.

[72] Title X, Draft Agreement on the Withdrawal of the United Kingdom of Great Britain and Northern Ireland from the European Union and the European Atomic Energy Community (19 March 2018).

[73] Such as those in the territory as its jurisdiction is not nationality-specific.

[74] Stephanie Reynolds, 'Explaining the Constitutional Drivers behind a Perceived Judicial Preference for Free Movement over Fundamental Rights' (2016) 53 *CML Rev* 643.

It is for this reason that the ECHR has also been highlighted as a useful course of action for individuals after Brexit to achieve justice through human rights protection. There are many unprecedented and unforeseeable scenarios, and flexibility is key. Article 8 ECHR has a long history before the ECtHR in many different areas.[75] Its interpretation is the subject of considerable attention, particularly concerning the legal culture of decision making and guiding principles for the ECtHR. The main principle that has emerged out of legislating Article 8 ECHR is the notion of an evolutive interpretation of the Convention's provisions.[76] This is something that was borne out of necessity because of the Convention's long history and modern-day developments since it was created. The flexibility under the ECHR and Article 8 has been to many individuals' benefit, and what is acknowledged is that this is particularly useful in the context of the unique and unprecedented situation of withdrawal from the EU. Similar to the evolutive interpretation of the Convention itself, this concept emerged out of the case law. It presents one of the clear advantages of having a (supposedly) apolitical entity governing universal concepts such as the protection of human rights – flexibility and adaptability to changing situations. It is therefore the natural choice to rely on for EU citizens in the UK.

It was in *Golder v UK*[77] that the notion of a living instrument was first considered by the ECtHR – it was later consolidated in *Tyrer v UK*.[78] Both were Article 8 ECHR cases. The idea that an international human rights treaty could be adapted to be interpreted consistently with developments of society today was a novel idea that gained a lot of traction and is widely considered to be one of the greatest benefits of the ECtHR system. Given that the ECHR itself is not a modern document, it was necessary for any judicial interpretation to keep up to date with modern-day developments. This characteristic is promising for any future applicant negatively affected by Brexit, since the situation of withdrawal from the EU is a novelty and would need the Court to adapt to its unique circumstances. As Bernardt argues, 'sometimes old problems need new answers or at least new considerations, and modern developments sometimes require the application of human rights guarantees to the new developments'.[79]

The evolutive nature of the ECHR has mainly been seen in cases that involve Article 8 ECHR. It has been broadly understood to include within its remit issues of family life, private life, criminal law, data protection, and privacy and home life.[80] This analysis will focus on three main sample sets of scenarios relevant to Brexit in the context of Article 8 ECHR. The first is nestled under the idea of

[75] Council of Europe, 'Guide on Article 8 of the European Convention on Human Rights' (31 December 2017), https://www.echr.coe.int/Documents/Guide_Art_8_ENG.pdf.

[76] Rudolf Bernhardt, 'Evolutive Treaty Interpretation, Especially of the European Convention on Human Rights' (1999) 42 *German Yearbook of International Law* 11.

[77] *Golder v UK* (1979) 1 EHRR 524, para 34.

[78] *Tyrer v UK* (1978) 2 EHRR 1.

[79] Bernhardt (n 76) 20.

[80] *Marckx v Belgium* (1979) 2 EHRR 330.

protecting the right to family life in more than one country and factors concerning dependency. The second is situations mentioned by the UK Immigration Rules which determine when foreign criminals can rebut the presumption of automatic deportation.[81] The third is the case of *Kuriç v Slovenia*,[82] a situation that bears the most parallels to Brexit as it concerned individuals becoming aliens after Slovenia's independence from the Socialist Federal Republic of Yugoslavia. Article 8 ECHR is the provision that is centre stage in these sample set of scenarios and, importantly, is also understood and interpreted in different ways by the ECtHR in order to truly demonstrate its flexibility and evolutive nature.

It is a positive sign for rights protection that the UK domestic courts have been cognisant of the fact that family life can continue even if partners and family members are in different countries. In this manner, they are able to protect rights for individuals who would be liable to separation by Brexit. In order to avoid being deported and separated from family in this way, an applicant must prove that insurmountable obstacles exist in relation to the continuation of their family life if they were not together, such as an adverse effect on one party's health.[83] The Scottish Court of Session stated that 'family life was not a fixed idea but was a wide ranging notion'.[84] This is a consistent message across various different interpretations of Article 8 ECHR both domestically and on the international stage with the notion of the ECHR as a living instrument. It seems that there has been a gradual evolution over time in the jurisprudence of the ECtHR, which takes into account the effects of globalisation and individuals wanting to move.[85] The EU itself can be considered largely responsible for encouraging this, and it is unlikely to simply disappear because of the UK's decision to withdraw.

This acknowledgement of dependency playing a factor in the balance and proportionality assessment of the ECtHR would be one of the sample set of scenarios that could arise out of the Brexit process for EU citizens in the UK. Coupled with the idea that family life was not a fixed concept, in the *Razgar* case before the House of Lords,[86] if the consequence of removal would seriously affect the applicant's mental health, then in some situations, Article 8 ECHR could be invoked.[87] It appears that the ECtHR has accepted that adverse effects on mental health are a part of the respect for one's private life, and given that there is already so much anxiety out of the Brexit vote for affected individuals,[88] there is a strong possibility that more vulnerable individuals could find themselves in this position.

[81] UK Borders Act 2007.

[82] *Kuriç v Slovenia* (2013) 56 EHRR 20.

[83] *R v Secretary of State for the Home Department ex parte Razgar* [2004] UKHL 27.

[84] *AH v Secretary of State for the Home Department* [2017] CSOH 154 2017, para 9.

[85] *Marckx v Belgium* (n 82).

[86] *Razgar* (n 85).

[87] *Bensaid v UK* (2001) 33 EHRR 205.

[88] Ben Quinn, 'Sleepless, Anxious, Depressed: EU Citizens in the Shadow of Brexit' *The Guardian* (24 June 2017), https://www.theguardian.com/politics/2017/jun/24/eu-citizens-shadow-brexit-sleepless-anxious-depressed.

Importantly, the ECtHR does not require it to amount to torture under Article 3 ECHR. It appears to recognise the serious consequences of adverse mental health on individual livelihoods, which transcends conventional 'treatment' for health problems to more holistic considerations like keeping a family together and not being asked to leave a Member State.

Applying the above to the DWA, the agreement does not address the question of returning to the UK after the transition period with a future EU citizen family member, which could include a future spouse or, indeed, children.[89] This would therefore also mean that carers would be put in a precarious position,[90] having their own and their dependant's family or private lives potentially permanently disrupted. Carers and their dependants represent a group of somewhat marginalised individuals, because under EU law they would not satisfy the economic criteria under Article 7(2) of the Directive.[91] The situation of future spouses and children has now been resolved by clarification from the Home Office on post-Brexit EU settlement. However, it does not address question of EU citizens who are either carers or dependants of a British carer (but not at the time of the transition period) who could easily also find themselves in a precarious situation. Known unofficially as '*Zambrano* carers', the argument is that these individuals' rights should also be given consideration post-Brexit because they are also guaranteed under the ECHR. *Zambrano* set a precedent for applying rights to private and family lives in situations of family reunification which derived originally from an international obligation.[92] By applying the judicial reasoning as set out by the House of Lords in *Razgar*, there is clearly a human rights claim for potential applicants. Had the EU settlement scheme also not addressed future spouses or children, there could be a case there too. However, given how closely linked the two situations are, the only difference that stands out is that *Zambrano* carers are less likely to satisfy the orthodox definition of a family life and therefore are more easily marginalised by interpretation of the protection under the ECHR's provisions.

A second sample set of scenarios that derive directly from the UK Immigration Rules are on deportation and the balancing exercise between deportation and rights under Article 8 ECHR. Under Articles 399 and 399A, various situations are cited in which Article 8 ECHR can help the claimant rebut the presumption of automatic deportation if they are found to be a 'foreign criminal'.[93] These mostly

[89] Also known as *Singh* returners from Judgment of 7 July 1992, *Singh* C-370/90, EU:C:1992:296.

[90] Often women as well.

[91] See art 7 of Council Directive on 2004/38/EC of 29 April 2004 on the right of citizens of the Union and their family members to move and reside freely within the territory of the Member States amending Regulation (EEC) 1612/68 and repealing Directives 64/221/EEC, 68/360/EEC, 72/194/EEC, 73/148/EEC, 75/34/EEC, 75/35/EEC, 90/364/EEC, 90/365/EEC 93/96/EEC [2004] OJ L158/77. These criteria refer to comprehensive health insurance and sufficient resources.

[92] And indeed it is also the original source.

[93] This is foreign criminals; s 32(1) of the UK Borders Act 2007 defines foreign criminals as non-British citizens who are convicted of an offence sentenced to imprisonment of 12 months or a serious criminal under s 72(4)(a) of the Nationality, Immigration and Asylum Act 2002 and sentenced to imprisonment.

include situations relating to family life, such as having young children where it would be unreasonable to ask the applicant to leave the country because there is no other adult to take care of the child; where they have a subsisting relationship with a British partner; where they have lived for 20 years continuously in the UK and have no ties with the country they would be deported to; and if they are under 25 years old and have spent at least half their life in the UK and have no ties with the country they would be deported to. Depending on what the Brexit process offers in terms of criminalising EU citizens in the UK who may become 'illegally' resident, this extensive and fairly generous list of factors seems promising.[94] For EU citizens post-Brexit, many of the situations included in Articles 399 and 399A are likely to apply to them should they fall within their scope. As such, the required balancing between these factors and the need to deport the individuals should in theory protect the individuals' rights.

It is already guaranteed that during the transition period, EU citizens in the UK will retain rights. Therefore, logically, there is no longer as much of a risk of falling automatically into the category of a 'foreign criminal' as the UK Borders Act 2007 sets out.[95] Recognising the existence of family life, having to care for children, long-term residency and that an individual may have no ties to the country to which they would be deported suggests that there is a more well-rounded consideration of Article 8 ECHR incorporated into domestic law.[96] This is despite the fact that the Immigration Rules are fairly punitive in terms of automatic deportation for criminals. Given that initially the concerns were that the UK was going to lose one of the most significant sources of rights protection when the Charter was no longer binding, it is somewhat reassuring that it is not the ECtHR that seeks to enforce Article 8 ECHR, but that the UK domestic courts take this right seriously. That this is also reflected in official government rules is also reassuring.[97] In *Huang*, the courts also confirmed that a test of 'exceptionality' was not required under the UK Immigration Rules.[98] Politically, the message is that Article 8 ECHR is a substantive right that requires thorough consideration and can potentially aid applicants post-Brexit by looking more holistically at social elements which may affect their rights and livelihoods.

There is another unique situation that bears some connection with the Brexit process before the ECtHR, as mentioned previously. In *Kuriç v Slovenia*, citizens of the former Socialist Federal Republic of Yugoslavia were 'erased' when Slovenia became independent.[99] Those who did not apply for Slovenian citizenship within a six-month period automatically became aliens. This affected 2,400 individuals.

[94] *Huang v Secretary of State for the Home Department* [2007] UKHL 11.

[95] UK Borders Act 2007, s 32(1).

[96] However, it does not discuss how often and how much weight these factors actually are given in terms of enforcement, and the fact that there is automatic deportation to begin with is an affront to EU law.

[97] Of course, this does not mean that enforcement is at all favourable to claimants.

[98] *Huang v Secretary of State for the Home Department* (n 94).

[99] *Kuriç v Slovenia* (n 82).

The similarities with this and the Brexit process are uncanny. The 'erased' individuals suffered various interferences to their private lives, including lost employment opportunities, lost health insurance and no ability to renew identity documents. Some were also deported. All these are risks that have been highlighted by EU citizens in the UK as ones they could (or currently) face. The ECtHR decided that the 'erasure' was an interference under Article 8 ECHR because the affected individuals were not able to foresee that the measures were going to be implemented and were not able to envisage repercussions on their private or family life, or both. This meant that because there was no knowledge of the potential change in domestic laws when applicants were building Article 8 ECHR rights, this strengthened their case. Brexit, which was not something necessarily foreseeable, would fall in this category. Given this, individuals in this position could possibly benefit from this line of reasoning if applied by the ECtHR.

Not being aware of interferences to private or family life appears to be a factor that the ECtHR takes into account when determining whether Article 8 ECHR interferences exist. This would have fed into the *Kuriç v Slovenia* decision. It was confirmed in *Jeunesse v The Netherlands*[100] that if there was prior knowledge of a potential situation in which immigration status would become precarious, then Article 8 ECHR could be exceptionally invoked.[101] In this sense, there is a possibility that the relatively unforeseen circumstances of Brexit may qualify as an interference to private or family life that would bring Article 8 ECHR into consideration. From the case law, there appears to be a clear pattern of decision making by the ECtHR, especially for situations where individuals want to bring family members to live with them. The relevant elements are that of knowledge of potentially changing circumstances, freedom to choose where to live, and the margin of appreciation of the relevant state. The more restrictive, cumbersome and inconvenient it is on the individual to be removed from the territory of the state in question, the more likely it is that Article 8 ECHR can help. Given that Brexit could be argued to have been unforeseeable and that this would also dictate where an individual may consider they are able or unable to call somewhere home, there is a chance the ECHR could also provide protection from undesirable effects of Brexit.

It is clear that there are two ways to envisage potential breaches of human rights and their outcomes for affected individuals as a result of Brexit. There is a domestic route, via the UK courts, and there is an international route, via the ECtHR. The fact that the UK courts rely upon the ECHR to apply protection of Article 8 ECHR demonstrates an appreciation of the rights under the international standards, and this is an important part of the methodology that will help make Brexit more just for affected individuals. Having recourse to a judicial body certainly helps, and having external standards and guarantees in place are also part of achieving justice. As concerns the currently marginalised individuals under

[100] *Jeunesse v The Netherlands* (2015) 60 EHRR 17, paras 115–23.
[101] *HA (Iraq) v Secretary of State for the Home Department* [2014] EWCA Civ 1304.

the current DWA regime, these judicial guarantees would be available. However, whilst there are clearly situations in which the rights may be of assistance, there are perhaps many more in which this optimistic view is not taken. In particular, these refer to the general dissatisfaction with the ECHR framework as applied by the ECtHR, as well as the UK government's inherent hostility against non-nationals as entrenched by certain provisions that exist in the law domestically.[102]

B. Weaknesses of the ECHR

The above section adopts an optimistic view of the ECHR and rights protection, highlighting situations in which the ECtHR and UK domestic courts have developed some principles that would serve future applicants well should they find themselves in a precarious situation post-Brexit. In particular, the private and family life element under Article 8 ECHR has been drawn upon the most, as not only is it the most obvious choice, but it is also the most adaptable to the varied and unique situations that Brexit may see individuals experiencing. The ECHR as a living instrument is the primary source of this flexibility and has thus far served certain situations well.[103] It is also clear that knowledge of one's rights, choice as to one's situation and the extent of the Contracting State's margin of appreciation have been influential in eventual decisions that come before the ECtHR. However, it is here where there is room for a more critical analysis, particularly of doctrines like the margin of appreciation. Whilst there has thus far been a positive portrayal of the application of the case law of the ECtHR or rights under the ECHR in the jurisprudence of the UK domestic courts, there are some serious substantive flaws that have undermined the enforcement of such rights protection, to the extent that academics and campaigners have denounced reliance upon the ECHR entirely as a rights protection mechanism.[104]

The weaknesses exhibited by the arguments proposed above for the protection of EU citizens' rights are as follows. The first concerns the *Razgar* case before the House of Lords. Whilst the notion of family life was considered to be a broad concept, the courts were careful to note that their standards for dependency affecting private and family life were those of exceptional circumstances. It would require a careful detailed analysis of specific situations in order to conclude whether in fact there were insurmountable obstacles to family life existing and being maintained if family members were to live apart from each other. The circumstances cited are those of dependency and adverse effects on mental health. However, upon

[102] UK Borders Act 2007.

[103] George Letsas, 'The ECHR as a Living Instrument: Its Meaning and Legitimacy' in Andreas Føllesdal, Birgit Peters and Geir Ulfstein (eds), *Constituting Europe: The European Court of Rights in a National, European and Global Context* (Cambridge University Press 2013); Bernhardt (n 76).

[104] Andrew Williams, 'The European Convention on Human Rights, the EU and the UK: Confronting a Heresy' (2013) 24 *European Journal of International Law* 1157.

closer inspection, this standard appears to be an exceptionally high one that is not easily satisfied. 'Insurmountable' has been interpreted fairly stringently,[105] and in this regard, accepting that family life may be present does not practically change much regarding the eventual outcome of the case and whether a family can be reunited. The reality of this means that the individual seeking to rely on these rights – potentially someone who may find themselves deported or whose family have been deported in post-Brexit Britain – would find themselves with relatively little protection. Comparing this potential future situation with the prior precedent of EU case law where this was previously a situation that was easily remedied emphasises how much will be lost after Brexit in terms of rights protection.

Considering this holistically, it becomes clear that whilst the broad definition of family life does mean that many situations of EU citizens in the UK post-Brexit could fall within the scope of Article 8 ECHR, the actual interpretation of the provision by the ECtHR has actually been less favourable towards claimants. This is particularly so when Article 8 ECHR is interpreted by domestic courts. Indeed, it seems that the obstacles to triggering Article 8 ECHR protection are not unlike those faced by claimants before the CJEU when applying the deprivation of genuine enjoyment test and seeking the application of Article 21 TFEU. Therefore, whilst in theory the guarantee of protection of private and family life should be a safeguard for individuals affected by Brexit, the troubling reality suggests – at least as analysed by looking at past interpretations of the domestic courts and the ECtHR – that perhaps relying wholly on the ECHR and its rights will not always provide the requisite level of protection as previously guaranteed under the EU framework.[106]

Furthermore, it was confirmed in *Ahmut v The Netherlands* that: 'Article 8 did not guarantee a right to choose the most suitable place to develop family life.'[107] This appeared to place certain limits on the scope of the notion that family life still exists even when family members live in different Member States.[108] Indeed, even though family life was a 'wide-ranging notion', it was held that there was not enough of an insurmountable obstacle demonstrated to allow family reunification in this situation. There are potentially a number of situations where EU citizens in the UK may find themselves separated from family members, whether they are EU citizens or not post-Brexit, and the risk that the mere fact of separation would not be enough to justify invoking the right to private and family life is problematic. It is especially so when it is the ECtHR that is the source of the disillusionment with rights protection, where the right to private and family life is primarily understood and interpreted.

[105] *Omoregie v Norway* App No 265/07 (ECHR, 31 July 2008); *R (on the Application of Agyarko & Ikuga) v Secretary of State for the Home Department* [2017] UKSC 11; *AH v Secretary of State for the Home Department* (n 84).

[106] Though the argument is that the CJEU has not been so generous to its citizens of late, see ch 4.

[107] *Ahmut v The Netherlands* App no 31465/96 (ECHR, 28 November 1996).

[108] *AH v Secretary of State for the Home Department* (n 84) para 9.

It is becoming increasingly evident that before the ECtHR and in domestic UK courts, family life seems to have been accepted politically as a factor that should carry some weight and deserve consideration, but in fact its protection in reality has little substantive effect. In practice, the right is often subject to a wide margin of appreciation, considering state interests or restricted by the ECtHR's high standards of what counts as a breach of Article 8 ECHR. This has thus led to a number of cases that are not in favour of the applicants' family lives and instead protect Member State interests. This is part of a broader criticism of the margin of appreciation doctrine and the ECtHR regime more generally, in that often in the balance between rights under the ECHR and the margin of appreciation, there has been a consistent deference to public interests in lieu of the enforcement of rights as the ECHR mandates. This, again, adds to the widespread criticism of the ECHR as a rights enforcement mechanism and even questions its standard of protection.

The main criticism about the margin of appreciation is that it is inconsistently applied by the ECtHR.[109] This would seem at odds with the main positive aspect of the ECHR and its provisions, in that it is a living instrument and is therefore able to be flexible and adaptable. However, it is clear from the commentary that this flexibility and adaptability has been taken too far. Whilst the margin exists primarily to account for and defer to Member State interests in culturally sensitive situations, it seems to have been invoked in so many situations that it has become unpredictable.[110] This has also led to criticism that it has been over-used, thereby limiting the Court's legitimacy.[111] Both these negative aspects of the ECtHR rulings do no favours for the protection of the human rights of individuals post-Brexit. Whilst there is a need for flexibility that the margin of appreciation can provide, if this comes at the cost of adding further unpredictability to an already unclear situation, then it is something that should be avoided, especially in the light of Brexit.

For the reasons stated above, there appears to be truth to the notion that 'the Court is often conceived of as an island disconnected from the polity or the general public in the member states'.[112] This is a troubling revelation because if it is to remain the main external standard of European human rights applicable to the UK, there needs to be a substantive rather than political effect on the private and family lives of the individuals potentially affected. McHarg argues for a narrow margin of appreciation in Article 8 ECHR case law,[113] which could go some way towards addressing the risk of potentially unhelpful decisions. However, until this becomes the normative argument underpinning the ECtHR's decisions, the

[109] Letsas (n 13) 2.

[110] Kanstantsin Dzehtsiarou, 'European Consensus and the Evolutive Interpretation of the European Convention on Human Rights' (2011) 12 *German Law Journal* 1730.

[111] Andreas Føllesdal, Birgit Peters and Geir Ulfstein, *Constituting Europe: The European Court of Human Rights in a Vational, European and Global Context* (Cambridge University Press, 2013).

[112] ibid 13.

[113] Aileen McHarg, 'Reconciling Human Rights and the Public Interest: Conceptual Problems and Doctrinal Uncertainty in the Jurisprudence of the European Court of Human Rights' (1999) 62 *MLR* 671, 690.

general consensus is that the ECtHR is not fit for the purposes of rights protection that it has the potential to be suited to in the context of Brexit. Specific to Brexit as well, it is highly foreseeable that given its unique nature, as well as how politically sensitive the entire process of withdrawal has been at both a domestic and a supranational level, it is entirely foreseeable that the ECtHR may wish to avoid getting involved. The likelihood of the ECtHR invoking the margin of appreciation to avoid having to decide on such sensitive matters is high,[114] but would be an undesirable outcome for EU citizens in the UK who may be looking to rely on this remedy.

The second sample set of scenarios post-Brexit was that of the UK Immigration Rules on automatic deportation of foreign criminals. What is interesting in this context is that the House of Lords in *Huang* declared that the situations under Article 8 ECHR that would rebut the presumption of automatic deportation were not intended to be exceptional. In and of itself, this suggests that the provision is not intended to be punitive, despite it being an automatic presumption in favour of deportation. However, in *AP (Trinidad and Tobago)*, Carnwarth LJ stated that the UK Borders Act 2007, which was the legislation passed implementing the UK Immigration Rules, 'is arguably a matter which should be taken into account in giving greater weight to [policy factors in favour of deportation] when drawing the balance of proportionality under Art 8'.[115] This is at odds with the dicta in *Huang*. It highlights the biggest problem with the UK Borders Act 2007: the fact that it allows automatic deportation for foreign criminals and that the burden of proof is on the individual to prove that Article 8 ECHR factors exist to rebut this presumption. The mere fact that automatic deportation is allowed should surely be considered an interference with Article 8 ECHR. Therefore, there is a lack of consistency in the understanding of the role of the Immigration Rules and its true intention – to allow a flexible consideration of factors that may affect deportation or to make concrete the idea of a hostile environment for foreign criminals in the UK. Carnwarth LJ seems to suggest that it fosters a hostile environment.

The fact that the Immigration Rules specifically references Article 8 ECHR is not likely to be enough to tip the balance in favour of individuals being protected from deportation is highly troubling for post-Brexit rights of EU citizens in the UK. Currently, under Citizens' Rights Directive 2004/38, there is a high level of protection for EU citizens in other Member States, and for those who are permanent, longer-term (10 years or more) residents or minors, the protection is even more enhanced.[116] An extensive list of factors is also set out in the provision, adding to the considerations needed before deporting an individual. Deportation from

[114] Ronald MacDonald, 'The Margin of Appreciation in the Jurisprudence of the European Court of Human Rights' in Ronald MacDonald, Herbet Petzold and Franz Matscher (eds), *The European System for the Protection of Human Rights* (Martinus Nijhoff, 1993) 85.

[115] *AP (Trinidad and Tobago) v Secretary of State for the Home Department* [2011] EWCA Civ 551, para 44.

[116] Directive 2004/38 (n 91), art 28.

the territory of an EU Member State is indeed the most punitive punishment in a Union that supports free movement at its central core. The fact that the UK does not subscribe to the same approach in favour of protecting from deportation is a significant disparity that will prove a huge barrier for rights protection in a post-Brexit Britain. In fact, it is even more troubling that the UK adopts the completely opposite approach – the EU favours protection against deportation, whilst UK law encompasses a presumption in favour of allowing it instead.

In the recent Home Office settlement guidance, it is clarified that after the implementation period, EU citizens in the UK – whether they have settled or pre-settled status – will be subject to the full force of the UK Immigration Rules, with no special treatment as EU citizens of a formerly more generous regime.[117] This means that there is no retention whatsoever of the protection against deportation. This is a significant loss of rights for EU citizens and a situation that can certainly foreseeably fall within the scope of protection under Article 8 ECHR. Furthermore, connected to this is the UK's retention of the criminality checks on individuals to determine their eligibility for settled or pre-settled status. This is another seemingly punitive measure that is in direct contradiction with the EU precedent on the matter, which has been established by the CJEU. In the *Tsakouridis* case, it was held that having a criminal background was not enough to justify deportation on the grounds of public security, nor could preventative deportation of ex-criminals be justified under EU law.[118] The general position adopted when applying a derogation to justify deportation is that it is extremely difficult to do so legally. This same standard should apply after Brexit to EU citizens in the UK, but the position currently is that after implementation, EU citizens will be treated as if they were any other foreign national in the UK's territory. In light of the human rights standards as set out in the ECHR, this is unacceptable.

As previously mentioned, the fact that Article 8 ECHR has been embedded into the UK Immigration Rules in theory has not necessarily translated into the provision's scope of protection applying in practice. Therefore, the concern is that whilst the UK authorities insist that there is adequate protection of rights under the ECHR, in practice, without the level of protection afforded by the EU framework in terms of its high level of enhanced protection against deportation for EU citizens, there are no legally certain guarantees after Brexit. It is this which needs to be addressed as part of the UK's negotiations on a post-Brexit regime and it is something of which the EU negotiators must also be cognisant. The argument is that whilst most EU citizens who are economically active with no criminal background will not be at risk, those who are on the margins (non-economically active individuals or anyone with a criminal background) will not be protected. This serves to highlight that the UK still considers some individuals undesirable, thereby excluding them from the territory of the UK after Brexit. However, as this

[117] Home Office (n 56) para 5.16.
[118] Judgment of 23 November 2010, *Tsakouridis* C-145/09, EU:C:2010:708.

is not what the EU regime promotes, it is not something that should so easily be lost simply because of withdrawal.

The analysis now draws parallels with *Kuriç v Slovenia* to the Brexit scenario, as this is the case which is closest to the situation of the UK's withdrawal from the EU. However, it is important here to highlight that the decision is also nuanced in such a way that it may not prove to be as helpful post-Brexit as it could be. This is because of the implementation of the ECHR rulings in domestic settings, and the relationship that the ECtHR has with its Contracting States in terms of enforcement. To clarify what is meant by this, it is necessary to compare the domestic implementation of the ECtHR decision in *Kuriç v Slovenia* with that of *Hirst v UK (No 2)*. The crucial points from *Hirst v UK (No 2)* are as follows. Hirst, a prisoner in the UK, had his case dismissed by the High Court and went before the ECtHR to protest against the ban on prisoners being allowed to vote. In theory, before the ECtHR, the UK government was defeated. It was held that the ban was an interference with private life under Article 8 ECHR. However, in practical reality, this defeat was a political one that has not changed the substance of the ban on prisoners' voting rights in the UK. The UK engaged in two rounds of consultation after the final decision was handed down by the ECtHR. However, these were subject to significant time delays and led to criticism that the UK government did not see this issue as a matter of priority.[119] Its eventual decision was to maintain the ban, with the effect that the UK therefore continues to breach the ECHR.

Hirst v UK (No 2) demonstrates a central problem with the effectiveness and enforcement of the ECHR as a mechanism of rights protection specifically in the UK. The political relationship between the Contracting States' national legal autonomies and the awkward constitutional position the ECtHR is in as a supranational international court has garnered great criticism of its value as a defender of human rights.[120] In particular, the fact that the ECHR continues to be breached by the UK despite its ruling in *Hirst v UK (No 2)* sheds considerable doubt on the ECtHR as an effective enforcement mechanism for those who may need protection after Brexit. The reference to the margin of appreciation and debate on this in the judgment of *Hirst v UK (No 2)* itself suggested that the ECtHR is struggling to reconcile its own constitutional relationship vis-a-vis the Contracting States.[121] Troublingly, until this is resolved, this will remain a problem that undermines the value of the ECHR as the main safeguard for international human rights protection after Brexit.

In contrast to *Hirst v UK (No 2)*, in *Kuriç v Slovenia*, a system of domestic compensation for those affected by the erasure was established after the ECtHR's

[119] Colin RG Murray, 'Playing for Time: Prisoner Disenfranchisement under the ECHR after *Hirst v United Kingdom*' (2011) 22 *King's Law Journal* 309; William Ashby Powers, '*Hirst v United Kingdom (No 2)*: A First Look at Prisoner Disenfranchisement by the European Court of Human Rights' (2005) 21 *Connecticut Journal of International Law* 243.

[120] McHarg (n 113) 672.

[121] See n 119.

ruling. This satisfied the requirement by the ECtHR of adequate compensation for those whose rights under Article 8 ECHR were breached. In contrast, *Hirst v UK (No 2)* changed virtually nothing for prisoners' votes. It was simply a political statement with no practical effect. Therefore, it is clear that whilst some Contracting States are pushed to change their laws by ECtHR rulings, the possibility that nothing will change after a ruling is a problem. The political undertones of the Brexit vote, particularly as to democratic power and political autonomy, may prove a barrier for the ECtHR should it be faced with such a question in future. However, the heart of the problem is that the ECHR and the ECtHR exist and operate in the political context of its constituent Contracting States. This has had a significant impact on many of its decisions.

In the UK in particular, there has been some attempt to bridge the political enforcement gap between the ECtHR and the UK domestic courts in the context of rights protection. The HRA 1998 itself explicitly includes obligations that are intended to provide more substantive effect to the international external standard of the ECHR. Section 3 sets out an interpretative obligation which requires that UK legislation must be interpreted consistently with Convention rights 'so far as it is possible to do so'. In general, section 3 has allowed for a wide scope of interpretation of Article 8 ECHR, famously broadening the definition of 'spouse' in *Ghaidan v Godin Mendoza*.[122] However, the reason for this wide scope was likely because section 4 sets out the provision regarding a declaration of incompatibility, which allows primary legislation to be declared incompatible if it contradicts a Convention right. It has been emphasised many times that this is a measure of last resort,[123] which would place more emphasis on section 3 of the HRA 1998.

However, whilst both provisions appear on the face of it to give substantial effect to the ECHR, in reality, the application of both has been less effective in terms of enforcement than the text of the provisions themselves would suggest. In *R v A (No 2)*, it was held that the interpretative obligation went beyond normal statutory interpretation, but later also held that it could not be invoked if it expressly contradicted what the legislation stated.[124] Regarding section 4(6), its effect is also limited as it states that the declaration of incompatibility does not affect the 'validity, continuing operation or enforcement of the provision'. Even when a declaration of incompatibility is issued, the authorities do not have to do anything in response.[125] Therefore, it seems that section 4 is used more as a signal that the UK authorities recognise there is a human rights violation, but are under no obligation to act to change it. Consistent with the reception of *Hirst v UK (No 2)* decision, this is an example of politics interfering with the desired outcome for any human rights violation of Article 8 ECHR on the part of the claimant – namely, a substantive change in their private or family lives.

[122] *Ghaidan v Godin Mendoza* [2004] UKHL 30.
[123] *R v A (No 2)* [2002] 1 AC 45, para 44.
[124] ibid para 108.
[125] *Bellinger v Bellinger* [2001] EWCA Civ 1140.

It is evident that there are some substantive flaws with the ECtHR's interpretation, undermining the claim that it will suffice as the main rights protection mechanism after Brexit. However, there are practical flaws that must also be considered. It has become a widespread fact that the ECtHR is collapsing under the weight of its own workload. The ECHR was originally hailed as the great human rights instrument of its time – a clear commitment demonstrated to human rights protection for all its signatories. This was particularly significant for Contracting States that had a less than stellar human rights record before signing up to the ECHR. It is understood that the ECHR was created to offer a wider range of protection to individuals in a specific state that might not offer the same safeguards domestically. However, despite the various procedural safeguards,[126] the existence of the ECHR has opened the floodgates for cases brought before the ECtHR by an overwhelming number of individuals. Whilst the intention was to offer greater protection to a larger number of individuals, the uptake has been unprecedented. Official guidance from the Council of Europe itself states that it receives over 50,000 applications a year and that: 'It is not possible to say how long it will take the Court, on average, to examine an application.'[127] As Greer notes, the 'road to judgment at Strasbourg is long and arduous'.[128]

Given that Brexit itself is unknown legal and political territory, the possibility that individuals will bring unique claims is a certain problem. The problem remains that the ECHR and the ECtHR exist and operate in the political context of the ECHR's constituent Contracting States. This has had a significant impact on many of its decisions. However, this tension does not affect individuals involved in Brexit as much as it can reveal what the troubles are for only having the ECtHR as adjudicator of rights.[129] Some of the present discussion on the statuses of EU citizens after Brexit focuses on the fact that there is no way to determine exactly how many EU citizens are in the UK.[130] The current plans for registering relevant individuals after Brexit will be extremely difficult for the already overwhelmed Home Office to handle because of the sheer number of potential applications. There is currently pressure on many of the governmental services related to regularising residency in the UK, including an uptake in permanent residency applications and many British citizens seeking Irish passports.[131] This does not bode well for EU citizens as there are also practical difficulties to getting cases heard before the ECtHR, limiting their remedial options.

[126] ECHR, arts 19ff.

[127] Council of Europe, 'Your Application to the ECHR', https://www.echr.coe.int/Documents/Your_Application_ENG.pdf.

[128] Steven Greer, *The European Convention on Human Rights: Achievements, Problems and Prospects* (Cambridge University Press, 2016) 72.

[129] This is especially so when the Charter is no longer available.

[130] 'EU immigration to the UK: What the National Insurance Numbers Reveal' *Full Fact* (12 May 2016), https://fullfact.org/immigration/eu-immigration-uk-whats-hidden-national-insurance-number-data.

[131] Alan Travis and Heather Stewart, 'Huge Backlog as EU Citizens Rush to Secure British Residency' *The Guardian* (30 November 2016), https://www.theguardian.com/uk-news/2016/nov/30/eu-citizens-in-uk-home-office-residency-applications-right-to-remain-before-brexit-talks.

There has also been debate as to whether there is a theoretical foundation for the enforcement of international human rights mechanism such as the ECHR. This is in relation to its enforcement in domestic legal systems. It has been a problematic democratic process because of the way in which some Contracting States incorporate the ECtHR reasoning into their own legal discourse. This is an especial problem for the UK. In particular, there is a dichotomy between the UK's HRA 1998 and the ECHR because of the tension on the part of judges in the UK as to how to strike the right balance between the two systems' interactions and yet remain neutral.[132] Political neutrality, as required by the judiciary, competes with the human rights *acquis* that is central to interpreting any international human rights obligations. McHarg argues that this has led to an emphasis instead on procedural certainty and doctrinal clarity to justify the application of international human rights.

In contrast, Orakhelashvili has noted that the ECtHR seems to choose between different methods of interpretation as if there is no hierarchy.[133] Indeed, both McHarg and Orakhelashvili have both recognised that by and large, a case-by-case assessment of situations before the ECtHR is often the method that generates the fairest outcomes to the affected parties.[134] However, this presents a normative difficulty in terms of theorising justice in light of human rights under the ECHR. Many commentators over the years have acknowledged that the ECHR jurisprudence comes under some scrutiny.[135] In particular, it is widely accepted that the ECtHR itself is under great pressure, a 'victim of its own success',[136] and that it has come under fire for its inconsistency in interpreting the margin of appreciation.[137] For Brexit, the problem with this is that anything that adds further uncertainty to the process itself should be avoided. If the judicial remedies are equally unclear, then it further highlights how crucial it is for the negotiations to consider and resolve all questions in order to really mitigate the negative effects on innocent parties like EU citizens in the UK.

If the guarantees of protection supposedly offered by the ECtHR as to rights protection are under pressure even before withdrawal has taken place, it serves as a prelude to what the situation may look like for the courts if EU citizens are in a position where their rights are collectively being breached. The fact that it is so difficult in practice to have a case before the ECtHR heard diminishes its value as an enforcement mechanism for human rights post-Brexit. Nonetheless, despite

[132] McHarg (n 113) 672.

[133] Alexander Orakhelashvili, 'Restrictive Interpretation of Human Rights Treaties in the Recent Jurisprudence of the European Court of Human Rights' (2003) 14 *European Journal of International Law* 529, 567.

[134] McHarg (n 113) 683; Orakhelashvili (n 134) 567.

[135] Williams (n 104).

[136] Lawrence Helfer, 'Redesigning the European Court of Human Rights: Embeddedness as a Deep Structural Principle of the European Human Rights Regime' (2008) 19 *European Journal of International Law* 125, 126.

[137] Letsas (n 13) 2.

these practical obstacles, it has not discouraged claimants from relying upon the judicial protection offered by the provisions of the ECHR. However, as seen from the above analysis, caution should be exercised before putting all the eggs in the ECtHR basket. However, since there are both substantive issues with relying upon the ECHR provisions and practical obstacles to getting one's case heard, it suggests overall that the ECHR is an inadequate form of protection for human rights post-Brexit.

IV. Conclusion

This chapter has aimed to demonstrate an existing correlation between the Court's declining interest in supporting a fundamental rights discourse and the increasing scepticism of EU citizens in the integrationist project of the EU. It has explained the crisis of faith in the EU as experienced by its citizens contextualised in the current situation of the UK's withdrawal from the EU. The argument was that there are parallels between the Court's lack of enthusiasm in protecting and giving effect to a broader scope of fundamental rights protection through EU citizenship, and the vote in favour of withdrawal from the EU. Though it cannot be said to be a direct result of the Court's case law, the argument is that the unsupportive attitude taken towards empowering the citizen has not helped matters. The argument is that the crisis of faith in the EU experienced by its citizens may have made less impact if the Court had not been so deferential to its Member States' interests in lieu of its citizens.

The normative value of human rights as it pertained to the arguments in favour of protecting citizens' rights in the Brexit negotiations was also discussed. This is why it was and remains so crucial that EU citizens' rights are brought to the forefront of considerations by the UK government. It is disappointing that this has not been the same attitude of the UK's team of negotiators, for it is clear from this analysis that they will risk breaching ECHR provisions. In particular, this has become a problem in the context of lacking protection for deportation of EU citizens after the implementation period, requiring criminality checks for eligibility of settled or pre-settled status and the uncertain post-Brexit residency status of *Zambrano* carers. It has been the intention of this chapter to highlight how problematic these omissions are for the future of EU citizens' rights protection in a post-Brexit Britain.

The chapter also evaluated the effectiveness of the ECHR as a means of protection and enforcement and as a rights protection mechanism after Brexit. Though there are situations where the ECHR may have proven effective as a means of protection, including the interesting position of *Kuriç v Slovenia* and the erasure of certain citizens of the former Yugoslavia, there are both substantive and practical barriers to the enforcement of the ECHR by the ECtHR that diminish its effectiveness. There are also nuances in the Brexit process which may prove to be bigger obstacles for the ECtHR than it can handle. These are likely to add pressure on expanding the margin of appreciation as applied to the UK should cases be brought by applicants concerning Brexit-related breaches. As discussed above, this is an inherent problem of the system of enforcement under the ECtHR, which has significantly undermined its value as a robust post-Brexit regime human rights regime after the loss of the EU framework.

The outlook is bleak as it stands for EU citizens' rights after Brexit. This chapter has highlighted the difficulties both normatively in terms of a correlation between the Brexit vote and the CJEU's attitude towards narrowing the scope of EU citizenship rights and the decline in fundamental rights, and substantively with an examination of the protection under the ECHR as applied by the ECtHR. It has highlighted both its potential as applied to post-Brexit scenarios and its flaws in terms of enforcement. The conclusion reached is that until the UK addresses the root of the problem – that is, seek to properly protect all the rights enjoyed pre-Brexit in a post-Brexit Britain – then rights protection will remain on the decline for EU citizens in the UK. This is, unfortunately, not dissimilar to how EU citizenship status itself has eventually developed, with the prospect for EU citizens and rights overall seeming fairly bleak.

7

Concluding Thoughts

This book has considered the entirety of the development of EU citizenship status from its very beginnings as a status for the economically active to its status now as an independent legal basis for rights. It has done so in relation to the discourse on EU fundamental rights that has been developing in tandem with the EU citizenship status and its requisite rights. This was done through a number of what could be argued to be activist decisions on the part of the CJEU, which elevated and substantiated the status of EU citizenship from primarily benefiting the economically active to applying more broadly to those who were non-economically active. This book has argued that this was done through invoking various different legal instruments and applying them to the different situations at hand. In this regard, the scope *ratione personae* and *ratione materiae* of EU citizenship was broadened. This has the effect of achieving different interpretations of what it meant to enjoy the status of EU citizenship. However, present throughout the development in case law was the fundamental rights discourse as an underlying trend in most cases on EU citizenship rights. It is for this reason that this book sought to analyse the growing trend of discourse of fundamental rights protection as applied to EU citizenship case law. The argument was that this has been present from the beginning and therefore had the potential to continue and develop as part of EU citizenship status itself.

However, the book then noted that despite the Court making more explicit its references to fundamental rights in EU citizenship cases, there was a shift in the political atmosphere in the EU which had a significant effect on the Court's legal culture of decision making. This in turn had an effect on the status of EU citizenship and the rights associated, as the Court began to narrow the scope of EU citizenship status. This is despite the trajectory that Court seemed to follow in cases immediately prior to this, particularly *Rottmann* and *Zambrano*, where it declared that EU citizenship status was now an independent legal basis for rights. It was argued that this backtracking was a result of the various different crises that the EU was experiencing, beginning with the Eurocrisis in the late 2000s and now culminating in the crisis of the UK's withdrawal from the EU. The interests of individuals began to wane in comparison to the needs of Member States because the EU project itself was perceived to be in crisis.

The phenomenon of Brexit forms the final part of the analysis in this book, as it is an apt case study for how the Court's unwillingness to expand the scope of EU citizenship status in its own case law can be compared and contrasted with the vote in favour of leaving the EU by the British electorate. The argument was that if there was greater support for the status of EU citizenship, then perhaps there would be less inclination to abandon a project which brings a certain number of benefits, including that of human rights protection. This book did not seek to recount the reasons for the Brexit vote; rather, it sought to bring together the analysis of EU citizenship status pre-Brexit to the situation of the EU citizens in the UK who are now facing loss of rights based upon a vote they could not participate in to abandon the EU project. There is a correlation in terms of time made between the decline of fundamental rights protection and the Brexit vote. The argument made was that it certainly was not in EU citizens' interests that the Court seemed to be narrowing the scope *ratione personae* and *ratione materiae* of EU citizenship after declaring the status and independent legal basis for rights. It was particularly difficult to reconcile when the UK was voting on withdrawing from the EU, and the fact that withdrawal was the eventual choice seems to suggest that there was not the trust in the status of EU citizenship as the book had shown there was the potential to be.

This book has discussed Brexit and citizens' rights protection after the UK withdraws because negotiations between the UK and the EU are still ongoing at the time of writing. The analysis carried out earlier on the history of the status of EU citizenship rights and their development and interpretation by the Court informs the eventual conclusions made as to why the UK needs to consider the fundamental rights considerations of the Brexit vote for EU citizens as a key priority as part of its deal for withdrawal. This book is written in a time of great political flux, both in the UK and EU contexts. In particular, what is important is that what is happening in the UK – and, indeed, the right-wing sentiment that is spreading across other parts of the EU as well – will have an impact on the way in which citizens' rights are protected and interpreted by the CJEU. This was made clear in understanding how the Court's legal culture operates and how influenced it is by the political atmosphere in the EU. However, because ultimately the UK will not be part of the EU, the book focused on the protection and enforcement of human rights protection as an 'alternative' to protection under EU citizenship status. Given the links between the two concepts, as demonstrated throughout, it seemed logical to consider human rights as part of the post-Brexit package of rights protection for EU citizens in the UK.

The argument made in the book, which was also foreshadowed in post-*Zambrano* cases that seemed to depart from the idea of integrating fundamental rights, was that there was a need to consider other sources of rights protection that could encourage the reintroduction of an effective system of protection of rights for individuals. The standalone interpretation of human rights has been shown to be possible through the obligations that the UK will remain bound by, namely, the ECHR and the domestic obligations under the HRA 1998. However, as the book has explained, although these rights represent a safeguard of protection for EU citizens in the UK after Brexit, the reality is such that whilst there is some precedent that may help the situation of individuals post-Brexit, the unfortunate reality is that there is less rights protection as a result of Brexit and, if possible, this should be a serious consideration for the negotiators as part of the post-Brexit deal. Given the underlying fundamental rights discourse that has arguably been present from the beginning, the argument is that after Brexit, fundamental rights protection should be brought to the fore and applied on its own.

There were two main types of fundamental rights protection as interpreted by the Court in EU citizenship case law. The first was the Charter of Fundamental Rights, whose role was developed by the Court in citizenship status. The second was the ECHR, which was applied prior to the Charter's existence to protect certain categories of rights when the Convention provisions were of relevance. The rights that were mainly relied upon were the widely interpreted rights to private and family life, and the right to non-discrimination. As the book has clarified, the ECHR has recently gained more attention because it is a non-EU human rights treaty closely connected to the EU and UK framework. The Court has been able to avoid its obligations under the Charter by means of a narrow interpretation of the provisions on the Charter's applicability and scope. The Charter will also not be binding on the UK after Brexit. This has meant that the ECHR is put back into the spotlight as the main source of human rights protection post-Brexit. However, whilst there may be precedent before the ECtHR in applying the Convention provisions that are promising in theory, in reality, enforcement of the ECHR has impeded its effectiveness significantly in terms of a just Brexit for EU citizens.

The weaknesses of the ECHR in terms of enforcement by its own European Court of Human Rights has been widely acknowledged as a problem outside the Brexit context. However, in the context of Brexit, these problems are amplified because of the high stakes for affected individuals' human rights. The fact that it will be the main source of rights protection is likely to be problematic for many reasons, not least the fact that there are practical barriers to bringing cases, but also that the scope of the ECHR provisions themselves is simply not broad enough to cover the wide variety of situations that Brexit may raise. This is both in terms of their substantive content as well as the interpretation by the ECtHR. In this regard, whilst there is some consideration of potentially comparable situations – including the secession of Slovenia from the former Yugoslavia and the many situations of deportation and family separation – the wide berth granted to the ECtHR alongside its highly politicised nature means that the likelihood of difficult cases being sidestepped by employing the margin of appreciation is high. Therefore, whilst in theory it seems that there will be human rights protection post-Brexit, the argument is that the reality in terms of actual enforcement of the ECHR and application of it by the ECtHR should be treated with caution.

The notion of a rise and decline of fundamental rights protection is not simply applicable to the EU citizenship status context; it can also be transposed onto the situation in which EU citizens in the UK will find themselves after Brexit. Indeed, the rise of fundamental rights protection as applied to EU citizenship case law covered EU citizens in the UK, and the fact that irrespective of Brexit, the Court still appears to be narrowing the scope of fundamental rights as applied to EU citizenship is clearly representative of the downwards trend of a decline. This is both in terms of the rights protection integrated into the status of EU citizenship and also the value and meaning of EU citizenship status as understood and appreciated by its subjects, the EU citizens and soon-to-be former EU citizens. The troubling conclusion is that the decline does not seem to be abating, and the fact that the rights protection mechanisms are few and far between after Brexit for EU citizens in the UK confirms this.

What the decline also indicates is that there is little appetite for further empowering the citizen by means of enforcing and making effective the rights that they enjoy by virtue of being humans – namely, human rights separate from citizens' rights. This is a particularly important point in the context of Brexit because EU citizens will lose the right to rights that were previously obligations that the national legal authorities in the UK had to adhere to as part of being under the EU framework. The decline is even more prominent when the alternatives for the non-EU human rights protection mechanisms are considered. As noted, whilst the ECHR was the original foundation for the Charter and the HRA 1998, its own enforcement by the ECtHR is simply not as effective as that of the EU instrument for rights protection. Therefore, doing away with the main source of effective rights protection alongside one's EU citizenship status no longer being relevant would suggest that there is very little to rely upon post-Brexit in terms of protection.

The ultimate conclusion reached by this book is that the status of fundamental rights protection as interpreted in the context of EU citizenship has undergone a tumultuous journey from its initial struggles to be understood as more than just a status for the economically active to becoming an independent legal basis for rights. However, once the Court declared that it was an independent legal basis for rights, the potential that this had in the context of fundamental rights protection and empowering the citizen was not realised. Instead of integrating the underlying discourse of fundamental rights protection that had been present in most cases since the beginning of the history of EU citizenship, the Court chose to limit the situations in which these rights could be relied upon. This is still ongoing at present, and therefore after the steady rise where fundamental rights and EU citizenship enjoyed their heyday, there is now a persistent and obvious decline as the EU is faced with crisis after crisis.

It is was not the intention of this book at the outset to paint such a bleak picture of the status of rights for EU citizens, whether they be in the EU or in a Member State that was formerly part of the EU. As the development goes, there is a lot to celebrate and congratulate the Court for in terms of embarking on the project of substantiating the status of EU citizenship. It has been argued that Euroscepticism already existed when the Maastricht Treaty introduced social and political rights to the EU, thereby suggesting an uphill battle for EU citizenship status to find its place amongst a predominantly economic Union. The strides made in this regard should not be downplayed. However, what has been criticised is the fact that the development has gone backwards in terms of the scope of EU citizenship rights and in particular in terms of its reliance and application of fundamental rights. This is not promising in light of the situation of the UK's withdrawal from the EU, where EU citizens will no longer be able to rely on their citizenship status to be protected in the UK. If human rights, particularly those outside the EU framework, cannot fill this gap, then there is the potential for significant difficulties for EU citizens in the future.

The hope for this book is to tell the story of EU citizenship case law and its fundamental rights influence in order to demonstrate the potential that there was for this to be a fulfilling and empowering relationship for rights protection of EU citizens, whose rights have not be the main priority of the EU since the beginning. It was the intention at the outset to demonstrate that the decline was not to be welcomed and that, if possible, it should be turned around. This is still the underlying message, particularly in a time of constant political change with Brexit and the EU's future. In particular, this was because there were various EU fundamental rights protection mechanisms which arguably required a robust form of protection. However, the loss of these rights has left EU citizens in post-Brexit Britain with very few viable options, and it is here where the decline persists. Whilst there is no way to conclusively state that the declining interest by the CJEU of integrating fundamental rights into citizenship was causally related to the Brexit vote, it is disappointing to acknowledge that there is such pessimism for the protection of citizens' rights – whether this is via EU citizenship status, through the protection of EU fundamental rights or through the wider framework of human rights in Europe.

BIBLIOGRAPHY

Adam, S and Van Elsuwege, P, 'Citizenship Rights and the Federal Balance between the European Union and its Member States: Comment on *Dereci*' (2012) 37 *European Law Review* 176

Alston, P and Weiler, J, 'An "Ever Closer Union" in Need of a Human Rights Policy: The European Union and Human Rights' in P Alston (ed), *The EU and Human Rights* (Oxford University Press, 1999)

Alter, KJ, *Establishing the Supremacy of European Law: The Making of an International Rule of Law in Europe* (Oxford University Press, 2001)

Amos, M, 'Problems with the Human Rights Act 1998 and How to Remedy Them: Is a Bill of Rights the Answer?' (2009) 72 *MLR* 883

Anderson, D and Murphy, CC, 'The Charter of Fundamental Rights' in A Biondi, P Eeckhout and S Ripley (eds), *EU Law after Lisbon* (Oxford University Press, 2012)

Arendt, H, *Imperialism: Part Two of the Origins of Totalitarianism* (Harcourt Brace Jovanovich, 1968)

——. *Totalitarianism: Part Three of the Origins of Totalitarianism* (Harcourt Brace Jovanovich, 1968)

Aristotle, *Politics*, E Barker E (trans) (Clarendon Press, 1948)

Azoulai, L, '"Euro-Bonds": The *Ruiz Zambrano* Judgment or the Real Invention of EU Citizenship' [2011] *Perspectives on Federalism* 31

——. 'The (Mis)Construction of the European Individual: Two Essays on Union Citizenship Law' [2014] *EUI Department of Law Research Paper 2014/14*

Baker, A, 'Article 14 ECHR: A Protector, Not a Prosecutor' (2006) 69 *MLR* 714

——. 'EU Citizenship and the Principle of Solidarity' in M Dougan and E Spaventa (eds), *Social Welfare and EU Law* (Hart Publishing, 2005)

Bauböck, R, 'Global Justice, Freedom of Movement and Democratic Citizenship' (2009) 50 *European Journal of Sociology* 1

Bellamy, R and Warleigh, A, *Citizenship and Governance in the European Union* (Bloomsbury Publishing, 2005)

Bernhardt, R, 'The Convention and Domestic Law' in R Macdonald, F Matscher and H Petzold (eds), *The European System for the Protection of Human Rights* (Kluwer, 1993)

——. 'Evolutive Treaty Interpretation, Especially of the European Convention on Human Rights' (1999) 42 *German Yearbook of International Law* 11

Berry, M, Garcia-Blanco, I and Moore, K, *Press Coverage of the Refugee and Migrant Crisis in the EU: A Content Analysis of Five European Countries* (United Nations High Commission for Refugees, 2015)

Besselink, LF, 'Dynamics of European and National Citizenship: Inclusive or Exclusive?' (2007) 3 *European Constitutional Law Review* 1

Besson, S, 'The Right to Have Rights: From Human Rights to Citizens' Rights and Back' in M Goldoni and C McCorkindale (eds), *Hannah Arendt and the Law* (Hart Publishing, 2012)

Besson, S and Utzinger, A, 'Introduction: Future Challenges of European Citizenship: Facing a Wide-Open Pandora's Box' (2007) 13 *European Law Journal* 573

Blauberger, M and Schmidt, SK, 'Welfare Migration? Free Movement of EU Citizens and Access to Social Benefits' (2014) 1 *Research & Politics* 1

Boyce, B, 'The Democratic Deficit of the European Community' (1993) 46 *Parliamentary Affairs* 458

Braun, D and Tausendpfund, M, 'The Impact of the Euro Crisis on Citizens' Support for the European Union' (2014) 36 *Journal of European Integration* 231

Brubaker, R, 'Membership without Citizenship: The Economic and Social Rights of Noncitizens' in R Brubaker (ed), *Immigration and the Politics of Citizenship in Europe and North America* (Rowman & Littlefield, 1989)

Calhoun, C, 'Imagining Solidarity: Cosmopolitanism, Constitutional Patriotism, and the Public Sphere' (2002) 14 *Public Culture* 147

Carlier, J-Y, 'Case C-200/02, *Kunqian Catherine Zhu, Man Lavette Chen v Secretary of State for the Home Department*' (2005) 42 *CML Rev* 1121

Carrubba, CJ, Gabel, M and Hankla, C, 'Judicial Behavior under Political Constraints: Evidence from the European Court of Justice' (2008) 102 *American Political Science Review* 435

Castro d'Oliveira, A, 'Workers and Other Persons: Step-by-Step from Movement to Citizenship – Case Law 1995–2001' (2002) 39 *CML Rev* 77

Coles, T, Burns, P and Novelli, M, 'Telling Tales of Tourism: Mobility, Media and Citizenship in the 2004 EU Enlargement' in P Burns and M Novelli (eds), *Tourism and Mobilities* (CABI, 2008)

Connelly, A, 'Problems of Interpretation of Article 8 of the European Convention on Human Rights' (1986) 35 *ICLQ* 567

Coppel, J and O'Neill, A, 'The European Court of Justice: Taking Rights Seriously?' (1992) 12 *Legal Studies* 227

Costello, C, '*Metock*: Free Movement and "Normal Family Life" in the Union' (2009) 46 *CML Rev* 587

Cotterrell, R, 'The Concept of Legal Culture' in D Nelken (ed), *Comparing Legal Cultures* (Dartmouth Publishing, 1997)

Cousins, M, 'Overview of Recent Cases before the European Court of Human Rights and the European Court of Justice (May–September 2008)' (2008) 10 *European Journal of Social Security* 295

Coutts, S, 'Union Citizenship as Probationary Citizenship: *Onuekwere*' (2015) 52 *CML Rev* 531

Cross, R and Harris, JW, *Precedent in English Law* (Clarendon Law Series, 1991)

Cygan, A, 'Citizenship and Fundamental Rights' (2009) 58 *ICLQ* 1002

D'Oliveira, H, 'European Citizenship: its Meaning, its Potential' in R Dehousse (ed), *Europe after Maastricht: An Ever Closer Union?* (Law Books in Europe, 1994)

——. *European Citizenship: Pie in the Sky* (SAGE Publications, 1995)

Dahl, R, *Democracy and its Critics* (Yale University Press, 1989)

Dautricourt, C and Thomas, S, 'Reverse Discrimination and Free Movement of Persons under Community Law: All for Ulysses, Nothing for Penelope?' (2009) 34 *European Law Review* 433

Davies, G, 'The Entirely Conventional Supremacy of Union Citizenship and Rights' [2011] *EUI Working Paper* RSCAS 2011/62

Dawson, M and de Witte, F, 'Constitutional Balance in the EU after the Euro-Crisis' (2013) 76 *MLR* 817

De Búrca, G, 'Fundamental Human Rights and the Reach of EC Law' [1993] *OJLS* 283

——. 'The Quest for Legitimacy in the European Union' (1996) 59 *MLR* 349

——. 'The Drafting of the EU Charter of Fundamental Rights' (2001) 26 *European Law Review* 126

De Groot, G-R and Luk, NC, 'Special Issue EU Citizenship: Twenty Years on. Twenty Years of CJEU Jurisprudence on Citizenship' (2014) 15 *German Law Journal* 821

De Groot, G-R and Seling, A, 'The Consequences of the *Rottmann* Judgment on Member State Autonomy: The European Court of Justice's Avant-Gardism in Nationality Matters' [2011] *European Constitutional Law Review* 138

De Waele, H, 'EU Citizenship: Revisiting its Meaning, Place and Potential' (2010) 12 *European Journal of Migration and Law* 319

Dougan, M, 'The Constitutional Dimension to the Case Law on Union Citizenship' (2006) 5 *Inter Alia* 77

——. 'Expanding the Frontiers of European Union Citizenship by Dismantling the Territorial Boundaries of the National Welfare States?' in C Barnard and O Odudu (eds), *The Outer Limits of European Union Law* (Hart Publishing, 2008)

——. 'The Spatial Restructuring of National Welfare States within the European Union: The Contribution of Union Citizenship and the Relevance of the Treaty of Lisbon' in R Nielsen,

U Neergaard and L Roseberry (eds), *Integrating Welfare Functions into EU Law: From Rome to Lisbon* (DJØF Publishing, 2009)
——. 'The Bubble That Burst: Exploring the Legitimacy of the Case Law on the Free Movement of Union Citizens' in M Adams et al (eds), *Judging Europe's Judges* (Hart Publishing, 2013)
Dougan, M and Spaventa, E, 'Educating Rudy and the (Non-)English Patient: A Double-Bill on Residency Rights under Article 18 EC' (2003) 28 *European Law Review* 699
——. '"Wish You Weren't Here ...": New Models of Social Solidarity in the European Union' in M Dougan and E Spaventa (eds), *Social Welfare and EU Law* (Bloomsbury Publishing, 2005)
Douglas-Scott, S, 'The European Union and Human Rights after the Treaty of Lisbon' (2011) 11 *Human Rights Law Review* 645
——. 'Fundamental Rights Not Euroscepticism: Why the UK Should Embrace the EU Charter' [2014] *Legal Research Paper Series* 1
Duxbury, N, *The Nature and Authority of Precedent* (Cambridge University Press, 2008)
Dzehtsiarou, K, 'European Consensus and the Evolutive Interpretation of the European Convention on Human Rights' (2011) 12 *German Law Journal* 1730
Editorial, 'Two-Speed European Citizenship? Can the Lisbon Treaty Help Close the Gap?' (2008) 45 *CML Rev* 1
Eeckhout, P, 'The EU Charter of Fundamental Rights and the Federal Question' (2002) 39 *CML Rev* 945
——. 'Opinion 2/13 on EU Accession to the ECHR and Judicial Dialogue: Autonomy or Autarky?' (2015) *Jean Monnet Working Paper 01/15*
Eriksen, EO and Fossum, JE, 'Europe in Search of Legitimacy: Strategies of Legitimation Assessed' (2004) 25 *International Political Science Review* 435
Evans, G and Menon, A, *Brexit and British Politics* (John Wiley & Sons, 2017)
Everson, M, 'The Legacy of the Market Citizen' in J Shaw and G More (eds), *New Legal Dynamics of the European Union* (Oxford University Press, 1995)
Finnis, J, *Natural Law & Natural Rights*, 2nd edn (Oxford University Press, 2011)
Follesdal, A and Hix, S, 'Why There is a Democratic deficit in the EU: A Response to Majone and Moravcsik' (2006) 44 *Journal of Common Market Studies* 533
Føllesdal, A, Peters, B and Ulfstein, G, *Constituting Europe: The European Court of Human Rights in a National, European and Global Context*, vol 2 (Cambridge University Press, 2013)
Frantziou, E, 'The Horizontal Effect of the Charter of Fundamental Rights of the EU: Rediscovering the Reasons for Horizontality' (2015) 21 *European Law Journal* 657
Fraser, N, 'Abnormal Justice' (2008) 34 *Critical Inquiry* 393
Friedman, LM, 'The Concept of Legal Culture' in D Nelken (ed), *Comparing Legal Cultures* (Dartmouth Publishing, 1997)
Fries, S and Shaw, J, 'Citizenship of the Union: First Steps in the European Court of Justice' (1998) 4 *EPL* 533
Gaja, G, 'Accession to the ECHR' in A Biondi, P Eeckhout and s Ripley (eds), *EU Law after Lisbon* (Oxford University Press, 2012)
Garland, D, *The Culture of Control: Crime and Social Order in Contemporary Society* (University of Chicago Press, 2012)
Gerards, J, 'The Discrimination Grounds of Article 14 of the European Convention on Human Rights' (2013) 13 *Human Rights Law Review* 99
Gerhards, J and Lengfeld, H, *European Citizenship and Social Integration in the European Union* (Routledge, 2015)
Golynker, O, 'The Correlation between the Status of Union Citizenship, the Rights Attached to it and Nationality in *Rottmann*' [2011] *EUI Working Paper* RSCAS 2011/62
Goodin, RE, 'Enfranchising All Affected Interests, and its Alternatives' (2007) 35 *Philosophy and Public Affairs* 40
Greer, S, *The European Convention on Human Rights: Achievements, Problems and Prospects* (Cambridge University Press, 2016)
Griffin, J, 'First Steps in an Account of Human Rights' (2001) 9 *European Journal of Philosophy* 306

Grimmel, A, '"This is Not Life as it is Lived Here": The European Court of Justice and the Myth of Judicial Activism in the Foundational Period of Integration through Law' (2014) 7 *European Journal of Legal Studies* 62

Groenendijk, K, 'Reverse Discrimination, Family Reunification and Union Citizens of Immigrant Origin' in E Guild, C Gortázar and D Kostakopoulou (eds), *The Reconceptualization of European Union Citizenship* (Martinus Nijhoff, 2014)

Guild, E, 'Does European Citizenship Blur the Borders of Solidarity?' in E Guild, C Gortázar and D Kostakopoulou (eds), *The Reconceptualization of European Union Citizenship* (Martinus Nijhoff, 2014)

Guild, E, Groenendijk, CA and, Carrera S, *Illiberal Liberal States: Immigration, Citizenship, And Integration in the EU* (Ashgate, 2009)

Gutmann, A and Thompson, D, 'Why Deliberative Democracy is Different' (2000) 17 *Social Philosophy and Policy* 161

Habermas, J, 'Citizenship and National Identity: Some Reflections on the Future of Europe' (1992) 12 *Praxis International* 255

——. 'Citizenship and National Identity' in B van Steenbergen (ed), *The Condition of Citizenship* (SAGE Publications, 1994)

Hailbronner, K, 'Union Citizenship and Access to Social Benefits' (2005) 42 *CML Rev* 1245

Hailbronner, K and Thym, D, 'Case C-34/09, *Gerardo Ruiz Zambrano v Office national de l'emploi* (ONEm), Judgment of the Court of Justice (Grand Chamber) of 8 March 2011' (2011) 48 *CML Rev* 1253

Hailbronner, M and Sánchez, SI, 'The European Court of Justice and Citizenship of the European Union: New Developments towards a Truly Fundamental Status' (2011) 5 *Vienna Journal on International Constitutional Law* 498

Hammar, T, *International Migration, Citizenship and Democracy* (Gower, 1990)

——. 'Denizen and Denizenship' [2003] *New Concepts of Citizenship* 93

Hanf, D, 'Reverse Discrimination in EU Law: Constitutional Aberration, Constitutional Necessity, or Judicial Choice' (2011) 18 *Maastricht Journal of European and Comparative Law* 29

Hansen, P and Hager, SB, *The Politics of European Citizenship: Deepening Contradictions in Social Rights and Migration Policy* (Berghahn Books, 2013)

Heater, D, *What is Citizenship?* (Polity Press, 1999)

Held, D, *Democracy and the Global Order: From the Modern State to Cosmopolitan Governance* (Stanford University Press, 1995)

Helfer, L, 'Redesigning the European Court of Human Rights: Embeddedness as a Deep Structural Principle of the European Human Rights Regime' (2008) 19 *European Journal of International Law* 125

Hinarejos, A, 'Extending Citizenship and the Scope of EU Law' (2011) 70 *CLJ* 309

——. 'Citizenship of the EU: Clarifying "Genuine Enjoyment of the Substance" of Citizenship Rights' (2012) 71 *CLJ* 279

——. 'Fiscal Federalism in the European Union: Evolution and Future Choices for EMU' (2013) 50 *CML Rev* 1621

Hofstotter, B, 'A Cascade of Rights, or Who Shall Care for Little Catherine? Some Reflections on the *Chen* Case' [2005] *European Law Review* 548

Horeth, M, 'No Way out for the Beast? The Unsolved Legitimacy Problem of European Governance' (1999) 6 *Journal of European Public Policy* 249

Isin, E and Turner, B, 'Citizenship Studies: An Introduction' in E Isin and B Turner (eds), *Handbook of Citizenship Studies* (SAGE Publications, 2002)

Jacobs, FG, 'Citizenship of the European Union: A Legal Analysis' (2007) 13 *European Law Journal* 591

Jacqueson, C, 'Union Citizenship and the Court of Justice: Something New under the Sun? Towards Social Citizenship' [2002] *European Law Review* 260

Jones, P, *Rights* (Macmillan, 1994)

Jourova, V, *2014 Report on the Application of the EU Charter of Fundamental Rights* (DG Justice, Consumers and Gender Equality, 2014)

Keller, H and Stone Sweet, A, 'The ECHR and National Legal Orders' in H Keller and A Stone Sweet (eds), *A Europe of Rights: The Impact of the ECHR on National Legal Systems* (Oxford University Press, 2008)

Kesby, A, *The Right to Have Rights: Citizenship, Humanity, and International Law* (Oxford University Press, 2012)

Kochenov, D, 'A Real European Citizenship; A New Jurisdiction Test; A Novel Chapter in the Development of the Union in Europe' (2011) 18 *Columbia Journal of European Law* 56

——. 'Two Sovereign States vs a Human Being: CJEU as a Guardian of Arbitrariness in Citizenship Matters' [2011] *EUI Working Paper* RSCAS 2011/62

——. 'The Right to Have What Rights? EU Citizenship in Need of Clarification' (2013) 19 *European Law Journal* 502

Kochenov, D and Lindeboom, J, 'Breaking Chinese Law – Making European One: The Story of *Chen*, or: Two Winners, Two Losers, Two Truths' in B Davies and F Nicola (eds), *EU Law Stories* (Cambridge University Press, 2017)

Kochenov, D and Plender, R, 'EU Citizenship: From an Incipient Form to an Incipient Substance? The Discovery of the Treaty Text' (2012) 37 *European Law Review* 369

Kokott, J and Sobotta, C, 'The Charter of Fundamental Rights of the European Union after Lisbon' [2010] *EUI Working Papers, Academy of European Law 2010/6*

Kostakopoulou, D, 'Ideas, Norms and European Citizenship: Explaining Institutional Change' (2005) 68 *MLR* 233

——. 'European Union Citizenship: Writing the Future' (2007) 13 *European Law Journal* 623

——. *The Future Governance of Citizenship* (Cambridge University Press, 2008)

Kurpas, S, *The Treaty of Lisbon: How Much 'Constitution' is Left?* (CEPS Policy Brief No 147, 2007)

Kymlicka, W, *Multicultural Citizenship: A Liberal Theory of Minority Rights* (Clarendon Press, 1995)

Lawson, R, 'Case C-168/91, *Christos Konstantinidis v Stadt Altensteig-Standesamt*, Judgment of 30 March 1993 [1993] 3 CMLR 401, Not Yet Reported in ECR' (1994) 31 *CMLR* 395

Leconte, C, 'The EU Fundamental Rights Policy as a Source of Euroscepticism' (2014) 15 *Human Rights Review* 83

Lehning, PB, 'European Citizenship: Towards a European Identity?' (2001) 20 *Law and Philosophy* 239

Lenaerts, K, 'European Union Citizenship, National Welfare Systems and Social Solidarity' (2011) 2 *Jurisprudencija* 397

——. 'The Court's Outer and Inner Selves: Exploring the External and Internal Legitimacy of the European Court of Justice' in M Adams et al (eds), *Judging Europe's Judges* (Hart Publishing, 2013)

Letsas, G, *A Theory of Interpretation of the European Convention on Human Rights* (Oxford University Press, 2009)

——. 'The ECHR as a Living Instrument: Its Meaning and Legitimacy' in A Føllesdal, B Peters and G Ulfstein (eds), *Constituting Europe: The European Court of Rights in a National, European and Global Context* (Cambridge University Press, 2013)

Lock, T, 'Human Rights Law in the UK after Brexit' [2017] *Public Law* 117

Locke, J, *Two Treatises of Government* (Cambridge University Press, 1963)

Lyons, C, 'A Voyage around Article 8: An Historical Evaluation on the Fate of European Union Citizenship' (1997) 17 *Yearbook of European Law* 135

MacDonald, R, 'The Margin of Appreciation in the Jurisprudence of the European Court of Human Rights' in R MacDonald, H Petzold and F Matscher (eds), *The European System for the Protection of Human Rights* (Martinus Nijhoff, 1993)

Magnette, P, *Citizenship: The History of an Idea* (ECPR, 2005)

Mantouvalou, V, 'Workers without Rights as Citizens at the Margins' (2013) 16 *Critical Review of International Social and Political Philosophy* 366

Mather, JD, 'The Court of Justice and the Union Citizen' (2005) 11 *European Law Journal* 722

McCauliff, C, 'EU Citizenship: Why Can't the Advocates General Keep Sheila McCarthy's Family Together' (2013) 36 *Fordham International Law Journal* 1372
McConnon, J, '*Dereci*: An Analysis of the Genuine Enjoyment Test and European Union Citizenship under Articles 20 and 21 TFEU' (2012) 15 *Trinity College Law Review* 119
McHarg, A, 'Reconciling Human Rights and the Public Interest: Conceptual Problems and Doctrinal Uncertainty in the Jurisprudence of the European Court of Human Rights' (1999) 62 *MLR* 671
Michelman, FI, 'Human Rights and the Limits of Constitutional Theory' (2000) 13 *Ratio Juris* 63
Miller, D, *On Nationality* (Clarendon Press, 1995)
——. *Citizenship and National Identity* (Polity Press, 2000)
Moravcsik, A, 'Liberal Intergovernmentalism and Integration: A Rejoinder' (1995) 33 *Journal of Common Market Studies* 611
——. 'Reassessing Legitimacy in the European Union' (2002) 40 *Journal of Common Market Studies* 603
Morijn, J, 'Balancing Fundamental Rights and Common Market Freedoms in Union Law: *Schmidberger and Omega* in the Light of the European Constitution' (2006) 12 *European Law Journal* 15
Morris, R, 'Case C-34/09-*Gerardo Ruiz Zambrano v Office National de l'Emploi* (ONEm), Judgment of the Court (Grand Chamber) of 8 March 2011, Not Yet Reported' (2011) 18 *Maastricht Journal of European and Comparative Law* 179
Muir, E, 'Fundamental Rights: An Unsettling EU Competence' (2014) 15 *Human Rights Review* 25
Murray, CR, 'Playing for Time: Prisoner Disenfranchisement under the ECHR after *Hirst v United Kingdom*' (2011) 22 *King's Law Journal* 309
Nelken, D, 'Using the Concept of Legal Culture' (2004) 29 *Australian Journal of Legal Philosophy* 1
Nic Shuibhne, N, 'Free Movement of Persons and the Wholly Internal Rule: Time to Move on?' (2002) 39 *CML Rev* 731
——. 'The Resilience of EU Market Citizenship' (2010) 47 *CML Rev* 1597
——. 'Seven Questions for Seven Paragraphs' (2011) 36 *European Law Review* 161
——. 'EU Citizenship after Lisbon' in D Ashiagbor, N Countouris and I Lianos (eds), *The European Union after the Treaty of Lisbon* (Cambridge University Press, 2012)
——. '(Some of) the Kids are All Right' (2012) 49 *CML Rev* 349
——. 'The Third Age of EU Citizenship' in P Syrpis (ed), *The Judiciary, the Legislature and the EU Internal Market* (Cambridge University Press, 2012)
——. *The Coherence of EU Free Movement Law* (Oxford University Press, 2013)
——. 'Limits Rising, Duties Ascending: The Changing Legal Shape of Union Citizenship' (2015) 52 *CML Rev* 889
O'Brien, C, 'Real Links, Abstract Rights and False Alarms: The Relationship between the ECJ's "Real Link" Case Law and National Solidarity' (2008) 33 *European Law Review* 643
O'Gorman, R, 'The Proportionality Principle and Union Citizenship' [2009] *Mitchell Working Papers 1/2009*
——. '*Ruiz-Zambrano, McCarthy* and the Purely Internal Rule' [2011] *Irish Jurist* 221
O'Leary, S, 'The Relationship between Community Citizenship and the Protection of Fundamental Rights in Community Law' (1995) 32 *CML Rev* 519
——. 'Putting Flesh on the Bones of European Union Citizenship' (1999) 24 *European Law Review* 68
——. 'The Past, Present and Future of the Purely Internal Rule in EU Law' [2010] *Irish Jurist* 13
O'Neill, P and Sandler, SR, 'The EU Citizenship *Acquis* and the Court of Justice: Citizenship Vigilante or Merely Vigilant Treaty Guardian' (2008) 7 *Richmond Journal of Global Law and Business* 205
Occhipinti, JD, 'Whither the Withering Democratic Deficit? The Impact of the Lisbon Treaty on the Area of Freedom, Security and Justice' [2013] *Cambridge Review of International Affairs* 1
Oliver, P and Roth, W-H, 'The Internal Market and the Four Freedoms' (2004) 41 *CML Rev* 407
Olsen, EDH, *Transnational Citizenship in the European Union* (Bloomsbury Publishing, 2012)
Orakhelashvili, A, 'Restrictive Interpretation of Human Rights Treaties in the Recent Jurisprudence of the European Court of Human Rights' (2003) 14 *European Journal of International Law* 529

Osiander, A, 'Sovereignty, International Relations, and the Westphalian Myth' (2001) 55 *International Organization* 251

Powers, WA, '*Hirst v United Kingdom (No 2)*: A First Look at Prisoner Disenfranchisement by the European Court of Human Rights' (2005) 21 *Connecticut Journal of International Law* 243

Preuss, UK, 'Problems of a Concept of European Citizenship' (1995) 1 *European Law Journal* 267

——. 'Two Challenges to European Citizenship' (1996) 44 *Political Studies* 534

Raucea, C, 'Fundamental Rights: The Missing Pieces of European Citizenship' (2013) 14 *German Law Journal* 2021

Reynolds, S, 'Explaining the Constitutional Drivers behind a Perceived Judicial Preference for Free Movement over Fundamental Rights' (2016) 53 *CML Rev* 643

Sacerdoti, G, 'The European Charter of Fundamental Rights: From a Nation-State Europe to a Citizen's Europe' (2002) 8 *ColumJEurLaw* 37

Safjan, M, 'Areas of Application of the Charter of Fundamental Rights of the European Union: Fields of Conflict?' [2012] *EUI Working Paper 2012/22*

Sánchez, SI, 'The Court and the Charter: The Impact of the Entry into Force of the Lisbon Treaty on the ECJ's Approach to Fundamental Rights' (2012) 49 *CML Rev* 1565

——. 'Fundamental Rights and Citizenship of the Union at a Crossroads: A Promising Alliance or a Dangerous Liaison?' (2014) 20 *European Law Journal* 464

Savino, M, 'EU Citizenship: Post-national or Post-nationalist? Revisiting the *Rottmann* Case through Administrative Lenses' (2011) 23 *European Review of Public Law* 39

Schmidt, SK, 'Who Cares about Nationality? The Path-Dependent Case Law of the ECJ from Goods to Citizens' (2012) 19 *Journal of European Public Policy* 8

Schönberger, C, 'European Citizenship as Federal Citizenship: Some Citizenship Lessons of Comparative Federalism' (2007) 1 *European Review of Public Law* 19

Schrauwen, A, 'European Union Citizenship in the Treaty of Lisbon: Any Change at All?' (2008) 15 *Maastricht Journal of European and Comparative Law* 55

Senden, L, *Soft Law in European Community Law* (Hart Publishing, 2004)

Shambaugh, JC, Reis, R and Rey, H, 'The Euro's Three Crises' [2012] *Brookings Papers on Economic Activity* 157

Shaw, J, 'The Many Pasts and Futures of Citizenship in the European Union' (1997) 22 *European Law Review* 554

——. 'The Interpretation of European Union Citizenship' (1998) 61 *MLR* 293

——. *The Transformation of Citizenship in the European Union: Electoral Rights and the Restructuring of Political Space* (Cambridge University Press, 2007)

Shaw, J et al, 'Has the European Court of Justice Challenged Member State Sovereignty in Nationality Law?' [2011] *EUI Working Paper* RSCAS 2011/62

Somek, A, 'Solidarity Decomposed: Being and Time in European Citizenship' (2007) 32 *European Law Review* 787

Spaventa, E, 'From *Gebhard* to *Carpenter*: Towards a (Non-)Economic European Constitution' (2004) 41 *CML Rev* 743

——. 'Seeing the Wood Despite the Trees? On the Scope of Union Citizenship and its Constitutional Effects' (2008) 45 *CML Rev* 13

——. 'Striving for Equality: Who "Deserves" to Be a Union Citizen?' in A Tizzano et al (eds), *Scritti in Onore di Giuseppe Tesauro* (Editoriale Scientifica, 2014)

——. 'Family Rights for Circular Migrants and Frontier Workers: *O and B, and S and G*' (2015) 52 *CML Rev* 753

——. 'Earned Citizenship: Understanding Union Citizenship through its Scope' in D Kochenov (ed), *EU Citizenship and Federalism: The Role of Rights* (Cambridge University Press, 2017)

Stone Sweet, A, 'The European Court of Justice and the Judicialization of EU Governance' (2010) 5 *Living Reviews in EU Governance* 5

Storey, H, 'The Right to Family Life and Immigration Case Law at Strasbourg' (1990) 39 *ICLQ* 328

Strus, J and Persak, N, 'The Charter of Fundamental Rights and EU Citizenship: The Link with EU Law Re-examined' in E Guild, C Gortázar and D Kostakopoulou (eds), *The Reconceptualization of European Union Citizenship* (Martinus Nijhoff, 2014)

Taggart, P, 'A Touchstone of Dissent: Euroscepticism in Contemporary Western European Party Systems' (1998) 33 *European Journal of Political Research* 363

Tetley, W, 'Mixed Jurisdictions: Common Law v Civil Law (Codified and Uncodified)' (1999) 60 *Louisiana Law Review* 677

Thompson, J, 'Community Identity and World Citizenship' in D Archibugi, D Held and M Köhler (eds), *Re-imagining Political Community: Studies in Cosmopolitan Democracy* (Stanford University Press, 1998)

Thym, D, 'Towards "Real" Citizenship? The Judicial Construction of Union Citizenship and its Limits' in M Adams et al (eds), *Judging Europe's Judges* (Hart Publishing, 2013)

——. 'The Elusive Limits of Solidarity: Residence Rights of and Social Benefits for Economically Inactive Union Citizens' (2015) 52 *CML Rev* 17

Tiilikainen, T, 'The Problem of Democracy in the European Union' in E Antola and A Rosas (eds), *A Citizen's Europe: In Search of a New Order* (SAGE Publications, 1995)

Tomuschat, C, 'Case C-85/96, *María Martinez Sala v. Freistaat Bayern*, Judgment of 12 May 1998, Full Court [1998] ECR I-2691' (2000) 37 *CML Rev* 449

Torreblanca, JI and Leonard, M, *The Continent-Wide Rise of Euroscepticism* (European Council on Foreign Relations Policy Memo, 2013)

Tridimas, T, *The General Principles of EU Law*, 2nd edn (Oxford University Press, 2006)

Tryfonidou, A, 'Family Reunification Rights of (Migrant) Union Citizens: Towards a More Liberal Approach' (2009) 15 *European Law Journal* 634

——. 'In Search of the Aim of the EC Free Movement of Persons Provisions: Has the Court of Justice Missed the Point?' (2009) 46 *CML Rev* 1591

Usherwood, S and Startin, N, 'Euroscepticism as a Persistent Phenomenon' (2013) 51 *Journal of Common Market Studies* 1

Van der Mei, AP, 'Freedom of Movement and Financial Aid for Students: Some Reflections on *Grzelczyk* and *Fahmi and Esmoris-Cerdeiro Pinedo Amoris*' (2001) 3 *European Journal of Social Security* 181

——. 'Overview of Recent Cases before the Court of Justice of the European Union (October–December 2014)' (2015) 17 *European Journal of Social Security* 103

Van Eijken, H, 'Case C-391/09, *Malgožata Runevič-Vardyn and Lukasz Pawel Wardyn v. Vilniaus miesto savivaldybes administracija and Others*, Judgment of the Court (Second Chamber) of 12 May 2011' (2012) 49 *CML Rev* 809

Van Eijken, H and de Vries, S, 'A New Route into the Promised Land? Being a European Citizen after *Ruiz Zambrano*' (2011) 36 *European Law Review* 704

Van Elsuwege, P, 'Court of Justice of the European Union European Union Citizenship and the Purely Internal Rule Revisited Decision of 5 May 2011, Case C-434/09 *Shirley McCarthy v. Secretary of State for the Home Department*' (2011) 7 *European Constitutional Law Review* 308

——. 'Shifting the Boundaries? European Union Citizenship and the Scope of Application of EU Law: Case No C-34/09, *Gerardo Ruiz Zambrano v Office national de l'emploi*' (2011) 38 *Legal Issues of Economic Integration* 263

Van Elsuwege, P and Kochenov, D, 'On the Limits of Judicial Intervention: EU Citizenship and Family Reunification Rights' (2011) 13 *European Journal of Migration and Law* 443

Verschueren, H, 'Preventing "Benefit Tourism" in the EU: A Narrow or Broad Interpretation of the Possibilities Offered by the ECJ in *Dano*?' (2015) 52 *CML Rev* 363

Von Bogdandy, A, 'The European Union as a Human Rights Organization? Human Rights and the Core of the European Union' (2000) 37 *CML Rev* 1307

Von Bogdandy, A et al, 'Reverse *Solange*: Protecting the Essence of Fundamental Rights against EU Member States' (2012) 49 *CML Rev* 489

Weatherill, S, 'After *Keck*: Some Thoughts on How to Clarify the Clarification' (1996) 33 *CML Rev* 887

——. 'Competence Creep and Competence Control' (2004) 23 *Yearbook of European Law* 1
Weiler, J, 'Eurocracy and Mistrust' [1986] 61 *Washington Law Review* 1103
——. 'Citizenship and Human Rights' in JA Winter et al (eds), *Reforming the Treaty on the European Union* (Kluwer Law International, 1996)
Wiener, A, *'European' Citizenship Practice* (Westview Press, 1998)
Wiesbrock, A, 'Disentangling the "Union Citizenship Puzzle"? The *McCarthy* Case' (2011) 36 *European Law Review* 861
——. 'Union Citizenship and the Redefinition of the "Internal Situations" Rule: The Implications of *Zambrano*' (2011) 12 *German Law Journal* 2077
——. 'Granting Citizenship-Related Rights to Third-Country Nationals: An Alternative to the Full Extension of European Union Citizenship' (2012) 14 *European Journal of Migration and Law* 63
——. 'The Self-Perpetuation of EU Constitutionalism in the Area of Free Movement of Persons: Virtuous or Vicious Cycle?' (2013) 2 *Global Constitutionalism* 125
Williams, A, 'The European Convention on Human Rights, the EU and the UK: Confronting a Heresy' (2013) 24 *European Journal of International Law* 1157
Wincott, D, 'Institutional Interaction and European Integration: Towards an Everyday Critique of Liberal Inter-governmentalism' (1995) 33 *Journal of Common Market Studies* 597
Yong, A, 'Opinion of AG Sharpston (12 December 2013) and Grand Chamber Judgment (12 March 2014) in Cases C-456/12 *O and B* and C-457/12 *S and G*' (2014) 25 *King's Law Journal* 155
——. 'Driving a Wedge between Friends? The Court of Justice of the EU and its Citizens in the Case of Welfare Benefits' (2016) 6 *European Human Rights Law Review* 664
——. 'Forgetting Human Rights: The Brexit Debate' (2017) 5 *European Human Rights Law Review* 469

INDEX